RENAISSANCE AND REFORMATION

RENAISSANCE AND REFORMATION

RENAISSANCE AND REFORMATION

Editor
James A. Patrick
Chancellor, College of Saint Thomas More

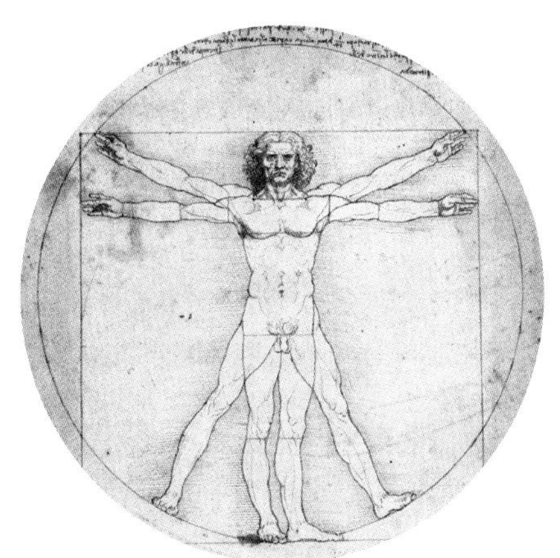

1

Agincourt, Battle of – Dams and Drainage

New York

Marshall Cavendish
99 White Plains Road
Tarrytown, New York 10591-9001

www.marshallcavendish.us

MARSHALL CAVENDISH
EDITOR: Thomas McCarthy
EDITORIAL DIRECTOR: Paul Bernabeo
PRODUCTION MANAGER: Michael Esposito

WHITE-THOMSON PUBLISHING
EDITORS: Steven Maddocks and Cath Senker
DESIGN: Derek Lee and Ross George
CARTOGRAPHER: Peter Bull Design
PICTURE RESEARCH: Amy Sparks
INDEXER: Cynthia Crippen, AEIOU, Inc.

Library of Congress Cataloging-in-Publication Data
Renaissance and Reformation / editor, James A. Patrick.
p. cm.
Includes bibliographical references.
Contents: 1. Agincourt, Battle of-Dams and drainage -- 2. Descartes, Rene-Households -- 3. Humanism and learning-Medicis, the -- 4. Michelangelo-Portugal -- 5. Preaching-Wren, Christopher -- 6. Index.
ISBN-13: 978-0-7614-7650-4 (set: alk. paper)
ISBN-10: 0-7614-7650-4 (set: alk. paper)
1. Renaissance--Encyclopedias. 2. Reformation--Encyclopedias. I. Patrick, James, 1933-

CB359.R455 2007
940.2'1--dc22

2006042600

ISBN-13: 978-0-7614-7650-4 (set)
ISBN-10: 0-7614-7650-4 (set)
ISBN-13: 978-0-7614-7651-1 (vol. 1)
ISBN-10: 0-7614-7651-2 (vol. 1)

Printed in Malaysia

10 09 08 07 06 5 4 3 2 1

ILLUSTRATION CREDITS
See page 288.

COVER: Raphael, *The School of Athens,* 1509–1511 (Art Archive/Vatican Museum, Rome).
TITLE PAGE: Quentin Massys, *The Banker and His Wife,* 1514 (Art Archive/Musée du Louvre, Paris/Harper Collins Publishers).

Directory of Contributors

Anna Bayman
Saint Hilda's College, Oxford University
English Civil Wars; Printing; Scotland; Stuarts, The

Brian Black
Penn State University
Agriculture; Disease; Machines; Manufacturing; Markets and Fairs; Science and Technology; Trade; Wren, Christopher

Hans Peter Broedel
University of North Dakota
Astrology; Bearbaiting and Blood Sports; Magic; Popular Culture; Preaching

Donald Carlson
Trinity Valley School
Agincourt, Battle of; Molière; Pico della Mirandola, Giovanni

Brian A. Carriere
Mississippi Gulf Coast Community College
Byzantium; Hanseatic League; Leonardo da Vinci; Maximilian I; Raphael; Reformation

Richard Cocke
Norwich, UK
Caravaggio; Michelangelo

Pierre de Craon
Paris, France
Leo X

Leif Dixon
Lady Margaret Hall, Oxford University
England

Daniel Horace Fernald
Georgia College and State University
Boccaccio, Giovanni; Descartes, René; Erasmus, Desiderius; Guilds and Companies; Hapsburg Empire; Households; Petrarch; Platonism; Universities

Charles Freeman
Suffolk, UK
Aristotle; Bramante, Donato; Brunelleschi, Filippo; Copernicus, Nicolaus; Galilei, Galileo; Languages, Classical

Alexandra Gajda
Saint Anne's College, Oxford University
Elizabeth I; Henry VIII

Rachel C. Gibbons
Bristol University (UK)
Hundred Years War; Peasants' Revolts

Kenneth Gouwens
University of Connecticut
Clement VII; Rome

Paul F. Grendler
University of Toronto (emeritus)
Medicine; Papacy; Renaissance

Jo Hall
Greenwich, London, UK
Gentileschi, Artemisia

John Haywood
Lancaster University (UK)
Armada, Spanish; Burgundy; Calendars; Christina; Lepanto, Battle of; Magellan, Ferdinand; Poland; Portugal; Sweden; Switzerland

Lisa R. Holliday
University of Kentucky
Spinoza, Baruch

Caroline S. Hull
Lancaster, UK
Bruegel, Pieter; Dürer, Albrecht; Giotto; Painting and Sculpture; Rembrandt; Rubens, Peter Paul; Velázquez, Diego Rodríguez de Silva

Phyllis G. Jestice
University of Southern Mississippi
Bohemia; Bosch, Hieronymus; Islam; Judaism; Monteverdi, Claudio; Music; Schütz, Heinrich

Susan Frances Jones
Caldwell College
Eyck, Jan van

Tom Lansford
University of Southern Mississippi
Banking; Education; Hobbes, Thomas; Machiavelli, Niccolò; Monarchy; More, Thomas; Shakespeare, William; Warfare

Jessica L. Malay
University of Huddersfield (UK)
Bacon, Francis; Borgia, Lucrezia; Catherine de Médicis; Cervantes, Miguel de; Literature; London; Marlowe, Christopher; Milton, John; Spain; Spenser, Edmund; Women

Kevin Marti
University of New Orleans
Chaucer, Geoffrey

Eric Nelson
Missouri State University
Botticelli, Sandro; France; Francis I; Henry IV; Heresy; Italian City-States; Joan of Arc; Paris; Population

Zachary C. Parmley
Georgia College and State University
Boccaccio, Giovanni; Households

James A. Patrick
College of Saint Thomas More
Architecture; Bernini, Gian Lorenzo; Bibles; Calvinism; Church of England; Constantinople; Established Churches; Iconoclasm; Jones, Inigo; Lutheranism; Missionaries; Palladio, Andrea; Philosophy; Thirty Years War

Robert J. Pauly Jr.
University of Southern Mississippi
Florence; German Towns; Medicis, The; Viscontis, The

Sheila J. Rabin
Saint Peter's College
Mathematics

Dylan Reid
University of Toronto
Humanism and Learning

Elizabeth D. Schafer
Loachapoka, Alabama
Calendars; Dams and Drainage; Exploration

Christine Shaw
Darwin College, Cambridge University
Charles V; Chivalry; Feudalism; Italian Wars; Lombardy; Nationalism; Nobility and Rank; Paul V; Pius II; Urbino; Venice

Andrew Spicer
Oxford Brookes University
Augsburg, Peace of; Philip II

Gretchen Starr-LeBeau
University of Kentucky
Ferdinand and Isabella; Pilgrimage

Joseph Sterrett
Cardiff University (UK)
Theater

John Swift
Saint Martin's College (UK)
Ivan IV Vasilyevich; Muscovy

Norman Tanner
Pontificia Università Gregoriana (Italy)
Florence, Council of; Religious Orders; Trent, Council of

Gordon C. Thomasson
Broome Community College, SUNY
Languages, Vernacular

Max von Habsburg
Oundle School (UK)
French Civil Wars; Holy Roman Empire; Rabelais, François

Douglas J. Weatherford
Brigham Young University
Columbus, Christopher

Set Contents

Volume 1

Volume 2

Volume 3

Volume 4

Volume 5

Volume 6

Thematic Contents

This thematic table of contents divides the articles in this encyclopedia into eleven groups. Within each group articles are arranged alphabetically; certain articles appear in more than one group. For each page listing, the number that precedes the colon is the volume number, and the number that follows it is the first page of the article.

Architecture, Painting, and Sculpture

Daily Life

Literature and Music

People

Philosophy, Religion, and Scholarship

Places

Politics and Economics

The Reformation and the Counter-Reformation

Rulers and Ruling Families

Science, Technology, and Exploration

Wars and Battles

Introduction

JAMES A. PATRICK

The articles in this encyclopedia constitute a critical survey of the ideas, events, and movements that marked European history between 1300 and 1700, the period from the first flowering of the Renaissance in Florence to the conclusion of the English civil wars. The set's title, *Renaissance and Reformation,* calls out the two defining movements of those centuries, movements whose great accomplishments in thought and deed at once summarized the achievement of the preceding two thousand years and laid the intellectual, social, and political foundations of the modern world.

An Age of Artistic Splendor. For many students of history, the meaning of the Renaissance is embodied in the achievements of its artists and architects. Preferring the glories of Rome and Greece to the traditions they had received from the Middle Ages, they midwifed a new world reborn out of ancient ideas. In Italy, France, and Spain the newly created wealth of the sixteenth century funded an artistic program that, while continuing to serve the interests of the church, as practically all medieval art had, was increasingly dedicated to creating a new secular art and to fulfilling the desires of Borgias, Medicis, and Viscontis for villas and country houses that were grandly built and lavishly painted. In the hands of Filippo Brunelleschi, Sandro Botticelli, Leonardo da Vinci, Donato Bramante, Raphael, Gian Lorenzo Bernini, Albrecht Dürer, Caravaggio, and Artemisia Gentileschi, a new European art was born—in architecture imitative of late Roman classical styles and in painting dedicated to a new realism in matters secular and to an illusionism of unparalleled beauty in matters religious. This beauty is particularly striking in the works of Italian painters—Michelangelo's Sistine Chapel is the great example—who brought heaven into the ceilings and domes of Italian churches. Within these pages are biographical studies of all these major figures and others; in addition, two overview articles examine developments in architecture and in painting and sculpture in close detail.

The radically new artistic styles that emerged in so short a time were an outgrowth of the radically new humanistic ideas of such thinkers as Petrarch, Desiderius Erasmus, Thomas More, and Pico della Mirandola, philosophers whose conceptions of God, human history, and most of all, the value of the individual life uprooted many of the approaches to being and learning that characterized the Middle Ages. A key philosophical battleground was language. Although many humanists were Latin and Greek scholars, their ultimate goal was to accurately translate classical works into the vernaculars of contemporary Europe. Their work paved the way for a flowering of vernacular literature and drama.

All of these developments, events, and trends receive careful examination herein. There are articles on both classical and vernacular languages. Overviews of literature and theater complement biographies of Giovanni Boccaccio, Miguel de Cervantes, Geoffrey Chaucer, John Milton, Molière, William Shakespeare, and others. An overview article on philosophy is supported by one on the works of Aristotle, who towers over the period, and another on Platonism, which gained ground as Greek manuscripts of Plato's work were unearthed. Articles on education and universities examine areas in which humanist ideas were extremely influential (many of Europe's great universities were founded during the Renaissance). Finally, those seventeenth-century thinkers whose ideas have the first ring of modernity are covered: Francis Bacon, René Descartes, Baruch Spinoza, and Thomas Hobbes.

Humanism and Religious Turmoil. The Reformation and humanism shared two important characteristics: an appeal to individual conscience and the notion that ancient texts contained truths that had become obscured by centuries of tradition. The translation of the Bible into vernacular languages was a key Reformation project, one that was aided enormously by the invention of mechanized printing in Germany in the 1450s. Nevertheless, whatever their common ground, Lutherans and Calvinists held a view of human nature far less optimistic than that of the humanists. Martin Luther—the German cleric who sparked the Reformation in 1517—John Calvin, Huldrych Zwingli, and like-minded Reformers stressed the weakness of a human nature flawed by original sin and entirely dependent for salvation on the grace of God. In stark contrast is the humanist thesis of Pico della Mirandola that the human being, as the natural lord of creation, is duty bound only to pursue specifically human ends.

Reformation met with Counter-Reformation, whose chief instrument was the Council of Trent, at which the Catholic Church formulated its response to the Reformers. An uneasy truce came with the Peace of Augsburg, which in 1555 decreed that the religion of a nation should be the religion of its ruler; attendant upon that peace was the spread of established churches, sponsored by princes and answerable only to them, in the Protestant countries of northern Europe. Although religion thrived in both Protestant and Catholic lands, by the second half of the sixteenth century, the idea that there was one church that had universal authority had been questioned and weakened. In the borderlands of the new Reformed religions there emerged groups, such as the Anabaptists and the Puritans, that challenged both Catholicism and the Reformed Christianity of Luther and Calvin. Catholic and Protestant rulers, who viewed heresy as political rebellion as much as religious dissent, often responded to it with violence. The attempt to preserve religious unity through law and punishment contributed to the outbreak in 1618 of the Thirty Years War, during which one-third of the population of Germany died. Yet its end in 1648 marked the beginning of an age of toleration that would lead in the West to religious freedom. These topics, too—from the specific (bibles, printing, and preaching) to the general (Lutheranism, Calvinism, and the Reformation and Counter-Reformation)—receive thorough attention in the volumes at hand. An overview of the papacy during this turbulent time is complemented by biographies of four critical occupants of the Chair of Peter: Leo X, Clement VII, Pius II, and Paul V.

War as the Forge of Modernity. Despite almost continual internal war, Europe flourished during the span of the Renaissance and the Reformation. Notable conflicts were many: the Hundred Years War, with its famous battle at Agincourt; the assault on England by the Spanish armada, as ill planned as it was executed; and those profoundly traumatic episodes—the Italian wars, the French and English civil wars, and the Thirty Years War—in which competing territorial and religious claims were inextricably bound up with one another. Although the wars of the Renaissance appeared to be pushing their participants to the brink of catastrophe, when seen in the rear-view mirror of history, they reveal themselves as the crucible in which modern Europe was forged. By the sixteenth century the medieval patchworks of sovereignties, dukedoms, and principalities held together by personal feudal loyalty had begun to give way to the consolidated nation-state: a geographically contiguous territory with one language, one religion, and an absolute ruler. Society was still hierarchical, and social rank—whether of the nobility or the gentry, of the freeholder or peasant class—was still inherited, but the notion of social hierarchy had been secularized: it tended away from an order in which the highest term was God and toward one based on political power. It was moving in fact toward a hierarchy of the kind advocated by Niccolò Machiavelli. Such sixteenth-century kings as Henry VIII of England and Francis I of France attained the long-sought goal of controlling the church and the nobility and thereby made themselves absolute rulers, but in attempting to govern without consent, they unwittingly sounded the death knell of monarchy. The rise of absolutism, the idea that the monarch was answerable to nobody but God (and to him only in theory), fanned the flames of popular demand for government based on constitutions and consent.

Externally, owing partly to structural weaknesses and corruption in the Turkish sultanate and partly to the courage and skill of Europe's warrior class (the inheritors of the chivalric tradition), the West finally broke the vise in which the armies and galleys of one Islamic power after another had held the Mediterranean world since the decisive failure of the Crusades in 1261. The long struggle between Islam and the Christian West is a book with many chapters, the *Reconquista*—the reconquest of Spain from the Moors, completed in 1492 by Ferdinand and Isabella—and the crucial naval battle fought at Lepanto in 1571 being only two of many. Still, European victory at Lepanto and in a series of battles in the Danube valley, extending as far west as Vienna, had far-reaching consequences for the Renaissance and the eras that followed it: by checking the expansion of Islam and the Ottomans, Europe's armies allowed Europe's nobles, merchants, and intellectuals the freedom to turn their attention to exploration and colonization, to religious controversy, and to the development of new philosophical, political, and artistic ideas. The final collapse of the Byzantine Empire and its millennia-old culture, an event marked by the conquest of Constantinople in 1453, while laying central Europe open to invasion, paradoxically strengthened the intellectual life of the West by forcing Byzantine scholars into exile in Italy.

Articles on all of the conflicts mentioned above examine not only the battles but also the causes and consequences of war. Advances in weaponry and trends in fighting are looked at in the overview article on warfare. Among the subjects of biographical articles are Machiavelli and all the monarchs mentioned on this page. Several articles cover what might be termed sociopolitical themes: feudalism, monarchy, nationalism, and nobility and rank are among these topics. Finally, the rich cultural legacy borne by the fleeing Byzantine scholars—notably a body of Greek texts long lost to the Latin West—is examined in an article called "Byzantium."

Looking Outward. Rooted in the Western character is a sense of adventure and a desire to push back boundaries; this set gives proper place to these yearnings. The mighty and expansive Roman Empire, the military campaigns of the Normans, and the far-ranging religious crusades and pilgrimages of the Middle Ages are all products of this mind-set. The adventurous spirit ultimately led to the Age of Exploration, which began in the mid-fifteenth century. Countless men (and later, women) embarked from Lisbon and Bristol—in ships usually no more than sixty feet long—to sail for weeks over the boundless ocean, ignorant save in the most general way of their location and with a food supply diminishing day by day as they looked for landfall. Among the unnamed many of these explorers and missionaries are a number of the famous, including Christopher

Columbus and Ferdinand Magellan. The complex motives that spurred them on included a desire for wealth, a determination to win the race for colonial territory at the expense of their European competitors, and for not a few, a genuine interest in saving souls by spreading Christianity among the native peoples of the New World.

As the sixteenth century wore on, maps of the world began to change. Gone were the mythical and misshapen landmasses; instead, the familiar picture of the world began to take shape. Medieval geographers had drawn maps according to an order of significance: they placed Jerusalem at the center of the earth because they believed that the most important event, the salvation of the world, had occurred there. By 1600 cartographers, basing their work on the findings of explorers and on the theoretical work of mathematicians, had begun to draw accurate representations of the continents and seas. Jerusalem appeared in the new maps at the remote edge of the Mediterranean—a city among cities.

Wealth and Commerce. The North and South American colonies of the Spanish and, later, the English, French, Portuguese, Dutch, and Danish, colonies established by generations of missionaries, explorers, and adventurers, generated an unexampled influx of wealth into their European mother countries. The new economy, one based on money rather than barter, encouraged elements of the system that would later be called capitalism. Pursued (albeit imperfectly) within the framework of an ethical system based on Christian principles and within the confines of the rule of law, capitalism produced unparalleled prosperity. The distinctive idea of the individual as a contract maker (the heart of the feudal system) was coupled with the increasing ability of the nobility and town dwellers to secure their property by denying absolute lordship to their prince or sovereign. The new understanding of contract and property combined with the spread of free markets—especially when markets were rationalized by a new accounting system that encouraged international banking—to make western Europe the most prosperous and dynamic civilization the world had yet known. These and other themes related to European economic development are explored in the articles dealing with markets and fairs, trade, the Hanseatic League, and banking.

New Knowledge and New Paradigms. During the Renaissance the foundations of modern science were laid by such men as Nicolaus Copernicus, whose calculations made the sun—not the earth—the center of the cosmos; Galileo Galilei, who argued that mathematics was the language in which nature was written; and Francis Bacon, who encouraged a new method of scientific enquiry based on observation and experimentation. The medieval view of nature as a wondrous witness to the glory of God was supplanted by a view of nature as an object of curiosity whose secrets were to be uncovered by the scientist and exploited for the benefit of all. Although this new approach produced a few technological results, notably in the field of agriculture, it was not until the eighteenth century that a sudden explosion in technological and mechanical innovation changed the world. The program of this industrial revolution, however, was laid out by the great figures of the seventeenth century.

At the end of that century, the world of the relatively new absolute kingdoms—still apparently religious, still hierarchically ordered—seemed secure. It was in fact on the verge of dissolution. Herein are numerous articles that examine empires (Holy Roman and Hapsburg), countries (England, France, Spain, and Portugal), sovereignties (Burgundy, Bohemia, and Muscovy), and cities (Florence, Venice, Rome, Urbino, London, and Paris) in which the intellectual, religious, and political status quo was overthrown and the modern world began to take shape. The future belonged to ideas and achievements rooted in the Renaissance and the Reformation: the new science, the nation-state, religious pluralism, capitalism, individual freedom, and government with the consent of the governed.

A New Past for a New Present. Civilizations are shaped by their ideas of their own past. History in 1300 tended to be an account less of what had actually happened, more of what ought to have happened. The extraordinarily rapid spread of printing—one library alone, the Bodleian at Oxford University, has in its collection six thousand books that were printed before 1500—together with a new critical approach to the texts that were printed, changed Europeans' view of their past. By the start of the seventeenth century the totality of human experience was beginning to be seen and written about in the light of evidence provided by books and artworks and to be arranged systematically along a time line that receded into the past. The modern student of history tackles his or her subject in much the same way. Indeed, this approach to picturing and interpreting the past, like so many ideas that were startlingly original during the Renaissance, is commonplace now. The time line that runs from 1350 to 1650 continues uninterrupted to the present day.

The people of the Renaissance and the Reformation, through their buildings and paintings, their treaties and treatises, remain alive, often vividly so. We of the present live along the fault line described by their partly old, partly very new ideas. What troubled them troubles us; what inspired them inspires us. May you, the reader, find in these volumes an insight into men and women who are, in every sense that matters, our contemporaries.

Reader's Guide

Renaissance and Reformation is a five-volume reference collection whose 158 articles survey European history from 1300 to 1700, with particular emphasis on the three centuries, 1350 to 1650, when the social, cultural, and political structures of the modern West took shape in the wake of, first, Europe's rediscovery of its classical past and then its religious fragmentation and reorientation.

As the site of these two transformative epochs, Europe is the focus of this encyclopedia—but not to the exclusion of those areas, especially the Americas and the Islamic world, to which the history of these centuries closely links it. Accordingly, along with the many articles on specific people, places, and conflicts of the European Renaissance and Reformation, there are others of a broader nature, on topics (astrology and manufacturing, to name but two) that provide background essential to understanding the period.

There are articles that examine the life, work, and influence of significant individuals: artists, architects, philosophers, writers, musicians, and figures of authority in the secular and ecclesiastical spheres (this last category includes articles on major dynasties and ruling families). Some articles describe historical events—battles, treaties, and church councils. Others provide an overview of an empire, kingdom, or city, with an emphasis on how the events of the Renaissance and the Reformation made themselves felt therein. Still others offer insight into cultural developments, political trends, or philosophical movements. As an aid to those who wish to carefully structure their inquiry, the Thematic Contents (pages 8–11 in this volume) organizes the articles by the type of subject treated.

All articles contain informational displays, or panels. An analysis panel provides detailed critical comment on a painting, building, sculpture, book, or point of debate among historians. A quotation panel offers an illuminating contemporary perspective drawn from a primary source. A biographical panel gives a brief account of the life and work of an individual who, though not covered in an article of his or her own, is important for a full understanding of the matter at hand—or indeed of the entire period. A feature panel focuses on a topic or theme that is especially germane to the subject of the article.

Each biographical article includes a chronology. This concise treatment of essential dates and other details allows the bulk of the article to be devoted to discussion and analysis. A map is provided wherever it will enrich the understanding of a place or an event (a battle, for example). Included within every article, under the heading Further Reading, is a short list of books, chosen by the contributor, for readers wishing to learn more about the article's subject. At the end of every article is a list of cross-references to other, related articles.

Each of the first five volumes concludes with an index specific to that volume. Volume 6, the final volume, contains a detailed time line of the Renaissance and Reformation, a glossary of unfamiliar terms, resources for further study (including Internet resources), a list and index of maps, numerous thematic indexes, and a comprehensive index.

A feature panel highlights an aspect of the subject that is of exceptional interest.

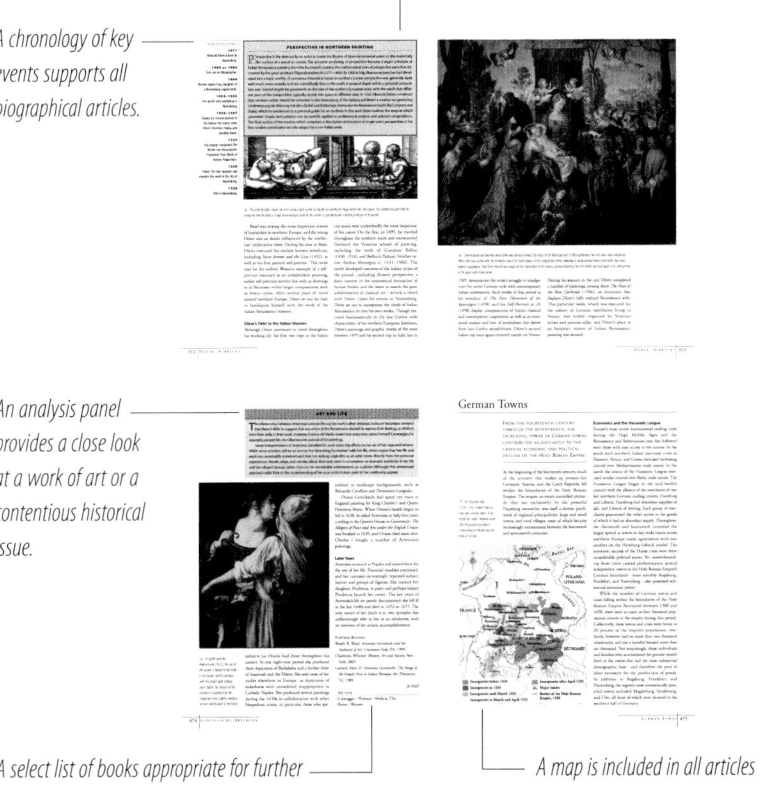

Agincourt, Battle of

AT THE BATTLE OF AGINCOURT (1415), A KEY CONFLICT OF THE HUNDRED YEARS WAR, KING HENRY V OF ENGLAND LED HIS SMALL AND EXHAUSTED ARMY TO VICTORY AGAINST A MUCH LARGER FRENCH FORCE.

In August 1415, two years after becoming king of England, Henry V attacked France. He had several possible motives for doing so: to reassert his family's claim to Normandy, Aquitaine, and Anjou; to quell doubts at home about the legitimacy of his succession by diverting the attention of the English barons toward a foreign war; and to exploit the weakness of the French king, Charles VI (reigned 1380–1422), who suffered from bouts of insanity.

Henry's decision to invade France opened the second stage of the Hundred Years War. The first stage had ended around thirty years earlier, when the French won back almost all of the territory lost to the English—whose arrival in Flanders in 1337 under King Edward III had set the Hundred Years War in motion.

Henry's army set sail from Portsmouth on August 11, 1415, in a large fleet of ships. They landed near Harfleur, at the mouth of the Seine River on France's northern coast, and laid siege to the city. Although Harfleur surrendered five weeks later, in late September, the English suffered heavy losses. More than one in three English soldiers died, and many survivors fell sick with dysentery.

Henry had initially planned, after the taking of Harfleur, to march his army along the Seine to Paris and then southwest all the way to Bordeaux. Yet with Harfleur conquered, Henry decided to turn northeast to Calais, possibly to emulate his great-grandfather Edward III—whose army had subdued that city in 1347—and to affirm his own claim to Normandy. The English had sustained too many losses to proceed with Henry's original plan, and so Calais, already in English hands, represented a haven. Taking a third of his remaining force and enough supplies to last eight days, Henry set out.

En route to Calais, Henry received intelligence that a French army, nearly five times the size of his own, blocked the way. The constable of

► *In the fourteenth and fifteenth centuries, the longbow afforded English armies a superior long-range weapon that often turned the tide of battle in their favor. Owing to the armor-piercing capabilities of the arrowheads when fired at short distances, archers were often strategically placed at the forefront of battle, as depicted in this illustration from a fourteenth-century manuscript by the great French chronicler Jean Froissart.*

France, Charles d'Albret, had mustered this force at Rouen, due east of Harfleur. The English continued to march in an attempt to avoid the French, who nevertheless managed to keep pace with the invaders. On October 19 the sick and hungry English finally crossed the Somme River. The following day, October 20 (which Henry had decreed a day of rest for his weary troops), French heralds arrived to make a formal challenge. Henry and his men resumed their march the next day. On October 24 Henry learned from his scouts that the French army had positioned itself between his army and Calais, which still lay around forty miles away.

Henry tried negotiating with the French, but their terms proved unacceptable to him. That night Henry ordered absolute silence in the English camp. English chroniclers report that, in contrast, the French soldiers were so confident that most of them stayed awake and noisily celebrated the victory to come. During the night it rained, as it had for several days previously, and the following day's battlefield turned into a sea of mud.

A youthful ruler, Henry V ascended the throne at age twenty-six. The scope of his ambitions is apparent in the Latin inscription around his image in this seventeenth-century engraving. In translation, the words read, "Henry V, king of England and France, lord of Ireland."

Henry V 1387–1422

Born at Monmouth, in southeastern Wales, on September 16, 1387, Henry Monmouth was the son of Henry Bolingbroke and Mary Bohun. In 1394 young Henry's mother died, and in 1398 his father was exiled by King Richard II. Nevertheless, Richard treated Henry kindly and took the boy under his protection. Henry's father returned the next year, deposed Richard, and as King Henry IV, established the House of Lancaster as the new royal family.

Some biographers portray Henry as a wild youth, a view lent credence by William Shakespeare's cycle of history plays treating the early phases of the Wars of the Roses (*Richard II; Henry IV, Part 1; Henry IV, Part 2;* and *Henry V* were written and first performed in the 1590s). However, given the great responsibilities Henry shouldered upon his father's elevation to the throne, the wildness of his youth was almost certainly overstated. In 1400 he was named prince of Wales, and in 1403, at age sixteen, he led the English forces at Shrewsbury against Henry Percy, known as Hotspur, who championed Edmund Mortimer, a rival claimant to the crown. In 1408 Henry helped end the Welsh rebellion led by Owen Glendower. His father's poor health brought Henry even more responsibility, and in 1410 he and his uncles Henry and Thomas Beaufort formed a ruling council that effectively placed control of the government in the young prince's hands. Henry and his father differed on domestic and foreign policy, and so the older Henry discharged his son from the council in 1411. Nevertheless, in 1413, upon his father's death, Henry became king.

Henry sought to solidify the Lancastrian succession by laying to rest some of the old enmities that had troubled his father's reign. He also turned his attention to France. In 1415 the invasion he led culminated in victory at Agincourt. Henry began his conquest of Normandy in 1417 and brought it to completion by capturing Rouen in 1419. Henry and Charles VI made peace in 1420 with the Treaty of Troyes, which named Henry heir and regent of France. Henry married Charles's daughter, Catherine of Valois, and returned to England but soon went back to France to quell renewed French opposition. A long winter siege at Meaux, southeast of Paris, ruined Henry's health. In August 1422 Henry died of dysentery at Vincennes. Had he lived two months longer, Henry V would have been crowned king of France.

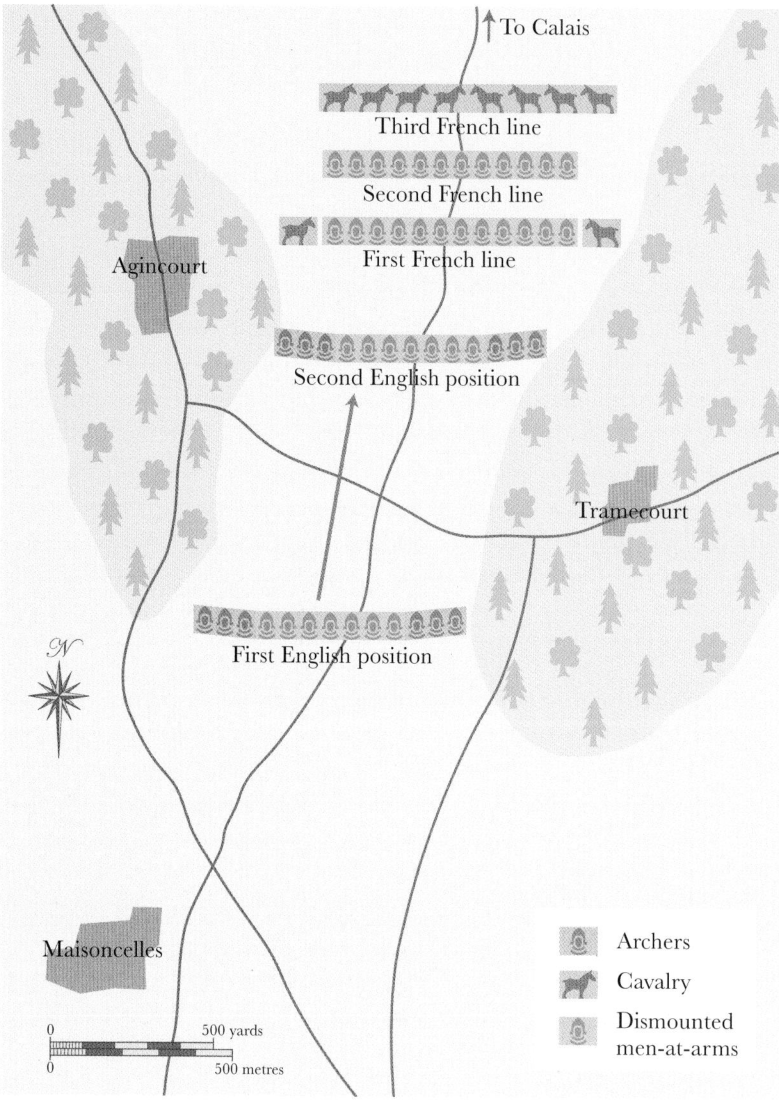

▲ *The Agincourt battlefield occcupied an inverted triangle whose vortices were formed by the villages of Agincourt to the west, Tramecourt to the east, and Maisoncelles to the south. Henry V's decision to advance his line, though risky, paid great dividends, since it allowed the English to provoke the French into attacking and narrowed the field of engagement, a distinct advantage for the outnumbered English force.*

The Day of the Battle

October 25 was the feast of Saint Crispin. As dawn broke, both armies prepared for battle. The English force numbered 5,000 archers and 900 men-at-arms, heavily armed mounted soldiers. The French numbered around 25,000. The armies faced off across a freshly plowed and planted field around a thousand yards from each other. The plain narrowed to around nine hundred yards, where forests bordered it on either side.

The English drew into a single line, four men deep, of men-at-arms and dismounted knights. Two wedges of bowmen may have divided the center of the line at equal distances from the left and right wings. Archers with longbows flanked the line. Sharpened stakes planted in rows protected the archers against cavalry charges. The woods on either side of the battlefield guarded the bowmen from a flanking maneuver by the French. Henry may have stationed a small group of archers in the woods behind the French position to cause confusion among the enemy. Thomas, Lord Camoys, and Edward, duke of York, commanded the left and right wings, respectively. Sir Thomas Erpingham commanded the archers. Henry himself took charge of the center.

The French deployed in three lines, two of infantry and one of cavalry. The French commanders also placed some artillery on the flanks toward the rear. Scattered between the first two lines were archers and crossbowmen. Lack of discipline proved to be a major weakness on the part of the French: the chivalric code demanded that mounted nobles place themselves at the forefront of a fighting army, and the efforts of the nobility, including Constable d'Albret himself, to join the first line created confusion and crowding.

The Battle

Once positioned, neither side moved for four hours. The French thought it advantageous to wait and perhaps even intended to delay until the English supplies ran out. Henry and his advisers agreed that they had to provoke a French attack. He ordered his men to advance quietly to within a longbow shot's distance from the French. The advance took about ten minutes. Had the French attacked at this point, they would have won.

Once in position, the archers received the order to fire on the French. Although they shot from too far away to inflict much damage, the arrows raining down probably caused outrage in the enemy camp. The French attacked: first the cavalry charged the bowmen on each English flank, and then the first line of infantry advanced on the English center. The charging knights rode their horses blindly into the thicket of stakes—moved and replanted during the general advance. The archers let fly with their longbows and struck horses as well as riders. Most of the frightened and injured animals turned in panic and, fleeing into the center of the advancing French line, disrupted their assault and churned up the muddy ground.

The first line of French infantrymen finally met their English opponents and briefly drove them back. Nevertheless, the French were crowded because the woods on either side narrowed the field by 150 yards, and the men-at-arms on the flanks moved in confusion to the center to avoid the English archers. The French were so packed that when they reached the English defenders, they were unable to wield their weapons to knock over their foes or to break the solid English formation. Soon enough, the English defenders were cutting through the French attackers. By pushing the French line back on itself, the English caused many of the French to lose their footing and fall into the mud. Each man wore sheet steel armor weighing an average of sixty to seventy pounds, and most were too exhausted and weighted down to get back up again.

After their arrows were spent, the English archers used swords, battle-axes, and maces to attack the French men-at-arms on both ends. In a short time the English had almost annihilated the French vanguard. Those who were not killed were taken prisoner.

Beset by mud and blocked by the bodies of their fallen comrades, the second French line, which moved in to attack, met the same fate as the first. Anthony of Burgundy, duke of Brabant, arriving late to the battle, led one more doomed French assault. In all, the decimation of the first two French lines and the repulsion of Brabant's charge took half an hour.

The battle took another bloody turn during the ensuing lull. The English had moved a number of French prisoners to the rear. With the threat of another assault from the third French line, Henry could ill afford to waste men guarding prisoners. If a third attack occurred, some thousand poorly guarded French prisoners—with discarded weapons scattered all around the battlefield—posed a threat to the English.

A group of peasants and three knights led by the lord of Agincourt ransacked the English baggage train and reportedly took one of Henry's crowns. It was at this point that Henry ordered

Among the most memorable moments in all of Shakespeare's work is the stirring speech Henry V delivers to his men just before the Battle of Agincourt:

And Crispin Crispian shall ne'er go by,
From this day to the ending of the world,
But we in it shall be remembered;
We few, we happy few, we band of brothers;
For he today that sheds his blood with me
Shall be my brother; be he ne'er so vile,
This day shall gentle his condition:
And gentlemen in England now a-bed
Shall think themselves accurs'd they were not here,
And hold their manhoods cheap whiles any speaks
That fought with us upon St. Crispin's day.

William Shakespeare, *Henry V*, act 4

At Agincourt much of the deadliest fighting was done at close quarters. This fifteenth-century French manuscript illustration vividly depicts the press of battle and the confusion of the French forces as they encountered successive waves of English fighters.

HOW DID THE ENGLISH WIN AT AGINCOURT?

Ironically, the advantage in numbers that the French enjoyed may have lost them the battle. As the French lines moved forward, the rear guard continued to press ahead, apparently oblivious that their comrades in front were taking heavy losses. The advancing second line hemmed in the first, the men of which had room neither to defend themselves nor to retreat. Owing to lack of discipline and leadership, the formation degenerated into a disordered mass that made easy pickings for the English men-at-arms and for the archers who engaged the French flanks in hand-to-hand combat. The terrain also helped turn the battle in Henry's favor. The mud was reported to be knee deep in places, and some of the horses sank up to the belly. These conditions severely handicapped the French.

► *The stunning victory at Agincourt may have been marred by the English army's brutal execution of French prisoners and looting of the dead, events that took place behind battle lines in the English camp. This fifteenth-century manuscript illustration shows some triumphant English soldiers hacking French prisoners to death while others pick over the belongings of their vanquished foes.*

the killing of the prisoners. He assigned the task of execution to two hundred archers. Not bound by the chivalric code, the archers were less reluctant than the men-at-arms to carry out this work. They bludgeoned, stabbed, and in some cases burned the prisoners to death. The executions ended when the third assault failed to materialize.

The Importance of Agincourt

The French lost perhaps as many as ten thousand men at Agincourt. The English also took some 1,500 noble prisoners back to England. The majority, who could not pay the ransom demanded, never returned to their homeland. In all, almost half of the French aristocracy was either killed or sent to England.

The English lost five hundred at most. Still, Henry was in no position to exploit the victory; he and his men proceeded to Calais and arrived there on October 29. From there they returned to England. Henry's campaign yielded little in territory. Nevertheless, the near-total destruction of the French army would allow Henry to achieve future victories far more easily.

Further Reading

Fowler, Kenneth Alan. *The Age of Plantagenet and Valois.* New York, 1980.

Keegan, John. *The Face of Battle.* New York, 1976.

Seward, Desmond. *Henry V: The Scourge of God.* New York, 1988.

Donald Carlson

SEE ALSO

• Burgundy • Chivalry • England • France

• Hundred Years War • Joan of Arc

• Shakespeare, William • Warfare

Agriculture

AGRICULTURAL INNOVATIONS HELPED TO STABILIZE LIFE IN MUCH OF EUROPE DURING THE RENAISSANCE AND REFORMATION ERAS.

As Europe emerged from the Middle Ages, agricultural technology remained relatively primitive. Most of the subsequent innovations in European agriculture derived from other parts of the world. In particular, the superior agricultural knowledge of the Muslim world was passed on to Europe. One of the main areas of contact was Spain, where Christian farmers picked up knowledge and techniques from Spanish Muslims.

▼ *Books of hours, prayer books that record important holy days, often include illustrations of the yearly agricultural cycle. On this page from a 1490 book of hours, the month of October is illustrated with an image of peasants plowing and sowing.*

Agriculture was a fundamental organizational principle of western European society in the Middle Ages. Peasant tillers made up the largest segment of the population. However, the chief basis of wealth and political power was ownership of land, and most peasants did not own the land that they tilled. During the Middle Ages industry and commerce dictated agrarian pursuits to a far lesser extent than they had done in Roman times or were to do in the modern era. After the 1300s, however, farmers adopted commercially oriented methods that began distinctly to alter European society. The primary changes were an increase in efficiency and, consequently, the regular production of surplus produce for sale.

Manorialism and Feudalism

The shape of agricultural life during the medieval era was determined by the manorial system. A typical manor consisted of a small village that was home to the peasants, the manor house that belonged to the lord, and a quantity of arable land. Often, the arable land was cultivated according to a primitive kind of crop rotation known as the three-field system.

Many peasants were serfs bonded to the land and thus were entirely subject to the will of the lord. Although they could tend a plot of land for their own benefit during free time, it was said that a peasant possessed *nihil praeter ventrem*—"nothing but his belly." The lands were cultivated by the peasants acting together, but they owned neither the tools nor the animals needed for cultivation. (Tools and animals were usually too expensive for peasants to own.) In some arrangements peasants were entitled to keep only what they made in their free time. In others the lord took only a portion of what was reaped.

Scholars mark the start of manorialism at the point when the German technique of working the land with a moldboard plow (one with an iron plate attached that turns up and mixes the topsoil) joined with the Roman system, in which poor farm laborers gave up their freedom in return for the protection of a lord who had the means to defend them in a situation of war or anarchy.

This Bohemian fresco of around 1400 is part of a cycle of months. The month depicted here is July; courtiers converse outside a manor house while peasants labor with scythes and rakes.

The agricultural system of manorialism was part of an overarching social system known as feudalism. Until the end of the thirteenth century, feudalism ordered much of European society. The word *feudalism* derives from the fief, which usually took the form of a grant of land from one nobleman to another. (A manor might be composed of multiple fiefs.) The one granting the fief was the lord; the recipient was his vassal. The lord protected the vassal, and the vassal repaid the lord with military service.The entire system was kept stable by the practice of primogeniture, according to which, upon the death of a landowner, all the lands were left to the eldest son. This system kept the large estates intact and left younger sons for the clergy or for a life of adventure.

Thus, agriculture perpetuated the class system that structured feudal society. However, the manorial system did not permeate all of medieval society. From the thirteenth century towns and cities grew steadily. Various urban centers emerged; besides London and Paris, there were Lübeck (in Germany), Naples (in Italy), Bruges (in Flanders), and Bergen (in Norway). Social changes that began in these and other urban areas would greatly alter life in the countryside.

With the development of towns came an increase in economic activity, and a money-based economy overtook the barter system that for centuries had been the rule in agricultural life. When transported to the towns and cities, agricultural produce became goods for sale. The emergence of capitalism—together with the increasing importance of the manufacturing sector—eventually disrupted feudal arrangements, which no longer met economic needs. Capital ceased to be concentrated in the hands of the nobility. Up-and-coming entrepreneurs began to gain a foothold in a society that had previously been dominated by feudal overlords. This shift in agricultural economics carried implications that rippled through almost every aspect of European life by the 1300s.

Agriculture and Commerce

From the eleventh century through the thirteenth, the farming population and the land under cultivation increased significantly. In many areas new tenure arrangements emerged. The number of freemen increased, and obligations of service were transformed into money payments. The lord's monopoly rights over milling, brewing, and cloth making became privatized concerns.

The wars and plagues of the fourteenth century upset virtually all commercial arrangements. Any crop failure could have far-reaching consequences. In addition, disease markedly decreased the number of laborers, and with fewer laborers, freemen had more and more opportunities to acquire land. By the beginning of the 1400s, however, the population of Europe had begun to rebound. With the changes in the agricultural system and the increasing population, lands under cultivation had to be in the best possible condition to produce enough food.

The following document itemizes the assets of a manor in Essex, east of London, in the early years of the fourteenth century.

Extent of the manor of Borley made there on Tuesday next after the feast of Saint Matthew the Apostle, A.D. 1308, in the first year of the reign of King Edward, son of King Edward, in the presence of John le Doo, steward by the hands of William of Folesham, clerk, on the oath of Philip, the reeve of Borley, Henry Lambert, Dennis Rolf, Richard at Mere, Walter Johan and Robert Ernald, tenants of the said vill of Borley. These all having been sworn, declare that there is there one messuage [a house, its outbuildings, and its grounds] well and suitably built; that it is sufficient for the products of the manor, and that it contains in itself, within the site of the manor, 4 acres, by estimation. The grass there is worth yearly by estimation, 2s [shillings]. And the curtilage [yard] there is worth yearly 12d [pence].... The fruit garden there is worth yearly as in apples, grapes, perhaps 5s and sometimes more. Total 8s.

... There is there a wood called le Hoo, which contains 10 acres, and the underbrush from it is worth yearly, without waste, 5s, and the grass from it is worth yearly, 5s; and the feeding of swine there is worth yearly, 12d. And there is there a certain other wood called Chalvecroft, which contains with the ditches, 5 acres. And the herbage there is worth yearly 2s 6d, and the underbrush there is worth 3s, and the feeding of swine there is worth yearly, 6d. Total value, 17s.

There are there, of arable land in demesne, in different fields, 300 acres of land, by the smaller hundred. And it is worth yearly, on lease, £15, at the price of 12d per acre. Total acreage, 300. Total value, £15.

And it is to be known that the perch of land in that manor contains 165 feet, in measuring land. And each acre can be sown suitably with 2½ bushels of wheat, with 2½ bushels of rye, with 2½ bushels of peas, with 3 bushels of oats, and this sown broadcast, and with 4 bushels of barley, even measure. And each plough should be joined with 4 oxen and 4 draught horses. And a plough is commonly able to plough an acre of land a day, and sometimes more.

Quoted in E. P. Cheyney, *Translations and Reprints from the Original Sources of European History*

◄ *This Italian fresco, executed in the late fifteenth century, shows fruit and vegetable traders selling their goods to well-to-do shoppers at a town market.*

▲ *As agriculture diversified, milling became a vital component of economic development. Some of the earliest mills were driven by wind power; this depiction of a windmill is from a manuscript of around 1340 called the* Romance of Alexander.

Technological advance was an important factor in making up the gap in production during the 1400s. Power generated by animals, wind, and water was used to drive mechanical mills that performed a huge range of tasks—laundering clothes, tanning hides, sawing wood, casting iron, mashing pulp for papermaking, operating cloth fullers' vats, powering bellows for blast furnaces, and driving hydraulic hammers in foundries. Indeed, the new clearings and cuttings for the fuel for blacksmiths' forges depleted forests and in some areas significantly reduced the surplus of immediately usable arable land. By the 1400s such basic mechanical tools as the lathe (for turning and shaping wood), the brace and bit (a primitive drill), and the spinning wheel were also in general use.

The Glorious (or Bloodless) Revolution, a series of events that took place in England in 1688 and 1689, resulted in the overthrow of James II and the accession of Mary II and William of Orange. The Glorious Revolution was an important stage in the development of a capital-based and surplus-generating agricultural sector in England. The Declaration of Rights, signed after the revolution by William of Orange (who became King William III), enshrined the rights of a parliament dominated by progressive middle-class landholders, who were exploiting new techniques in speculative, market-oriented ventures. From that point forward, Parliament and the courts were dominated by capitalistic agricultural and commercial interests.

Another factor in the commercialization of agriculture was the emergence of colonialism. In the sixteenth century European agriculturalists began to take the agricultural practices of Europe overseas—often to distant places whose climates were more amenable to the growing of certain desirable (and therefore profitable) crops.

BEASTS OF BURDEN

Domesticated horses and oxen were a vital component of agriculture during the Renaissance and the Reformation. Although oxen had been used in the field for many years, new hardware was needed to involve horses, which were much more flexible and adaptable (the use of oxen did not entirely disappear, however).

In addition to pulling carts, oxen since antiquity had been used to pull what was called a heavy plow. This plow was often mounted on wheels, a setup that allowed the plowshare to be matched to the furrow being plowed. Another innovation was to have the plow pulled by several oxen harnessed in tandem. In later years, oxen were frequently replaced by horses in tandem.

To enable horses to be used in place of oxen, farmers first used a classical harness, in which a horse pulled against a strap placed around its neck. This harness significantly limited the load the horse could pull before it became distressed. By the sixth century a device known as a breast strap moved the load point to the horse's chest and, by removing the stress on the neck, allowed the horse to pull much greater loads. Nevertheless, the breast strap was not a perfect solution: it tended to ride up the neck when the horse pulled a heavy load that was attached high on the back. To prevent the breast strap from riding up, it was held down by another strap that passed from the breast strap, between the front legs of the horse, and back to a girth strap.

The harness most widely used in the Middle Ages rested on the shoulders and the breast of the horse. Thus, the pressure points fell across the horse's shoulders, not high on its back. This harness allowed the horse to pull much greater loads without putting any pressure on its neck. With this improvement horses could pull a number of different devices, including a harrow, a heavy cultivating implement. This design was modified to include a horse collar, which went around the horse's neck and prevented the harness from shifting. Use of this modified harness spread rapidly—though not uniformly—through European agriculture. It also allowed horses to be used for heavy freight hauling.

Plantations became a vital part of the mercantilist system, in which European powers rigorously controlled the market in valuable commodities produced in their overseas colonies and directed all colonial wealth back to the mother country. By the 1600s European colonies in the Atlantic and Caribbean would in turn export the techniques and hardware of European agriculture to the American mainland.

▼ Using the limited tools of the era, agriculturalists cared for and managed plants in a variety of ways. This sixteenth-century manuscript illumination, from a treatise on agriculture by Pietro de Crescenzi (c. 1230–c. 1310), depicts an agricultural worker grafting fruit trees (affixing part of one plant onto another in such a way that the two fuse and grow together).

Gardens and Horticulture

Another development in agriculture during the later Middle Ages and early Renaissance was the division of the single field of agriculture into the various fields of agronomy, horticulture, and forestry—divisions that would become more pronounced after 1350, when scientific knowledge and experimental methodology was applied much more rigorously to land and plant management.

Agronomists came to specialize in the management of open fields and meadows for the best production of grain and fodder for animals. The kitchen gardens of tree and vine fruits, vegetables, herbs, medicinal plants, and ornamental plants became the domain of horticulture. The forests

▲ *Many of the developments in plant management took place in controlled herb gardens that were often contained within walled towns. In this fifteenth-century illustration from a French manuscript of Pietro de Crescenzi's agricultural treatise, a nobleman oversees his gardeners planting herbs in parterre.*

that produced timber and game became the particular purview of forestry.

As European cities became larger, an increasing segment of the population had to work on farms in order to grow sufficient food to feed everyone. This trend helped to make horticulture a major industry. Large croplands were developed in the countryside to supply cities. Influences from foreign trade brought in new crops, such as artichokes and citrus from India and watermelons from Africa.

Foreign influence also spurred Europeans to make ornamental gardens of increasing complexity. In formal Renaissance gardens, the patterns of planting were as important as the plants themselves. The French name for this approach, particularly where numerous beds are separated by paths, is parterre. Changes in European landscape design culminated in the seventeenth century with the intricate geometric patterns of the grand gardens built by King Louis XIV of France. His gardens at Versailles, outside Paris, remain one of the world's great horticultural feats. The stylistic hallmarks of the gardens of Elizabethan England were sculpted shrubs, mazes, statues, and patterned knot gardens, in which herbs and other plants were arranged into exotic designs.

European ornamental gardening became something of a craze in the seventeenth century, when international trade brought new plants from Asia and the Americas. Tulips, for example, came to Europe from Turkey in the mid-1500s. People in the Netherlands found the tulips so attractive that demand outstripped supply; the result was the *tulpenwoede,* a Dutch word that means something akin to "tulip mania." Tulips were traded for extremely high prices: some Dutch traders even mortgaged their home and business to buy a single bulb.

In the seventeenth and eighteeenth centuries, the English moved away from strict symmetrical formality in garden design and developed a more natural look. They preferred extensive grassy lawns and parks and planted large areas of trees in the countryside.

New Husbandry

In agriculture a series of innovations known collectively as new husbandry were introduced between 1500 and 1750. These new methods made their first European appearance in the Low Countries and by 1750 had been adopted in most European countries—with the exception of France, where farmers tended to resist agricultural innovation.

Among the most important new techniques was the elimination of fallowing (the custom of leaving a field unplanted for a period of time). In medieval agricultural practice, nearly a third of the available arable land needed to be left fallow each year in order to exterminate weeds accumulated from two successive years of growing grain. It proved useful instead to alternate new fodder crops, including alfalfa, clover, turnips, and new grasses, with more soil-intensive grain crops. Alternating crops not only improved the soil by increasing its level of nitrogen (clover and alfalfa contain nitrogen-fixing bacteria) but also broke disease and pest cycles.

In addition to the elimination of fallowing and the cultivation of new fodder crops, another new practice was the stall feeding of cattle. The overall result of these changes was more numerous and better-fed cattle—and thus, the supply of

Jethro Tull 1674–1741

Born into gentry in Berkshire, west of London, Jethro Tull studied law at Gray's Inn in preparation for a political career. However, when illness stalled these plans in 1699, he began farming with his father in Wallingford, in Oxfordshire.

At that time cereals were distributed into furrows by hand, a process known as drilling. Not only was this process time-consuming, Tull also noticed that the heavy sowing densities traditionally associated with drilling were not very efficient. (This wasteful distribution of seeds over a wide area is known as broadcast spreading.) Tull therefore instructed his workers to drill very precisely and at low densities. By 1701 his frustration with their lack of cooperation prompted him to invent a machine to regulate the exact placement of seeds.

Inspired by the memory of an organ he had taken apart when he was younger, Tull designed his drill with a rotating cylinder. Grooves were cut into the cylinder that allowed seeds to pass from the hopper above to a funnel below. The funnel directed the seeds into the channel that had been dug by a plow that was located at the front of the same machine. Instead of broadcasting the seed, the drill used sticks to make a hole into which a single seed could be placed. The seed was then immediately covered by dirt by a harrow attached to the rear of Tull's device.

Eventually, as agricultural improvement became fashionable, people began to take more interest in Tull's ideas. In 1731 he published a book, *The New Horse Hoeing Husbandry,* in which he detailed his system and machinery. While several other mechanical seed drills had also been invented, Tull's complete system was a major influence on the agricultural revolution.

animal products was increased. Better animals produced more fertilizer, a development that helped to increase cereal yields. Additional food helped to make animals stronger. With new, improved plows, a single team of horses could now do work that had previously required four to seven oxen.

Although these gradual changes in agricultural practice did not amount to a rapid revolution in many areas, England did undergo an agricultural revolution in the eighteenth century. England's revolution was founded on a more intensive use of land through the substitution of crop rotation for fallowing. English crop rotation was successful because it involved the use of artificial legume fodders that not only restored the fertility of soil but also provided additional fodder.

This change in England effectively broke what is often referred to as the dung-fodder cycle: more dung improves soil fertility; more fertile soil produces more fodder; more fodder feeds more cattle; more cattle produce more dung; and so on. The rotation of new crops was the crucial factor in the production of agricultural surpluses. These surpluses fed the ever-increasing population of nonfarmers and thus enabled the massive increase in nonagricultural pursuits that sparked the industrial revolution in the late eighteenth century.

An unattributed contemporary portrait of the English agriculturalist Jethro Tull, whose innovative mechanical seed drill made planting far more efficient and productive than it had ever been.

A map of enclosed fields in Laxton, a community in Nottinghamshire, in central England; it was drawn in 1635 by Mark Pierce. The various activities depicted include plowing and deer hunting.

Revolutions in Agriculture

Over the centuries property and land ownership rights in Europe had evolved from a system of serfdom and peasant tenancy toward one of individual and absolute tenure. By 1500 these trends in private ownership had led courts to enforce the enclosure of fields that had previously been communally owned and farmed. These new enclosures, which passed into individual ownership and management, were parceled into sufficiently large units to accommodate the demand for foodstuffs in rapidly developing towns. This agricultural revolution occurred first in England, where the process of defeudalization had gone farther than it had in any other European nation. Thereafter, as England's middle-class entrepreneurs applied their energy to manufacturing, agricultural revolution followed in France.

The success of agriculture—that is, its ability to produce a surplus for investment—depended on the elimination of feudal institutions. This development was achieved almost two centuries after settlement began in the American colonies of France and Britain. The French Revolution followed hard upon the American Revolution; both entailed the formal abolition of feudal tenure. The difference was that significantly greater informal erosion had occurred in New England than had occurred in New France (present-day Canada).

Throughout Europe changes in agriculture triggered social changes. Drainage and flood-control systems, experimentation with a variety of fertilizers, and the improved design of nearly every agricultural implement (including wagons, scythes, spades, and plows) increased production. The most important change in agricultural hardware was the curving of the moldboard on the new iron plows after 1650; this innovation reduced friction with the soil and thus improved the efficency of plows.

Generally speaking, however, the changes in agriculture did not reduce the time that men and women spent in the fields. Most of the new techniques saved money and land but increased labor.

Further Changes

Europe's expansion into new parts of the world also introduced Europeans to new foods. Maize and potatoes, brought from the Americas, became very important in Europe and Africa. Tobacco from the Americas generated major new social habits in Europe and Turkey. Tomatoes became popular in India and throughout the

Beginning in the earliest days of the continental Renaissance, information about plant species was disseminated in writing. This description of the apple tree dates from the 1500s.

The Apple loveth to be digged twice, especially the first yeare, but it needeth no dung, and yet notwithstanding dung and ashes cause it prosper better, especially the dung of Sheepe, or for lesse charges sake, the dust which in Sommer is gathered up in the high waies. You must many times set at libertie the boughes which intangle themselves one within another; for it is nothing else but aboundance of Wood, wherewith it being so replenished and bepestred, it becometh mossie, and bearing lesse fruit. It is verie subject to be eaten and spoyled of Pismires and little wormes, but the remedie is to set neere unto it the Sea-onion: or else if you lay swines dung at the roots, mingled with mans urine, in as much as the Apple-tree doth rejoyce much to be watered with urine. And to the end it may beare fruit aboundantly, before it begin to blossome, compasse his stocke about, and tie unto it some peece of lead taken from some spout, but when it beginneth to blossome, take it away. . . .

Apples must be gathered when the moone is at the full, in faire weather, and about the fifteenth of September, and that by hand without any pole or pealing downe: because otherwise the fruit would be much martred, and the young siences broken or bruised, and so the Apple-tree by that meanes should be spoyled of his young wood which would cause the losse of the Tree.

Charles Stevens and John Liebault, *Maison Rustique; or, The Countrey Farme*

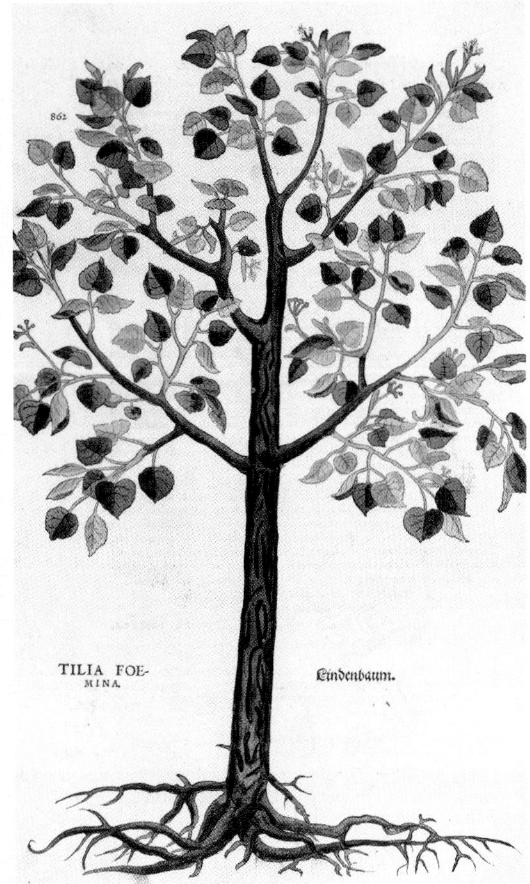

By the 1500s agricultural and botanical knowledge was being exchanged through published writings and drawings. This illustration of a European linden, also known as the lime tree, is taken from a 1542 work that was extremely influential in the development of natural history: De historia stirpium (On the History of Plants), by the German botanist Leonhard Fuchs (1501–1566).

Mediterranean. As the food supply increased and diversified, epidemic diseases decreased.

The intrinsic relationship between agriculturalists and their land underwent a significant change during the Renaissance and Reformation. During the Middle Ages farming had been carried out by laborers without a personal interest in the undertaking. Farmers kept journals, exchanged ideas, and helped other practitioners whenever possible, but their drive for improvement was not comparable to what followed when farmers tilled their own lands.

Even though colonial settlement abroad enabled the development of specialized agriculture, farmers in Europe continued to supply the public's primary food needs during the seventeenth and eighteenth centuries. They filled this role for a growing population by approaching their task with new tools and a new understanding of the natural world. Their newfound efficiency and commercialism proved to be the foundation for numerous social and cultural changes that would grow from European roots after 1700.

Further Reading

Abel, Wilhelm. *Agricultural Fluctuations in Europe from the Thirteenth to the Twentieth Centuries.* New York, 1980.

Albala, Ken. *Food in Early Modern Europe.* Westport, CT, 2003.

Ambrosoli, Mauro. *The Wild and the Sown: Botany and Agriculture in Western Europe, 1350–1850.* New York, 1997.

Astill, Grenville, and John Langdon, eds. *Medieval Farming and Technology: The Impact of Agricultural Change in Northwest Europe.* New York, 1997.

Mokyr, Joel. *Twenty-five Centuries of Technological Change: An Historical Survey.* New York, 1990.

Solbrig, Otto T., and Dorothy J. Solbrig. *So Shall You Reap: Farming and Crops in Human Affairs.* Washington, DC, 1994.

Usher, Abbott Payson. *A History of Mechanical Inventions.* Rev. ed. New York, 1988.

Brian Black

SEE ALSO

• Dams and Drainage • Feudalism • Machines
• Markets and Fairs • Trade

Architecture

WITH ITS APPEAL TO ANCIENT ROMAN MODELS, ARCHITECTURE WAS THE MASTER ART THAT TRULY ANNOUNCED THE IDEALS OF RENAISSANCE CIVILIZATION.

Using the materials and building techniques a culture offers, architecture interprets place through the lens of imagination, transcending mere function so as to express the aesthetic, political, and religious ideals of civilization. In the 1400s these ideals were changing. Before the mid-fifteenth century, buildings in southern Europe were designed on traditional patterns, particularly the Roman house and the *insula* (urban apartment block) and the long basilican church with its center aisle running toward a semicircular apse in which the altar stood. In northern Europe, from Milan and Venice north throughout France, Germany, and England, there flourished a style of exceptional beauty that contemporaries called German or modern but that Renaissance writers, critical of the style's lack of clear classical references and assuming an association between this architecture and the invasions of the barbarian Ostrogoths, named Gothic. Late Gothic, called perpendicular because of its use of pronounced verticals in window mullions (slender elements dividing sections of a window) and stone details, persisted in England, where such masterpieces of Gothic architecture as the chapel of King's College, Cambridge, and the chapel of Henry VII at Westminster Abbey were still under construction in the 1510s, just as Donato Bramante (1444–1514) was introducing High Renaissance style to Rome.

▼ *Though the Italian Gothic style of the cathedral at Siena (built between 1284 and 1299) is neither as pronounced nor as complex as the great French and English Gothic cathedrals, this building's finials (crowning ornaments) and triangular gables nevertheless trumpet its Gothic inspiration.*

Renaissance Styles

In Italy, beginning in the 1420s, buildings designed with the self-conscious intention of imitating ancient Roman models began to replace the traditional southern architectural styles and patterns. The core vocabulary of Renaissance style was formed by the five orders of Roman architecture: Doric, Ionic, Corinthian, Tuscan, and Composite. Each order was defined according to its characteristic columns (including their capitals and bases) and the entablatures the columns supported (including cornices and moldings). Within the broad movement to re-create an architecture based on the five orders and on antique building patterns in general, there are identifiable modes: early Renaissance, High Renaissance, mannerism, and baroque. The development of Renaissance style through these phases is clearly illustrated in Italy, where fifteenth-century architects were intrigued not only with ancient Roman architecture but also with geometry and mathematical proportion.

This interest in geometry was especially evident in the design by Leon Battista Alberti (1404–1472) for the Church of Santa Maria Novella in Florence and in such buildings in Rome as the Cancelleria Palace and the Church of Sant'Agostino. In these early Renaissance

The influential Italian architect and theorist Sebastiano Serlio (1475–1554) wrote seven enormously important treatises dealing with virtually every aspect of architecture past and present. The following passage extols the importance of geometry in architecture:

How needful and necessary the most secret art of Geometry is for every artificer and workman, as those that for a long time have studied and wrought without the same can sufficiently witness, who since that time have attained unto any knowledge of the said art, do not only laugh and smile at their own former simplicities, but in truth may very well acknowledge that all whatsoever had been formerly done by them, was not worth the looking on.

Seeing then the learning of architecture comprehendeth in it many notable Artes, it is necessary that the architector or workeman, should first, or at the least (if he cannot attain unto any more) know so much thereof, as that he may understand the principles of geometry, that he may not be accounted among the number of stonespoilers, who bear the name of workemen, and scarce know how to make an answer what a point, line, or plane, or body is, and cannot tell what harmony or correspondency means, but follow after their own mind, or other blind conductors that have led to work without rule or reason, they make bad work.

Complete Works on Architecture and Perspective

This plate, published in the 1540 edition of Sebastiano Serlio's First Book of Architecture, *clearly displays the features that distinguished each of the five orders of architecture: (from left to right) the plain frieze of Tuscan; the deep and decorated architrave, or high beam, of Doric; the scroll-like capital of Ionic; the eucalyptus leaf capital of Corinthian; and finally the combination of Corinthian and Ionic features that marked the Composite style.*

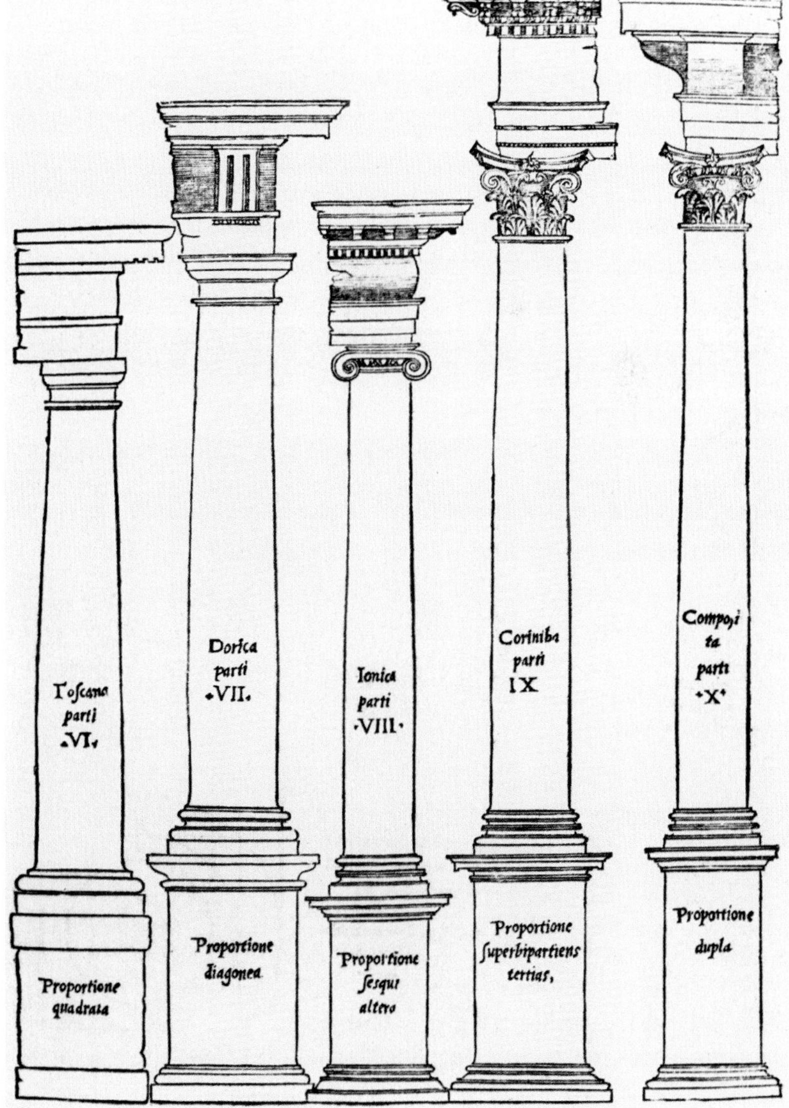

buildings the elevations, or facades, are often divided into bays by pilasters (columns built into the wall) that barely break the surface of the underlying wall so that the design is expressed linearly on a two-dimensional surface, not by three dimensional volume. In these buildings there is evidence of an emergent concern for the correct use of orders and proportions. Windows are often arched or arcuated, and rustication, the use of rough unfinished stone on the ground floor, is common.

Circles and Central Plans

Every well-educated humanist—a category that included Alberti, Bramante, and other architects—knew that Plato had described the circle as the most perfect form. When Nicolaus Copernicus, the fifteenth-century Polish astronomer who originated the theory that the sun, not the earth, was the center of the planetary system, pondered the path of the planets, he concluded that they must move along a circular path, for they were the most perfect of creatures and therefore must move in the most perfect way. Sforzinda, the theoretical city Filarete (c. 1400–c. 1469) proposed for his Sforza patrons, was designed as a perfect circle, and when Tommaso Campanella (1568–1639) described his City of the Sun, a utopia based on Plato's *Republic,* it was a vast circular city.

CIRCLES IN RENAISSANCE CHURCH DESIGN

"It is obvious," Leon Battista Alberti wrote in his seventh book, "from all that is fashioned, produced, or created under her influence that Nature delights primarily in the circle." When Alberti designed the Church of Santissima Annunziata in Florence in 1470, he would provide a circular plan. The Church of Santa Maria di Loreto, later much embellished by Antonio da Sangallo the Younger (1483–1546), was built in 1501 at the foot of the Capitoline Hill; the octagonal church bears a ribbed dome that seems to imitate the magnificent dome designed by Filippo Brunelleschi (1377–1446) for the cathedral in Florence. Bramante's Tempietto was a single circular space on a circular platform, and he intended the structure to be set within a circular colonnade or cloister; Bramante's plan for the Basilica of Saint Peter in Rome was a central plan beneath a hemispherical dome.

Since the interest in the circle included designs that could be inscribed in a circle, it extended to centrally planned churches of various geometries. Michelangelo followed the scheme of Baldassare Peruzzi (1481–1536) for completing Saint Peter's as a centrally planned church, a Greek cross with equal arms, and also proposed a circular domed structure for the San Giovanni dei Fiorentini, the Roman church of the Florentines. Gian Lorenzo Bernini (1598–1680) built the Church of Santa Maria della Assunzione in the town of Ariccia, southeast of Rome, with a circular nave, and his Sant'Andrea al Quirinale, in Rome, was designed as an ellipse. The first plan proposed by Pietro da Cortona (1596–1669) for the Church of Santi Luca e Martina by the old Roman forum was a circle. The first design made by Andrea Palladio (1518–1580) for il Redentore, the Church of the Redeemer, in Venice, was a central plan surmounted by a great dome. For Saint Paul's Cathedral in London, in 1673 Christopher Wren (1632–1723) proposed a central plan, a Greek cross with arms joined by concave walls. This plan came to be called the Great Model.

The only pre-Renaissance church in the round in Rome was the fifth-century San Stephano Rotondo, an attempt on the part of its designers to build in accordance with the design for the heavenly Jerusalem suggested in the last two chapters of the Book of Revelation. The interest in circular or centrally planned spaces, so much in evidence throughout the architectural Renaissance, faded after the seventeenth century owing to resistance by such powerful churchmen as Cardinal Charles Borromeo of Milan, who, in his *Instructions to Ecclesiastical Builders and Furniture Makers* (1577), expressed a preference for the Latin cross—that is, a design in which the nave is longer than the transept (the arms of the cross).

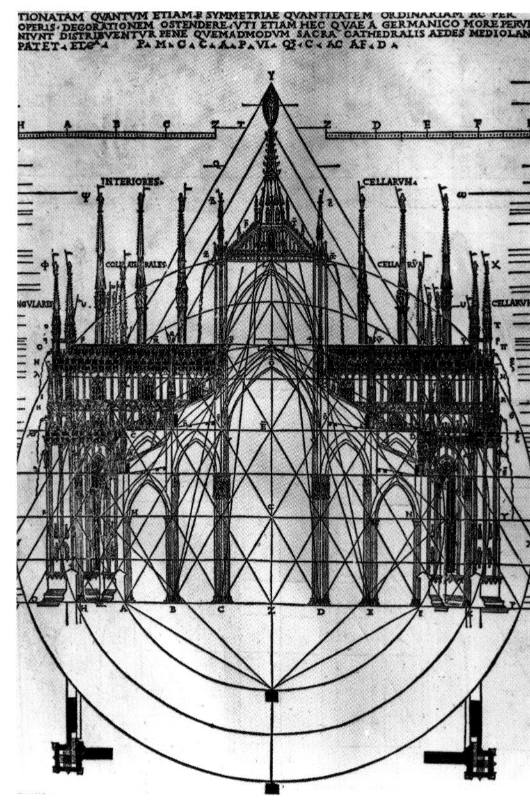

▶ *The cathedral in Milan (begun in 1386 but not completed until the nineteenth century) was one of the last Gothic cathedrals; its construction involved long theoretical arguments about the geometry that underlay the design and the structure. This plate from a sixteenth-century edition of Vitruvius illustrates the attempt to make design rational by making it geometrical.*

The High Renaissance of the early sixteenth century, still loyal to classical models, saw the development of more fully modeled forms and the use of circular central plans in church design. At the house of Raphael in Rome, designed by Bramante, the facade has depth, and the bays are divided by columns—which rest on a rusticated base extending to the level of the first floor—that are freestanding rather than being engaged, that is, built into the wall. Bramante's circular Tempietto, a small chapel in the courtyard of the Church of San Pietro in the Montorio district of Rome, is an early essay in central-plan church design, an idea that would fascinate architects until the late 1600s.

Mannerism

With the career of Michelangelo Buonarroti (1475–1564), adherence to classical precedents and scholarly interest in proportion gave way to an exuberant style called mannerism. Mannerists

▲ *The Church of Santa Maria di Loreto, situated near the Forum of Trajan in Rome. Built around 1501 and attributed to Antonio da Sangallo the Younger, this church is one of the few in Rome that fulfilled the aspiration of early-sixteenth-century architects to build round-domed structures.*

used architectural elements without reference to antique Roman models and often disregarded function and concentrated their efforts instead on producing a dramatic effect. Michelangelo's stairway at the Laurentian Library in Florence is a remarkable example of mannerist design. A triple stairway, it is first and foremost a piece of sculpture; two-thirds of it has no function, since it leads only to a single doorway. Michelangelo's career was followed by a dry, academic form of mannerism, complicated but not always inspired, that gave way around 1620 to the Roman baroque of Gian Lorenzo Bernini (1598–1680) and Francesco Borromini (1599–1667), an assertive and dynamic architectural style that confidently used references to classical elements in novel ways.

Theories and Books

When the Renaissance began, most architects had risen from among the ranks of stonecutters and wood carvers, and thus an architect was a higher sort of workman. By the beginning of the seventeenth century, many architects were gentlemen. This new status was a reward for service to the state; Gian Lorenzo Bernini was ennobled by Pope Gregory XV with the Order of Christ, and Christopher Wren was knighted by Charles II of England in 1673. However, the elevated idea of the profession depended less on architects' laying aside the hammer and chisel—neither Michelangelo or Bernini ever did so—than it did upon the claim Renaissance architects made to knowledge of a body of theory. Because a principal source of inspiration for Renaissance endeavor was the scholarly appropriation of ancient texts, architecture became bookish; many of the famous Renaissance architects published treatises that advocated and illustrated their theories. Only one text offered architects an ancient precedent. Vitruvius Pollio was a Roman architect and military engineer who wrote a treatise called *De architectura (On Architecture)* during the reign of Augustus, perhaps around 20 CE. Vitruvius's books included a treatment of town planning that discussed the orders, proportion, and materials and methods of construction. This text, found by the manuscript hunter Poggio Bracciolini in 1415, was first published in 1486, and the first Italian text was prepared by Fra Giacondo and published in Venice in 1511 and 1513. The edition published by Daniele Barbarao in Venice in 1556 was illustrated by Andrea Palladio (1518–1580).

▶ *This view of the interior of the Pantheon, built during the first and second centuries CE as a place in which the gods of the Roman Empire might be represented, conveys the majestic quality of the all-encompassing dome and something of the color and polish of the marble-encased interior.*

In the wake of the publication of Vitruvius, there followed a series of printed treatises on architecture. Leon Battista Alberti's *Ten Books on Architecture* was presented to Pope Nicholas V in 1452 and first printed in 1485. Filarete wrote a treatise before 1464; an illustrated copy of his work was dedicated to Piero de' Medici in 1465. Francesco di Giorgio (1439–1502) published his treatise on architecture after 1456. The Bolognese painter and architect Sebastiano Serlio (1475–1554) wrote a popular treatise titled *The General Rules of Architecture* that appeared in sections between 1540 and 1575. *The Rules of the Five Orders of Architecture* by Giacomo Barozzi, who is usually known as Giacomo da Vignola, was published in 1562. In 1563 a slim treatise titled the *First and Chief Groundes of Architecture* was published in London by John Shute, who had traveled in Italy under the patronage of the duke of Northumberland some time before 1550. Palladio's *Four Books* followed in 1570, and the *Idea of a Universal Architecture* by Vincenzio Scamozzi (1552–1616) was published in 1615. These treatises defined the profession by offering theoretical rules, discussed types of buildings, and included illustrations of ancient and contemporary architecture.

During the Renaissance, for the first time architecture was seen as an art with a history. Almost everything modern scholars know of the great Italian architects of the period runs back to Giorgio Vasari's *Lives of the Painters, Sculptors, and Architects* (first published in 1550). Biographies of architects published during the Renaissance include the *Life of Brunelleschi* by Antonio Mannetti (written during the 1480s) and the *Life of Bernini* by Filippo Baldinucci (c. 1624–1696).

Brunelleschi in Florence

Filippo Brunelleschi (1377–1446) was twenty-seven when, in 1404, he was first consulted about a small matter concerning the cathedral in Florence. He had already entered and lost the competition to design the baptistery doors. After losing out to Lorenzo Ghiberti in 1401, he spent thirteen years in Rome studying ancient buildings, his interest being chiefly in the structural techniques that enabled the Romans to build the great dome of the Pantheon and the vaulted ceilings of Nero's Golden House. A member of the

The conviction that the architect must combine practical skill with theoretical insight was a commonplace in the seventeenth century. Robert Hooke said of Christopher Wren that, since Archimedes, "there scarce ever has met in one man, in so great perfection, such a mechanical hand and so philosophical a mind." The notion may have its root in this passage from a first-century-BCE work on architecture that, after its rediscovery and publication in 1486, proved extremely influential.

The architect's expertise is enhanced by many disciplines and various sorts of specialized knowledge; all the works using the other skills are evaluated by his seasoned judgement. This expertise is born both of practice and reasoning. Practice is the constant, repeated exercise of the hands by which the work is brought to completion in whatever medium is required for the proposed design. Reasoning, however, is what can demonstrate and explain the proportions of executed works skillfully and systematically.

Thus architects who strove to obtain practical manual skills but lacked an education have never been able to achieve an influence equal to the quality of their exertions; on the other hand, those who placed their trust entirely in theory and writing seem to have chased after a shadow, not something real. But those who have mastered both skills, armed, if you will, in full panoply, those architects have reached the goal more quickly and influentially.

Vitruvius, *De architectura,* book 1

silk workers and goldsmith's guild, Brunelleschi worked as both a sculptor and a painter, but in 1419 he also created one of the first Renaissance designs, the cloister of the Ospedale degli Innocenti (Foundling Hospital) in Florence, a series of arches that shows the continuity in Italy between the revivals of the fifteenth century and the architecture of late antiquity.

Brunelleschi's fame was secured by his construction of the magnificent dome of the cathedral at Florence, but this spectacular achievement took place amid numerous other successes in Florence: the Old Sacristy in the Church of San Lorenzo, the parish church of the Medici family, and the Church of Santa Croce are among his most noteworthy projects.

▲ *The main body of the Pantheon, shown here, is a cube in which a sphere can be inscribed. The knowledge that the architects of the classical period had designed through geometry fed the desire of Renaissance architects to measure and imitate.*

Alberti: Arches and Geometry

Leon Battista Alberti was the illegitimate son of a Florentine family temporarily exiled to Genoa. He was educated in Latin and Greek at Padua and in law at Bologna. By age twenty he was the author of a comedy that passed briefly as antique. Arriving in Florence in 1428, he entered the papal civil service and was given several benefices that produced income, among them an appointment as canon of Florence's cathedral. In Florence he met Brunelleschi, the sculptor Donatello, and probably the painter Masaccio, and there he began to write his work *Ten Books on Architecture,* the first Renaissance treatise modeled on Vitruvius. Unlike Brunelleschi, who studied Roman ruins in order to discover building techniques, Alberti employed an assistant to supervise the construction of his designs while he devoted himself to such theoretical aspects of architecture as determining proportions and ratios and investigating the use of geometry. Always something of a rationalist, Alberti rejected the advice of an assistant with the words, "I have more faith in the men who built the baths and the Pantheon and all those noble edifices than I have in him, and a great deal more in reason than in any man." Alberti clearly equated reason in architecture with mathematics and geometry.

Roman church builders had learned to span considerable distances with a framework of wooden trusses, but there was no permanent way to span an opening in a brick wall without an arch. Where such an opening appeared to have a flat horizontal lintel, the appearance was usually deceptive, for often there would be a relieving arch over the door or window that carried the weight of all the masonry above. The lintel would carry only the weight of the small semicircle beneath the relieving arch.

Visually, Rome was a city of arches: aqueducts were raised off the ground on arches; great military victories were commemorated in triumphal arches; arches marched down the side aisles of churches. Thus, it is not surprising that Alberti's architecture defines a theme of the early Renaissance in its use of the arch as the dominant element in the composition of facades. Alberti's first patron was Giovanni Rucellai (1475–1525), a well-off Florentine who liked to build because doing so honored "God, the city, and my own memory." Under his patronage Alberti would provide the design for the facade of the Church of Santa Maria Novella in Florence and for the Rucellai Palace. Alberti's design for the Rucellai Palace featured numerous arched window openings, each subdivided into two tall arched shapes. Alberti designed two churches in Mantua, San Sebastiano and Sant'Andrea. The facade of Sant'Andrea was composed of a tall central archway leading into the church flanked by smaller blind arches (that is, purely decorative arches built into the wall).

At Santa Maria Novella the striking characteristic of the flat facade is not dynamism but geometry. The facade is composed on three squares, two side by side at the height of the side aisles and a third centered above. Alberti's use of giant consoles, or brackets, in the angle formed by the intersection of the horizontal line of the lower story with the vertical of the central nave became the standard device for joining visually the first story of a church, at the height of the lower aisle, to the tall nave.

The Renaissance Comes to Rome

Donato Bramante's patron, Ludovico Sforza, lost control of Milan in 1499. When Bramante, accompanied by Donatello, came to Rome, he brought the architectural Renaissance with him. Under Pope Julius II the city was once again the political capital of Italy, and it was the intention of the pope, who at various times employed Raphael (Raffaello Sanzio; 1483–1520) and Michelangelo, as well as Bramante, to make

◀ *Alberti's design for the Palazzo Rucellai, in Florence, illustrates the tendency of fifteenth-century architects to create two-dimensional designs inspired by geometry.*

Rome the artistic capital of the Christian world. Bramante's first Roman work, the cloister of the Church of Santa Maria della Pace (1500–1504), was an unremarkable design reminiscent of Brunelleschi's colonnade at the Foundling Hospital. Bramante's commanding reputation was established by two completed works: the tiny circular Tempietto (1502)—a chapel in the cloister of the Church of San Pietro in Montorio, Rome—and the palazzo-like house Bramante built for himself that was later occupied by Raphael and has been known ever since as the house of Raphael. The Tempietto was intended to mark the spot of Saint Peter's crucifixion, a location, fancifully computed, that was, according to tradition, *inter duas metas* ("between two small pyramids"). One *meta* was identifed as a pyramid-shaped tomb near Castel Sant'Angelo, and the other was the pyramid of Caius Cestius at the Porta San Paolo. Intended not as a church but rather as a *martyrium,* a commemorative monument marking the spot of Peter's martyrdom, the Tempietto's perfection engaged and influenced Renaissance architects. Bramante had meant it to stand not in the present square courtyard but in a circular colonnade. Its fully modeled design distinguishes it from the first generation of Roman Renaissance buildings, whose facades are merely delineated. The house of Raphael is a mature Renaissance design. Its ground floor is a series of heavily rusticated arches, and its *piano nobile*, or principal floor, is divided into bays by paired Doric columns placed against the wall but not engaged.

▲ *This bronze medallion, a self-portrait of Leon Battista Alberti, is evidence of the new sense of importance enjoyed by fifteenth-century architects, who considered themselves artists rather than mere workmen.*

Leon Battista Alberti 1404–1472

With his broad interests and wide-ranging talents, Leon Battista Alberti, a priest of the Catholic Church, is often cited as the ideal example of the Renaissance man. His book on architecture formed only a fraction of his published output; Alberti's works included the titles *Philodoxeus* (*Lover of Glory*; 1424), *Theogenius* (*The Origin of the Gods*; 1440), *De iciarchia* (*On the Prince*; 1468), and a work on painting, *Della pittura* (1436). His architectural successes in Florence and Mantua aside, Alberti was the first to undertake a scientific mapmaking project for the city of Rome, in which he located the ancient monuments, as seen from the Capitoline Hill, with a system of coordinates. He made the Aqua Virgo, Rome's only working aqueduct, operable by repairing the channel that carried its water under the Pincian Hill to a site near the present-day Trevi fountain. He almost succeeded in raising one of the two ceremonial barges that had lain on the bottom of Lake Nemi for a thousand years. By suspending winches from a bridge of floating barrels, Alberti was able to raise the prow of one of the two barges to the surface briefly, although he was unable to bring the waterlogged boat to land. Neither barge would be seen again until the twentieth century, when both were recovered—only to be destroyed in 1945.

▲ *The open loggia (porch) and rusticated basement and foundation of Giulio Romano's Palazzo del Tè, built between 1525 and 1535 in Mantua, anticipated the country house designs Palladio would make famous.*

The project that should have brought Bramante fame, the Basilica of Saint Peter, has secured him only a place of honor in the long succession of renowned architects who worked on the church between 1506 and 1665. Appointed architect of the proposed new church around 1506, Bramante contributed the central-plan design, an equal-armed Greek cross crowned by a dome. The four central piers, reinforced as architect followed architect, were located as they stand by Bramante, whose influence upon the building of the great church was thus made permanent.

Raphael may have been related to Bramante; in any event the two men worked closely together. Joint projects in Rome included designing Sant'Eligio degli Orefici, a tiny, domed Greek-cross church just off the Via Giulia that perhaps presaged Bramante's Saint Peter's. It is also often pointed out that the building depicted in Raphael's famous fresco *The School of Athens* is very much like Bramante's plan for Saint Peter's.

SAINT PETER'S AND THE SUCCESSION OF RENAISSANCE STYLES

During the Renaissance, the Basilica of Saint Peter, a pilgrimage church built in Rome by Constantine the Great around 330 at the place of Peter's burial, came to overshadow Saint John Lateran, the site of the pope's palace and hence of the government of the church. By 1585, when the dome was added, Saint Peter's was arguably the most important building in Europe.

Saint Peter's embodied a succession of Renaissance styles; it was the work of a dozen architects whose efforts spanned the period from the groundbreaking under Pope Julius II in 1506 to the completion of the colonnade by Gian Lorenzo Bernini in 1665. Bramante, the winner of the original competition of 1501, proposed a central plan under a high dome—a plan for which his Tempietto may be a sketch. In 1513 Julius II died, and his successor, Leo X, appointed a triumvirate of Raphael, Giuliano da Sangallo (Antonio the Elder's brother; c. 1445–1516), and Fra Giocondo (1435–1515). Raphael, who was capo (chief builder) for seven years, proposed a plan in a Latin cross. Baldassare Peruzzi, appointed his successor, planned to revert to a Greek cross, but the sacking of Rome by Charles V in 1527, during which Peruzzi was taken prisoner, delayed the work. Antonio da Sangallo the Elder, the architect for the next ten years, strengthened the central piers and proposed an awkward beehive-shaped dome, which was fortunately never built. Then in 1546 Michelangelo was appointed. Michelangelo would give the building its final form; he designed the dome, the nave, the chapels, and the side aisles with their distinctive and characteristically mannerist segmental lintels.

Michelangelo's dome, altered from the hemisphere he had proposed to a shape that gave a higher and more easily stabilized profile, was erected by Giacomo della Porta (1537–1602) and Domenico Fontana (1543–1607). The facade was built in 1612 by Carlo Maderna (1556–1629). Cupolas were added by Vignola in 1564, and between 1606 and 1612 Carlo Maderna lengthened the nave and added the baroque facade. Bernini then overlaid this complex composition with his own dramatic elements: the Chair of Peter in the apse, the baldachin—a canopy over the altar—at the crossing, the holy water stoups (basins), the colonnade, and the angels that guard the bridge over the Tiber River. During Bernini's years the other master of the baroque, Francesco Borromini, still a stonecarver, produced architectural ornamentation. At least eight master architects working in virtually the entire range of Renaissance styles produced a work of impressive, if unanticipated, unity and enduring beauty.

Agostino Chigi employed Raphael to fresco the walls and ceilings of his villa beginning in 1508, and after Bramante's death in 1514, Raphael designed the Chigi chapel in Santa Maria del Popolo and, with Antonio da Sangallo the Elder (1455–1535), the Villa Madama on Rome's Monte Mario, intended to be a great villa built around a circular courtyard but left half finished.

Giulio Pippi de' Gianuzzi, usually known as Giulio Romano (c. 1499–1546), was Raphael's assistant for some years before 1520 and took part in many of Raphael's works, among them the decoration of his Villa Madama. Four years after Raphael's death, Giulio accepted the invitation of the duke of Mantua and spent the remainder of his life (until 1546) in Mantua, where he designed the magnificent Palazzo del Tè.

Palaces and Families

For Italians of the Middle Ages and the Renaissance, the family was the bedrock of life, and many actions were conceived and undertaken in order to improve the success and wealth of the family. Headed by a great nobleman, often a prince of the Holy Roman Empire, the important families staked out territories and defended their property with great towers, such as the Torre delle Milzie, which still stands guard over the Market of Trajan. Sometimes families occupied the ancient monuments; in 1240 the Frangipanes and the Annibaldis both held parts of the Colosseum.

After the papal court returned to Rome from Avignon in 1407, after the Papal Schism was resolved in 1417, and after Nicholas V was elected pope in 1447, the great Roman families abandoned their fortresses and built palaces. By the end of the fifteenth century, Rome was a city of palaces. Four from that period still stand within a stone's throw of one another near the flower market (the Campo dei Fiore), between the Corso (a major thoroughfare) and the Tiber River: the Palazzo Massimi, the Cancelleria, the Palazzo Farnese, and the Palazzo Spada.

After Saint Peter's was completed around 1630, it became the architectural center of the Catholic world. In 1730 Giovanni Paolo Pannini (1691–1765) painted this scene depicting the visit of the French cardinal Melchior de Polignac to the basilica.

The immense Cancelleria, which abuts the Corso, was built by Raffaele Riario, a nephew of Pope Sixtus V, between 1486 and 1498 to a design by either Andrea Bregno or Antonio Montecavallo. After 1515 Pope Leo X confiscated the palace from the Riarios and made it the papal chancery. In the eighteenth century it became the residence of the Stuart pretenders to the English throne, who had taken refuge in Rome. The cliff-like facade of the Cancelleria, elegant but static and divided into bays by pilasters that barely break the surface of the wall, shows the geometric articulation of the early Renaissance. The second-story windows are arches set in a rectangular frame, a device common in the period before the sack of Rome (1527).

Just across the Corso from the Cancelleria is the Palazzo Massimi (1535). Built for Piero Massimi by Peruzzi in an awkward curve of the street, the Palazzo Massimi displays an early example of irregular column spacing. The Palazzo Farnese, begun by Antonio da Sangallo the Younger, is almost in sight of the Cancelleria across the Campo dei Fiori. As completed by Michelangelo, the Palazzo Farnese represents the beginning of mannerist style in palace design; its mannerist character is indicated by the dramatic contrast between the plain wall, unarticulated by pilasters, and the rich window frames and also by Michelangelo's central window, which includes a cartouche, or shield, bearing the Farnese arms and an exaggerated cornice. A few steps south of the Palazzo Farnese is the Palazzo Spada, built in 1550 and owned by the Spada family from 1632 to 1926. The striking facade of the Palazzo Spada is decorated with statues of Roman heroes, and its garden contains Borromini's trompe l'oeil vista (a form of optical illusion in which a small distance is made to look like a much larger one). Between the Farnese Palace and the Tiber River and parallel to the river is the Via Giulia, a street containing such smaller palaces as Borromini's Palazzo Falconieri.

The Galleria Prospettica in the garden of the Palazzo Spada in Rome, built after 1632 by Francesco Borromini. The garden walk seems to disappear into the distance; in fact, the colonnade is just thirty feet (9 m) long.

In the sixteenth and seventeenth centuries numerous palaces dotted the urban landscape, including the Palazzo Barberini (1504), by Bernini and Carlo Maderna; the Palazzo Borghese, designed by Vignola but completed by Martino Longhi the Elder by 1614; and Bernini's monumental Palazzo Chigi-Odescalchi. Each was home to the large household of a great noble Roman family and was thus a center of art, political influence and power, and employment.

Peruzzi's Painted Villa

Trastevere, the district west of the Tiber River that in Roman times had been the site of elegant suburban houses, had lapsed into a region of small gardens and orchards by the turn of the sixteenth century. In 1506 Agostino Chigi, one of Europe's wealthiest men, decided to build his summer house on the Tiber just opposite Raphael's Sant'Eligio degli Orefici. The site sloped gently toward the river's bank (the embankment that now contains the river would not be built until 1888). The building was not to be a palazzo built around a courtyard containing a garden but rather a small house surrounded by gardens and containing only six public spaces and one bedroom.

For the work Chigi chose Baldassare Peruzzi, who created a block of reticent delicacy with the stories delineated by deep cornices and bays divided by flat pilasters. Peruzzi designed the house in such a way that the visitor would enter by the Loggia (a room open on one side) of Psyche and Cupid, which was separated from the garden by five open arches.

The Loggia di Galatea, in the Villa Farnesina, was painted by Peruzzi and other architects of the early sixteenth century about 1506, when the villa was still the property of its builder, the wealthy banker Agostino Chigi.

BRINGING MYTHS TO LIFE

The spaces Baldassare Peruzzi designed for Agostino Chigi's villa by the Tiber have a grandeur of their own, but they are perfected by the ambitious painting program executed between 1508 and 1516 by Raphael, Sebastiano del Piombo, and Peruzzi himself. The scenes painted in the so-called Loggia of Psyche are derived from Apuleius's second-century prose narrative *The Golden Ass*, which had been translated into Italian in 1500 with a commentary by Agostino Chigi's friend Filippo Beroaldo the Younger. In order to humiliate her mortal rival, the beautiful Psyche, Venus orders her son Eros to make Psyche fall in love with an ugly suitor. However, Eros falls in love with Psyche and, without revealing himself to her, leads her to an enchanted castle. Overcome by curiosity about the identity of her sleeping spouse, Psyche lights a lamp. Eros wakes and flees; much of the story follows Psyche's pursuit of him. On the ceiling are two great panels: the *Council of the Gods*, at which the assembled deities contemplate the wedding of Psyche and Eros, and the *Banquet of the Gods*, a feast at which Psyche and Eros are at last united.

The other great room on the ground floor is the Loggia of Galatea, named for the river nymph who is pursued by the cyclops Polyphemus. The hexagons between the arches that run along all four sides of the room display the astrological signs representing the horoscope of Agostino Chigi. The ceiling is decorated with octagons displaying Peruzzi's own *Perseus and the Gorgon and Callisto*. The glory of the room is Raphael's *Triumph of the Galatea*, a depiction of the nymph's triumphant escape. The second story of the villa contains the great Hall of Perspectives, in which every wall is a trompe l'oeil scene of Trastevere. The other small room depicts scenes from the life of Alexander the Great.

The tendency to make historical and literary subjects part of the architecture was universal. Annibale Carracci decorated the Farnese palace with scenes from Apuleius, and the facade of the Spada Palace displayed in stucco the statues of Roman heroes.

Giorgio Vasari had been taken as a pupil to Michelangelo at age fourteen, when Michelangelo was at work on the sacristy for the Church of San Lorenzo in Florence.

Since he wished to make it in imitation of the Old Sacristy that Filippo Brunelleschi had built, but with another kind of ornament, he made a composite ornament, in a more varied and more original manner than any other master at any time, whether ancient or modern, had been able to achieve, for in the novelty of the beautiful cornices, capitals, bases, doors, tabernacles, and tombs, he made it very different from the work regulated by measure, order, and rule, which other men did according to normal usage and following Vitruvius and the antiquities, to which he would not conform. That license has done much to give courage to imitate him to those who have seen his methods, and new fantasies have since been seen which have more of the grotesque than of reason and rule in their ornaments. Therefore the craftsmen owe him an infinite and everlasting obligation, because he broke the bonds and chains of usage they had always followed.

Giorgio Vasari, *Lives of the Painters*

▼ *Palladio's Villa Rotonda, illustrated in plan and section in the 1570 edition of his* Four Books of Architecture, *was frequently copied in England and North America for at least three hundred years.*

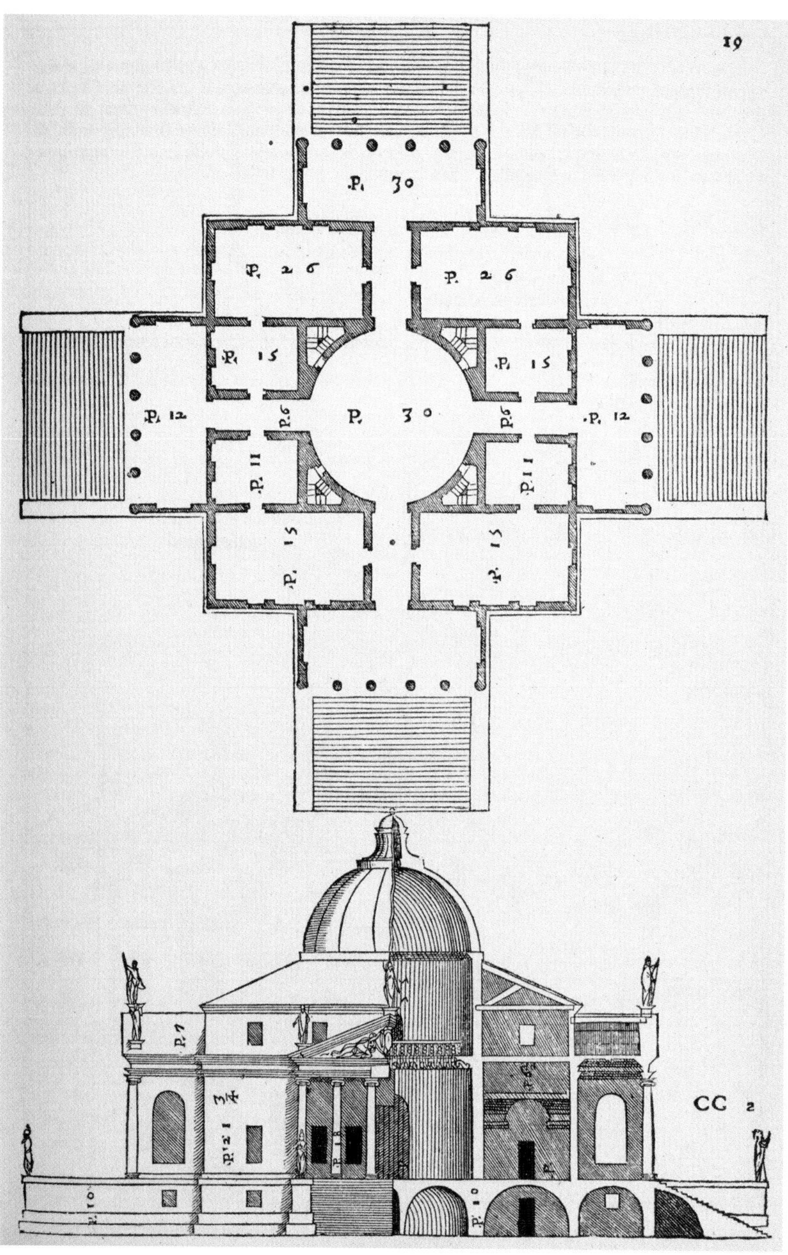

Michelangelo

Most famous as the painter of the ceiling of the Sistine Chapel in the Vatican, Michelangelo was, in common with many of the great Renaissance architects, first a sculptor. As an architect his distinctive mannerist style was established in the 1520s by his work at San Lorenzo, the Medici church in Florence. There he built a chapel that features his tomb of Giuliano de' Medici. The tomb's broken, curved pediment supports reclining figures of Night and Day; facing it is a statue of Lorenzo, seated above his own sarcophagus, which also supports the figures of Dusk and Dawn.

At the end of his career, in such works as the Porta Pia (a city gate) and the Sforza Chapel at the Church of Santa Maria Maggiore, Michelangelo anticipated the fully developed baroque.

Palladio in Venice

In the sixteenth century the draining of the marshes in the Veneto, Venice's mainland territory, to make arable land brought about an agricultural boom in the area. The newfound prosperity made Vicenza an important provincial city, and a new generation of great country houses soon sprang up.

Andrea di Pietro della Gondola, born in Padua in 1508, was apprenticed at age thirteen to a stone carver. In 1524 he broke his apprenticeship and fled to Vicenza, where he worked in the shop of the local carvers. At thirty he was employed as a mason to work on a villa at Cricoli, where Count Giangiorgio Trissino was erecting the first building in Vicenza designed in the new Renaissance style. Trissino's interest in the work at Cricoli brought him into contact with Andrea; the count took on the young mason as a protegé, gave him the name Palladio, and decided to give him a humanist education alongside the young nobles of his household.

Palladio's work matured during the 1550s, when he worked on several country houses: Palazzo Chieracati, Villa Thiene, and the Rotonda. If there had ever been a traditional architecture of the Roman country house, that tradition had been exhausted in the rough, castellated farmhouses of the Middle Ages, and so Palladio, free to consider each project afresh, created designs of great variety. Some of these designs—for example, the type of country house represented by the Villa Coronaro and the Villa Pisani, the long two-story block with a central porch of four or six columns—would be influential in the design of country houses in England and America until 1860. Other houses—Villa Barbaro, Villa Polano, and Villa Thiene, for instance—were one-of-a-kind designs crafted as the solutions to particular problems. The influence of Palladio's Villa Rotonda, the four-square domed villa with porches on each side, would be seen in the architecture of churches, universities, and courthouses into the twentieth century—a suitable destiny, perhaps, for a house built not for a landowner but for a retired monsignor of the Roman Church.

Inspired by the education provided by Count Trissino, Palladio became a humanist and a founding member of Vicenza's Academia Olympica, for which he designed an academic building containing a theater. His journeys to Rome with Trissino in 1541 and again in 1547 and 1554 put him in touch with both ancient architecture and contemporary buildings in the mannerist mode. His *Antiquities of Rome,* a guidebook to the ancient monuments, was published in 1554. His acquaintance with the works of Jacopo Sansovino (1486–1570)—notably the basilica in Vicenza and library in Venice—and his friendship with Sebastiano Serlio, who had come to Venice to oversee the printing and publication of *Antiquities of Rome,* were important to Palladio's development.

▲ Il Redentore, the Church of the Redeemer, in Venice, a building that displays the distinctive clarity that Palladio was able to achieve by setting a few bold elements (the columns, triangular pediments, and niches flanking the doorway) against severely plain wall surfaces.

While Palladio had tried and failed to secure a government post in Venice in 1554, Sansovino had secured commissions for the Scala d'Oro (golden staircase) in the doge's palace and the Rialto bridge. After Sansovino's death, Palladio became the most capable and available architect in the republic. In 1570 he moved to Venice; in 1572 both his sons died, and he became reclusive. His *Commentaries on Caesar,* a testimony to his humanist scholarship that was illustrated with his sons' drawings, was published as their memorial in 1573. The only work completed according to design during his time in Venice would be il Redentore, the great church commissioned by the senate of Venice in thanksgiving for deliverance from the plague of 1577. The church's hemispherical dome seems to float over the waters of the Grand Canal; in building the church, Palladio achieved at last an important goal of sixteenth-century architects by erecting a raised, perfectly hemispherical dome that defined a central space. Palladio's influence in England was secured through his *Four Books of Architecture*, published in Venice in 1570.

A FAMILY BUSINESS

The custom that a son succeeded his father in a family enterprise was especially prevalent in the building trades and among architects, many of whom never completely laid aside the stonecutter's hammer and sculptor's chisel. Gian Lorenzo Bernini came to sculpture and architecture by way of his father, Pietro, an ornamental stonecutter, and Gian Lorenzo's brother Luigi di Pietro Bernini was his assistant. Francesco Borromini was related to Carlo Maderna and to Domenico Fontana, and when he came to Rome, he was first employed by another relative, Leone Garovo, who was working under Carlo Maderna on the decoration of the portico of Saint Peter's. Borromini inherited much of Maderna's work after the latter's death in 1629. Giuliano da Sangallo (c. 1445–1516), originally a woodworker, took on such projects as the Church of Santa Maria delle Carceri in Prato, near Florence, and a sacristy for Brunelleschi's Church of Santa Croce in Florence. Giuliano's brother, Antonio the Elder, was born in 1455; their nephew Antonio the Younger was born in 1483.

The facade of the Church of Santa Susanna in Rome, built in 1603 to a design by Carlo Maderna that displays the depth and sense of movement that could be achieved through the use of dramatically assertive cornices and columns.

Michelangelo to Maderna

After the death of Michelangelo in 1564, the architecture of Rome was in the hands of Vignola, whose reputation was secured by his design for the facade of il Jesu, the principal church of the Jesuits in Rome. Giacomo della Porta and Domenico Fontana together built the dome of Saint Peter's in 1585. Fontana, with Pope Sixtus V as his patron, produced the tomb of Nicholas IV in the Church of Santa Maria Maggiore. He also worked at the Church of San Luigi dei Francesci. Fontana's career ended when he was accused of misappropriating funds on a bridge project, and his practice was taken over by his nephew, Carlo Maderna. Maderna rose to fame in the 1590s, when he designed the facade of the Church of Santa Susanna from 1597 to 1603, the Church of San Giorgio dei Fiorentini in 1598, and the Palazzo Barberini in the 1620s. He is remembered principally as the architect of the facade of Saint Peter's.

Borromini and Bernini

The near contemporaries Francesco Borromini and Gian Lorenzo Bernini together created in Rome a triumphant baroque style that announced the recovery of the Catholic Church signaled by the Council of Trent (1545–1563). Bernini, first a sculptor, had completed all his marble portraits and narrative sculptures by age twenty. He then worked at Saint Peter's for around fifty years. Borromini was born in 1599 into a family of stonecutters. Domenico Fontana was his uncle and Carlo Maderna his cousin. After several years in Milan, Borromini went to Rome, where his work as a decorative sculptor for his relatives culminated in employment in the shop of Carlo Maderna at the time when Maderna was completing Saint Peter's. Several of the architectural elements of that great church are Borromini's work, notably the putto (a figure of an infant boy) over the Holy Door and the iron gates of the Blessed Sacrament chapel.

In Rome, Borromini was to some degree overshadowed by Gian Lorenzo Bernini, who was as amiable and courteous as Borromini was melancholy and reclusive. Their relationship began when Borromini worked under Bernini at the Barberini Palace and later at Saint Peter's. Historians tend to accept Borromini's claims that Bernini took credit for several inventions that were Borromini's own.

In 1634 Borromini won the first of the commissions that secured his reputation as an originator of the baroque. Pope Sixtus V had laid out streets that crossed on the shoulder of the Quirinal hill, and fountains had been placed at each corner of the intersection. The church that would be San Carlo alle Quatro Fontane was designed by Borromini in 1634 and built between 1635 and 1640. By now Borromini was using classical elements with considerable freedom; in San Carlo many such elements are no more than reminiscent of their originals. San Carlo and the slightly later Sant'Agnese, in the Piazza Navona, were centrally planned churches whose designs, developed using complex overlapping geometries to create dramatically new spaces, represented an advance from the academism of the late sixteenth century. San Carlo was one unified space, its ceiling twice as high as the width of the nave.

The second great Borromini church was Sant'Ivo, the chapel dedicated to Saint Yves of Chartres that completes the courtyard of Sapientia University. Topped by a distinctive corkscrew tower, Sant'Ivo presented yet another novel and compelling set of geometries. Sant'Andrea delle Fratte, Borromini's third great Roman church, was distinguished by a fanciful facade composed in a spirit of baroque freedom.

France: Châteaux and Royal Palaces

The architectural Renaissance spread north and west from Rome. In such countries as France, England, and Germany, where there had been a strong tradition of Gothic architecture, the first essays in Renaissance classicism always incorporated medieval elements. The great architectural projects of the French Renaissance are royal palaces; among the finest are the Louvre in Paris, the rural palaces at Versailles and Fontainebleau, and the country houses of the great nobles in the valley of the Loire River—notably Chambord, Chenonceaux, and Blois. Fontainebleau was begun by Gilles le Breton in 1528, and additions were made by Serlio and Vignola. The Louvre occupied the great architects of the time for more than a hundred years. Begun by Pierre Lescot (1516–1578) in 1546, it was still incomplete when Bernini came to Paris in 1665 and would not be finished until François Mansart (1598–1666) undertook the completion of the project. The Palladianism that permeated English architecture in the seventeenth century had little influence on the architecture of France during the same period. A distinctive development of French Renaissance architecture was the tall double-sloped mansard roof that added another story beneath the rafters.

The clock pavilion wing of the Louvre in Paris. Built by Pierre Lescot between 1549 and 1555, this wing has the delicacy and complexity characteristic of sixteenth-century French palace architecture. Its most notable features are its triangular and segmental pediments, its arched and square window heads, its three stories with an additional fourth story above the main entrance, and a curved mansard roof that makes visual reference to the segmental window heads.

▲ *The almost endless succession of identical windows marching down the facade of the monastery at the Escorial, designed by Juan de Herrera and Juan Bautista de Toledo and built between 1563 and 1584, evokes the autocratic power and religious seriousness of the Spanish monarchy in the sixteenth century.*

Spain: Architecture for the Kings

In 1492 Columbus sailed on his first voyage, the expedition that would launch Spanish territorial expansion in the New World (the Americas), and earlier that year Granada, the last Moorish stronghold in Spain, fell to the Christians. The Renaissance coincided with a period of increasing Spanish power and self-confidence that began around 1500 and ended with the Peace of Westphalia, which concluded the Thirty Years War in 1648. Although Spain had no effective centralized bureaucracy, the Spanish kings ruled absolutely, and the architecture of the period bears the stamp of their authority.

As Holy Roman emperor, Charles V ruled Germany, Austria, and the Netherlands, and as the Hapsburg king of Spain, he ruled the Iberian Peninsula and Sicily as well as the extensive Spanish possessions in the New World. The palace of Charles V in Granada is perhaps the finest example of High Renaissance architecture in Spain. A two-story building some two hundred feet (61 m) square with a circular central courtyard, its facades are divided vertically by paired columns and horizontally by heavy cornices. The alternating triangular and segmental pediments over the windows would become a European convention. Charles's son, King Philip II, sponsored the Escorial, a group of buildings that embody the austerity of the king—whose Catholicism permeated every aspect of his life—as well as the ambitiousness of Spain itself in the sixteenth century. At the center of the composition was a domed church with twin west towers flanked by a college and a monastery. Philip's bedroom opened directly onto the altar of the church.

Both the Escorial and Charles V's palace are distinctly and exclusively Renaissance buildings, but most Spanish architecture of the sixteenth century displayed a unique character, one born of the melding of Moorish elements and native exuberance. This character was expressed in a surface decoration called Plateresque and a local Spanish baroque style called Churrigueresque. Among the great exponents of this Spanish style are the architects Juan de Herrera (c. 1530–1597), who designed the Valladolid Cathedral and is sometimes called the Spanish Palladio, and Juan Bautista de Toledo (d. 1567), the first architect of the Escorial.

England

The English architectural Renaissance was mostly the work of two great architects, Inigo Jones (1573–1652) and Christopher Wren (1632–1723). It was not until the 1610s that the new architecture was well represented in England. At the beginning of that decade, Jones designed the prince of Wales's lodging at Newmarket, in eastern England, and thereby inaugurated an English Palladianism that would characterize the reign of the first two Stuart monarchs, James I (reigned 1603–1625) and Charles I (reigned 1625–1645).

▲ *Wilton House in Wiltshire, in southern England. Rebuilt in Palladian style by Inigo Jones, Wilton House is typical of the rural palaces the seventeenth-century English aristocracy preferred.*

NEW STRUCTURAL TECHNIQUES

Concrete in compression, transferring weight from above to the ground, is strong, but concrete in bending—used, for example, to make a beam over an opening—is weak. By 1530 architects had realized that, by embedding iron in concrete, they would increase its ability to resist tension. When subsidence in its foundations threatened the Sistine Chapel in Saint Peter's, Giuliano da Sangallo halted the movement by inserting iron rods into the masonry of the ceiling vault and beneath the floor. In doing so, he anticipated the modern use of reinforced concrete.

As the desire to copy Roman buildings developed, the problem of constructing domes, which have a natural tendency to collapse outward at the base, became paramount. The problem was typically solved by surrounding the dome-bearing structure with lower secondary elements that countered the outward thrust. In the great Gothic churches external buttresses, sometimes of dramatic reach, solved the problem by pushing back against the walls of upper stories. Another solution was to set the dome low so that its outward thrust could be resisted by the surrounding parts of the building. However, among Renaissance architects anxious to imitate classical models, neither solution seemed appropriate.

Antiquity offered structural precedents. In building the dome of the Pantheon, which stood stable for a thousand years, architects had used a combination of solutions. The dome was concrete, a material that is to some degree internally stable. A surrounding cylindrical structure counteracted the tendency of the dome to collapse outward at the base. The tendency to buckle along the curve of the dome was resisted by extra weight cleverly built into the lower third of the dome itself. When Brunelleschi built the dome of the cathedral in Florence in the 1430s, the design included no surrounding structure that might have resolved, at least partially, the thrust of the dome. Either Brunelleschi or his employers solved the problem in part by designing a dome that was not strictly hemispherical but rather taller, so that thrust was minimized. Vertical ribs connected by masonry stiffened the dome and thus resolved internally—or, at least, limited—the dome's outward thrust. Finally, a stone chain was used at the base of the dome, and an iron chain was also added.

In order to minimize thrust at the spring line (the point at which the dome begins to curve) in Saint Peter's, the profile of Michelangelo's hemisphere was altered (it was made taller) by Giacomo della Porta and Domenico Fontana in 1585, and at various times ten iron chains were added to keep the dome as it had been built from collapsing outward.

Raphael wrote the following in a letter of 1514:

That your Lordship has honored me [with a commission] that has placed a great weight on my shoulders, as the Fabbrica di San Pietro [the building of Saint Peter's] has done. I hope not to fall under this weight, all the more since the model I made of it pleases his Holiness [Pope Leo X] and is praised by many fine minds. But my thoughts soar still higher. I would like to rediscover the fine forms of ancient buildings. Vitruvius has thrown much light on the subject for me, but not enough.

Letter to Baldassare Castiglione

This engraving of Christopher Wren's Saint Paul's Cathedral (c. 1750), viewed from a vantage point south of the Thames River, tells the viewer more about the importance the building held in English imagination as a native Protestant answer to Saint Peter's in Rome than it does about the exact proportions of the famous cathedral.

Jones's career was developed mostly before the revolution of 1642, which deposed the Stuarts and ruined Jones's practice. His most important designs were the Queen's House in Greenwich (1616–1619) and the Banqueting House in Whitehall (1619–1622). The link between Jones and Christopher Wren was Jones's assistant John Webb (1611–1674). Webb was employed by Inigo Jones at Wilton House and Durham House, both undertaken between the restoration of the Stuarts in 1661 and Webb's death in 1674. By that time Christopher Wren, a fellow of All Soul's, Oxford, who was well known for his studies in astronomy and anatomy, had developed an interest in architecture and had come to the attention of King Charles II. Wren began his architectural career with the design of the chapel at Pembroke College, Cambridge. In 1665 and 1666 he traveled to France, where he met François Mansart and also Gian Lorenzo Bernini, who had been in Paris since June 1665 at the behest of King Louis XIV. While in France, Wren also visited Versailles and the country houses of the Loire valley.

Wren had already commited to paper several designs for covering the crossing of Saint Paul's Cathedral with a dome like those he had seen in France at Jacques Lemercier's Church of the Sorbonne and François Mansard's Church of the Val-de-Grâce. However, it was the great fire of London (1666) that gave him the opportunity to provide the design for the new Saint Paul's Cathedral and indeed for the other city churches destroyed by the fire. His scheme for Saint Paul's, which is rightly considered his most important work, was imposing and monumental, although it was somewhat somber in comparison with baroque churches elsewhere. There would be no statues of saints or any trompe l'oeil paintings of saints ascending, since England had just emerged from a decade of Puritan government (Puritans condemned the use of images of Christ and the saints in worship). Masterly in composition, all Wren's work has a delicacy that echoes the French Renaissance; one of his favorite devices is the paired column, which he preferred to the bold orders of Inigo Jones's Palladianism.

In addition to the great cathedral in London, Wren designed fifty-two churches to replace those destroyed in the great fire. These churches followed Jones's centrally planned design for the Queen's Chapel and also the Roman baroque style of Bernini and Borromini. Each was arrranged around a central space with the altar the dominant feature on the east wall and a pulpit placed high toward the middle of the nave to ensure that the sermons that were central to Protestant worship could be easily heard. The variety of Wren's spatial solutions, dictated by the restricted urban sites, gave the London skyline its distinctive character until tall buildings obscured the forest of spires in the twentieth century. Among Wren's churches, two that seem especially evocative of his architectural imagination are Saint-Mary-le-Bow, famous for its steeple as well as for its bells (a Cockney was defined as anyone living within hearing range of Bow Bells), and Saint Martin's, Ludgate, the spire of which would be frequently imitated in seventeenth-century New England.

Renaissance Borderlands

Generally speaking, as the Renaissance spirit crossed the Alps into Germany and the Low Countries, the architecture it produced was a hybrid of medieval detail and half-understood Renaissance themes. The result in Germany and the Low Countries was a charming and picturesque architecture represented in such a municipal building as the Rathaus (town hall) in Bremen and in such a church as the Marienkirche at Wolfenbüttel, buildings whose design is far removed from the Renaissance classicism of Italy or the Palladianism of seventeenth century England. Exceptions to this trend may be found in Russia, where Peter the Great simply commanded that neoclassicism be adopted. In Mexico City, Lima, and other major cities in Spain's colonial dependencies, despite a certain localism, a recognizable and powerful baroque style appeared.

The Rathaus in Bremen, built between 1602 and 1612 by Luder von Bentheim, typifies the tendency of German architects to subordinate Renaissance architectural styles to local themes and tastes. The facade carries statues of Charlemagne and the seven electors of the Holy Roman Empire.

The Enduring Renaissance

The architectural Renaissance that began in fifteenth-century Florence has never ended. The baroque of the 1600s gave way in the eighteenth century to neoclassicism, an architecture using the classical orders but based on a claim to reasonableness that characterized the Enlightenment. Even after neoclassicism gave way in the 1780s to romanticism, which scorned rule and precedent, there were repeated classical revivals, notably the Greek revival of 1790 to 1840 and the later Renaissance revivals associated with the French École des Beaux-Arts. As late as 1850, public buildings in the United States were more likely to be Palladian than of any modern design. Varieties of classicism persisted into the 1940s.

FURTHER READING

Benevolo, Leonardo. *The Architecture of the Renaissance.* New York, 2002.

Murray, Peter. *The Architecture of the Italian Renaissance.* New York, 1986.

Norberg-Schulz, Christian. *Baroque Architecture.* New York, 2003.

Wittkower, Rudolf. *Architectural Principles in the Age of Humanism.* New York, 1965.

Wölfflin, Heinrich. *Renaissance and Baroque.* Ithaca, NY, 1966.

James A. Patrick

SEE ALSO

- Bernini, Gian Lorenzo • Bramante, Donato
- Brunelleschi, Filippo • Michelangelo
- Painting and Sculpture • Renaissance

Aristotle

Rediscovered in the 1200s, the works of the Greek philosopher Aristotle (384–322 BCE) were the intellectual backbone of academic life in Europe until Aristotelian science was challenged in the seventeenth century.

Aristotle was born in Stagira, in northern Greece, in 384 BCE and as a young man went to study at the Academy in Athens, a school run by the great philosopher Plato (c. 428–c. 348). While Plato believed that beyond the material world was a world of ideals that could be understood by the reasoning mind, Aristotle was primarily concerned with what it was possible to know about the material world from direct experience of it.

The range of Aristotle's interests was extraordinary. He divided knowledge into three classes. In the productive class he included such skills as rhetoric (the skill of persuasion, especially in public speaking) and art, a field that included the writing of plays. In the practical class of skills, he placed politics and ethics (the field of philosophy that deals with questions of duty and of good and bad conduct, whether of individuals or groups). In the third, the theoretical class of knowledge, Aristotle placed natural science, a category of learning that included physics, biology, botany, and chemistry. He argued that it was essential to accumulate as much factual knowledge as possible about the world and living creatures, both plants and animals, and he himself made vast compilations of his observations of animals as varied as bees and bison. Theoretical knowledge also encompassed mathematics, a discipline that offered the possibility of certainty—through geometrical proofs, for instance. In addition, the theoretical class included logic, the application of formal principles to philosophical reasoning and argument, and metaphysics, the inquiry into the fundamental abstract nature of reality and existence. What was remarkable about Aristotle was that he pioneered new ideas in almost all of these fields, from botany to ethics and from poetry to logic. In the field of logic, he is remembered in particular for his definition of the syllogism. The classic example of an Aristotelian syllogism is as follows: All men are mortal. Socrates is a man. Therefore, Socrates is mortal.

However, Aristotle's works often proved difficult to understand. Many were no more than lecture notes and were concerned with such

◄ *By the early 1500s Greek philosophy in general had been so well established that Pope Julius II could commission* The School of Athens *(1508–1511), a fresco by Raphael. In this detail Aristotle's hand points downward to the material earth, while Plato looks upward to an ideal world beyond this one.*

As the following passages demonstrate, Aristotle believed that the desire for knowledge was a natural characteristic of humanity. For Aristotle the gaining of knowledge was a collaborative exercise in which all those with a reasoning mind could share.

All men by nature desire to know. An indication of this is the delight we take in our senses; for even apart from their usefulness they are loved for themselves; and above all others the sense of sight. For not only with a view to action, but even when we are not going to do anything, we prefer sight to almost everything else. The reason is this, most of all the senses, makes us know and brings to light many differences between things....

The investigation of the truth is in one way hard, in another easy. An indication of this is found in the fact that no one is able to attain the truth adequately, while, on the other hand, no one fails entirely, but everyone says something true about the nature of things, and while individually they contribute little or nothing to the truth, by the union of all a considerable amount is amassed.

***Metaphysics* I and II**

complex issues that their real meaning remained unclear. As the English political thinker Thomas Hobbes (1588–1679) wrote two thousand years later, "None of the ancient philosophers' writings are comparable to those of Aristotle for their aptness to puzzle and entangle men with words and to breed disputation." Later scholars would produce commentaries on Aristotle's works in an attempt to make them accessible to the ordinary reader.

Aristotle believed that every organism had a potential, the state it would grow into if left to flourish. An acorn, if left free to grow, would become a great oak tree. A fully developed human being would become a reasoning creature (there are indications that Aristotle did not believe that women or slaves could ever develop a reasoning mind). From its early days Christianity taught that the path to truth lay through faith rather than through reasoning; by the fourth century CE, as Christian teachings spread throughout Europe, Aristotle's emphasis on reason had become discredited. In the West, where few could read Greek, his works had disappeared almost completely by the sixth century. At the beginning of the twelfth century, only two of Aristotle's many works were known to Europeans.

The Medieval Rediscovery

Aristotle remained popular in the Arab and Jewish world, where a number of important philosophers preserved and commented on his work. The most influential of these Islamic Aristotelians was the Spanish Arab Ibn Rushd (known in the West as Averroës; 1126–1198), whose commentaries were particularly thorough and sophisticated. When the Christians reconquered Islamic Spain, they came across Ibn Rushd's writings in libraries. Thus, European scholars gradually rediscovered Aristotle, even though, at first, they had to use Latin translations of the Arabic translations of the original works in order to gain access to them.

▲ *The works of Aristotle were deeply respected in the Arab world. In this thirteenth-century Seljuk Turkish manuscript, Aristotle is portrayed as an Islamic teacher explaining a scientific problem to his students.*

▼ *In his* Triumph of Saint Thomas Aquinas, *of which this is a detail, the Italian artist Benozzo di Lese Gozzoli (1420–1497) places the great Christian philosopher between Aristotle (on Thomas's right) and Plato. Beneath Thomas's feet is Averroës (Ibn Rushd), whose Arabic commentaries on Aristotle, though enormously influential, are shown to have been superseded by Thomas's.*

Aristotle's works reflected the prevailing beliefs of the pagan era in which he had lived, and within the church, there was some resistance to their reintroduction. Aristotle's first major Christian champion was the German Dominican friar Albertus Magnus (c. 1200–1280), who collected those works of Aristotle he knew together with Arab commentaries on them. Albertus was careful to point out that, while he thought people should know of Aristotle, he did not necessarily endorse what Aristotle wrote. Albertus's most famous pupil, Thomas Aquinas (1225–1274), went much farther and embraced Aristotle's philosophy. Aristotle himself had argued that there must logically exist an Unmoving Mover who set the universe in motion. For Aquinas and other Christians, this hypothesis demonstrated that Aristotle's beliefs were consistent with the existence of the Christian God. Far from seeing Aristotle's elevation of reason as a threat to Christian doctrine, Aquinas argued that reason had been given to mankind as a gift of God, and thus, used correctly, reasoning would never contradict what God had revealed. Aquinas wrote commentaries on many of Aristotle's works and incorporated Aristotelian ideas into his great work, the *Summa theologiae*.

Nevertheless, the problem remained that Aristotle had held beliefs that contradicted Christianity. He had argued, for example, that the world had always existed and that there had been no distinct moment of creation. He had also believed that the soul was inseparably bound up with the body. Christians, on the other hand, believe that the soul can separate from the body and continues to exist after the death of the body. Aquinas glossed over these difficulties, and, despite some continuing opposition, the Catholic Church adopted Aquinas's theology, which was infused with Aristotelian ideas.

Indeed, Aquinas's work was used to strengthen Catholic doctrine. For example, Aristotle had made the distinction between substance (the underlying properties of a thing) and accidents (the particular visible aspects of a thing). For Aristotle the substance of a human being is a reasoning mind, and that mind might be contained in a tall or short body or a black or white body without the substance being affected. The crucial Catholic doctrine of transubstantiation, the belief that bread and wine are transformed into the body and blood of Jesus at the Eucharist, was explained in terms of the contrary Aristotelian view that the substance of a thing could change while the accidents remain unchanged. Thomas Aquinas's version of Aristotle remained at the core of Catholic teaching for centuries.

Other scholars continued to be impressed by Ibn Rushd's vast and erudite commentaries, first translated into Latin in the mid-thirteenth century. Ibn Rushd, a Muslim, had laid stress on aspects of Aristotle's thought—such as the eternity of the world and the union of the body and soul—that did not fit with Christianity. His followers, the Averroists, also placed more stress on the possibility of a person finding happiness on earth through the use of reason. (Aristotle had put forward this view in his *Nicomachean Ethics,* so called because one Nicomachus was the first editor of the work). Averroistic Aristotelianism became established as a distinct approach to the philosopher, one that the great Italian poet Dante was sympathetic to. Ibn Rushd's interpretations of Aristotle appealed particularly to those studying medicine and other sciences.

It was also possible to use Aristotle to resist the power in the secular realm of the Catholic Church. In one of his most famous works, the *Politics,* Aristotle argued that the highest state of communal living was the city (in Greek, *polis*) and that a successful city depended on free men concentrating their energies on living in harmony. This ideal of the self-sufficient community had been challenged by Saint Augustine's *City of God* (413–427), which claimed that the only true city was that instituted by God in heaven—an argument the papacy endorsed.

Marsilius of Padua (c. 1280–1343) was rector of the University of Paris at a time when the French monarchs were challenging the secular authority of the papacy. In *Defender of Peace* (c. 1324), he used Aristotle's *Politics* as the basis for his argument that a state should be ruled by its own citizens and that the church should be subject to civil law, not above it. Although Marsilius was excommunicated in 1327, the *Defender* became an extremely influential text.

▲ *According to the principles of Aristotelian ethics, justice should always be applied with moderation and balance. In the upper portion of this illustration from a fifteenth-century philosophical manuscript, an allegorical figure representing legal justice shelters all comers. Below, goods are fairly measured out (left), and retribution is threatened to a wrongdoer (right).*

Marsilius of Padua drew on Aristotle's *Politics* when he argued that citizens should be the ultimate authority in the making of law.

Now we declare according to the truth and on the authority of Aristotle that the law-making power or the first and real effective source of law is the people or the body of citizens or the prevailing part of the people according to its election or its will expressed in general convention by vote, commanding or deciding that something be done or omitted in regard to human civil acts under penalty or temporal punishment.... On the authority of Aristotle by a citizen I mean him who has a part in the civil community, either in the government, or the council, or the judiciary, according to his position. By this definition boys, slaves, foreigners, and women are excluded, though according to different limitations. Having thus defined citizen and the prevailing section of the citizens, let us return to the object proposed, namely to demonstrate that the human authority of making laws belongs only to the whole body of citizens as the prevailing part of it.

Defender of Peace

▲ This colored engraving of Aristotle comes from a book by the Hungarian scholar Johannes Sambucus, published in Antwerp in 1574, on ancient and modern figures of eminence in philosophy and medicine. The breadth of Aristotle's work, which encompassed discussions of the human body and mind, qualifies him for inclusion under either heading.

Scholasticism

The medieval universities that taught Aristotle used a system of questions and answers. A class might start with the question, "What is physics?" The answer would be a definition from Aristotle's work on physics. Further questions and answers would follow, and the issue would be fully explored until a logically defensible definition of physics had been achieved, one that would usually take account of the role of God as the ultimate arbiter of all created things.

This method of intellecual inquiry was known as Scholasticism. Although Aristotle's views were often accepted without much criticism, in some cases—such as, for example, Aristotle's view that a vacuum is physically impossible—they were challenged by the Scholastics. It was certainly possible to make progress in knowledge by using the Scholastic method, but Scholasticism also gained the reputation for being conservative and much too concerned with minute distinctions between terms.

The Humanist Reaction

While almost all of Aristotle's works were known in the West by 1300, the translations from the original Greek were often crude, many having been taken from Arabic translations and commentaries and then reinterpreted, through Scholastic methods, to fit with Catholic teaching. Humanist scholars set themselves the task of rediscovering the original texts of classical authors and interpreting them according to the original intentions of those authors. Humanists derided the medieval Latin the Scolastics used to conduct their debates and the narrowness of their perspective. In the words of the classical scholar Angelo Poliziano (1454–1494), who lectured on Aristotle at the University of Florence, "On account of their ignorance of both Latin and Greek, [the Scholastics] polluted the purity of Aristotle's works with their vile and dreadful hair splitting to such an extent that sometimes it made me laugh and at other times it made me angry." For their part the humanists tried to track down the best surviving manuscripts of Aristotle and translate them into classical Latin; at the same time they revived Aristotle's works on ethics, poetry, and rhetoric, which the Scholastics had neglected. One early translator was Leonardo Bruni (c. 1370–1444). In his *Life of Aristotle* (c. 1428), Bruni portrays his subject as an ideal model for the humanists: a man of high moral principles, thoughtful but active in politics, of wide intellectual interests, and true to his friends. One of Bruni's most influential translations was his 1416 edition of Aristotle's *Nicomachean Ethics*, an important work (then as now) for those who believe that it is possible to use reason to define the nature of the good life and of rightful action.

Though widely read, even by Scholastics, Bruni's translation of the *Ethics* was also criticized. Bruni had assumed that there must be an equivalent Latin word for every Greek term, but often there was not, and so in many instances Aristotle's true meaning was lost in the translation. A more sweeping criticism, made by Alfonso of Cartagena, a Spanish bishop, was that Aristotle should always be interpreted to fit in with the revealed truth of God. This view conflicted with the humanist position that the

The humanist Leonardo Bruni, an important champion of Aristotle, believed the great philosopher's works had been abused by Scholastic philosophers and their clumsy Latin.

But there are many masters of this knowledge [philosophy] who promise to teach it. But if anyone should ask them on whose authority and precepts they rely in this splendid wisdom of theirs, they say the Philosopher's, by which they mean Aristotle's. And when there is need to confirm something or other, they bring forth the sayings in those books which they claim to be Aristotle's—words, harsh, awkward, dissonant, which would wear out anyone's ears. . . . The Philosopher says this, they tell us. It is impious to contradict him, and for them ipse dixit has the force of truth [i. e., merely because Aristotle himself has said something, it is true], as if he had been the only philosopher, or his sayings were as fixed as those which Pythian Apollo gave forth from the Holy Sanctuary [the site of the Greek oracle at Delphi]. . . . Not that I say this to censure Aristotle; I have no war with that very wise man, only with the folly of those Aristotelians. . . . Not even in the least thing do I believe that they rightly grasp what Aristotle taught.

Leonardo Bruni, *The Dialogues*

scholar should try to find exactly what Aristotle had written, whether or not Aristotle's beliefs agreed with church teaching. Indeed, the debate over how Aristotle should be translated became a major issue of the day. Was it better to have a translation of Aristotle's works that reflected the fact that the original might have been difficult to interpret and that retained those difficulties, or should the translation aim to produce a perfect example of polished Latin that glossed over the difficulties in Aristotle's original texts?

To some extent the issue was solved by the appearance of new texts and translators when the Ottoman Turks took Constantinople in 1453. Many of the Greek-speaking refugees who fled Constantinople and arrived in Italy were fine scholars. One of them, Johannes Argyropoulos (1415–1487), made more translations of Aristotle into Latin than any other fifteenth-century humanist. Many of these translations remained standard throughout the sixteenth century. The translation of the *Nicomachean Ethics* by Argyropoulos went through sixty-five editions, most of which were published in France and Italy.

Many classical Greek and Roman cities and even the households of educated men would display busts of the great philosophers. Pictured here is a Roman copy in marble of a Greek original that probably dates from the late fourth century BCE, when such busts first became popular. This image, which gives Aristotle a beard—the recognized hallmark of a philosopher—served as a model for later representations of its subject.

One of the main achievements of the humanists was to discover commentaries on Aristotle written during classical times. The earliest humanist translation of a classical commentary on Aristotle was the Venetian Ermolao Barbaro's 1481 Latin version of the *Paraphrases,* a work written in the fourth century CE by an orator named Themistius. Even though Themistius was writing some seven hundred years after Aristotle, it was assumed by the humanists that Greek commentaries on Aristotle by writers of the classical era were bound to be superior to medieval European and Arab commentaries. Barbaro (1454–1493) went on to criticize the commentaries of Albertus Magnus and Thomas Aquinas. This development further distanced the humanists from the Christianized version of Aristotle.

Another classical commentary, one written around 200 CE by Alexander of Aphrodisias on Aristotle's views of the soul, prompted the Mantuan scholar Pietro Pomponazzi (1462–1525) to argue in a treatise that Aristotle did not support the Christian view of the soul. Francesco Vimercati, a Milanese who held the chair of Greek and Latin philosophy at the University of Paris, argued in 1543 that scholars should not try to make pagan philosophers compatible with Christianity. "I think our faith is much more imperiled," Pomponazzi wrote, "when we try to confirm and protect it with the testimonies of Aristotle, Plato, or other outsiders which are inappropriate, unsuitable, and not written by them for that purpose." This statement was typical of the humanist position.

▲ *Although this seventeenth-century engraving shows Aristotle writing in a notebook, most scholars assume that the philosopher's works were either dictated in rough form or noted during his lectures. For this reason many have found his writings difficult to interpret (Plato's works, on the other hand, are beautifully written).*

Aristotle in the Sixteenth Century

The arrival of mechanized printing in the latter part of the fifteenth century boosted the dissemination of Aristotle's works—as it did the works of all classical authors. The great Venetian publisher Aldus Manutius printed the first full edition of Aristotle in its original Greek between 1493 and 1498. As a result, scholars could always refer back to the original texts (insofar as the manuscripts used by Aldus were correct; unfortunately, Aldus's texts were so densely printed as to make them hard to use). In 1497 Niccolò Leonico Tomeo, another Venetian, began using the original Greek texts for his lectures on Aristotle at the University of Padua. Padua, which boasted Europe's foremost medical school, was a stronghold of Aristotelianism, which was not, by and large, taught within any Christian context. The university there was one of the first to concen-

ARISTOTLE AND THE PLATONISTS

The great philosopher Plato (428–347 BCE) had argued that beyond the material world there existed an eternal realm of perfect ideas—such abstract qualities as Beauty, Justice, and Goodness. What might be considered beautiful in nature was only an imitation of the perfect idea of Beauty. Plato's works, in common with those of Aristotle, had been lost to the West. However, in the 1480s there arose an important revival of Platonism that was centered in the city of Florence, where the scholar Marsilio Ficino (1433–1499) had translated Plato from Greek into Latin and made Plato fashionable in the intellectual circle that surrounded Lorenzo "the Magnificent" de' Medici (1449–1492), Florence's ruler. Plato's works were easy to read, and by comparison, Aristotle and his interpreters seemed stuffy. Plato offered a vision of an ideal world beyond this one—a vision that many found spiritually uplifting. As so much art of the period bears witness, the Platonists breathed new life into the study of ancient mythology, a subject in which Aristotle had shown no interest.

Although Plato, like Aristotle, wrote of the importance of reason in discovering truth, many Platonists of the sixteenth century preferred to find ancient wisdom in other sources. Giordano Bruno (1548–1600), for instance, attempted to trace Christianity back to ancient Egypt, where, he claimed, it had existed in a pure form. For Bruno, Aristotelian rationalism was a corruption of religion. (Bruno's views were so unsettling to the church that he was burned as a heretic in Rome.) Other Platonists drew for their inspiration on the Kabbalah, the sprawling body of Jewish commentaries on the Hebrew scriptures.

Although the Platonists failed to produce any coherent alternative to Aristotle, whose works continued to form the core of the academic curriculum, they showed that imagination and creativity, however undisciplined, did offer an avenue to other forms of truth. As such, they contributed to the growing disillusionment by intellectuals with Scholasticism and hence with the authority of Aristotle.

A sixteenth-century engraving of Giordano Bruno (1548–1600). A freethinking Dominican monk, Bruno fell afoul of the church for a number of reasons, chief among them his complaints about the absolute and unquestionable status of Aristotle's works within Catholicism. He agreed with the Polish astronomer Nicolaus Copernicus that direct observation of the universe, for instance, might show that Aristotle's views had been superseded. In 1600, after many years of imprisonment, Bruno was finally burned as a heretic in Rome.

trate on the classical rather than the medieval commentaries.

Even within the University of Padua, there remained differences in the way that Aristotle was approached. Jacopo Zabarella (1533–1589), a professor of natural philosophy at the university, declared that he followed Aristotle because he believed that the philosopher used reason extremely successfully. However, in Zabarella's view, one had to observe the natural world continually, and if new observations were forthcoming, Aristotle's own observations and the theories he deduced from them could be discarded. Zabarella's successor, Cesare Cremonini (1552–1631), took a completely different line. For Cremonini, Aristotle's texts were sacred; what Aristotle had written must stand for all time. Cremonini told the Inquisition, the papal court that investigated him for heresy, that his job was simply to pass on what Aristotle had written and not to question it. It was Cremonini who refused to look through Galileo's telescope, saying that nothing he would see through it could ever supersede what Aristotle had written. Such obstinate views served to alienate Aristotelians from the academic mainstream during the scientific revolution of the seventeenth century.

In general, the trend at the more secular universities, such as Padua, was to move away from the Scholastic approach to Aristotle. Even Ibn Rushd's commentaries became redundant. There was some resistance to this trend, however. The Venetian publisher Tommaso Giunta mourned the neglect of Ibn Rushd: "So addicted are they [the humanists] to the [commentaries of] the Greeks that they proclaim the writings of the Arabs to be no better than dregs and useless trash." Between 1550 and 1552, Giunta printed a major edition of Aristotle together with Ibn Rushd's commentaries. After 1575, however, Ibn Rushd was little used. Still, the work of producing accurate original texts continued; a great edition of Aristotle, with parallel texts in Greek and Latin, was published in Lyons in 1590 by the scholar Isaac Casaubon (1559–1614).

▼ *It was in Venice that many of Aristotle's works were printed for the first time in their original Greek. The Venetian publisher Tommaso Giunta, the subject of this 1563 oil by Benedetto Caliari (1538–1598), printed Aristotle's text alongside Arabic commentaries, such as that of Ibn Rushd, at a time when these commentaries were being derided by the Catholic authorities.*

Aristotle and the Church

Aristotle had become so closely tied to the authority of the Catholic Church that with the Reformation, Aristotelianism was inevitably called into question. When the Dutch humanist scholar Desiderius Erasmus (c. 1466–1536) traveled to Paris in 1495 to study theology, he was horrified by the bickering between rival groups of Scholastics over tiny issues that seemed to him to have no relevance to Christian life. He argued that Scholasticism had been an unwelcome innovation in the history of Christianity and that Aristotle and theology did not necessarily fit together. "It is something new to exclude from the Holy of Holies of Theology anyone who has not sweated for years over Averroes or Aristotle," he later wrote. Instead, Erasmus believed, Christians should engage directly with the scriptures—and his own translations of the Bible were designed to enable them to do so. The Reformer Martin Luther (1483–1546) was even more dismissive of Aristotle. Luther believed that the Christian should live by faith only—in his words, "reason is the devil's whore." Luther held that the Christian depended entirely on God for salvation and that scripture is the only way to find God's will. He vehemently rejected Aristotle and, in common with Erasmus, Scholasticism. Interestingly, however, the Reformers had great difficulty in finding alternatives to Aristotle. The rambling *Natural History* written by the Roman scholar Pliny the Elder (23–79 CE) was used by some in place of Aristotle as an introduction to the science of the natural world, but Pliny's work lacked any kind of systematic approach. Soon even the Reformers had returned to Aristotle; his work was so wide ranging that he tended to be the starting point for any scholarly debate.

The traditional Scholastic approach to Aristotle endured in most parts of Europe and even spread, with the Catholic Church, to the Spanish colonies that were gaining a firm foothold in the Americas in the early sixteenth century. During the Counter-Reformation, Scholasticism received a boost when the Catholic

Church revitalized its education system in order to defend traditional Catholicism. The Society of Jesus (the Jesuits), founded by Ignatius Loyola in 1540, was the intellectual powerhouse of the Counter-Reformation. The Jesuits based the theological component of their curriculum on Aquinas (who was, of course, heavily influenced by Aristotle) and returned to Aristotle himself for natural sciences. Many Jesuits proved to be important scholars of Aristotle. One Jesuit, Tarquinio Galluzzi (1574–1649), wrote an extensive commentary on the *Nicomachean Ethics;* to the original Greek text and a Latin translation, Galluzzi added medieval commentaries, especially those of Thomas Aquinas, as well as classical ones. Such major works kept Aristotle embedded within Catholic doctrine. In the seventeenth century the English philosopher Thomas Hobbes complained, "Philosophy hath no other place than as the handmaiden to the Roman religion; and since the authority of Aristotle is only current there, that study is not properly philosophy but Aristotelity." Louis XIV of France (reigned 1643–1715), the so-called Sun King, noted that Aristotle and Catholicism were "so tightly joined that one could not overthrow one without the other."

▲ *In Rembrandt's majestic oil* Aristotle with a Bust of Homer *(1653), the medallion hanging from Aristotle's neck bears the image of Alexander the Great, whom Aristotle apparently tutored. According to the Roman biographer Plutarch (c. 46–c. 119 CE), Aristotle prepared a special edition of Homer's* Iliad *in order to teach Alexander the art of war. This story, which Rembrandt would have known, provides the link between the three great figures of antiquity featured in this painting.*

THE REDISCOVERY OF ARISTOTLE'S *POETICS*

Aristotle's wide-ranging interests included poetry, which in ancient Greece was primarily an oral art form that included tragic drama as well as such epic poems as Homer's *Iliad* and *Odyssey.* In the *Poetics,* Aristotle wrote what can be seen as the earliest handbook of literary criticism. For Aristotle all art is imitation of nature. (In other words, he does not believe that art is purely the product of the human imagination). The purpose of art, in Aristotle's view, is to arouse emotion. While upbeat poetry may arouse delight, great tragedy may arouse pity or fear; by releasing these emotions, the spectator may be spiritually purged (a process known in Greek as *katharsis* and in English as catharsis). Aristotle goes on to analyze the structure of a successful play—its plot, characters, staging, and so on.

The *Poetics* had been largely ignored by the Scholastics, even though a commentary on the work by Ibn Rushd had been printed in 1481. The process of its rediscovery provides a good example of how knowledge of Aristotle's work gradually spread. The first printed Latin translation of the *Poetics* appeared in 1498, and then the original Greek text (which had been left out of Aldus's edition) appeared in 1508. Other Latin translations, including one by Erasmus, followed. In 1536 an edition by Alessandro de' Pazzi was the first to place the Greek original and Latin translation together in one volume. The earliest evidence of public lectures on the work—at Padua—dates to 1541. The first major commentary on the *Poetics* was by Francesco Robertello in 1548. A year later Bernardo Segni published an Italian translation, the first translation in a language other than Latin. By the 1560s the *Poetics* was being talked of, in Italy at least, as the standard work on poetry (it supplanted the *Ars Poetica* by the first-century-BCE Latin poet Horace). From that point forward, the *Poetics* became more widely available throughout Europe and increasingly important, especially to the French tragedians of the seventeenth century.

The Challenge to Aristotle's Science

Aristotle had argued, in common with other ancient Greek scientists, that the earth was the center of the universe, that the sun and the other planets orbited the earth, that the universe was unchanging, and that the planets themselves were perfect spheres that moved in perfect circles. In 1543 the Polish astronomer Nicolaus Copernicus (1473–1543) challenged the earth-centered view of the universe in his *De revolutionibus orbium coelestium (On the Revolution of Heavenly Spheres),* but this work remained virtually unknown to contemporaries. Then in 1604 the discovery of a supernova suggested that the universe was indeed subject to change. Soon after, Galileo Galilei shattered Aristotle's conception of the universe by pointing his telescope at the sky and revealing that the moon had an irregular surface and that Jupiter had its own moons. The arguments for a sun-centered solar system gradually became stronger. Many of Aristotle's other assertions—for example, those about the nature of motion and the dynamic properties of falling bodies and projectiles—were also being challenged by Galileo's experimentation and calculations. Experiments with air pumps proved that vacuums could exist, while the mechanical view of the physical world offered by René Descartes (1596–1650) challenged Aristotle's theory of a world governed by a chain of causes. The English scientist and philosopher Francis Bacon (1561–1626) accused Aristotle of the greatest scientific sin of all—interpreting and modifying observations in order that they might fit in with conclusions already drawn. Bacon's own scientific method was founded on experience, specifically observation—whether of the natural world or of carefully planned experiments. Although Bacon's approach does not differ greatly from Aristotle's and although his attack was somewhat unfair (he certainly borrowed more from Aristotle than he acknowledged), his work tended to advance the impression that Aristotelianism and modern science were incompatible. In short, during the scientific revolution of the seventeenth century, Aristotle's teachings were steadily superseded by a host of new discoveries and ways of conceiving the physical and metaphysical world.

▼ *This copper engraving by Joseph Mulder (1659–1718) adorns the title page of the 1700 Leiden edition of Galileo's* Dialogue concerning the Two Chief World Systems *(first published in 1632). Aristotle is shown seated alongside Ptolemy and Copernicus, whose contrasting views on the universe are explored in the* Dialogue. *Galileo points out that if Aristotle had been able to view the heavens with seventeenth-century instruments, he would have bowed to observation and changed his ideas.*

A Coherent View of the World

From 1450 to 1600, between three and four thousand editions of works by Aristotle were published (by comparison, fewer than five hundred editions of Plato's works were published in the same period). The sheer number of editions demonstrates the extent to which Aristotle dominated the academic curriculum in Europe throughout that period. As a matter of course, most educated men knew Aristotle's works on ethics, politics, and later, poetry. Aristotle is often considered as being in decline during the seventeenth century, but outside the field of physics, this view is not strictly true. Aristotelian logic and biology continued to hold their own into the

As this excerpt from his 1620 work demonstrates, the English scientist and philosopher Francis Bacon condemned the work of Aristotle and the Scholastics (Schoolmen):

Nor let any weight be given to the fact that in his [Aristotle's] books on animals and his problems, and other of his treatises, there is frequent dealing with experiments. For he had come to his conclusion before; he did not consult experience, as he should have done, for the purpose of framing his decisions and axioms, but having first determined the question according to his will, he then resorts to experience, and bending her into conformity with his placets, leads her about like a captive in a procession. So that even on this count he is more guilty than his modern followers, the Schoolmen, who have abandoned experience altogether.

Novum organum, 63

◀ *Aristotle's ethical works included explorations of the nature of human relationships. On this page from a fifteenth-century French illuminated manuscript, the different forms of friendship are portrayed. They include: (above, from left to right) friendship for profit, friendship for pleasure, virtuous friendship between equals, (below, from left to right) friendship between a prince and his subject, friendship among relatives, and friendship between a husband and a wife.*

nineteenth century, and the *Poetics* reached the peak of its influence in the seventeenth. The *Nicomachean Ethics* was a key text in nineteenth-century British universities, and it remains an important work to this day. Francis Bacon's comments notwithstanding, Aristotle's lasting contribution is to have been the first philosopher to set out coherent approaches to understanding all aspects of the world. In a letter that he wrote toward the end of his life, Galileo is generous in his assessment of his ancient forebear: "If Aristotle should see the new discoveries in the sky, he would change his opinions and correct his books and embrace the most sensible doctrines, casting away from himself those people so weak-minded as to be induced to go on maintaining everything he had ever said."

FURTHER READING

Barnes, Jonathan. *Aristotle.* New York, 1982.

Rubenstein, Richard E. *Aristotle's Children: How Christians, Muslims, and Jews Rediscovered Ancient Wisdom and Illuminated the Dark Ages.* Orlando, FL, 2003.

Schmitt, Charles B. *Aristotle and the Renaissance.* Cambridge, MA, 1983.

Tarnas, Richard. *The Passion of the Western Mind: Understanding the Ideas That Have Shaped Our World View.* New York, 1991.

Charles Freeman

SEE ALSO

• Bacon, Francis • Education • Galilei, Galileo
• Humanism and Learning
• Literature • Philosophy • Platonism • Universities

Armada, Spanish

In 1588 the armada, a fleet sent by Catholic Spain, made an unsuccessful attempt to invade England and overthrow its Protestant queen, Elizabeth I.

▼ This miniature of Charles Howard (Second Baron Howard of Effingham; 1536–1624) was painted in 1605 by Rowland Lockley. Although his father had been an admiral under Mary I, Howard's experience had been mainly as a courtier and diplomat before he became lord high admiral in 1587 (a position he held until 1618, when he was eighty-two).

The Enterprise of England

Spanish kings traditionally saw England as a natural ally in Spain's struggles against France. The Spanish kings also saw themselves as defenders of the Roman Catholic Church; after the English church broke with Rome and began to move in the direction of Protestantism under King Henry VIII in the 1530s, relations between England and Spain became more difficult. Henry's daughter Mary I restored Catholicism in 1553. To secure a Catholic succession, Mary married the future king Philip II of Spain, but when she died childless in 1558, her sister, Elizabeth, came to the throne, and England reverted to Protestantism.

Elizabeth's support for Protestant rebels in the Spanish Netherlands and her refusal to stop Francis Drake and other pirates from raiding Spanish shipping and Spanish colonies in the Caribbean brought Spain's relations with England to a crisis point. After war broke out in 1585, Philip II decided to invade England, depose Elizabeth, and replace her with her Catholic cousin, Mary, Queen of Scots. However, Elizabeth undercut this plan by having Mary executed for treason in 1587. Since Philip had a reasonable claim to the English throne through his earlier marriage to Mary I, he decided to conquer England and make himself king.

Philip's plan, which he called the Enterprise of England, seemed straightforward. He would send a great fleet—the armada—to the Netherlands, where it would link up with the Spanish army under the duke of Parma and escort that army to England. The Spanish army, the most professional of its day, was more than a match for England's small contingent of mainly part-time soldiers.

However, Philip's plan had a number of weaknesses. One weakness lay in the actual conveying of the army across the English Channel. England might have had a feeble army, but as the Spanish were painfully aware, its formidable navy comprised by far the best warships in Europe. Also, owing to the shallowness of the sea off the coast of the Netherlands, the large Spanish ships could not sail close in to the shore. The Spanish planned to transport the duke of Parma's army to the warships in barges—a plan that was feasible only in calm weather. Furthermore, for the first part of their journey, the barges would be vulnerable to attack from so-called sea beggars, Dutch Protestants who patrolled the coast in specially built shallow-draft warships. Many historians believe that the problems facing the Spanish were so great that the armada was doomed to fail even before it sailed. Many Spanish officers also had their doubts. Though they called their fleet the invincible armada, they did so ironically.

The Armada Sets Sail

The Spanish carried out their preparations on such a scale that they could not keep them secret. In April 1587, in a daring attack on Spain's main naval base at Cadiz, in southwestern Spain, Francis Drake destroyed over forty ships and a vast quantity of stores. This attack, known as the singeing of the king of Spain's beard, set back the armada for a year. The Spanish ships finally sailed from Lisbon on May 28, 1588. The fleet consisted of 130 ships, around 40 of which were warships and the rest armed transports, and around 30,000 sailors and soldiers. The commander of the armada, the duke of Medina Sidonia, was not a professional sailor (in fact, he suffered from chronic seasickness), but he was a brave and competent officer. The admiral commanding the English fleet, Charles Howard (Second Baron Howard of Effingham), was also not a professional seaman, but he was ideally suited to the task of reining in some of the more reckless captains, such as Drake and Martin Frobisher.

Bad weather forced the armada to shelter for over a month at La Coruña, in northwestern Spain, and it was not until July 29 that an English scout ship sighted the Spanish ships as they entered the Channel. The main English fleet, including twenty powerful royal galleons and one hundred smaller ships, hastily left its base at Plymouth, in southwestern England, to avoid

▲ A contemporary drawing of an English galleon of the Elizabethan period. The drawing shows clearly the sleek lines and low forecastle that made the English ships superior in speed and agility to the higher, broader, Spanish ships. This innovative design is believed to have been introduced by the privateer captain John Hawkins (1532–1595), who commanded the *Victory* during the engagements with the armada.

TO BOARD OR TO BATTER?

The English and Spanish had quite different approaches toward naval warfare. The Spanish saw sea battles simply as infantry engagements on shipboard. Ships were expected to grapple together as a prelude to boarding, at which point soldiers fought with the aim of capturing the enemy ship by means of hand-to-hand fighting. By this method the Turks had been defeated by an alliance of Christians at the Battle of Lepanto, nearly twenty years earlier. Spanish warships were built broad to accommodate as many soldiers and stores as possible, and they had high fore and aft castles to provide good fighting platforms. Spanish ships carried plenty of light cannon for use against enemy crews but few heavy guns capable of holing a ship's hull. In contrast, the main armament of an English warship was a battery of heavy cannon mounted on the broadside. English ships carried few soldiers: the English hoped to avoid being boarded by using their cannon to sink or batter enemy ships into submission from as far away as possible. By imitating the shapes of fish, English shipbuilders streamlined the underwater portion of their ships and thus made them considerably faster than Spanish ships. English ships were also more maneuverable than Spanish ships—high forecastles made ships clumsy and unstable in crosswinds, and so the English did away with them.

Shortly before the armada set sail, a Spanish captain named Martín de Bertendona wrote a confidential letter to a papal diplomat expressing his fears about the expedition and accurately summarizing the tactics each side hoped to use.

It is well known that we fight in God's cause. So, when we meet the English, God will surely arrange matters so that we can grapple and board them, either by sending some strange freak of weather or, more likely, just by depriving the English of their wits. If we can come to close quarters, Spanish valor and Spanish steel (and the great masses of soldiers we have on board) will make our victory certain. But unless God helps us by a miracle the English, who have faster and handier ships than ours, and many more long range guns, and who know their advantage just as well as we do, will never close with us at all, but stand aloof and knock us to pieces with their culverins [a type of cannon], without our being able to do them any serious hurt. So, we are sailing against England in the confident hope of a miracle.

Quoted in N. A. M. Rodger, *The Safeguard of the Sea: A Naval History of Britain, 660–1649*

▼ *In this contemporary engraving by the Dutch mapmaker and maritime artist Franz Hogenberg (c. 1535–c. 1590), English fireships are sent against the armada while it lies at anchor off Calais. The attack caused panic and forced the armada to break its strong defensive formation. Spanish fear of the fireships was magnified by the memory of a Dutch fireship attack on the port of Antwerp in 1585, an attack that killed thousands of Spanish troops.*

being trapped by the armada. Legend has it that Drake, who was playing a game of bowls when the alarm was raised, coolly refused to sail until he had finished his game. The English attacked the armada persistently as it sailed down the Channel but enjoyed little success. The English found it very difficult to penetrate the armada's crescent-shaped defensive formation, with the weaker ships in the center and the stronger ones on the horns. The English also found that wooden ships

were much harder to sink with iron cannonballs from long range than both they and the Spanish had expected. By the time the armada reached the French port of Calais on August 6, it had lost only three ships.

Nevertheless, the Spanish were frustrated and demoralized by their failure to inflict any damage on the nimble English ships. At Calais the armada anchored—Spanish diplomacy had secured French neutrality—to await news from the duke of Parma. The English saw their chance and sent fireships (old ships packed with tar and gunpowder and set alight) against the armada on the night of August 7/8. Fire was the greatest of all threats to wooden sailing ships. Many Spanish captains cut their anchor cables to escape, and the armada scattered in disorder.

The Armada Fails

While the armada was trying to re-form off Gravelines, to the east of Calais, the English attacked again. This time the English pressed their attacks much closer, waiting until they were less than a hundred yards away from the Spanish ships before firing their cannons. In one day three Spanish ships were sunk, one was captured, and twelve more were so badly damaged that they would sink later. Worse luck was in store for the Spanish. On August 9 the armada narrowly avoided being swept onto sandbanks, and on the following day a strong south wind prevented the Spanish ships from returning to the coast of the Netherlands to link up with the army, which was now ready to embark for England.

▲ *This map shows the route of the Spanish armada from Spain into the English Channel and then in flight around the coast of Britain.*

It was now clear to Medina Sidonia that he could not execute his king's instructions, and he ordered the armada to return to Spain by sailing north around Scotland and west into the Atlantic Ocean. The English pursued the Spanish as far as the coast of Scotland before returning to port. By now the armada was low on supplies of food and fresh water, and many ships were leaking badly from damage inflicted by English cannonballs. As the armada entered the Atlantic on August 21, the weather turned stormy, and the fleet broke up. Dozens of ships were blown off course and wrecked on the rocky western coasts of Scotland and Ireland. Thousands were drowned, and in Ireland most of those who made it to land were killed by the English garrisons or Irish looters.

By the time Medina Sidonia's ship returned to Spain on September 22, half his crew were dead or dying of disease and starvation. Over the course of the next few weeks, the remainder of the surviving ships straggled in; the last arrived home on October 14. In all, the armada had lost at least sixty-three ships, and nearly two-thirds of the sailors and soldiers had died—far more of them from disease and hunger than in battle. The whole of Spain plunged into mourning for the scale of the defeat. No English ship suffered serious damage, and there were fewer than a hundred English casualties (though hundreds more sailors died of an epidemic that broke out when the fleet returned to port).

THE WEATHER GAUGE

In the age of sailing warships, the strength and direction of the wind could decide the outcome of a sea battle. Naval commanders would try to use the wind to gain a tactical advantage. A ship that was upwind of its opponent was said to have the weather gauge. Having the weather gauge brought many advantages. Because smoke from cannon fire blew away from the ship, it was easier to aim guns and to signal other ships. Aggressive sea captains liked to have the weather gauge so that they could bear down fast on enemy ships, fire a broadside, and sweep away to reload for another pass. A disadvantage of the weather gauge was that a damaged ship would be blown helplessly toward the enemy fleet and be captured.

The Spanish knew that they could not prevent the faster, more maneuverable English ships from winning the weather gauge. However, the crescent formation adopted by the armada was designed to prevent the English from using the weather gauge to their best advantage. The Spanish placed their strongest ships on the horns of the crescent, their weakest in the center. The English could safely attack only the horns. If an English ship attempted to attack the center from behind, it would lose the weather gauge to the big Spanish ships on the horns, which could close in behind and surround it; if it attempted to attack from the front, the whole armada would bear down on it with the wind. The crescent formation was clearly a strong one: the English sank and captured very few Spanish ships as the armada advanced along the Channel.

A detail of an engraving by John Pine of the Armada Tapestry (1739). Commissioned by Charles Howard to be displayed in the House of Lords, the tapestry was made in Flanders, then the leading center of tapestry work, to a design by the Dutch maritime painter Hendrik Vroom (1566–1640). The original tapestry was destroyed when the Houses of Parliament burned down in 1834.

The Significance of the Armada

If the armada had succeeded, it would have scored a great victory for the Counter-Reformation by winning England back for Catholicism. Deprived of English support, the Dutch rebellion would probably have failed. However, no blame for the armada's failure can be attached to Medina Sidonia; few commanders could have done better under the circumstances. Though some contemporaries did blame Medina Sidonia, Philip II was not among them. The English believed that they had struck the Spanish empire a mortal blow, but their attempts to exploit the victory were unsuccessful. The decline of Spanish power in the seventeenth century was due more to the huge debts the country built up in paying for the defense of its vast empire than it was to any single military defeat. While the English cannon had not proved as deadly as had been hoped, the English had gained an early lead in naval gunnery, and they kept that lead throughout the age of sail.

FURTHER READING

Hanson, Neil. *The Confident Hope of a Miracle: The True History of the Spanish Armada.* New York, 2005.

Mattingly, Garrett. *The Defeat of the Spanish Armada.* Boston, 1984.

Rodger, N. A. M. *The Safeguard of the Sea: A Naval History of Britain, 660–1649.* New York, 1998.

John Haywood

SEE ALSO

• Elizabeth I • England • Lepanto, Battle of • Philip II • Spain • Warfare

Astrology

IN RENAISSANCE EUROPE, ASTROLOGY, THE STUDY OF THE STARS AND PLANETS AND THEIR PURPORTED INFLUENCE UPON HUMAN AFFAIRS, WAS QUITE INFLUENTIAL, AND ITS USE TO PREDICT THE FUTURE, THOUGH CONTROVERSIAL, WAS WIDESPREAD.

Astrologers assumed that a careful study of celestial bodies would give them a better understanding of the terrestrial world and would enable them to make accurate predictions about both natural and human events. Some believed that God revealed his divine plan through changes in the heavens—the star of Bethlehem, which had guided wise men to Jesus's birthplace, was the most important and spectacular example of such a revelation. Others (the majority), while accepting that God sometimes used the stars as signs, held that the stars and planets had an independent influence on the world. The majority view also held that each celestial object had its own particular character and properties, which it imparted in subtle ways to everything under its influence.

Astrology depended upon accurate knowledge of the positions of heavenly bodies, and this technical information was provided by the related but far less controversial field of astronomy. All the better schools offered astronomical instruction, since knowledge of the stars was also important to navigation, timekeeping, medicine, and agriculture. In their observations of the sky, astronomers distinguished between celestial bodies of two kinds: the stars moved across the sky from east to west while seeming to be fixed in place in the bowl of the heavens, whereas the planets (from the Greek word *planetes*, which means "wanderers") traveled in the same general direction but at different speeds and in ever-changing relationships with one another. The most important stars were the constellations of the zodiac: Aries, Taurus, Gemini, Cancer, Leo, Virgo, Libra, Scorpio, Sagittarius, Capricorn, Aquarius, and Pisces. Renaissance astronomers counted the sun and the moon as planets, together with Mercury, Venus, Mars, Jupiter and Saturn (Uranus, Neptune, and Pluto were as yet undiscovered). As the relationship between these bodies in the heavens changed, so, it was assumed, did their effects upon the earth. The astrologer's job, through a combination of theory, analogy, and long practice, was to understand and to predict these effects.

On this celestial chart, which he made in 1590, the astrologer Thomas Hood used conventional iconography to depict the constellations of the night sky as seen from somewhere in northern Europe. Most of the constellations of the zodiac can be glimpsed just within the outer edge of the horizon.

Natural Astrology

Astrologers and their critics alike distinguished between predictions concerning the stars' and planets' influence on the natural world and predictions having to do with human affairs. The former kind was, almost universally, more acceptable, since predictions about the natural world did not infringe upon human free will. Moreover, the effects of celestial bodies on the physical world were readily observed. The sun bathed the world in light and heat, the moon controlled the tides, and the seasons also responded to the motion of the heavens.

▲ *This fifteenth-century French miniature illustrates the relationship that was believed to exist between the human body and the cosmos. Such information was essential for physicians and useful for ordinary people, since the positions of the stars and planets were held to have vital effects on human health.*

Indeed, since weather, agriculture, and even human health seemed tied to seasonal change, almost everyone accepted that it was legitimate for astrologers to study the celestial origins of seasonal change. The resulting predictions were gratefully received; most people at this time were directly engaged in agriculture, and all farmers were desperate for the kind of information that only the astrologers could then provide: such information included weather forecasts for the coming year, the dates of the first and last frosts, the best times to sow and to harvest, and whether the year would bring dearth or plenty. Those who could not afford a modest consulting fee could buy an almanac, a convenient collation of raw astrological data and a calendar bound together with agricultural and meteorological predictions for the coming year. Almanacs were cheap and hugely popular—hundreds of thousands were sold each year—and they brought astrological learning within the reach of almost every farmer. Of course, a detailed weather prediction offered by an almanac or an astrologer would often be completely wrong; so to avoid making embarrassing gaffes, astrologers were prone to couch their predictions in language so general that they could easily be satirized—as indeed they were in the 1664 satirical almanac, *Poor Robin*, which predicted for February that "we may expect some showers of rain either this month or the next, or the next after that, or else we shall have a very dry spring."

Astrological influence was most pervasive, though, in the study of medicine, since the ever-changing influence of the stars kept earthly matter, including human bodies, in constant flux. Early physicians understood human health in terms of fluctuations of four basic bodily fluids, or humors: blood, phlegm, black bile (or melancholy), and yellow bile (or choler). The balance of the humors in the body determined a person's health and temperament in terms of four physical conditions: hot, cold, moist, and dry. These physical conditions also characterized the stars and planets. Therefore, a physician had to know which moments were astrologically propitious and which dangerous for a particular remedy: for example, when it was best to let a certain patient's blood, when to prescribe a cold bath, and so on. Astrology was taught systematically at medical schools, and a great many Renaissance astrologers were or at least started out as medical practitioners. As was the case with most astrological matters, the role of the stars in medicine became enormously complicated. The constellation Libra, for example, was thought to govern the kidneys, thighs, and buttocks. Saturn ruled black bile and the spleen, stomach, bladder, womb, and right ear (Jupiter ruled the left) and was responsible for sadness, depression, dysen-

ORIGINS OF EUROPEAN ASTROLOGY

Renaissance humanists commonly assumed that learning and wisdom tended to decay over time—just as living organisms did—and so they generally valued older traditions more highly than recent ones. Most were convinced that astrology originated with the ancient Babylonians or Egyptians, and a great deal of its prestige as an intellectual system came from its presumed antiquity. In reality, however, while the accurate mapping of the heavens may have begun at a very early date, horoscopes and the related arts of judicial astrology originated mainly with the Greeks, not much earlier than the fourth century BCE. The subsequent refinement and systemization of astrology by the Greeks and Romans culminated in the *Tetrabiblos*, a textbook written by the second-century Greco-Egyptian astrologer Claudius Ptolemy that set out exactly how the heavens affect human lives and provided the rules necessary for making predictions on that basis.

During the Middle Ages, Europeans practiced a simplified form of astrology based on the classical Roman tradition, but the *Tetrabiblos* and the other great texts of astrological learning were lost to Europeans until Latin translations from Arabic editions began to filter back into Europe in the twelfth century. European astrology remained grounded in medieval Arab texts until the fourteenth century, when Renaissance scholars began to delve once again into the Greek originals. The challenge for the most learned European astrologers was how to reconcile current astrological practice with Christianity and with the work of such esteemed classical philosophers as Aristotle and Plato. As a result, while there was considerable consensus concerning essential astrological principles, in matters of theory and detail, astrologers often disagreed.

tery, the sniffles, and several other conditions and illnesses. Astrologers could predict who would be prone to these particular ailments and warn patients to take precautions when the influence of Saturn was strong. Although, in all probability, few physicians let astrology rule their work, few dismissed it altogether, and until the seventeenth century a great many would take astrological data of at least a simple sort into account during diagnosis and treatment.

Judicial Astrology

The same principle that required physicians to consider the stars, when applied more ambitiously, was used in judicial astrology to make detailed assessments of an individual's personality and his or her future prospects. Astrologers maintained that the influence of the heavens was particularly strong at birth. Personality, they believed, was determined by the planet that was dominant at the moment of birth: people born under Jupiter (also called Jove), for instance, were destined to be good-humored (jovial). Those born under Mercury would be changeable (mercurial). The person born under Saturn would be gloomy or surly (saturnine). A person's birth stars also revealed hidden aptitudes. One English scholar even proposed that all prospective university students undergo an astrological evaluation to determine their fitness for advanced study.

This celestial chart, which includes depictions of the twelve signs of the zodiac and the twenty-eight phases of the moon, is from a 1583 manuscript by the Arab philosopher and poet Loqman entitled The Fine Flower of Histories.

Girolamo Cardano 1501–1576

The illegitimate son of Fazio Cardano, a Milanese lawyer, Girolamo (also known as Geronimo or Gerolamo) Cardano trained to be a physician but found that the circumstances of his birth and his prickly personality made him unwelcome in that profession. He found work only as a poor country doctor and supplemented his income by writing a small book of astrological predictions, the *Pronostico*, which was published in 1534. The book was well received, and Cardano went on to write voluminously on astrology, medicine, mathematics, and various other subjects, including no less than four versions of his own autobiography. He championed a scientifically exact astrology, grounded in astronomical precision and sophisticated theory; a good humanist, Cardano also argued for an astrology based upon classical principles and purged of recent accretions. For Cardano astrology was the noblest, most divine, and most beneficial of all the arts and sciences. Respected as both a physician and an astrologer, he treated an impressive international clientele but resisted the temptation to take lucrative positions outside Italy. He lectured and wrote until 1570, when he was arrested and briefly imprisoned on charges of impiety. He had published a detailed horoscope of Jesus Christ, and the notion that the Lord's singular gifts might have been determined by the stars offended many, despite Cardano's reasonable claim that God would have had the good sense to be born at a moment when the stars reflected his dignity. Cardano was released but was forced to spend his last years in Rome, forbidden to publish and closely watched by the Inquisition.

▼ *Girolamo Cardano was one of the most learned and intellectually gifted astrologers of his day. By his own account, this contemporary engraving (from the frontispiece to* The Book of My Life, *1654) is flattering: he described himself in the same book as having a narrow chest, skinny arms, a long thin neck, a wide forehead, beady eyes, and a dangling lip. He further wrote, "I have accustomed my features always to belie me."*

Such well-regarded astrologers as the Italian Girolamo Cardano (1501–1576), the Frenchman Michel de Nostredame (usually known as Nostradamus; 1503–1566), and the Englishman William Lilly (1602–1681) responded to hundreds or even thousands of queries every year. John Booker, a busy but not atypical English astrologer of the seventeenth century, fielded around 16,500 inquiries in seventeen years. A great many of these questions were extremely mundane but doubtless of the first importance to those who asked them: they covered such topics as the parentage of children, the love of a master for his maidservant, the location of stolen merchandise, and so on. That so many people consulted astrologers to help them make important decisions accounts for a great deal of astrology's tenacious appeal.

To make predictions, astrologers relied upon a horoscope, a map of the heavens at a particular moment in time as seen from a particular point on earth. To cast a horoscope, the astrologer first divided the sky into twelve arcs, called houses, aligned with the path of the sun as it crossed the horizon relative to an earthly observer over the course of the year. Next, using complex formulas combined with antique (and generally inaccurate) tables of astronomical data, the astrologer determined the positions of the planets, the constellations, and the brightest stars within the various houses. Finally, the astrologer interpreted the chart according to a vast number of rules and precedents in order to arrive at a series of predictions and conclusions. Each house, for example, had its own particular set of meanings, one having especially to do with health, one with love, one with relatives, and so forth. The first house, which corresponded to the section of the heavens just under the eastern horizon, was particularly important. Any planet in that house was said to be ascendant, or rising. The house in which the sun was traveling at the time of birth was also important, and the corresponding constellation of the zodiac had special significance for a person said to have been born under that sign. This particular aspect of horoscope prediction—the influence on a person of their sun, or birth, sign—is the only part of the whole system that survives in the astrological forecasts of modern newspapers.

Casting a proper horoscope was enormously complicated, and mistakes were easily made. Girolamo Cardano spent over one hundred hours working on his horoscope for the English king Edward VI (reigned 1547–1553). He eventually predicted a long and successful life for the young monarch. When Edward unexpectedly died shortly after, at the tender age of fifteen, Cardano admitted his mistake and claimed that his error had arisen from taking one too many shortcuts in his calculations. Likewise, the horoscopes drawn up by Nostradamus, his subsequent fame as a prophet notwithstanding, were riddled with basic errors. Nonetheless, people from all walks of life continued to consult astrologers. After all, the complexity of the whole process provided a ready excuse for failures: an astrologer whose predictions were faulty could always blame some countervailing celestial influence, previously unrecognized but now all too plain.

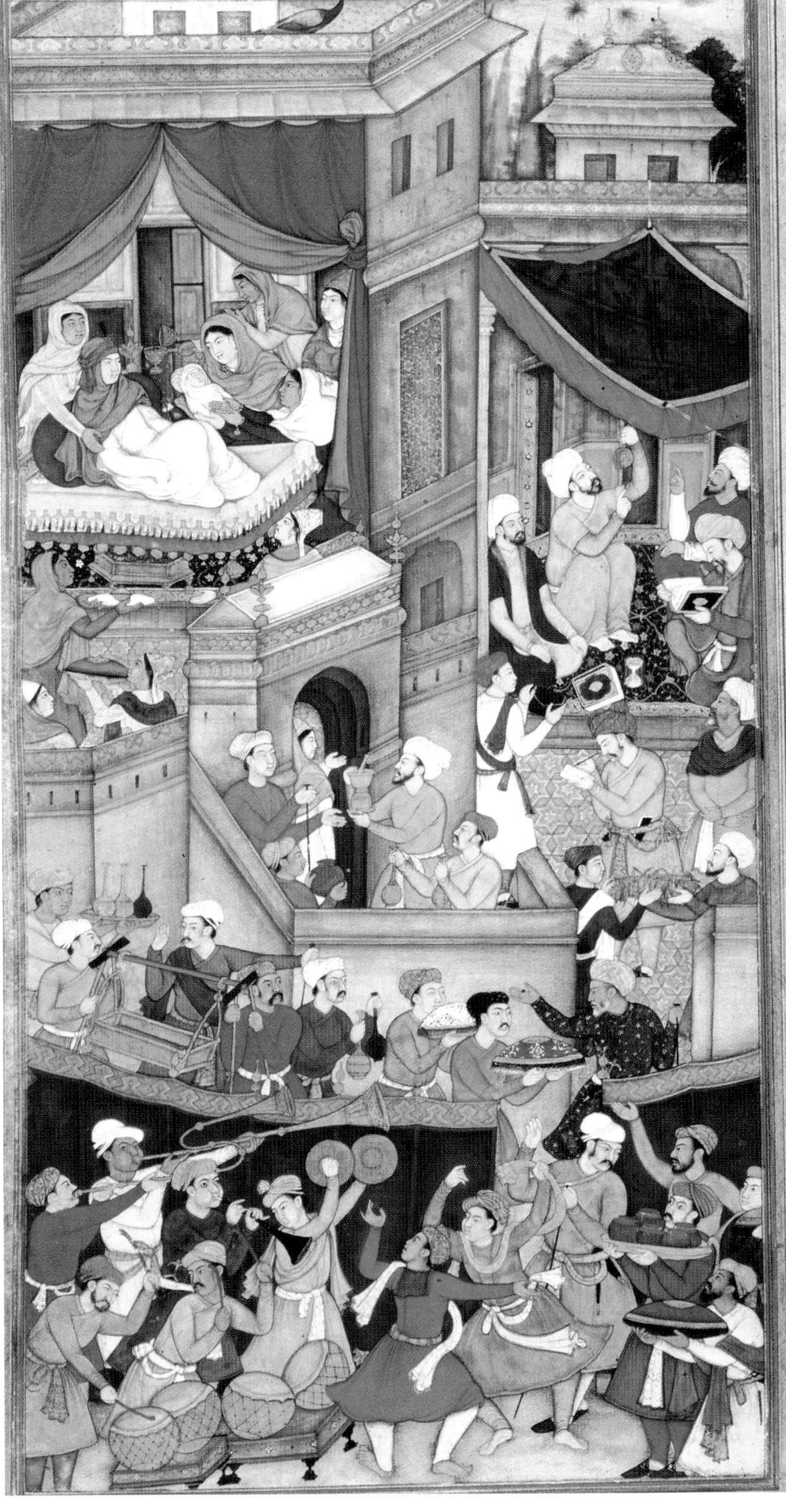

▲ *This illustration is from a history of Akbar, a ruler of India from 1556 to 1605. As part of the festivities celebrating the birth of Timur, to whom the Mogul line traced its origin, astrologers (upper right) cast Timur's horoscope.*

Astrology and the Courts

Most European princes employed either official or semiofficial astrologers; since astrologers were cheap and their advice potentially valuable, it made good sense to do so. In common with most people, though, rulers turned to astrologers only in certain situations and only in the absence of alternative guidance. No ruler went to war because an astrologer recommended it. Nonetheless, all things being equal, most nobles followed the advice of the stars when that advice was available. A study of aristocratic marriages, for instance, reveals that most nobles chose to marry on astrologically propitious days. As there was no sense in taking chances, Elizabeth I of England, by no means the most credulous of

The following passage from the 1554 work in which Girolamo Cardano published his horoscope of Christ (the work's Latin title means "On the Laws of the Stars") is a typically complex explication of a single astrological calculation:

Take the nocturnal horary part of Jupiter's place . . . you will find this under the number of days, which is most necessary for this calculation, under 48° polar altitude [for Paris]. You will discover a semi-diurnal arc of the thirteenth part of Gemini, or 7 hours 49 minutes, whose remainder of 12 is the semi-nocturnal arc, that is, 4 hours, 11 minutes, which was sought. Multiply this by 2. It is as if you were to reduce hours to minutes by multiplying by 60 and dividing by 24 the product of 6 hours, which is the number of the semi-diurnal arc, or 4, the number of minutes of an hour of the semi-nocturnal arc in which 1° ascends. The result is 10° 28'. These are the horary times. Observe therefore, how far Jupiter is distant from the degree of the occident.

De astrorum iudiciis

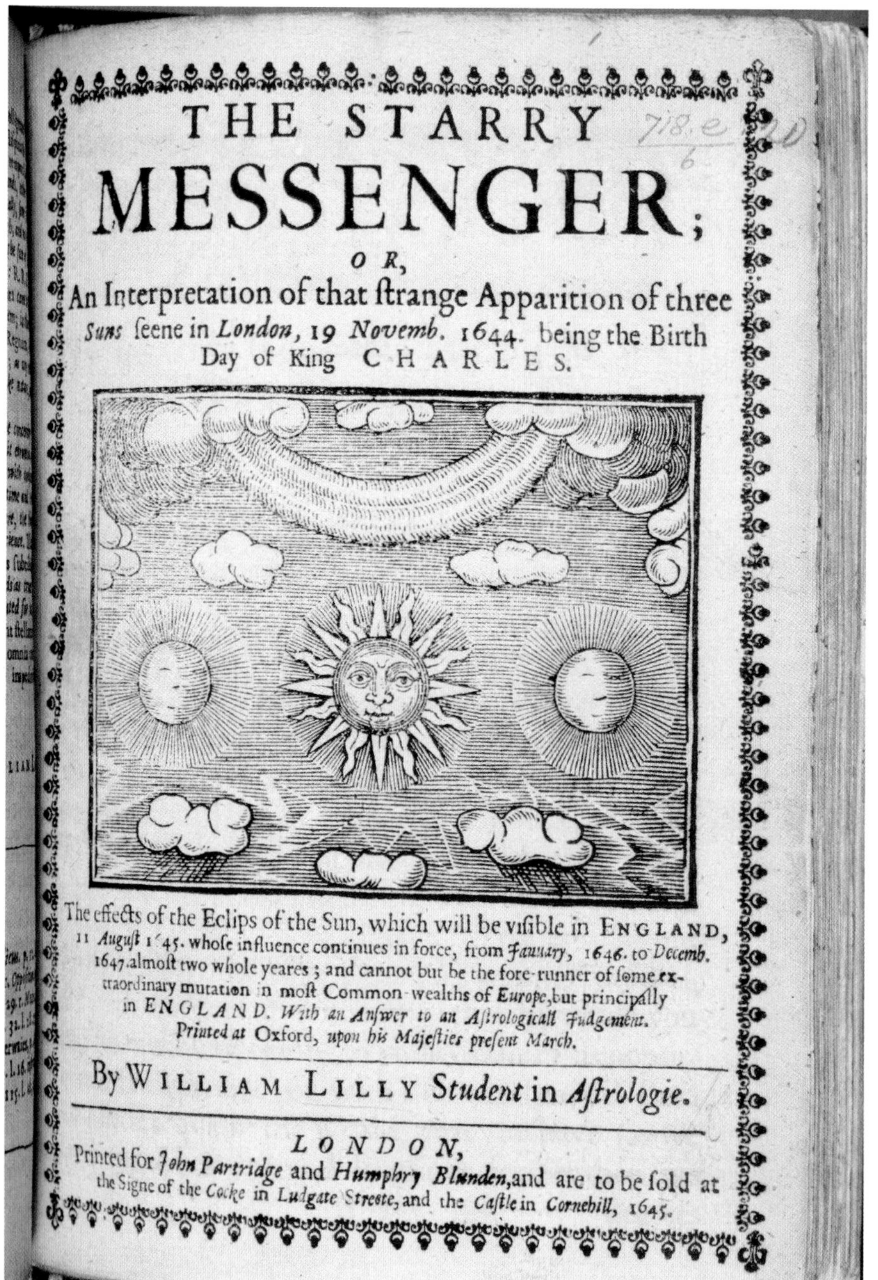

THE STARRY MESSENGER; OR, An Interpretation of that ſtrange Apparition of three *Suns* ſeene in *London*, 19 *Novemb.* 1644. being the Birth Day of King CHARLES.

The effects of the Eclips of the Sun, which will be viſible in ENGLAND, 11 *Auguſt* 1645. whoſe influence continues in force, from *January*, 1646. to *Decemb.* 1647. almoſt two whole yeares; and cannot but be the fore-runner of ſome extraordinary mutation in moſt Common-wealths of *Europe*, but principally in ENGLAND. *With an Anſwer to an Aſtrologicall Judgement. Printed at* Oxford, *upon his Majeſties preſent March.*

By WILLIAM LILLY *Student* in *Aſtrologie.*

LONDON, Printed for *John Partridge* and *Humphry Blunden*, and are to be ſold at the Signe of the *Cocke* in *Ludgate Streete*, and the *Caſtle* in *Cornehill*, 1645.

◀ *The leading English astrologer William Lilly (1602–1681) allegedly forecast the great fire of London (1666) fourteen years before it occurred. In the broadsheet pictured here, called* The Starry Messenger, *Lilly gives vent to his political views; he predicts not only an eclipse of the sun but also a parliamentarian victory in the English civil wars.*

rulers, had her astrologer, John Dee, set the date of her coronation. Another English monarch, Charles II, asked his astrologer to give him auspicious dates on which to make important speeches to Parliament. Alessandro Farnese thought the secrets of the stars so important that he brought his favorite astrologer to Rome with him when he was elected pope and took the name Paul III.

Despite their usefulness, though, astrologers were not warmly welcomed at the highest reaches of court. A primary reason for this state of affairs was that, fairly or not, astrologers were associated with magic and spirits and, as such, were at least faintly disreputable. A second and perhaps more serious reason was that monarchs and princes often felt threatened by astrological predictions regarding their rule. Would-be assassins and plotters, for example, would find nothing more encouraging than a horoscope predicting a ruler's imminent demise. In England conspirators against Henry VII, Elizabeth I, James I, and Charles II were all fortified by confident astrological predictions of their success (none of which were ultimately fulfilled). Understandably, then, astrologers caught casting potentially subversive royal horoscopes were severely punished.

More generally, political rivals and dissidents used astrological predictions to bolster their arguments, encourage their supporters, and persuade the undecided. During the English civil wars, Parliamentarians and Royalists alike aggressively recruited astrologers to their cause and used astrologers' writings in their propaganda. William Lilly, the leading English astrologer of his day, was a confirmed Parliamentarian, and his politically charged predictions were said to be worth more than half a dozen regiments. Likewise, in France, Nostradamus prophesied on behalf of Catherine de Médicis, his patron. Nostradamus's prophecies must have been invaluable given that he was consulted by some of the most important noble families of Europe. The most serious astrologers were appalled that some might use their art to promote a personal or political agenda, but owing to the enormous complexity of astrological forecasting and the lack of precise astronomical data and universally recognized rules of interpretation, anyone with a command of the terminology could read virtually anything into the stars.

Cardano's horosocope of Christ (1554) gives a map of the heavens at the moment of Jesus's birth, which he assumed to have been midnight on December 25, 1 CE. The various houses are depicted as triangles. The first house, the triangle on the left side pointing left, shows Jupiter ascendant; the sun is in Capricorn with Mercury in conjunction. The comet in Libra could be interpreted as the star of Bethlehem, while the rest of the horoscope predicts Jesus's divinity, fame, and violent death.

Astrology and Religion

Christianity was hostile to astrology almost from the first. In many ways the two systems of belief were incompatible; first, astrology was in origin a pagan practice; second, astrologers deemed the stars, and not God, directly responsible for the course of natural events; and finally, by arguing that the stars control people's actions, astrologers seemed to abnegate free will. Nonetheless, astrology was less objectionable than other divinatory practices, and it eventually found grudging acceptance in the medieval church. Thomas Aquinas (1225–1274) reconciled free will with astrology by arguing that, while stars might predispose men to do certain things, all people were capable of resisting their influence: celestial objects might have power over the human body but not over the soul. Indeed, Aquinas noted, astrologers themselves claimed that the wise man is master of the stars because he is the master of his passions. If many forecasts came true, it was simply that few men were wise; most chose to gratify their passions.

Nevertheless, most medieval and early modern clerics—Aquinas included—remained deeply suspicious of astrology. Astrologers routinely practiced as if matters were settled solely according to the dictates of the stars, and their clients expected no less. Still worse for the church was the fact that the bread and butter of the astrologer was precisely that of the local parish priest: a family crisis or misfortune that a churchman might explain as a warning—or punishment—from God might be more attractively explained by the astrologer as the result of an unfortunate assemblage of unlucky stars.

After the Reformation clerical antagonism to astrology intensified gradually, especially among Calvinists and Presbyterians, whose determinist theology most closely resembled astrologers' own views on fate. The important difference was that for Calvin, it was absolutely necessary that God's unalterable and foreordained plan remain secret. Any attempt to learn what divine providence had in store was blasphemous and futile. In the Calvinists' view, the accuracy of an astrologer's predictions demonstrated collusion with the devil rather than talent or skill.

Catholics, too, accused astrologers of heresy, diabolism, and superstition. Several popes issued bulls (papal proclamations) condemning astrology in almost all its forms, partly because the papacy felt that judicial astrology in particular was incompatible with doctrine and partly because the popes were concerned about unpalatable predictions. Pope Urban VIII (reigned 1623–1644), an accomplished astrologer himself, pun-

WHY DID BELIEF IN ASTROLOGY DECLINE?

After the seventeenth century the influence of astrology dwindled remarkably. The traditional explanation—that astrological belief fell before the onslaught of modern scientific thinking—may to an extent be true. Astrology was surprisingly well-equipped to deal with the new reality of a sun-centered cosmos, but associated changes in the way people thought about the heavens represented more of a challenge. Astrology's fundamental assumption was that celestial objects were both physically and metaphysically higher than those of the earth. However, as the use of the telescope revealed that the moon was not a perfect sphere and that objects in the sky were not necessarily permanent and unchanging, scientists increasingly viewed stars and planets as essentially the same as the earth—composed of the same matter and subject to the same laws. By 1700 most serious astronomers no longer practiced astrology, and in the scientific community at large, the influence of astrology had all but evaporated.

Yet it is unclear whether or not the disdain of scientists was entirely the result of simple intellectual evolution. Astrologers had always worked and lived on the disreputable fringes of the academic mainstream; they competed with their respectable colleagues rather than join them. The new scientists of the seventeenth century, perhaps less hostile to astrological theory than to its practitioners, may well have sought simply to rid the field of their less prestigious competitors. Among the social elite, disdain for astrology grew in response to its tremendous popularity as well as to its associations with radical politics. Although almanacs and astrological forecasts continued to sell in huge numbers, educated men and women began to view astrology as an addiction or fetish of the uneducated masses. To renounce astrology was therefore to make a statement about one's education and position in society.

Despite his personal fondness for astrology, Pope Urban VIII, the subject of this unattributed contemporary engraving (colored later), was so alarmed by an astrological forecast of his death that he ordered the arrest and incarceration of its author, Orazio Morandi. Urban's hostility toward Morandi—and astrologers in general—may have influenced the pope's role in the 1633 trial for heresy of Galileo, a friend of Morandi's.

ished astrologers severely when their persistent predictions of his own death sparked unrest in Rome. In his bull *Inscrutabilis* (1630), Urban attacked astrology in terms that Catholics and Protestants alike could readily understand: astrology was the height of blasphemous human arrogance because "the unfathomable depth of God's judgments does not tolerate the human intellect, locked as it is in the shadowy prison of the body, to rise above the stars."

FURTHER READING

Grafton, Anthony. *Cardano's Cosmos: The Worlds and Works of a Renaissance Astrologer.* Cambridge, MA, 1999.

Maxwell-Stuart, P. G., ed. *The Occult in Early Modern Europe: A Documentary History.* New York, 1998.

Tester, S. J. *A History of Western Astrology.* New York, 1989.

Thomas, Keith. *Religion and the Decline of Magic: Studies in Popular Beliefs in Sixteenth- and Seventeenth-Century England.* New York, 1997.

Hans Peter Broedel

SEE ALSO

• Calendars • Copernicus, Nicolaus • Galilei, Galileo • Magic • Medicine • Popular Culture • Science and Technology

Augsburg, Peace of

PROMULGATED ON SEPTEMBER 25, 1555, THE PEACE OF AUGSBURG BROUGHT AN END TO YEARS OF RELIGIOUS TENSION AND CONFLICT IN GERMANY AND ESTABLISHED THE BASIS FOR THE LEGAL COEXISTENCE OF CATHOLICISM AND LUTHERANISM IN THE HOLY ROMAN EMPIRE.

The origins of the Peace of Augsburg can be traced not only to earlier attempts to resolve the religious tensions within the Holy Roman Empire but also to the compromises that the Holy Roman emperor Charles V agreed to in order to gain the support of the Lutheran princes in his campaigns against the Ottoman Turks and also against the French. Following his defeat of the Lutheran princes at the Battle of Mühlberg in 1547, Charles V attempted to impose a temporary solution to the religious divisions, a solution that would stand until the decisions of the Council of Trent became known (the Catholic Church had convened that council in December 1545; sessions were held on and off for the next eighteen years). Though the Interim of Augsburg (1548), as it was called, dealt with practical matters concerning religious practice rather than doctrinal differences, it made some concessions to the Protestants. Nevertheless, various Protestant groups opposed the interim, and it was finally overthrown by the Second Schmalkaldic War (1552), in which the Lutheran princes were led by Duke Maurice of Saxony. The need for a lasting settlement was recognized in the Treaty of Passau, which ended the latest conflict and established peace until the next meeting of the imperial diet (the assembly of princes).

This engraving by Matthäus Merien the Elder (1593–1650) first appeared in a Frankfurt chronicle published in 1630. It depicts the Battle of Mühlberg, fought on April 24, 1547, at which the forces of Charles V defeated the Lutheran princes and captured their leader, John Frederick of Saxony. The princes, however, regrouped, and after further fighting, the Peace of Augsburg was signed at an imperial diet held in 1555.

The Diet of Augsburg and Terms of the Peace

Charles V absented himself from the meeting of the diet, which assembled at Augsburg in February 1555. The emperor was opposed to anything "by which [the] true, ancient, Christian and Catholic religion might be offended, injured, weakened or disgraced." It was therefore left to Ferdinand, the emperor's brother and the future successor in Germany, to forge a religious compromise between the Protestant and Catholic powers. Although the papacy warned about the danger of a godless peace, the influence of Rome on the negotiations was limited. As a result, the discussions were largely left to the German princes, and of them only the Catholic cardinal of Augsburg and the evangelical duke Christopher of Württemberg could really be said to be motivated by religious rather than personal concerns.

The Peace of Ausgburg stated that the "religious belief, liturgy and ceremonies" of the Confession of Augsburg (the statement of Lutheran belief drawn up in 1530) and Catholicism were both permitted in the Holy Roman Empire and that this edict was to be enforceable under imperial law. War within the empire for religious reasons was forbidden, and one state was not allowed to interfere in the religious practices of another. The religion of each territory was to be uniformly either Catholic or Lutheran, depending on the religion of its ruler. This principle was enshrined at the end of the sixteenth century in the maxim *cuius regio, eius religio,* a Latin phrase that means "whose the rule, his the religion." This idea was not a new one—

it had been discussed as early as 1526 at the Diet of Speyer but had been rejected by the emperor. The princes were granted *ius reformandi,* the right to introduce religious reforms in their lands. The agreement also sought to deal with the problem posed by ecclesiastical (church-owned) lands that had been seized by the Lutherans. It was determined that Lutherans would retain any lands that had been in continuous Lutheran possession since the Treaty of Passau (August 2, 1552).

Several clauses on which agreement was not reached were issued under Ferdinand's authority. They included the ecclesiastical reservation *(reservatum ecclesiasticum),* which stated that any bishop or abbot who converted to Protestantism was required to relinquish his office and lands. Under the *Declaratio Ferdinandei,* protection was provided to Lutheran knights or towns within ecclesiastical lands.

Limitations

Ambiguities and loopholes in the terms of the Peace of Augsburg prompted numerous appeals to imperial courts. The definition of a territorial ruler was ambiguous, and as the empire was composed of a variety of different jurisdictions and states, it was unclear which rulers had the right to enact religious reform in their lands.

One of the fundamental problems with the Peace of Augsburg was that it applied only to Catholics and the adherents of the Confession of Augsburg. It therefore excluded other Protestant groups, notably Zwinglians, Calvinists, and Anabaptists. At the time when the peace was concluded in the mid-1550s, Calvinism had certainly not reached the level of popularity that it was to achieve in the second half of the sixteenth century. Nonetheless, only ten years after the agreement had been reached, no less prominent a figure than the elector Frederick III of the Palatinate became a Calvinist. Frederick did not fall afoul of the terms of the peace because he was able to accept a more radical version of the Confession of Augsburg, the Variata (1540), which similarly allowed other more radical Protestants to remain within the terms of the settlement. The Palatinate became an important center for Calvinism in the empire, and by the early seventeenth century, an important core of Calvinist princes also included the elector of Brandenburg, who had converted in 1613. These princes had intervened in the French wars of reli-

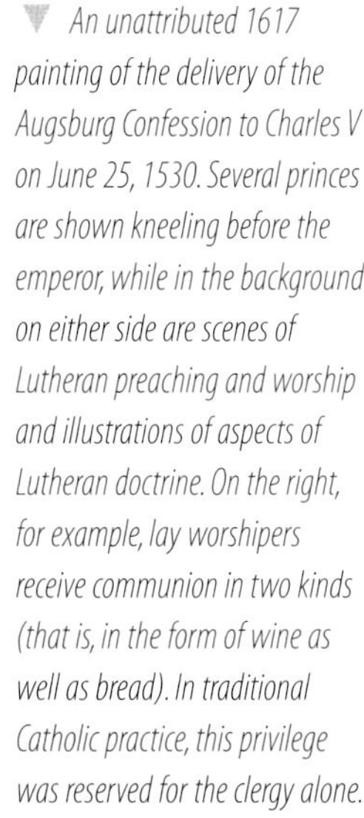

▼ *An unattributed 1617 painting of the delivery of the Augsburg Confession to Charles V on June 25, 1530. Several princes are shown kneeling before the emperor, while in the background on either side are scenes of Lutheran preaching and worship and illustrations of aspects of Lutheran doctrine. On the right, for example, lay worshipers receive communion in two kinds (that is, in the form of wine as well as bread). In traditional Catholic practice, this privilege was reserved for the clergy alone.*

The fact that Charles did not attend the diet at Augsburg suggests that he had given up all hope of maintaining the religious uniformity of the empire. Instead he gave his brother and successor to the imperial throne, Ferdinand I, whose signature and seal feature in this photograph of the original document, responsibility for negotiating a settlement.

gion and the Dutch revolt on behalf of their coreligionists and had formed alliances with ruling houses outside the empire. Such alliances increased the religious tensions within the empire in the period before the outbreak of the Thirty Years War in 1618.

The Peace of Augsburg was not a general act of toleration that permitted freedom of conscience to all the inhabitants of a state; the faith of the state was that of its ruler, and it could change with the accession of a new ruler. In the Palatinate, for example, Lutheran church government was introduced in 1556, but when in 1563 the elector Frederick III declared himself a Calvinist, Lutheranism was overthrown; on Frederick's death in 1576, Lutheranism was briefly restored by his successor, only to be abandoned again in 1583. The inhabitants of a particular state either conformed to the religion of their prince or could exercise their right to leave *(ius emigrandi).* Evidence of the exercise of this right can be found in the Palatinate, where the confessional shifts of the electors were matched by changes in the academic staff at the renowned University of Heidelberg. Emigration was regarded more as a punishment than a religious concession and was certainly exploited by some rulers, such as the cardinal of Augsburg, as a means of threatening or compelling the religious conversion of the inhabitants of their territory.

A number of disputes also arose over Protestant attempts to secularize ecclesiastical territories. In 1576 the bishop of Würzburg invaded the principality of Fulda to prevent its secularization. The Lutheran princes and the emperor almost went to war when the archbishop-elector of Cologne converted to Lutheranism and extended the freedom of worship to his Lutheran subjects. The archbishop was deposed by the pope in 1583 to prevent the secularization of the archdiocese. There were further similar disputes over Aachen, Magdeburg, Paderborn, Osnabrück, and Strasbourg.

The following excerpts illustrate key terms of the Peace of Augsburg:

15. In order to bring peace into the holy Empire of the Germanic Nation between the Roman Imperial Majesty and the Electors, Princes and Estates: let neither his Imperial Majesty nor the Electors, Princes &c do any violence or harm to any estate of the empire on account of the Augsburg Confession, but let them enjoy their religious belief, liturgy and ceremonies as well as their estates and other rights and privileges in peace; and complete religious peace shall be obtained only by Christian means of amity, or under threat of the punishment of the imperial ban.

16. Likewise the Estates espousing the Augsburg Confession shall let all the Estates and Princes who cling to the old religion live in absolute peace and in the enjoyment of all their estates, rights and privileges.

17. However all such as do not belong to the two above named religions shall not be included in the present peace but be totally excluded from it.

24. In case our subjects whether belonging to the old religion or the Augsburg Confession should intend leaving their homes with their wives and children in order to settle in another place, they shall be hindered neither in the sale of their estates after due payment of the local taxes nor injured in their honour.

Quoted in E. Reich, ed., *Select Documents Illustrating Medieval and Modern History*

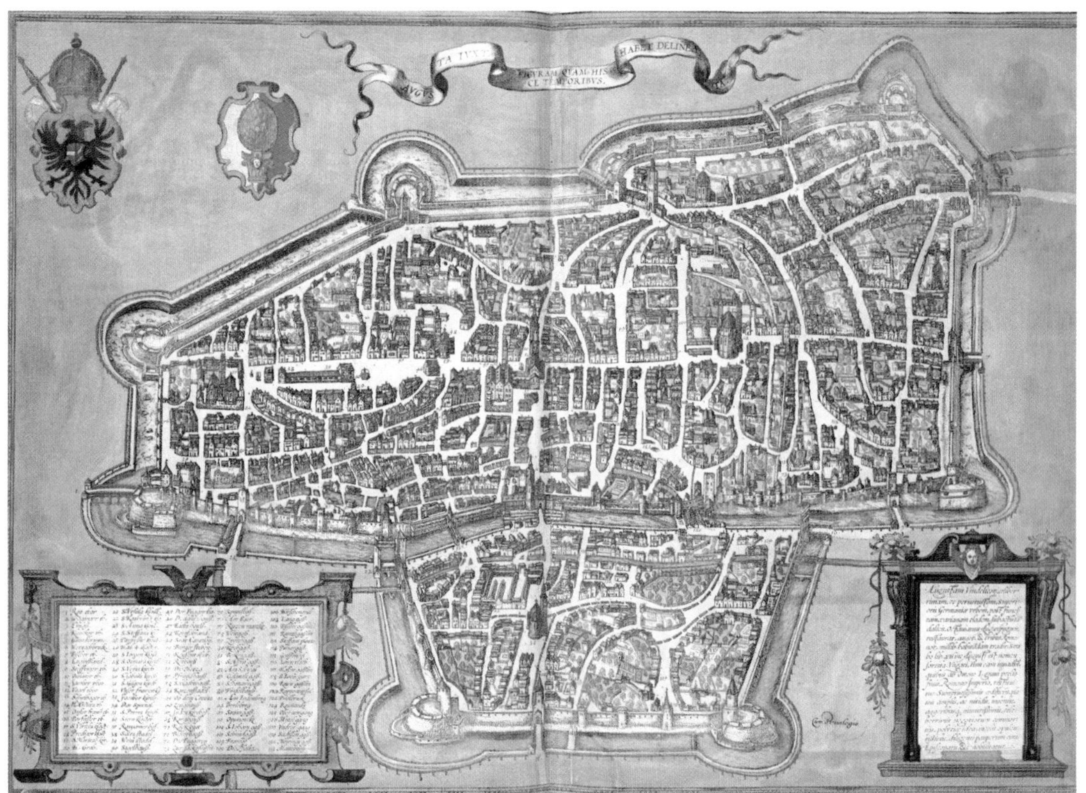

This map of Augsburg appears in *Civitates orbis terrarum* (1572), a pioneering work of cartography engraved by Franz Hogenberg and edited by Georg Braun.

IMPERIAL CITIES

The Peace of Augsburg did not grant religious toleration, but the imperial free cities that had adopted Lutheranism were required to allow Catholic minorities the right to worship. The eight cities already divided between Catholics and Protestants were to remain biconfessional. The peace terms were interpreted by the imperial cities variously and in some cases breached. In the city of Ulm—dominated by the highest cathedral spire in Europe—Catholics were at first allowed to worship at the Franciscan friary and then were banished completely in 1569.

Religious coexistence was not always easy to maintain in practice. In April 1606 a Catholic procession was attacked by the Lutheran inhabitants of the city of Donauwörth. Following an appeal by the bishop of Augsburg, the largely Protestant city was forcibly occupied by the duke of Bavaria in defense of Catholicism in 1607. A number of Protestants protested that this occupation was in breach of the terms of the Peace of Augsburg. The forcible re-Catholicization of the city led to the formation of a Protestant military alliance in 1608 and a Catholic alliance the following year. Such military escalations prepared the way for the outbreak of the Thirty Years War (1618–1648).

While there were clearly a number of ambiguities and unresolved issues in the terms of the Peace of Augsburg, it did manage to maintain a degree of religious equilibrium within the empire during the second half of the sixteenth century, at a time when France and the Low Countries were being torn apart by wars that had a strongly religious dimension. However, the weaknesses in the peace later contributed directly to the outbreak of the Thirty Years War (1618–1648), a bitter conflict fought largely (although not exclusively) on religious grounds.

Further Reading

Asch, Ronald G. *The Thirty Years War: The Holy Roman Empire and Europe, 1618–48.* New York, 1997.

Dixon, C. Scott. *The Reformation in Germany.* Malden, MA, 2002.

Reich, Emil. *Select Documents Illustrating Mediæval and Modern History.* London, 1905.

Andrew Spicer

SEE ALSO

• Calvinism • Charles V • Holy Roman Empire • Lutheranism • Reformation • Thirty Years War • Trent, Council of

Bacon, Francis

THE ENGLISH PHILOSOPHER AND WRITER FRANCIS BACON (1561–1626) ORIGINATED A NEW METHOD OF SCIENTIFIC INQUIRY AND PLAYED A KEY ROLE IN THE POLITICAL WORLD OF QUEEN ELIZABETH I AND KING JAMES I.

This marble bust by Louis-François Roubillac (1702–1762), an idealized representation of Bacon the philosopher, reveals the high esteem in which its subject was held a century after his death.

Francis Bacon was born in London on January 22, 1561, at York House on the Strand, the traditional home of the lord keeper of the great seal of England—an officer of the crown whose custodianship of the royal seal conferred upon him important rights and privileges. In 1617, when, following in his father's footsteps, he secured promotion to the position of lord keeper, Bacon returned to his birthplace and declared, "I was born there and am like to end my days there." His prediction turned out to be very wide of the mark.

Early Life, Education, and Career

Francis's father was Nicholas Bacon, and his mother was Anne Cooke, one of the learned daughters of Anthony Cooke (who had been King Edward VI's tutor). At Gorhambury, near Saint Albans in Hertfordshire (north of London), Bacon received an early education in Latin and Greek. At age twelve he was sent to Trinity College, Cambridge, under the tutelage of John Whitgift, the future archbishop of Canterbury. After leaving Cambridge in 1575, Bacon was admitted to London's Gray's Inn, one of the four Inns of Court, at which students trained in law, to prepare for a career in government. However, instead of embarking on his legal studies, Bacon went to France with Amias Paulet, the English ambassador. The Roman law Bacon encountered in France greatly influenced his later ideas about legal reform. In 1579 Nicholas Bacon died unexpectedly, and Francis was forced to look about for a way to earn a living and gain a respectable position. Since the obvious choice was the law, he finally took up his place at Gray's Inn.

At Gray's Inn, Bacon's natural talent and energetic dedication to his studies ensured rapid progress. Bacon also began to pursue a political career and was first elected to Parliament in 1581.

In the 1587 Parliament, Bacon participated in discussions concerning Mary, Queen of Scots, the cause of much Catholic unrest in England; he was on the committee that drew up the petition for Mary's execution. In 1594 he was appointed a learned counsel, a key legal adviser to Queen Elizabeth I. Yet Bacon, always ambitious, was not content simply to serve as a lawyer: he hoped to play a more central role in government, as his father had done before him. Also in 1594, Robert Devereux, the earl of Essex, a favorite of the queen's, campaigned for Bacon to become attorney general (the crown prosecutor), but the position went to Edward Coke, who was to become Bacon's bitter long-term rival.

CHRONOLOGY

January 22, 1561
Francis Bacon is born at York House, London.

1584
Is elected member of Parliament for Dorsetshire.

1597
Essayes, Colours of Good and Evil, and *Meditationes sacrae* are published.

1605
The Advancement of Learning is published.

1620
Novum organum is published.

1621
Charged with bribery, Bacon is politically disgraced.

1622
The Historie of the Raigne of King Henry the Seventh and *Historia naturalis* are published.

1623
Historia vitae et mortis and *De augmentis scientiarum* are published.

1625
New Atlantis and *The Essayes, or Counsels, Civill and Morall* are published.

1626
Bacon dies at the earl of Arundel's house in Highgate.

1630
Maxims of the Law and *Elements of the Common Laws of England* are published.

1642
Reading on the Statute of Uses is published.

Despite this setback Bacon's legal career continued to flourish. He also began seriously to pursue his interests in science and more general scholarly pursuits. His *Essayes,* a masterful collection of observations on a variety of moral themes, was first published in 1597. In 1597 he presented Elizabeth with a work entitled *Maxims of the Law* (it was eventually published in 1630). In it Bacon explored how English law might be restructured in order to work more efficiently and fairly. Even with these successes Bacon continued to suffer from financial problems. His attempts to court and marry the rich widow Elizabeth Hatton were unsuccessful, and when he was arrested on charges of debt in 1598, he barely avoided imprisonment.

Bacon in the Reign of James I

After the death of Elizabeth I in 1603, Bacon looked to King James I for political favor. In writing *A Brief Discourse Touching the Happy Union of the Kingdoms of England and Scotland,* Bacon hoped to impress James with an intellectual treatise that promoted one of the king's most important projects. Bacon also improved his financial position by marrying the fourteen-year-old heiress Alice Barnham.

By June 1607 Bacon had gained the office of solicitor general, the king's principal legal adviser, and a year later he was granted the clerkship of the star chamber, a judicial body that reviewed judgments made by other courts and heard direct appeals. Bacon was also continuing his lifelong intellectual project, a major work on natural philosophy (his name for the entire body of terrestrial knowledge, somewhat akin to the modern term *natural science*). In 1605 he had already published *The Two Bookes of Francis Bacon: Of the Proficience and Advancement of Learning Divine and Humane,* commonly known as *The Advancement of Learning.* During the next decade he was to develop the ideas begun in this work.

By 1613 Bacon's long years of service to the crown finally saw him appointed attorney general. By 1616 he was a privy counselor (the privy council was the king's most powerful body of advisers). Finally, in 1617 he attained the position of lord keeper, an office held by his father before him. In 1618 Bacon was created Baron Verulam; he was also made lord chancellor, the preeminent judge in the country. As lord chancellor he was involved in several high-profile cases, including the death sentence of Walter Raleigh, as well as numerous smaller cases. By 1620 Bacon had reached the pinnacle of his career. He celebrated his sixtieth birthday with an extravagant feast held in York House on January 22, 1621. Five days later he gained the title of Viscount Saint Alban.

Bacon's Scientific Method and the Advancement of Knowledge

Throughout his public career, Bacon continued to work privately on the development and elaboration of a new scientific method. Intellectual life

Essayes.

Religious Meditations

Places of perswasion an

disswasion.

Seene and allowed.

At London,
Printed for Humfrey Hooper, and a
to be sold at the blacke Beare
in Chauncery Lane.
1597.

Bacon modeled his essays on those of the French writer Michel de Montaigne (1533–1592). The simplicity of the title page of the first edition of Bacon's Essayes (1597), pictured here, suggests that the publisher, one H. Hooper, had relatively modest expectations of success.

In a letter he wrote to his uncle in 1592, Francis Bacon set out the scope of his intellectual pursuits:

I have taken all knowledge to be my province. . . . I hope I should bring in industrious observations, grounded conclusions, and profitable inventions and discoveries; the best state of that province. This, whether it be curiosity, or vain glory, or nature, or (if one take it favourably) philanthropia, *is so fixed in my mind as it cannot be removed.*

Letter to William Cecil, Lord Burghley

In this oil portrait by Paul van Somer (c. 1576–1621), painted around the time of Bacon's elevation to lord chancellor in 1618, a mature Francis Bacon confidently surveys his political successes.

in England was still based heavily on medieval Scholasticism, a form of logical inquiry conducted in Latin that derived mainly from the work of the ancient Greek philosopher Aristotle. One of the keystones of Scholastic learning was the syllogism, a logical device that consists of a major premise, a minor premise, and a conclusion. The most famous of Aristotle's syllogisms is as follows: all men are mortal (major premise); Socrates is a man (minor premise); therefore, Socrates is mortal (conclusion). Bacon's principal criticism of this deductive method of reasoning was that if the major premise is incorrect, then everything derived from the premise is also incorrect. Bacon insisted on a radical departure from this method of ascertaining truth.

In the *Novum organum* (1620), Bacon sought to provide a new method of attaining knowledge. He rejected the logic of the syllogism and proposed instead a logic based on the classification of data provided by the senses. For Bacon, the true natural philosopher is one who painstakingly observes natural phenomena and "by slow and faithful toil gathers information from things and brings it into understanding." Instead of expounding upon nature through abstract argument, Bacon proposed a method of inquiry in which the inquirer investigates nature itself empirically—that is, with no preconceptions as to what he or she might find.

Bacon's inductive method of reasoning begins, then, with observations, meticulously noted and ordered into tables of classification. Once sufficient data has been collected, recorded, and categorized, the natural philosopher moves on to explore the relationships between the observed phenomena and to form general rules, or axioms. An essential feature of Bacon's method at this point is the use of exclusion. Through a process of analysis, those axioms that are found not to be true of the observed phenomena are ruled out. The natural philosopher moves from axioms that describe specific data to axioms of increasing generality that encompass greater bodies of data until he finally arrives at fundamental laws of nature (or, in Bacon's words, a knowledge of forms). This sequence of steps creates a systematic methodology that attests to the reliability of the final laws, or forms. The chain of reasoning also provides a firm grounding upon which the natural philosopher can proceed to develop practical uses for and applications of these laws.

▼ *The title page of the London edition of the* Instauratio magna, *published by John Bill in 1620, illustrates the ambition of the work, which was no less than to present a classification of all the sciences. The work was never completed, but the portions that were published influenced European thought for centuries.*

The revolutionary aspect of Bacon's methodology lay in his realization that it is not sufficient simply to gather facts directly from nature. Rather, natural phenomena must be observed and then processed into axioms through a thorough methodological system. While traditional methods of deductive logic proved inadequate in the field of natural science, Bacon's inductive reasoning provided a model that later philosophers and scientists could use and develop. Bacon's method has been criticized and his contribution to science undervalued because of its onerous dependence upon the painstaking gathering of evidence and its lack of appreciation for intuition and imagination. However, these criticisms aside, Bacon's work may be seen in retrospect as a necessary departure from an essentially medieval way of exploring the world. His work inspired others, freed from the shackles of tradition, to continue developing empirical scientific methods using observation, experimentation, and analysis. Bacon's work is seen by some as a starting point for modern science, the beginning of a process that culminated in the many great scientific achievements of the seventeenth century and beyond.

Fall from Power and Retirement

In 1621 Bacon became embroiled in a political scandal concerning patents (legal documents allowing somebody to exercise a monopoly on a certain item or service). An investigation discovered that a patent issued for gold and silver thread channeled considerable profits to the king. In order to protect the king, the blame was shifted to Bacon, who had drawn up the patents. He was imprisoned in the Tower of London, fined £40,000, removed from public office, and barred from holding government positions and from sitting in Parliament. The sentence was

BACON'S INDUCTIVE STUDY OF HEAT

Francis Bacon not only expounded upon method and theory but also sought to show his method at work. In his famous study of heat in the *Novum organum,* he constructs a "table of presence" in which he lists all those natural phenomena in which heat is observable. The table includes such entries as the rays of the sun, a flame, rotting vegetation, quicklime, and hot oils. Alongside this table he constructed another, made up of related phenomena in which heat is not observable—moonlight, for example. He also constructed a third table, "Degrees or Comparison in Heat," where he notes differences in the intensity of heat. For instance, "the anvil grows very hot under the hammer," and "some ignited bodies are found to be much hotter than some flames." Using these three tables, he applies his method of exclusion and eliminates all entries that are not common to all instances of the presence of heat. Bacon then interprets the findings in order to identify a fundamental law or form: "Heat is a motion, expansive, restrained and acting in its strife upon the smaller particles of the body." While a modern scientist might see this particular exercise as rather simplistic, the methodology Bacon introduced was a radical departure from traditional practices.

◀ *This engraving of the ruins of Gorhambury, the medieval manor house in which Francis Bacon grew up, was made in 1803. Some of these ruins still stand (Bacon's descendants built a new Palladian mansion nearby in 1777).*

harsh; although the fine was never collected and his imprisonment lasted only three days, Bacon's public career was over, and his finances were in shambles. He retreated to his country home, Gorhambury, and spent the next years on his philosophical pursuits.

By December 1625 Bacon was so ill that he drew up his final will, in which he disinherited his wife. His marriage, like his political career, had begun so carefully and hopefully but ended in ruin. When Bacon died on April 9, 1626, he left a letter, half finished, like so much of his writing, apologizing to the earl of Arundel for having arrived without due notice at the earl's house in Highgate, in northern London. His last words form a fitting epitaph for this man of great intellect and even greater ambition, "I was not able to go back, and therefore was forced to take up my lodging here."

FURTHER READING

Coquillette, Daniel R. *Francis Bacon.* Stanford, CA, 1992.

Farrington, B. *The Philosophy of Francis Bacon.* Liverpool, 1964.

Jardine, Lisa. *Francis Bacon: The Discovery and the Arts of Discourse.* Cambridge, 1974.

Jardine, Lisa, and Alan Stewart. *Hostage to Fortune: The Troubled Life of Francis Bacon.* New York, 1999.

Martin, Julian. *Francis Bacon, the State, and the Reform of Natural Philosophy.* New York, 1992.

Jessica L. Malay

SEE ALSO

• Elizabeth I • England • Hobbes, Thomas
• Humanism and Learning • London
• Philosophy

Banking

THE FOUNDATIONS OF MODERN BANKING SYSTEMS EMERGED DURING THE RENAISSANCE, AND REFORMATION-ERA INNOVATIONS IN THE FIELD OF FINANCE LED THE WAY TO A DRAMATIC EXPANSION IN EUROPEAN BUSINESS AND COMMERCE.

During the Middle Ages many areas of Europe began to make the transition from a barter system of commerce (one in which traders exchange goods for other goods of equivalent value) to one based on the payment of money for goods and services. As continent-wide trade expanded, there was a concurrent increase in the types and forms of financial commerce. The emergence of standardized currencies and organizations offering such financial services as banking and insurance facilitated this rise in economic activity. The most significant innovations occurred first in Florence, Genoa, and other Italian city-states and then spread throughout Europe. A secure banking system and financial-services sector provided the economic basis for the commercial activity that fueled Europe dur-ing both the Renaissance and the Reformation.

Money and Credit

Early money was in the form of coins. Coins were usually named after their weight—as was the case with the British pound—or after the sovereign who issued the coins—as was the case with the Venetian ducat, which was named after the doge of Venice. At first, many kingdoms had coins minted by private firms under license from royal

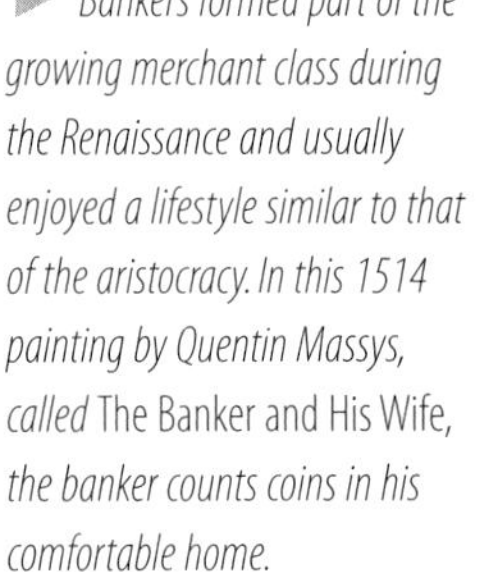

Bankers formed part of the growing merchant class during the Renaissance and usually enjoyed a lifestyle similar to that of the aristocracy. In this 1514 painting by Quentin Massys, called The Banker and His Wife, *the banker counts coins in his comfortable home.*

authority. Only in the later Renaissance did kingdoms and other political units begin establishing their own mints.

These early coins presented merchants with a number of problems. First, there was a large number of different types of coins in circulation. Coins were often minted with the current sovereign stamped on them. The arrival of a new ruler usually entailed the minting of new coins. It was often difficult to assess the value of coins from different eras. Second, the coins were seldom uniform, even when they were minted by the same firm. The actual worth of coins with the same nominal value could vary widely depending upon the minting techniques employed, differences in the quality of ore used, or the wear that came from use. Third, merchants often faced problems in trying to determine the value of coins from other countries or cities.

In order to address these problems, a new class of merchant emerged: the money changer. Money changers exchanged foreign currency into local coins and replaced worn or damaged currency. Over time, money changers began to develop a system of coinless transactions. When traders brought in coins, the money changer would simply open an account for the merchant instead of providing new or converted currency. The merchant could use that account to pay suppliers who also had accounts with the money changer. Hence, items could be bought or sold and payments and credits made without coins ever changing hands. In return for this service, money changers often charged a small fee, but they also allowed merchants short-term credit.

This illustration of a usurer, from a fifteenth-century book by Jacques le Grant called Le livre des bonnes moeurs *(The Book of Good Manners), reinforces the social taboo against usury by conveying the greed associated with the practice.*

USURY AND EARLY BANKING

Under the influence of the church, most European states developed laws that forbade usury, the charging of excessive interest on loans (excessive interest was usually defined as any rate of 25 percent or higher). The canonical laws of the Middle Ages and early Renaissance outlawed usury, and among the church edicts against the charging of high interest were those issued at the Council of Lyon (1274) and the Council of Vienna (1312). Some secular restrictions forbade the charging of any interest whatsoever. As late as 1546, the Holy Roman emperor Charles V forbade anybody who charged interest on loans or received loans that charged interest from attending mass or even entering church property (a restriction that prevented such people from being buried in a church cemetery).

Usury laws were designed to prevent bankers or other financiers from taking advantage of people in economic difficulties. Particularly troubling for church leaders was the notion that one person would benefit from the misfortunes of another. At the same time, these restrictions on charging interest limited the potential of many firms and companies to expand their business and move into new markets—since there was little incentive to provide capital to fuel the expansion. Even the church made regular use of banks to finance projects and maintain the solvency of the papacy.

During the Reformation secular usury laws began to be loosened. In 1545 King Henry VIII of England permitted the charging of interest with an upper limit of 10 percent (this limit was later lowered to 8 percent). Other Reformation states, including Holland and several of the German states, also relaxed usury laws, although most German states set the limit on interest at 5 percent. Many Catholic countries continued to forbid usury; France did not approve charging interest on loans until 1789. Reformation thinkers had mixed views on the subject of usury. Martin Luther condemned usury, but John Calvin endorsed the loosening of restrictions on interest loans.

The church's restrictions on usury did not apply to Jews. Owing to this factor and to the secular restrictions on land ownership by Jews in many European states, money changing and loan provision were among the very few commercial opportunities open to Jews in Europe. Interestingly, most kings and rulers held that usury laws did not apply to monarchs or governments (in order to ensure that the state had ready access to loans). Conversely, sovereigns repeatedly used prohibitions against usury as a means to avoid repaying loans, especially when they were in danger of default.

could try to defraud their creditors. At the same time, dishonest money changers could also try to cheat customers by pretending to overextend themselves through false loans and then declaring themselves insolvent, going out of business, and absconding with the money.

▲ *A detail from a 1468 manuscript illustration by Benvenuto di Giovanni entitled* The Finances of the Commune of Siena, in Time of Peace and in Time of War. *In the detail, which illustrates financial transactions during peacetime, a heavenly figure oversees a banker dealing with noblemen.*

One of the earliest forms of regular business credit came in the form of overdrafts. Money changers extended credit or made small loans by allowing their clients to overdraw their account for short periods. In exchange for these loans, the merchants were charged a percentage of the loan, although this charge did not amount to interest in the traditional sense. The particular method of charging was designed to avoid accusations of usury. The system was very informal: there was no legal obligation on the part of the money changer to honor the overdraft. However, this means of providing loans became a regular feature of commerce.

Since money changers oversaw their clients' accounts, they would have a good sense of their clients' creditworthiness and their ability to repay an overdraft. Still, these short-term loans were very risky, as businesses could fail, merchants could die, and unscrupulous traders could try to defraud their creditors.

Early Banks and Pawnbrokers

By the dawn of the Renaissance, there were three sources for personal and commercial loans. During the Middle Ages, in addition to money changers, some merchants and wealthy families with large amounts of capital had begun to issue large loans to governments and individual sovereigns. Few countries or kingdoms had anything like a modern treasury system, and so the authorities were often forced to rely on private loans to finance construction projects, wars, and famine relief. Over time, these family loan enterprises developed into the first modern banks. Unlike money changers, these banking firms were typically international in nature and lent very substantial sums of money. Since governments and individual rulers often exempted themselves from usury laws, these early banks were able to make substantial profits from their loans. For particularly large loans, it was not uncommon for a group of bankers to form a syndicate or cartel in order to provide the necessary funds. This pooling of resources had the added advantage of spreading the risk of the loan among several financiers in the event of default.

The large banking firms were able to ensure that their loans were repaid by insisting that the loans were secured with substantial collateral, such as royal jewels or property. For instance, the king of Cyprus offered the port of Famagusta as collateral for a loan from a group of Genoese bankers. When the king defaulted on the loan, the bankers took control of the port. On the other hand, many powerful sovereigns defaulted on loans without suffering the ramifications. At different times the kings of England and Spain defaulted on loans from international firms. The bankers were unable to do anything about the default because of the political and military power of the kingdoms.

These large international banking firms also provided a degree of security and safety that helped spur cross-border commerce. Many firms established branches in all of the major commercial centers of the day. For example, the Medici Bank had branches in the Italian cities of Pisa, Milan, Florence, Rome, and Venice; Bruges (in the Low Countries); London; Geneva (in present-day Switzerland); and the French cities of Paris, Avignon, and Lyons. Over the course of the Renaissance, two main centers for international banking emerged: the Italian city-states and Geneva. The Italian states dominated trade and commerce in the Mediterranean region, while trade north of the Alps tended to center around Geneva.

The title of Vittorio Carpaccio's work The Healing of the Madman *(c. 1496) refers to a miraculous healing depicted in the upper left of this tempera painting. Carpaccio captures the splendor, majesty, and bustling activity of fifteenth-century Venice, which was rapidly becoming one of Europe's financial centers. Straddling the Grand Canal is the wooden Rialto bridge, which was built in 1458 and collapsed in 1524 (the current stone bridge was erected in 1592).*

Giovanni di Bicci de' Medici 1360–1429

Giovanni di Bicci de' Medici, the founder of the great Medici dynasty, was the father of Cosimo de' Medici and the great-grandfather of Lorenzo the Magnificent. Giovanni laid the basis for the dramatic rise in the family's prominence by overseeing the Medici Bank. Having worked as money changers during the early 1300s, the Medicis established a small bank in Rome to work with the church. Giovanni worked for a relative in his youth and then used his connections and financial acumen to create his own firm.

Giovanni quickly rose through the ranks to become one of the most important papal bankers. Although his business with the papacy initially provided the main source of income for the bank, Giovanni correctly foresaw the rise of Florence as a commercial center and established a branch of his bank there in 1397. This branch became the core of the great Medici Bank. He later established branches throughout Italy and the Mediterranean.

In 1410 Giovanni's friend Baldassare Cossa was elected pope as John XXIII (the manner of his election being irregular, the Catholic Church regards him as an antipope). He made the Medici firm the principal papal bank and granted Giovanni a range of concessions, including contracts for tax collecting and the supervision of mining. These new opportunities made Giovanni, already wealthy, one of the richest men in Italy and ensured the rise of the Medici dynasty.

Giovanni was not interested in politics; he strenuously sought to avoid public service. He even preferred to pay fines rather than accept government offices. After Giovanni's death in 1429, his son Cosimo further expanded the wealth and prominence of the bank, which survived until 1494—when financial losses forced it to close.

THE FUGGER BANK

The Fugger Bank of Augsburg was created by a trading company that specialized in exchanging textile products (such as wool) and local silver for goods from the Orient—mainly spices and silk. As the firm acquired more and more money, it began to make loans to the nobility of the Tyrol (a region of Austria and Italy) in return for mortgages on the nobility's silver mines (in several cases, the family was able to acquire the mines). The Fuggers later even issued loans to the Hapsburgs. Their banking success soon eclipsed their trade business, and they began to open branches of their bank throughout Europe in such cities as Leipzig, in eastern Germany; Antwerp, in the Low Countries; Rome; and Lyons.

During the 1500s the Fuggers started to extend substantial loans to Spain. Initially they made large profits, owing to the large amount of gold and silver being brought into Spain from its colonies in the Americas. The Fuggers made the miscalculation of taking out long-term loans in Augsburg in order to provide Spain with short-term loans and then relying on the Spanish payments to service their bank's own growing debt. In 1557 Philip II of Spain ordered two payments of silver confiscated for his own use. The Fuggers could do little in response except renegotiate with Spain on the monarch's terms, which included reduced interest rates and a longer period of repayment. In 1575 Spain again stopped payments and then in 1596 defaulted a third time. The third default caused the collapse of the Fugger Bank, which could no longer repay the loans it had taken out in order to finance its own loans to Spain.

This portrait of Jakob Fugger (1459–1525), painted around 1518, is by the celebrated German artist Albrecht Dürer. The Fugger Bank, one of the most successful lending firms in Germany, reached its height under Jakob, who was often called Jakob the Rich.

The first major international firm, the Medici Bank, was established in 1397 by the powerful Medici family of Florence. The Medici Bank was followed in 1407 by the Bank of Saint George in Genoa and in 1487 by the Fugger Bank in Augsburg, in southern Germany. Later, in the 1600s, a number of firms were established in northern Europe. The early Italian banks were established for both commercial and political reasons. The Medici Bank served not only to generate profits for the family but also, by providing loans to prominent citizens and to international firms, to enhance the family's political power and influence.

Among the three classes of bankers, pawnbrokers were considered the lowest form and the least reputable. Pawnbrokers offered small loans that were secured by such collateral as jewels, tools, and household items. A customer would give an item to the pawnbroker in return for a loan that was usually less than the value of the item. If the customer did not repay the loan within an agreed amount of time, the item was forfeit. Thus, the pawnbroker was assured a profit, either through the interest payments on the loan or, in the case of default, by the money recouped through the sale of the item. Many pawnbrokers committed usury by charging interest rates of 30 percent or more, in spite of laws to the contrary. That pawnbroking had an unsavory reputation is therefore hardly surprising.

Pawnbrokers provided an important service to nobles, especially in areas where usury laws prevented the rise of commercial banks. This illustration of a Venetian pawnbroker is from a seventeenth-century book of costumes by Jan van Grevenbroeck.

Until well into the seventeenth century pawnbrokers frequently provided the only means for the poor or noncreditworthy to gain loans. Many private pawnbrokers were considered disreputable; however, some pawnbrokers became wealthy and prominent by offering their services to royalty and the nobility. For instance, the house of the Lombards was granted the exclusive right to serve as pawnbroker to the royal houses of Europe. The Lombards provided pawn services to a range of royal clients, including Edward III of England (reigned 1327–1377). As a result, the firm became wealthy and its members accepted among the highest social circles. Its crest, three suspended golden balls, remains the international symbol for pawnbrokers.

During the early Renaissance, the church began actively to encourage the formation of charitable pawnshops as alternatives to the private pawnbrokers who offered interest-based loans. Most of these pawn operations were operated by the church, and they were officially allowed to charge interest rates of between 6 and 15 percent on loans in order to finance their operations. The later rise of commercial banks would relegate pawn operations to the margins of the banking system.

Public and Municipal Banks

Repeated efforts to create public banks during the later Middle Ages and early Renaissance failed. Governments sought to establish public banks in order to increase economic growth and to lessen the damaging effects of economic panics and depressions. States also wanted a secure source of funding to bolster or augment public revenues. The Spanish city of Barcelona, for instance, created a bank of deposit, the Taula. The Taula received surplus tax revenues during prosperous economic times and was expected to lend money back to the city during economic downturns. The bank made no loans to the general public; it lent money only to the government and to businesses or guilds. Its financial solvency was supported by the government, which required the bank to back its deposits with 100 percent capital. Its loans had to be based on any profits it made. Because it could not provide the overdraft loans that were popular at the time, the Taula was unable to attract customers other than the government. In 1345, when Barcelona's rulers needed a substantial amount of cash, they forced the bank to provide the city with excessive loans. This overstretching caused the bank to fail; in response the city executed the bank's leaders.

When the Bank of England was originally chartered in 1694, it was still acceptable for borrowers to offer collateral, or pawns, to secure their loans. One bylaw of the bank's original charter regulates the use of pawns and reserves the bank's right to sell items if loans are not repaid within three months of the due date:

It is resolved and ordained, that all jewels, plate, bullion, or other goods, chattels or merchandizes whatsoever, which shall be pawned unto this corporation, or left and deposited therewith, as pawns, or pledges for money to be lent or advanced thereon, and not redeemed at the time agreed on, or within three months afterwards, shall (whensoever they are sold) be sold at a public sale, by inch of candle, in manner as in such cases is usual, upon three days notice thereof, first given by writing, on the Royal Exchange, or upon such other public notice as the court of directors shall think fit. And no sale of any such goods, chattels, or merchandizes (not redeemed as aforesaid) shall be had or made in any other manner.

Bylaw 9 of the charter of the Bank of England

▼ *Coins were the main form of currency during the Renaissance. To ensure authenticity and standardization, royal mints were chartered to produce coins that usually bore a royal impression. This 1644 gold three-pound coin, which is embossed with an image of King Charles I of England, was minted in Oxford.*

The Barcelona incident stands as an example of why public banks usually failed during the Renaissance and the early decades of the Reformation: rulers repeatedly raided the financial reserves of the banks when they needed cash or revenues. In England in 1640, Charles I confiscated 200,000 pounds sterling from the Royal Mint, which had been acting as a depository for English merchants. He agreed to return the funds only after the merchants in turn agreed to loan the crown 40,000 pounds. Monarchs often caused the demise of private banks as well. The famed Fugger Bank of Augsburg failed in 1596 when Spain refused to repay loans.

The Rise of National Banks and the Modern Banking System

Central to the development of modern financial systems was the evolution of national or central banks that controlled monetary policy. There was a concurrent rise in banking regulations to ensure the stability of banks and the safety of deposits. Chartered in 1609, the Bank of Amsterdam, for example, served to exchange currency and to oversee minting. In 1656 Sweden formed the Riksbank (or Bank of Sweden), which became the world's first true national bank when the crown took complete control of it in 1668. The Riksbank had two departments. One, based on the Bank of Amsterdam, oversaw currency issues. The other was a true lending bank that provided loans to the government and other bodies and issued securities. The Riksbank served as the model for other national banks, including the Bank of England (established in 1694). These national banks regulated monetary policy and currency. They also helped establish the guidelines and principles that governed the conduct of private banks. With the rise of national banks, there was

▲ *The setting for Vittorio Carpaccio's 1502* Calling of Saint Matthew *is the Venice of the artist's day. Saint Matthew accepts the call of Jesus Christ and the disciples to abandon his job as a tax collector and join them instead.*

a corresponding increase in regulations that governed private banks. For instance, in some countries banks were required to keep a certain amount of their deposits on hand in order to ensure their solvency. In other cases banks had to provide the civil government with a deposit in silver or gold as insurance in case they failed. Such regulations gave merchants more confidence in banks, and with an increase in the amount of credit available, trade in turn expanded.

Banking and Insurance

Banks provided another major benefit for commerce by leading the effort to establish insurance systems. For instance, in 1252, tired of losing money on loans for products that were lost at sea, major banks pressured the Venetian government to start charging merchants a premium and then using these funds to reimburse banks that lost money after maritime losses. In 1384 private banking firms began offering insurance policies to merchants to cover products and supplies being shipped. Finally, in 1688 Lloyd's of London, a private firm devoted entirely to offering maritime insurance, was formed. The creation of Lloyd's of London launched the major expansion in insurance services that also helped fuel the economic expansion of Europe in the eighteenth and nineteenth centuries. The spread of insurance companies reduced the financial risks associated with shipping and overseas commerce and thus prompted an increasing number of merchants to engage in foreign trade.

Further Reading

Chiappelli, Fredi, ed. *The Dawn of Modern Banking.* New Haven, CT, 1979.

Goldthwaite, Richard A. *The Building of Renaissance Florence: An Economic and Social History.* Baltimore, 1980.

Kirshner, Julius, ed. *Business, Banking, and Economic Thought in Late Medieval and Early Modern Europe: Selected Studies of Raymond de Roover.* Chicago, 1974.

Lane, Frederic C., and Reinhold C. Mueller. *Money and Banking in Medieval and Renaissance Venice.* Vol. 1, *Coins and Moneys of Account.* Baltimore, 1985.

Mueller, Reinhold C. *Money and Banking in Medieval and Renaissance Venice.* Vol. 2, *The Venetian Money Market: Banks, Panics, and the Public Debt, 1200–1500.* Baltimore, 1997.

Tom Lansford

SEE ALSO

• Florence • Hanseatic League • Italian City States • Judaism • Markets and Fairs • Medicis, The • Trade • Venice

Bearbaiting and Blood Sports

IN EARLY MODERN EUROPE BAITING BEARS AND OTHER DANGEROUS ANIMALS BY TETHERING THEM TO POSTS AND SETTING DOGS ON THEM WAS A POPULAR AMUSEMENT. AMONG THE OTHER BLOODSPORTS ENJOYED BY MEN AND WOMEN OF ALL SOCIAL CLASSES WERE COCKFIGHTING, DOGFIGHTING, FALCONRY, AND HUNTING.

The long history of baiting animals for entertainment goes back at least to Roman times, and throughout medieval Europe baitings and other sorts of organized animal torments were an accepted part of many holiday celebrations. Baitings were traditional features of the festive communal calendar (the regular civic celebration of holy days), and on such occasions towns, guilds, and even churches would often chip in to fund a full day of animal sports. By the sixteenth century, however, as cities became larger and their culture more urban, animal baiting was increasingly seen as a purely commercial entertainment.

Bearbaiting and Monkey Baiting

In a bearbaiting a bear was first secured to a post with around twelve feet of chain; the crowd then either formed a circle or watched from beyond a fence while dogs were let in (either one at a time or together as a pack) to worry and harass the bear. Points were scored for effective hits (the dogs were trained, for example, to go for the bear's eyes, with the result that many baited bears were soon blinded); meanwhile masters and bystanders could wager on the dogs' performance. Although combat generally ended before the bear was mortally injured—bears were, after all, both difficult and expensive to replace—the bear was almost always badly bitten. Monkey baitings were similar: a pack of dogs was set on a monkey mounted on a cheap horse within a fenced ring; as the horse galloped frantically around the circle, the dogs would try to take down either the horse or its rider.

▼ Although bear wards, men who took bears from town to town, tried to keep their animals alive, their bears were usually sadly dilapidated, as the name Blind Hunk (a well-known London bear) suggests. In this depiction of bearbaiting from the Luttrell Psalter (c. 1340), three men release their dogs onto the tethered bear under the direction of the bear ward.

Although to the modern eye such entertainments appear to be mere pointless exercises in animal cruelty, in origin they had a more practical—and deadly—purpose: the dogs used in bearbaitings and monkey baitings were mastiffs, the huge, shaggy, ferocious, homicidal beasts that the English aristocracy used as war dogs. By pitting their dogs against monkeys on horseback and against bears (whose upright, two-legged fighting stance mimicked that of a man), medieval English aristocrats were in fact training their dogs to kill men in combat.

By the sixteenth century entertainment had become by far the most important reason for animal baiting, and the fondness of the English for baitings was well known. Eventually London could boast three different bear gardens at which bears and monkeys were baited several times a week before large and appreciative crowds of paying spectators. Still, in Renaissance England, practical reasons remained for training dogs to kill: in 1598, when the earl of Essex led an army into Ireland to subdue the rebellion, he brought with him three thousand mastiffs to hunt not bears or monkeys but Irish rebels.

▲ *This anonymous Elizabethan woodcut depicts a bear garden, an arena where animals were baited before large crowds of paying spectators. Bearbaiting rivaled the theater as a popular form of inexpensive urban entertainment in Renaissance England.*

THE POPULARITY OF BLOOD SPORTS

The appeal of many Renaissance blood sports, in which deliberate cruelty to animals seems to be the whole point of the exercise, is lost on most people in the twenty-first century, but for this reason it is important to make the effort to understand why these entertainments were so popular. First, most people in Renaissance Europe did not think blood sports cruel at all: they regarded animals as soulless creatures that God had created exclusively for the benefit of people. For many people of the Renaissance, the notion of cruelty simply did not apply to animals—in precisely the same way that, to the modern sensibility, it does not apply to plants. Many scholars, including such brilliant thinkers as René Descartes, even argued that animals did not feel pain and that the shrieking of a whipped dog was simply that animal's reaction to stimuli, akin to the noise made by a drum when beaten. Furthermore, people of all ranks were accustomed to the sight of bloodshed, as well as to the sight of animals being butchered for food or for sport. The attitude of most people was thus what some scholars have termed a cruelty of indifference rather than outright malice.

Many witnesses claimed to have had an aesthetic appreciation for blood sports that is difficult for modern observers to comprehend. When Queen Elizabeth of England witnessed a bearbaiting in 1575, one of her companions remarked that it was a matter of "goodly relief" to see the bear shake the blood from his head and ears. An Italian tourist found a London monkey baiting quite "wonderful to see"—although he confessed that the bearbaiting that followed was "not very pleasant." Others thought the sight of the terrified monkey, screaming while trying desperately to avoid the dogs, an amusing spectacle.

Bearbaiting and bull baiting may also have given the lower classes a sort of vicarious thrill: for a poor man to see such a powerful animal as a bear or a bull torn apart by a pack of smaller dogs may well have seemed a pleasurable inversion of the usual rules of social hierarchy. The thought at least occurred to Shakespeare's contemporary Thomas Dekker when he went to the bear garden; in 1609 he wrote in *Work for Armourers,* "for the Bears, or the Bulls fighting with the dogs, was a lively representation, me thought, of poor men going to law [taking to court] the rich and mighty."

Bull Baiting

Bulls were probably baited more often than any other large animal. The origins of bull baiting (and bullfighting) may lie in pagan religious ceremonies, perhaps those dedicated to Mithra, the chief god of pre-Zoroastrian Persia. Mithraism enjoyed widespread appeal in Roman Europe in the first centuries CE, and surviving reliefs from sites of worship depict the sacrifice of a bull, the cult's sacred animal. Mithra's holy day was in midwinter, when medieval bull baitings and bullfights were especially common. However, by the Renaissance any such ancient origin had been forgotten, and bulls were baited for reasons of entertainment—and also of hygiene: bulls, physicians advised, were by nature extremely cold and dense, and as a result, their meat was almost inedible and certainly unhealthy. Baiting, the physicians said, would warm the bull and make its meat more tender and palatable. Thus, many communities legally required butchers to bait their bulls before slaughter in the interests of public health. For this reason if a market had a butcher, it generally had a bullring, too.

In a bull baiting, a bull was tethered by around twelve feet (3.7 m) of rope or chain to an iron ring set in the ground. Bulldogs—hence the breed's name—were then set upon the bull: the dogs would crouch low to the ground and rapidly but cautiously approach the bull. The bull would try to hook a dog under its horns and toss the animal high into the air (whereupon its unfortunate owner would attempt to catch it in order to save it from more serious harm). If a dog evaded the horns, it would seize the bull by its throat, nose, or dewlap and hang on for dear life until it finally tore out a part of the bull's face or throat or was shaken free by the bull's frantic bucks and twists. Sometimes the dogs would kill the bull, but more often they would just maim it—and "warm" it enough for slaughter and safe consumption.

Hunting

Hunting, unquestionably the most aristocratic of the blood sports, remained the chief amusement of Europe's noble classes throughout the Renaissance. Aristocrats argued (probably correctly) that hunting was excellent training for war: it tested their horsemanship, their skill with weapons, and their knowledge of the land. Nevertheless, it was also true that as the military importance of cavalry diminished, so did the practical value of the hunt. By the sixteenth century whatever importance hunting had was almost entirely social; men who had never gone near a battlefield, as well as women and members of the clergy, might be avid hunters. Aristocratic

This anonymous Flemish tapestry panel, made around the turn of the seventeenth century, depicts a bull-baiting scene.

hunting took two main forms. In the first mounted men working with dogs drove game animals through a wood or park toward a waiting line of hunters on foot. This form of hunting was the least strenuous and could provide large amounts of game for the table. It did not, however, provide much in the way of sport. Indeed, there was often nothing remotely sporting about it. Large numbers of Renaissance game parks had tame inhabitants, a fact that permitted even the least skilled huntsman to make a kill. One Englishman invited to an Italian boar hunting party reported that he was disgusted to discover that not only was the beast less fierce than expected, but it would even come when he whistled. In the alternative form of hunting known as coursing, dogs chased after a suitable prey animal (generally a stag, deer, boar, or hare). The dogs and the quarry were then in turn pursued by the mounted hunters, who communicated with their dogs (and each other) by calls and horns. When the quarry was finally brought to bay, one of the hunters would kill it with a sword or spear.

Noblemen and their ladies are depicted coursing with hounds in Lucas Cranach the Elder's 1544 oil painting Hunt in Honor of Charles V at the Castle of Torgau. *Renaissance aristocrats of all kinds—kings and queens, bishops and popes, children, and even near invalids—were enthusiastic hunters. The French essayist Michel de Montaigne, who hated cruelty in any form, nonetheless adored the hunt.*

A PAPAL HUNTING ENTHUSIAST

Leo X, who was pope from 1513 to 1521, enjoyed bullfights and other blood sports and was passionately fond of hunting, despite the canonical decrees that forbade priests to hunt. Unfortunately, Leo's nearsightedness made hunting difficult for him, and so instead he liked to ride up to a piece of high ground and watch the proceedings through a telescope. Well beforehand, his servants would have collected and confined to a large pen numerous animals of all kinds—deer, boars, rabbits, goats, and even porcupines. When Leo gave the signal, underlings with horns and dogs drove the animals through a gap in the pen and toward the waiting sportsmen, who would fall on the beasts with axes, swords, and spears. Any creature fortunate enough to evade the slaughter would be chased down with dogs.

One day was particularly memorable. First, an unusually dim courtier mistook a hunting dog for a wolf and killed it; then, during a brawl that broke out among the hunters, one man lost an eye; and finally, a drunken huntsman speared his own dog instead of the boar he had been aiming at and became so enraged that he leaped from his horse and attempted to strangle the huge creature with his own hands. The boar gored him to death. Leo, viewing the carnage, mildly observed, "What a glorious day!"

COCKFIGHTING

Like bull- and bearbaiting, cockfighting was a festive entertainment that featured regularly at fairs and horse races, on holidays, and as school treats. One church in Wiltshire, in southern England, paid for cockfights at Easter for over a century (a reflection, perhaps, of a popular fable that a rooster crowed at the moment of Jesus's death and hence the animal was deserving of punishment).

Cocks were bred and raised specifically to be fighters: their wings were clipped, their beaks were filed sharp, and they were outfitted with long razor-sharp steel spurs. A cockfight was a series of one-on-one matches between members of two rival teams; a battle royal was a melee in which a large number of cocks were simply thrown into a pit together. King James I of England saw one such battle in 1617 and commented that he "was made very merry" by the sight.

Unlike most blood sports, in which wagering on the outcome was subordinate to the sheer enjoyment of the spectacle, much of cockfighting's popularity derived from the predilection of the gentry for betting. Cockfighting was also extremely popular among boys of school age: on Shrove Tuesday many children took their roosters to school, where the masters would supervise the contests. Cock throwing was yet another boyish holiday pastime. A simple sport, it consisted simply of throwing things at a tethered rooster until it died.

▲ *Blood sports—particularly cockfighting—provided rare opportunities for the lower classes to rub shoulders with nobles. Even kings and queens enjoyed the spectacle and festive atmosphere of the cockpit, as did Charles I, pictured in this anonymous seventeenth-century Dutch oil.*

Criticisms

Despite the popularity of blood sports, they were condemned by many. Some critics, such as the medieval theologian Thomas Aquinas, cautioned that those who were excessively cruel to animals might acquire the habit and be cruel to humans, too. Others argued on religious grounds that, although killing animals for food or necessity was permissible, it was wrong to cause unnecessary suffering. According to this point of view, as stewards of God's creation, people were given lordship over animals only on the condition, as the French Reformer John Calvin remarked, that "our rule be gentle." Evangelical Protestants disliked the culture that was often associated with blood sports—the gambling, drinking, and swearing—but they also argued that it was wrong to derive pleasure from the bloodlust of animals: since all animals were tame at creation, their ferocity was a consequence of human sin. Certain critics argued on ethical grounds against cruelty in all its forms. The great French essayist Michel de Montaigne (1533–1592), in his essay "On Cruelty," wrote, "We owe justice to men: and to the other creatures who are able to receive them we owe gentleness and kindness. Between them and us there is some sort of intercourse and a degree of mutual obligation." Criticisms of blood sports intensified in the seventeenth and eighteenth centuries; eventually some were abolished and others regulated.

FURTHER READING

Fudge, Erica. *Perceiving Animals: Humans and Beasts in Early Modern English Culture.* New York, 2000.

Holt, Richard. *Sport and the British: A Modern History.* New York, 1993.

Thomas, Keith. *Man and the Natural World: Changing Attitudes in England, 1500–1800.* New York, 1996.

Hans Peter Broedel

SEE ALSO

• Descartes, René • Leo X • Popular Culture • Warfare

Bernini, Gian Lorenzo

GIAN LORENZO BERNINI (1598–1680) CROWNED THE RENAISSANCE WITH A STYLE OF ARCHITECTURE AND SCULPTURE THAT GAVE SEVENTEENTH-CENTURY ROME A DISTINCTIVE BEAUTY AND GRANDEUR.

Gian Lorenzo Bernini's talent was established by the time he was eight. His father, the Neapolitan sculptor Pietro Bernini, was called to Rome in 1605. It is likely that Pietro received a commission to work at the Pauline Chapel, in the Church of Santa Maria Maggiore, from Cardinal Camillo Borghese, who would be elected pope as Paul V later that same year. Gian Lorenzo's long relationship with the church was personal as well as professional. A devout Catholic, he attended Mass three times a week, and his eldest son became a priest.

Bernini created the baroque style, which was characterized by a confident, unconventional use of classical elements. He produced architecture and sculpture that expressed the dynamism and optimism of the Catholic Counter-Reformation, the movement for the renewal of the church that was begun by the Council of Trent (which met from 1546 to 1563).

As a young man Bernini spent three years sketching ancient marbles as well as the paintings of the great sixteenth-century Italian artists Michelangelo, Raphael, and Giulio Romano. About 150 of Bernini's paintings are known to have existed at one time, but most are now lost, and sculpture, rather than painting, is the medium for which he is most celebrated. Before Bernini reached the age of seventeen, he had produced for the pope's nephew, Cardinal Scipione Borghese, a sculpture called *The Goat Amalthea with the Infant Jupiter and a Faun*, a piece of such beauty and technical perfection that it was long considered the work of a sculptor of classical antiquity.

Portraits in Marble

During Bernini's long career, he carved at least thirty-nine portrait busts, of which the most famous is his sculpture of Cardinal Scipione Borghese (1632). Bernini was supremely skilled at capturing in marble a living, thinking person; this celebrated bust leaves the impression that the cardinal is engaging the onlooker in conversation. He catches Borghese in a pose that perfectly combines authority with geniality. With the same skill Bernini sculpted Paul V, Urban VIII, and other popes, as well as Kings Charles I of England and Louis XIV of France.

◄ *This self-portrait of Bernini as a young man strongly evokes the architect's intensity and self-confidence.*

CHRONOLOGY

December 7, 1598
Gian Lorenzo Bernini is born in Naples.

1613
At fifteen, carves the figure of Saint Lawrence, his name saint.

1624
Designs the Church of Santa Bibiana, his first architectural commission.

1628
Begins the tomb of Urban VIII in Saint Peter's Basilica.

1637
Begins the bell tower atop the facade of Saint Peter's; his only unsuccessful project, it was pulled down in 1646.

1639
Bernini marries the daughter of Paulo Tezio, a union that would produce many children.

1647
Wins the commission for the *Fountain of Four Rivers* in the Piazza Navona.

1663
Designs the Scala Regia, the staircase linking the papal apartments to Saint Peter's.

April 1665–November 1666
Is resident in Paris, where he creates a portrait bust of Louis XIV and proposes designs for the Louvre.

November 28, 1680
Dies in Rome and is buried in the family vault in Santa Maria Maggiore, where he had come as a boy to watch his father work in the Pauline Chapel.

Great Stories in Stone

Inspired by the true-to-life sculpture of the late Roman Empire, Bernini began early in his career to create sculptures that told a story. The subjects of these narrative sculptures are caught in motion at a particular moment and often express vivid emotions ranging from hope to terror. In *Apollo and Daphne* (1622–1624), Daphne is caught as she is turned into a laurel tree in answer to her prayer that she be saved from the unwanted attentions of Apollo. In *Aeneas, Anchises, and Ascanius Fleeing Troy* (1619), Bernini depicted a Roman founding myth that was fundamental to the classical (and thus to the Renaissance) imagination. Aeneas is portrayed carrying his father Anchises and leading his son Ascanius; Anchises carries the household gods and Ascanius the hearth-fire that would make Rome another Troy. In his *David* (1623–1624), Bernini captures the moment before David's sling is discharged

A work in marble must be composed for a viewer who will see it from every side. The compositional genius Bernini would display as an architect was evident in the young sculptor, who created complex three-dimensional pieces, such as this Abduction of Proserpina *(1621).*

toward the giant Goliath. All these works, together with *The Abduction of Proserpina* (1621–1622), may well have been completed before the sculptor was twenty-five.

Bernini and Saint Peter's

In 1623 Cardinal Maffeo Barberini was elected pope (he took the title Urban VIII). Throughout Urban's pontificate, which lasted until 1644, Bernini would be the pope's architect. Saint Peter's Basilica had been left unfinished at Michelangelo's death in 1564, and Carlo Maderno's facade would not be complete until 1632. For fifty years Bernini would never be without some project related to the completion of Saint Peter's.

According to tradition, in Saint Peter's the altar must stand exactly over the spot where the apostle Peter, the founder of the Roman Church, had been buried after his execution in the nearby Circus of Nero. Bernini's task was to give this most important altar in Christendom a visual power that matched its religious significance, and his solution was the dramatic baldachin, the monumental bronze canopy that dominates the space beneath Michelangelo's dome. Built between 1624 and 1633, the baldachin is as much a work of architecture as it is a sculpture. The four twisted columns supporting the canopy were inspired by much smaller marble columns that had formed a screen between the altar and the main body of the church in the first Saint Peter's, built by Constantine around 330.

After the city of Jerusalem, which had numerous memorials to events in the life of Jesus Christ—particularly those of Holy Week—the altar of Saint Peter's, located atop the relics of the apostle and crowned by the great dome, was probably considered the most important place in Christendom during the Renaissance. Bernini designed the altar and its canopy, or baldachin, and the Chair of Peter in the apse.

BERNINI AND THE COUNCIL OF TRENT

The Council of Trent had been convened in 1546 to set right the failures that had, in the eyes of many, provided justification for the German Reformer Martin Luther's rejection of Roman authority and to channel a renewed missionary zeal. Lutheran Protestantism emphasized the individual's experience of God's forgiveness in preference to an unquestioning assent to church authority; so in a climate in which personal feeling and subjectivity had a new importance, the Council of Trent envisioned a new kind of naturalistic Catholic art that would inspire piety by evoking emotion.

In Bernini the council found a sculptor who shared its religious goals and whose art was both true to life and inspirational. Bernini read Thomas à Kempis's *Imitation of Christ,* a classic of the fifteenth-century *devotio moderna* ("modern devotion") that had anticipated both Martin Luther and the Council of Trent by encouraging a heartfelt piety that went beyond conventional assent to religious doctrine.

When Bernini traveled to France in 1665, he took with him Ignatius Loyola's *Spiritual Exercises,* a work that sought to spark the believer's imagination through meditations on the specific scenes of Christ's life as they were described in the Gospels. Every Bernini sculpture of a saint displays that union of naturalism and emotion that the church looked for in the period of renewal that followed the Council of Trent.

▲ Bernini's grand colonnade of Saint Peter's, seen from above in this photograph, harks back to the atriums of early Christian churches, transitional spaces that led the worshiper from the busy world of the street into the church proper. It is also difficult to ignore the reference the colonnade makes to encircling arms welcoming the pilgrim.

Seen beyond and through the baldachin, the monumental Chair of Peter occupies the apse. Working between 1658 and 1666, Bernini encased the small wooden cathedra (throne) of the apostle in a monumental bronze chair and made it the center of a composition designed to express the authority and wisdom of Peter in particular and the Roman Catholic Church in general. The single window, centered in a "glory" of golden rays that seem to materialize light, depicts the descent of the Holy Spirit upon the Chair of Peter.

The papal altar marked the beginning of Bernini's career at Saint Peter's; the Chair of Peter was begun in 1658, more than thirty years later. In the interval Bernini designed the magnificent colonnade that framed Carlo Maderno's facade, the holy water containers (or stoups), the tombs of Popes Alexander VII and Urban VIII, the marble pavement, and the angels that stand guard on the bridge leading away from Saint Peter's across the Tiber River.

Bernini's Saints

To depict a saint in the period of Bernini's maturity was to depict the transforming influence of God's love in the human heart, which in the saints produced a kind of ecstasy so joyous as to be painful. The Spanish Carmelite mystic Teresa of Ávila had died in 1582, and her fame was still spreading when in 1628 Bernini represented her mystical encounter with a cherub who had plunged a spear into her heart several times and left Teresa "utterly consumed by the great love of God." Almost thirty years later Bernini produced a second piece with a similar theme, his sculpture of the Blessed Ludovica Albertoni (1473–1533), a lay associate of the Franciscan order who spent her wealth ministering to the poor and sick. Bernini placed the statue above the altar and beneath and in front of a painting by Giovanni Gaulli in the Altieri Chapel in the Church of San Francesco a Ripa. Putti, winged heads depicting angelic intelligences, intrude across the frame of Gaulli's painting and bind the painting to the sculpture below. The entire complex composition, a unified combination of architecture, sculpture, and painting, is illuminated from windows placed at either side.

Bernini's Churches

In his designs for two churches, Sant'Andrea al Quirinale in Rome, begun in 1658, and Santa Maria dell'Assunzione in Ariccia, begun in 1662, Bernini helped invent a new kind of space for Christian worship. The typical Italian church, descended from the Constantinian basilica, had a long central axis culminating in the semicircular apse, in which, usually on an elevated platform, stood the altar. The Gothic churches of medieval France and England were also designed around a long central axis. Often worshipers were separated from the area in which the action of the Mass took place by a screen or wall. In great churches such as Canterbury Cathedral and King's College Chapel, Cambridge, this separation was established by a thick stone wall with only one door, an arrangement that reflected a hierarchical society in which it did not seem

The following excerpt is from a biography of Gian Lorenzo Bernini published in 1682, just two years after his death.

Bernini used to say that the worthy man was not he who made no errors, since that is an impossibility for those who do things, but he who made fewer errors than others; and that he himself has made more errors than any other artist, since he had made more works than any other. To one of his disciples who questioned him because he criticized beautiful things, he replied that there was no need to criticize ugly things, but rather the blameworthy aspects of beautiful things, thus seeking the perfect. It is not easy to describe the love Bernini brought to his work. He said that, when he began to work, it was for him like entering a pleasure garden.

Filippo Baldinucci, *The Life of Bernini*

◄ *Bernini's* Ecstasy of Saint Teresa, *in the Coronaro Chapel of Santa Maria della Vittoria, illustrates in marble the ideal of the saint transformed by charity, a virtue represented here by the smiling angel.*

unusual that choir monks and nobles should be closer to God's presence—symbolized by the altar—than ordinary worshipers.

Part of the Renaissance experience, Catholic as well as Protestant, was the new idea that each individual enjoyed a personal experience of God. As sculptural essays in individualism, Bernini's saints reflect this idea, and his churches are explicit statements of it. At both Sant'Andrea and Santa Maria, the church is a single round or elliptical space that the worshiper enters directly. The separation between the altar and ordinary worshipers has been stripped away; all are equally in the presence of God, and the boundaries between earthly life and heaven have been erased.

Further Reading

Baldinucci, Filippo. *The Life of Bernini.* Translated by Catherine Enggass. University Park, PA, 1966.

Lavin, Irving. *Bernini and the Unity of the Visual Arts.* New York, 1980.

Marder, Tod A. *Bernini and the Art of Architecture.* New York, 1998.

Wittkower, Rudolf. *Gian Lorenzo Bernini: The Sculptor of the Roman Baroque.* 3rd ed. Ithaca, NY, 1981.

James A. Patrick

SEE ALSO

• Architecture • Bramante, Donato
• Brunelleschi, Filippo • Michelangelo • Rome

Bibles

AFTER JOHANNES GUTENBERG PERFECTED PRINTING IN 1448, BIBLES BECAME COMMONPLACE POSSESSIONS. THEIR WIDE AVAILABILITY AIDED THE ESTABLISHMENT OF NEW FORMS OF CHRISTIANITY THAT CLAIMED SCRIPTURE AS THE SOLE AUTHORITY.

▶ *The first page of the book of Exodus in the magnificently illustrated Bible of Borso d'Este (1455–1461).*

Before printing made it possible for ordinary Christians to own a copy of the New Testament or the entire Bible, only very few might have access to a manuscript of part of the Bible, which would have been carefully copied by hand and perhaps embellished with illuminated capital letters. Churches would have possessed a lectionary, a book that included biblical passages designated for reading on specific Sundays and feast days. Before paper became readily available around 1350, manuscripts were written on vellum, the bleached hide of lambs or calves. There were few complete bibles: a volume containing perhaps eighty-one individual books written on vellum was unmanageably bulky.

In the thirteenth century the decline of Latin as the European lingua franca (common language) and the development of vernaculars (particularly French, English, Italian, and German) encouraged translations of the Bible from Latin into the vernaculars. However, perhaps the most important factor that encouraged biblical translation was the new theory that the source of revelation was Sacred Scripture alone, read and interpreted by the individual Christian—not read and interpreted on the Christian's behalf by church authorities. In the 1370s the English theologian John Wycliffe (c. 1330–1384) argued that the Bible was the only source of Christian doctrine and that the authority of the pope as head of the Roman Catholic Church was not

SOLA SCRIPTURA: SCRIPTURE ALONE

Reformation theologians relied on the idea that scripture was the only source of knowledge of God and insisted that the pope had denied believers access to the Bible. In his *Table Talk*, Martin Luther wrote, "The ungodly papists prefer the authority of the church far above God's Word, a blasphemy abominable and not to be endured." More than any single specific doctrine (justification by faith alone, for example), the idea of scripture alone *(sola scriptura)* was the linchpin of Protestant theology, and any doctrine the Reformers did not find supported by the Bible was relegated to the realm of superstition and idolatry.

However, ordinary readers were probably not so much interested in the theological points that engaged Luther and the other great Reformers as they were in the message of hope they found in the newly accessible pages of the Bible, which offered a path to knowledge of God that did not rely on the clergy. The *sola scriptura* theory was revolutionary not merely in terms of theology but also in terms of religious practice, since it initiated the conversion of the objective faith of the late Middle Ages, which rested on assent to the authority of the church, to the subjective faith of the Reformation, which found its authority in individual interpretations of the Bible and in the personal convictions of the believer.

supported by scripture. Although Wycliffe played no direct part in the translation that bears his name, the translation of the Bible into English made by his followers between 1390 and 1407 was important to the dissemination of his reforming theories. Wycliffe sponsored or perhaps was adopted by the Lollard movement, whose adherents shared his convictions that the Bible was the only source of doctrine and that every Christian should be free to form a private interpretation of the text. Wycliffe was declared heretical—unsurprising, given that he and the Lollards equated the pope with the Antichrist and foresaw the destruction of the papacy. His close association with translation of the Bible tended to promote a conviction among church authorities that biblical translations in general were linked to heresy.

Printing: The Technology of Reformation

The first printed edition of the Latin Bible was produced at Mainz, Germany, by Johannes Gutenberg between 1453 and 1455. Called the Mazarin Bible because the copy that gained scholarly attention was found in Cardinal Mazarin's library in Paris, the text was reprinted often after 1458. An Italian translation was printed in Venice in 1471, and eighteen German editions were printed prior to 1522, four of them in the Low German ordinary believers were likely to read and speak. However, it was not until the translations of the New Testament made by the German Reformer Martin Luther in 1522 and the Englishman William Tyndale in 1525 and 1526, both of whom rejected traditional teaching in their text and notes, that the printing and publication of bibles alarmed church authorities.

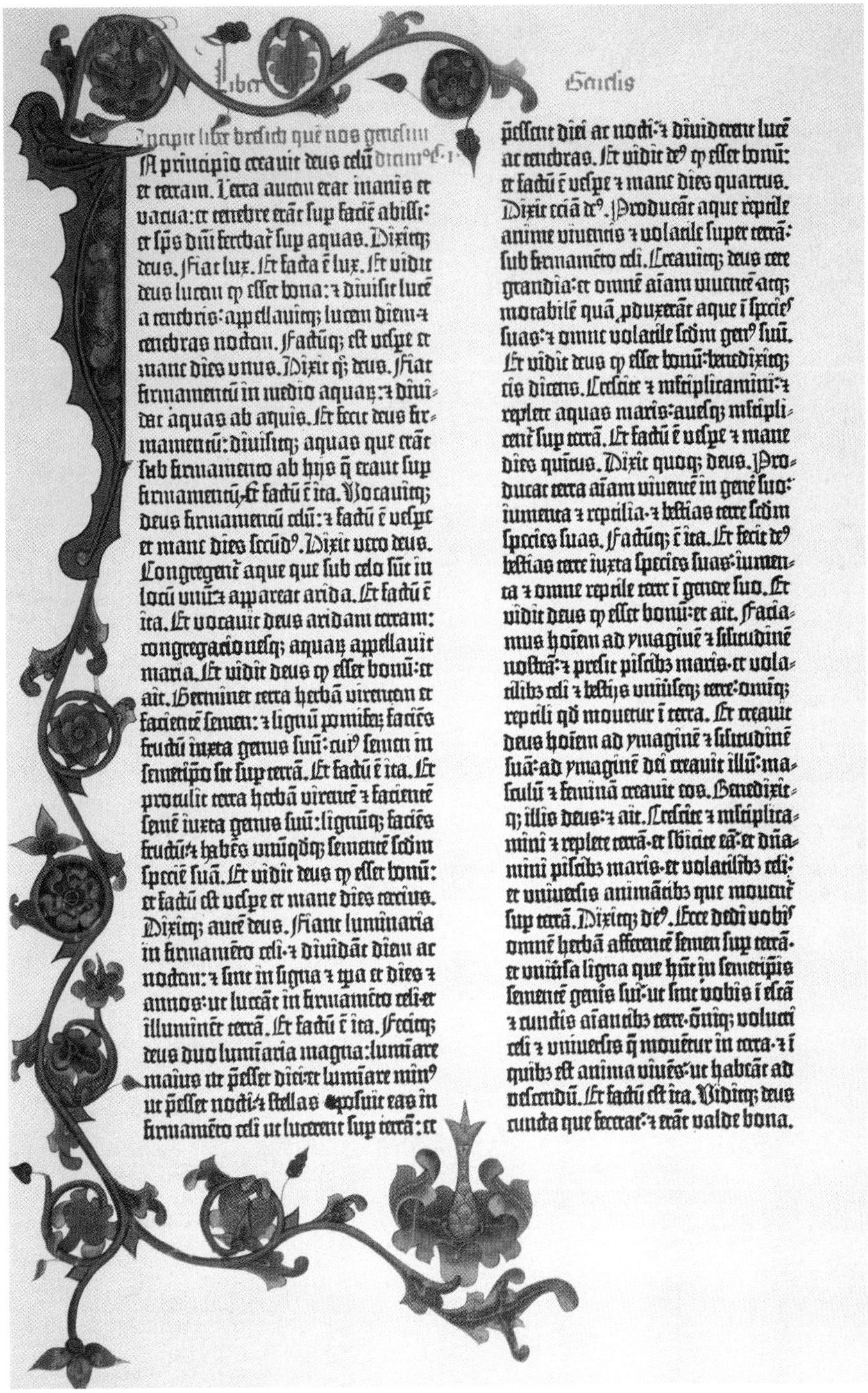

▲ *This first page of the first printed Bible, the two-column, forty-two-line edition printed by Gutenberg from 1455, has an embellished first letter—the "I" in the Latin phrase* In principio *("In the beginning").*

The Problem of the Apocrypha

The version of the Old Testament that Christians were using at the time when the New Testament was being written—between 50 and 150 CE—was the Greek Septuagint; its name is derived from the tradition that the number of translators required was seventy (in Latin, *septuaginta*). Compiled in Alexandria around 200 BCE, the Septuagint included Greek translations of the thirty-nine Hebrew books, as well as fifteen books accepted in Judaism before 100 CE that survived only in Greek. These Greek books, which came to be called the Apocrypha, or hidden books, included history (for example, two books that recount the Maccabean revolt of the second century BCE) and proverbial good advice (for example, the Wisdom of Solomon and the book of Ecclesiasticus).

Around 100 CE Jewish rabbinic leaders decided that these Greek books lacked authority and dropped them from the Hebrew canon. The books rejected by the rabbis were still included in the Christian Septuagint, but for many the distinction the rabbis had made suggested that the fifteen Greek books of the Old Testament were somehow less valuable than the thirty-nine Hebrew books. Saint Jerome, the translator of the Vulgate (the official Latin Bible used by the Catholic Church), followed the Jewish authorities in doubting the canonical status of the Apocrypha, but the Western church did not recognize this distinction. Saint Augustine considered the Apocrypha canonical, and in 1546 the Roman Catholic Council of Trent included the apocryphal books in the Old Testament.

In the fourteenth century some, whether scholars or critics, began to group the apocryphal books in a separate section. Luther did so in 1534, although he called the books "useful and good to be read." The apocryphal books were included in the 1611 Authorized Version, the Bible produced for the Church of England under the auspices of King James I, even though the English church's sixteenth-century doctrinal summary, the Thirty-nine Articles, had viewed the apocryphal books as being of secondary value (an opinion for which Jerome's authority was claimed) and suggested that they be read "for example of life and instruction of manners," but not "to establish any doctrine." In 1646 the Westminister Confession, the statement of faith of English-speaking Presbyterians, rejected the Apocrypha, and soon Protestant editors and publishers were routinely omitting the apocryphal books from their editions of the Bible.

The illuminated roundels of the Bible moralisée, *produced in France between around 1235 and around 1245, tell the story of Tobit and his wife, Anna.*

Luther's German Bible

Luther's theology depended upon asserting the authority of the Bible against the older idea that both scripture and tradition—doctrine interpreted by the church and therefore ultimately by the pope—were sources of revelation. Between May 26, 1521, when his teachings were formally condemned by the Edict of Worms, and September 1522, Luther translated into German the Greek translation of the New Testament made by the Dutch humanist scholar Desiderius Erasmus (c. 1466–1536). By 1534 Luther's translation of the Hebrew text of the Old Testament was complete. Luther's brilliant effort established a Protestant canon. He contemplated dropping the Epistle of James from the Bible because it emphasized good works as well as faith and collected the apocryphal books in a kind of appendix introduced by a note that weakened their authority. Perhaps Luther removed the apocryphal Greek books because they were later than the Hebrew books, not ancient in the sense that Renaissance scholars valued so highly. However, the Greek books also recommended prayers for the dead (2 Maccabees 12:43-45), a practice that supported the Catholic teaching that the departed, including those lesser sinners ultimately destined to enter heaven, would endure temporary suffering in purgatory and that, by offering prayers for those in purgatory, Christians still living might reduce the terms of this period of punishment. For Luther praying for the dead was futile; the practice conjured up the entire Catholic apparatus of penances and pardons and thus also the idea that good works were effective before God—the idea against which Luther had originally rebelled.

Inherent in Luther's translation were recommendations of Lutheran doctrine. By inserting

Luther's German Bible included woodcuts that were intended to advance his theology pictorially. The seven-headed beast of chapter 13 of the book of Revelation was often identified with the church of Rome.

the word *alone* in the texts of Romans 3:25 and 28, Luther ensured that his doctrine of justification by faith alone found biblical support. Luther also established his interpretation of certain important texts through the inclusion of explanatory notes. His introduction to Paul's Epistle to the Romans, slightly longer than the book it introduced, further established the Lutheran doctrine that faith alone is required for salvation, and a system of marginal notes provided a Lutheran interpretation of controversial passages. Several of the woodcuts that illustrated Luther's text depicted the tiara, the tall papal crown, on the head of the beast of Revelation, whose attempt to wreak destruction on mankind in the apocalyptic struggle between good and evil is described in the Revelation of Saint John. Between 1530 and 1540 there were thirty-four Wittenberg impressions of Luther's Bible and seventy-two reprints for the rest of Germany. One press in Wittenberg produced at least 100,000 bibles between 1534 and 1584.

MARGINAL NOTES

The writing of notes or glosses in the margins of manuscripts was a well-established practice in the Middle Ages that had little influence outside scholarly circles. The introductory prefaces and the notes printed in the margins of bibles in the sixteenth century had a larger purpose: to establish the meanings the Reformist translators intended. In his English New Testament (1526), William Tyndale reproduced forty-five of Luther's ninety notes, as well as Luther's introduction to Romans. The most popular Bible in England during the reign of Queen Elizabeth I (1558–1603) was the Geneva Bible (1560). One famous note explained Matthew 16:17–19, a passage in which Peter has just confessed that Jesus is the Messiah. Jesus replies, "Thou art Peter, and upon this rock I will build my church." According to the traditional Catholic interpretation, the rock was Peter himself: the passage made Peter the first pope and justified the entire institution of the papacy. The Geneva note, following Luther, offers the explanation that the rock is Peter's faith and thus casts the passage in a totally different light. By publishing bibles that included marginal notes, Luther, Tyndale, and others thus attempted to influence the reader's understanding of scripture.

The bishop of London commissioned the humanist Thomas More to demonstrate the errors of William Tyndale's translation of the New Testament. In this passage More attacks the idea, central to Tyndale's work, that everything Christ had commanded was or must be written.

Now this I say, since many things were taught first unwritten, if any of them be yet left unwritten, then say I that Tyndale is at the least wise temerarious and over bold so certainly to affirm that any sacrament that the Church uses, or has so long used; or ceremony either, is idolatry.... [God] was not of any necessity compelled to write any one ceremony or sacrament or weighty point of belief, for any fear lest it should fall away and that he could not with his own spirit keep it in men's hearts and useage without writing.

Thomas More, *Confutation of Tyndale's Answer*

English Printed Editions

Around 1522 William Tyndale (c. 1494–1536) conceived the project of making an English translation of the Bible and sought the support of the bishop of London, Cuthbert Tunstall. When Tunstall withheld his sponsorship, Tyndale went to Germany, where his translation was greatly influenced by Luther's in its system of notes as well as its text. The first copies of Tyndale's New Testament reached England in March 1526. The work was greeted with official hostility, partly because it was considered inaccurate. The response of Archbishop William Warham was to purchase copies and have them burned. The unintended consequence of this act was to turn Bible printing into a profitable business and provide Tyndale with the resources to continue revising his work.

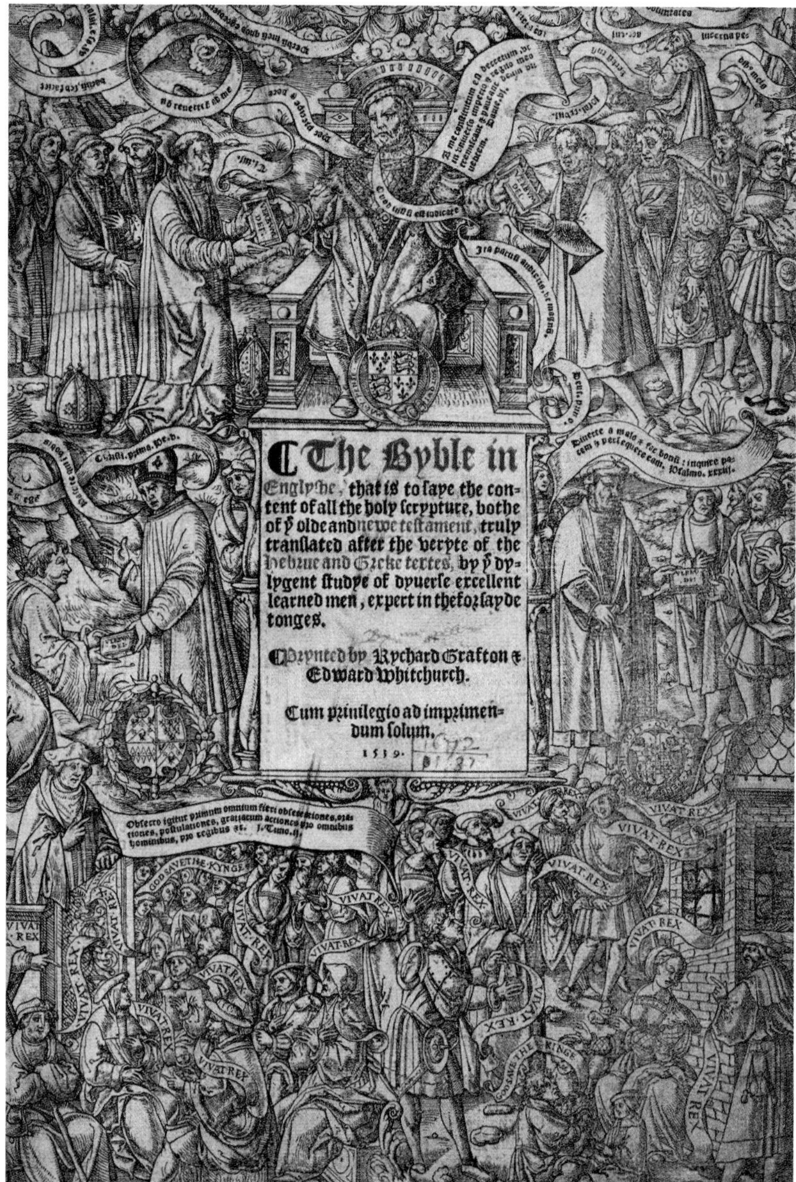

▼ The first printed English Bible published with the authority of the English crown featured this elaborate frontispiece. Commissioned by Thomas Cromwell, chancellor of England, and translated into English by Miles Coverdale in 1539, this Bible was intended by the government to promote Bible reading and thus reinforce the newly popular theory that scripture, not tradition, was the principal source of Christian doctrine.

Tyndale's death in 1536 at the hands of Catholic imperial authorities at Vilvoorde, in the Spanish Netherlands, fixed in the minds of Protestant Europe an association between the effort to make an English translation of the Bible and martyrdom. Tyndale's translation was the basis of the 1611 Authorized Version (also known as the King James Version) and through it influenced the Revised Version of 1881 and the Revised Standard Version of 1946.

King Henry VIII at first had no interest in promoting Lutheran ideas—indeed, he described the marginal notes in Tyndale's New Testament as "pestilent glosses." However, after about 1532 Henry wanted to destroy the power of the papacy in England. After the final break with Rome in 1534, the publication of an English text became an important political project for the king and his chancellor, Thomas Cromwell. The project had the religious support of Henry's archbishop of Canterbury, Thomas Cranmer, who had been sympathetic to Lutheran ideas since his undergraduate days at

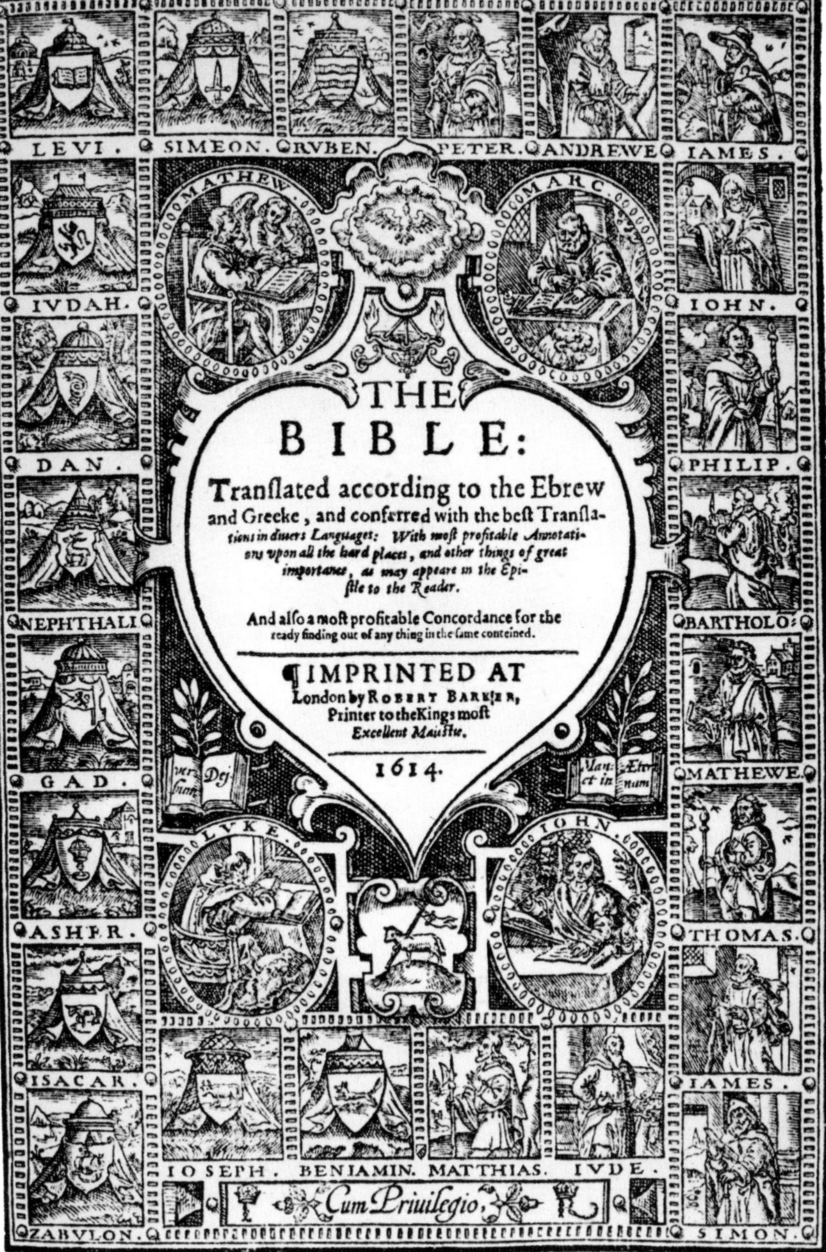
LEVI. SIMEON. RVBEN. PETER. ANDREWE IAMES.
MATHEW MARC
IVDAH. IOHN.
THE BIBLE:
Tranſlated according to the Ebrew and Greeke, and conferred with the beſt Tranſlations in diuers Languages: With moſt profitable Annotations vpon all the hard places, and other things of great importance, as may appeare in the Epiſtle to the Reader.
And alſo a moſt profitable Concordance for the ready finding out of any thing in the ſame conteined.
IMPRINTED AT
London by ROBERT BARKER, Printer to the Kings moſt Excellent Maieſtie.
1614.
DAN. PHILIP.
NEPHTHALI BARTHOLO.
GAD. MATHEWE.
LVKE IOHN
ASHER. THOMAS.
ISACAR. IAMES.
IOSEPH. BENIAMIN. MATTHIAS. IVDE.
Cum Priuilegio.
ZABVLON. SIMON.

▲ *Originally published in 1560, the Geneva Bible remained a competitor of the 1611 Authorized Version. The edition of the Geneva Bible pictured here was published in 1614.*

Cambridge. In 1535 Miles Coverdale published a complete Bible based on Tyndale, with the Old Testament translated into English from Luther's German. In 1537 John Rogers, under the pseudonym Thomas Matthew, published by royal authority Matthew's Bible, a combination of Tyndale's New Testament and Coverdale's Old Testament. In September 1538, when Thomas Cromwell ordered that a new translation of the Bible be provided for every parish church, Miles Coverdale produced a new version that relied heavily on Matthew's Bible. This Coverdale version, which came to be known as the Great Bible, was published in 1539 and reissued with a preface by Thomas Cranmer in 1540. Nevertheless, at the end of Henry's reign, the place of the English Bible was still not secure: in 1546 the king forbade the use of either Tyndale's or Coverdale's translations in favor of the Latin Vulgate (this policy was reversed upon Henry's death the following year).

During the reign of Edward VI (1547–1553), although no new translation or version was published, the Bible religion of England became rooted. The privy council, the king's senior advisory body, repealed the laws against the Lollards and commanded that a copy of the Great Bible be set up in every parish church. Although Queen Mary Tudor (reigned 1553–1558) would in turn repeal the Edwardian laws, the idea that English religion was based upon Bible reading by the individual Christian was by now established. The last year of Edward's reign saw the publication of the Forty-two Articles, which declared, "Holy Scripture containeth all things necessary to salvation; so that whatsoever is not read therein, nor may be proved thereby, is not to be required of any man." This seemingly straightforward assertion inaugurated a century of controversy as to just what was contained and what might be proved, but that the Bible was the only basis of doctrine became the core idea of English Protestantism, an idea that would survive the reign of Mary Tudor, the last Catholic queen.

Mary of course opposed the publication of the English Bible, but the parade of versions and translations did not stop. In 1557 William Whittingham published for the English Protestant exiles in Geneva a New Testament, divided for the first time into verses. When completed by the publication in 1560 of the Old Testament, this Geneva Bible became the most popular translation of the Elizabethan reign. Within days of her accession in 1559, Elizabeth I made it clear that if she was not a zealous Protestant, she was certainly not a Catholic; so Whittingham felt free to dedicate the Geneva Bible to her. The text, based on Tyndale and the Great Bible, also bore the influence of the continental Reformers John Calvin (1509–1564) and Théodore de Bèze (1519–1605) and contained marginal notes of a decidedly Protestant tenor.

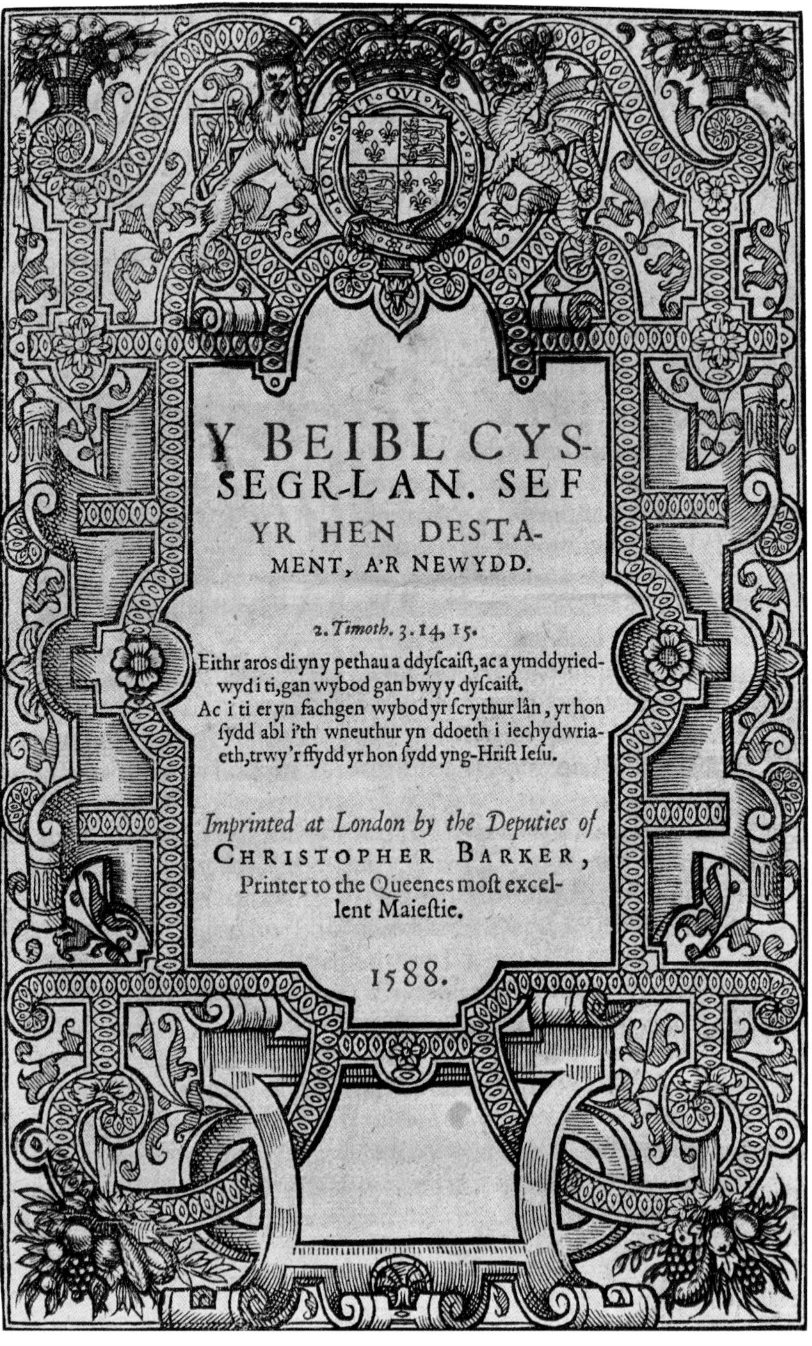

Y BEIBL CYS-
SEGR-LAN. SEF
YR HEN DESTA-
MENT, A'R NEWYDD.

2. *Timoth*. 3. 14, 15.

Eithr aros di yn y pethau a ddyſcaiſt, ac a ymddyried-
wyd i ti, gan wybod gan bwy y dyſcaiſt.
Ac i ti er yn fachgen wybod yr ſcrythur lân, yr hon
ſydd abl i'th wneuthur yn ddoeth i iechydwria-
eth, trwy 'r ffydd yr hon ſydd yng-Hriſt Ieſu.

Imprinted at London by the Deputies of
CHRISTOPHER BARKER,
Printer to the Queenes moſt excel-
lent Maieſtie.

1588.

▲ *Since Welsh was the common language of a good number of people in western Britain, it was important that the Bible be made available in that language. The Welsh translation whose strapwork title page is pictured here was published in 1582.*

Douay-Reims

It became clear to Roman Catholic authorities that it was their duty to sustain the significant minority in England who remained Catholic in the face of official pressure and persecution. For them, a Catholic English translation of the Bible was essential, and the task was taken up by the English College, the seminary in which English exiles trained for the priesthood. The translation of the New Testament was begun at Douai (or Douay), in the Spanish Netherlands, in 1578, and completed when the college was at Reims, in northeastern France, from 1578 to 1593. The translator, Gregory Martin, completed the New Testament just before his death in 1582. The Old Testament was published after the college returned to Douai in 1609. The Douay-Reims Bible, a literal translation from the Latin Vulgate, influenced every Catholic English Bible made before the twentieth century.

The Authorized Version of 1611

In 1603 England's new monarch, James I, inherited the religious controversy that divided radical English Protestants, by now called Puritans, from the established Church of England. The Hampton Court Conference of 1604, called to settle differences between Puritans and church authorities, settled nothing, but one concession to the Puritans was royal encouragement for a new translation of the Bible. The translators were instructed to take into account the Reims New Testament, the Bishops' Bible, and the Geneva Bible and to omit notes unless required to explain a technical term. The book included the Apocrypha. Called the Authorized Version in England and the King James Version in the United States, its text, together with the Book of Common Prayer and the plays of William Shakespeare, did much to stabilize and standardize the English language.

Bibles in Other Languages

Printed translations of the Bible were issued in every European country in the fifteenth and sixteenth centuries. The first French New Testament, published anonymously in 1523, was probably the work of Jacques Lefèvre d'Étaples. In 1535 another version was published by Pierre-Robert Olivétan, a cousin of John Calvin. Olivétan's Bible became the basis of the text published in Geneva; its 1588 edition, which was edited by Théodore de Bèze (1519–1605), remained unchanged until 1693. In 1550 the faculty of the University of Louvain, in present-day Belgium, published a Catholic translation, the 1578 edition of which was reprinted two hundred times. By 1600 the Bible had been published even in the languages of such small populations as the Maltese, the Welsh, the Bretons, and the Catalans.

The following passage is part of the translators' preface to the Authorized Version:

How shall men meditate in that which they cannot understand? How shall they understand that which is kept close in an unknown tongue?... Translation it is that openeth the window, to let in the light; that breaketh the shell that we may eat the kernel; that putteth aside the curtain, that we may look into the most holy place; that removeth the cover of the well, that we may come by water; even as Jacob rolled away the stone from the mouth of the well, by which means the flocks of Laban were watered. Indeed without translation into the Vulgar tongue, the unlearned are like children at Jacob's well (which was deep) without a bucket or something to draw with.

Establishing the Text

The first printed editions of the Bible were made either from the Vulgate or the Textus Receptus ("received text"), the traditional Greek text that was published by Erasmus in 1516. Throughout the Renaissance, scholars examined the small differences between important manuscripts in an effort to establish the best possible text. As early as 250 CE, the Alexandrian scholar Origen had produced the Hexapla, which placed several versions of the Septuagint, together with the Hebrew, in parallel columns. The first multilingual Renaissance text was the Complutensian Polyglot. Named for the university at Alcalá (in Latin, Complutum), where it was produced between 1514 and 1517, this version displayed the complete Bible in different languages in parallel columns with interlinear Latin. Several great Greek manuscripts came to light for the first time in Europe during this period. Around 1625 the fifth-century Codex Alexandrinus was presented to James I by Kyrillos Loukaris (in English, Cyril Lucaris), the patriarch of Constantinople, and the fourth-century Codex Vaticanus was in the catalog of the Vatican Library after 1481.

Bible Religion

After the publication of the Authorized Version, knowledge of the scriptures permeated the language and culture of English speakers. Possession of the text did not, however, settle all questions of interpretation. Religion in England splintered over time into a dozen or more sects, often as a result of disagreements over the meaning of certain biblical passages. Interpretation of the Bible was at the heart of the controversy between the Puritans and the more moderate Protestants of the Church of England. The Thirty-nine Articles never asserted the exclusive right of the church to interpret scripture, and the nineteenth article pointed out that, in the past, great churches had erred in matters of faith. The Puritans argued that customs not based on scriptural texts should not be followed. Scripture did not mention the sign of the cross in baptism or clerical vestments, for example, and so the insistence of the Church of England on such customs was taken by Puritans as evidence of its reprobation. The English civil wars (1642–1649) were in good part a prolonged conflict between, on the one hand, Puritans, Independents, and Presbyterians, all with Bible in hand, and on the other, the Stuart monarchy with its nonbiblical bishops and customs.

◀ *This page, from the fifth-century Greek Codex Alexandrinus, is typical of the manuscripts from which the New Testament was translated into English from the sixteenth century on.*

TRANSLATIONS AND NEW IDEAS

Both Wycliffe and Tyndale translated the Greek word *ecclesia* as "congregation" (as opposed to "church," used in the Douay Bible of 1582 and the Authorized Version of 1611). The Greek *ecclesia* (from *ek*, "out," plus *kalein*, "call") had always been taken to mean "called out" in the sense of "elected" (the word described the assembly of ancient Athens, whose members were indeed chosen, or called out); it is probably in this sense that the Gospel of Matthew and the letters of Saint Paul use the word *ecclesia* in the New Testament. By translating *ecclesia* as "congregation," a word that means "those gathered together," Wycliffe and Tyndale were encouraging the idea that the church consisted not of those chosen by God but rather by the faithful, who, having read God's word and been persuaded by it, voluntarily assembled. Conversely, Catholic translators working on the Reims New Testament of 1585 used the phrase *do penance* in Luke 13:3 for a Greek word that could mean simply "repent." The exhortation to do penance reinforced an important aspect of Catholic theology, the necessity of making reparation for sin—an idea rejected by the Reformers, who argued that human works were unnecessary to salvation.

Archbishop James Ussher (1581–1656) of Armagh, in Ireland, provided in his *Annals of the Old and New Testament* a chronology of biblical events that dated the creation of the world to 4004 BCE. From 1701 many editions of the Authorized Version included marginal dates derived from Ussher's book that readers sometimes took to be part of the text. It was this chronology that was fixed in the public mind when, in the nineteenth century, Charles Lyell and other geologists announced that the earth was millions of years old and Charles Darwin published his theory that all creatures—including humans, the biblical account notwithstanding—had evolved from earlier animals. The apparent contradiction between science and scripture damaged but did not destroy the authority of the Bible. The Bible has been translated more often since 1611 than it was before, and the principal argument of the sixteenth-century Reformers—that the Bible is an inspired source of knowledge of God—endures.

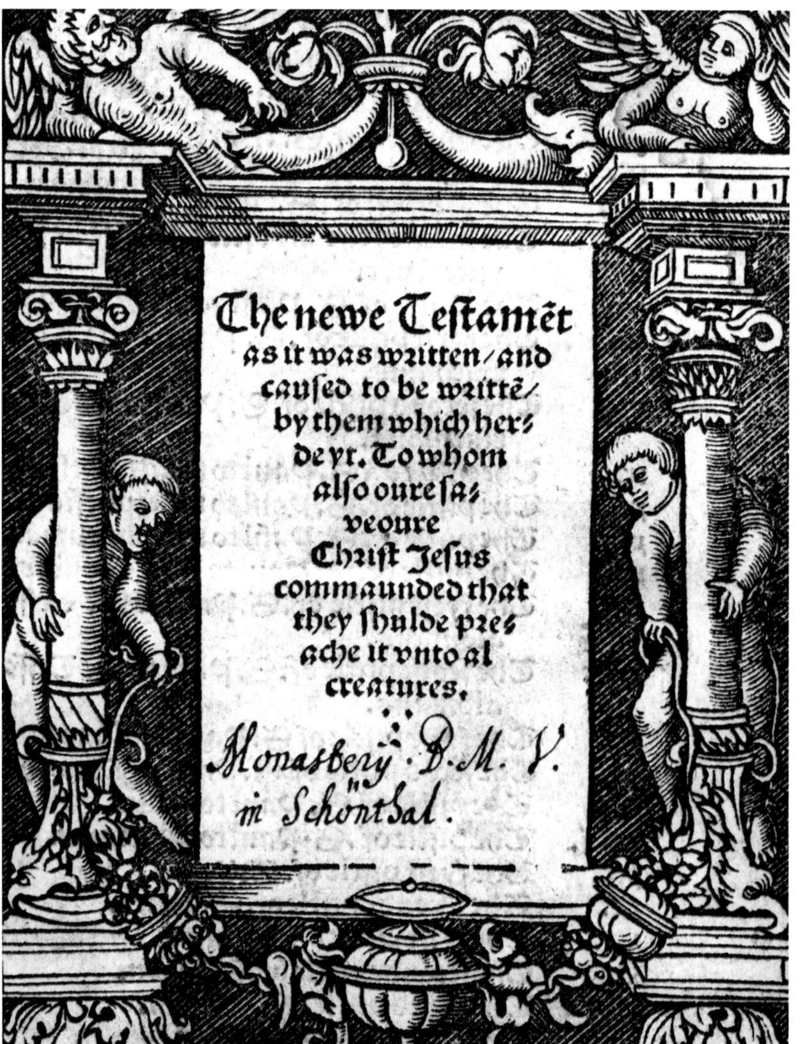

▼ *The first printed English New Testament, published at Worms in 1526, bore this elaborate title page. Inspired, if not actually translated, by William Tyndale, its publication gave impetus to Bible reading. On the other hand, its novel translations of some theological words made English bishops suspicious of any new translation.*

FURTHER READING

Bruce, F. F. *The English Bible: A History of Translations from the Earliest English Versions to the New English Bible.* Rev. ed. New York, 1970.

Daniell, David. *The Bible in English.* New Haven, CT, 2003.

Kenny, Anthony, ed. *Wyclif in His Times.* New York, 1986.

Nicolson, Adam. *God's Secretaries: The Making of the King James Bible.* New York, 2003.

James A. Patrick

SEE ALSO

• Calvinism • Church of England
• Humanism and Learning • Lutheranism • Printing
• Trent, Council of

Boccaccio, Giovanni

A FIGURE OF CONSIDERABLE STATURE WHOSE INFLUENCE EXTENDED WELL BEYOND HIS OWN LIFETIME, GIOVANNI BOCCACCIO (1313–1375) PRODUCED AN IMPRESSIVE CORPUS OF VERSE AND OF PROSE FICTION, AMONG OTHER LITERARY FORMS.

Giovanni Boccaccio was born to a merchant father and a mother whose background is uncertain. Although his exact birthplace is not known, Certaldo (the family hometown) and Florence are the most likely candidates.

Around the age of fifteen, Bocaccio moved with his father from Florence to Naples in order to facilitate his father's commercial pursuits. At his father's urging, Boccaccio pursued an education that was typical of Italy in the period, with an emphasis on the study of banking and canon (church) law. Boccaccio devoted approximately six years to studying banking and six to law, but eventually, and much to the chagrin of his business-minded father, he succumbed to his deep-rooted literary inclinations.

This portrait of Boccaccio, painted seventy-five years after his death, is part of a fresco by Andrea del Castagno (1421–1457) that also features the two other great Italian poets of the late Middle Ages and early Renaissance, Petrarch and Dante.

During his years in Naples, Boccaccio made many friends and acquaintances whose influence on him would prove to be long lasting. As a student of canon law, Boccaccio studied under the well-known Tuscan poet Cino dei Sighibuldi (usually known as Cino da Pistoia; c. 1270–c. 1336). Cino may have encouraged Boccaccio's interest in literature and introduced him to a variety of poetry from the region. During his education Boccaccio also made the acquaintance of numerous men of letters at the courts as well as at the university. He was introduced to the poet and philosopher Petrach (1304–1374) by the theologian Dionigi da Sansepolcro .

Boccaccio formed another influential friendship during this period, with the royal librarian Paolo de Perugia, who began the massive *Genealogia deorum gentilium* (Genealogy of the Gods of the Gentiles), which Boccaccio would later complete. Within the *Genealogia,* Boccaccio mentions several men who influenced his life, including Petrarch, Paolo de Perugia, and the great Italian poet of the Middle Ages Dante Alighieri (1265–1321).

It was during his stay in Naples that Boccaccio first began writing. Thus, his writings were produced within and influenced by the two great political and cultural centers of Renaissance Italy in which he spent most of his life—Naples and Florence. Also while in Naples, Boccaccio met and fell in love with the woman he called Fiammetta, who would appear in many of the writings he produced throughout his life. It has been speculated that this Fiammetta was actually Maria d'Aquino, the illegitimate daughter of the king of Naples, Robert of Anjou. This theory has not been proven, however, and the true identity of Fiammetta remains a matter of speculation.

CHRONOLOGY

1313
Giovanni Boccaccio is born.

c. 1328
Moves with his father to Naples.

c. 1341
Moves back to Florence with his father.

1348
Experiences the devastation of the Black Death.

1350
Is appointed Florence's ambassador to the lords of Romagna; meets Petrarch for the first time.

1351
Is appointed ambassador and municipal counselor to Louis, duke of Bavaria.

1354
Is appointed ambassador to the court of Pope Innocent VI.

1362
Briefly returns to Naples.

1363
Retires to the family hometown of Certaldo.

1365
Is ambassador to Pope Urban V's court at Avignon.

1367
Is ambassador to Pope Urban V's court at Rome.

1370–1371
Returns again to Naples.

1374
Dies and is buried in the Church of Santi Michele e Jacopo, in Certaldo.

Early Writings

In his early writings Boccaccio followed varied models. His earliest Latin poem, "Elegia de Costanza" (Elegy of Costanza), was modeled around a funeral inscription. *La caccia di Diana* (Diana's Hunt), written in 1333 and 1334, shows the influence of Dante and of the Roman poets Ovid (43 BCE–17 CE) and Claudian (c. 370–c. 404). *Il Filostrato,* written around 1335, demonstrates Boccaccio's love for the culture of classical Greece. Written in ottava rima, a stanza form consisting of eight lines of eleven syllables, the poem tells the story of Troilus, a prince of Troy who loved Cressida, the daughter of a deceptive priest. Despite the story's Trojan setting and Greek narrator, the style of *Il Filostrato* is more reminiscent of contemporary Tuscan poetry. Boccaccio's poem would later become the basis for the English poet Geoffrey Chaucer's celebrated work *Troilus and Criseyde* (written during the 1380s).

Il Filocolo, a prose work written around 1336, tells the story of Biancifiore, who is loved by Prince Florio. Florio's father, who does not approve of the match, puts an end to the prince's infatuation by selling Biancifiore into slavery. Florio seeks out his love and eventually finds her stowed away in a tower belonging to the admiral of Alexandria. Upon reuniting, the two are married and are then caught by the furious admiral. Fortune aids the young couple, and their lives are spared. At this point the two lovers, who have learned of Biancifiore's Christian heritage, convert to Christianity. The story blends many Christian themes with elements of Greek mythology, as well as styles modeled after Ovid and Virgil and contemporary popular romance. *Il Filocolo,* apparently composed at the request of a daughter of King Robert, is written in the ornate and elegant dialect of Italian spoken at the Neapolitan court. It remained popular at least into the sixteenth century, when Beatrice del

▶ *This manuscript illustration of Pandarus talking to Cressida is from a late-fifteenth-century French translation of* Il Filostrato *by Pierre de Beauveau.*

TERZA RIMA

Terza rima was a verse form used by many Italian poets of the Renaissance, notably Dante, who employed it in his *Divina commedia (Divine Comedy).* It consists of three-line stanzas whose first and last lines rhyme. The sound that terminates the middle line becomes the rhyming sound for the first and third lines of the following stanza. Thus, the rhyme scheme is *aba, bcb, cdc, ded,* and so on. Terza rima verse typically ends with a single line that rhymes with the middle line of the stanza immediately preceding.

Since Italian has more rhymes than English, the terza rima style fits much more comfortably with Italian poetry than it does with English. When terza rima poetry is translated into English, the verse form is generally abandoned. At times, however, English authors have found ways to use terza rima. Robert Pinsky, who translated the *Divine Comedy* in 1994, opted for a looser translation in order to maintain the verse form. The great English Romantic poet Percy Bysshe Shelley (1792–1822) made beautiful use of terza rima in his "Ode to the West Wind" (1819).

Sera, a Florentine nun, adapted and modified the story to create a convent play.

The *Teseida* (Book of Theseus), composed around 1341, was the first classical epic poem written in vernacular Italian. Divided into twelve cantos of ottava rima stanzas, the narrative begins where Statius's *Thebaid* (Book of Thebes), a first-century Latin epic, ends. *Teseida* interweaves numerous classical myths and historical and cultural references into a tale of two friends competing for the love of the same woman, Emilia. The work had a profound effect on the literature of the Renaissance and greatly boosted the status of Italian as a literary language. Geoffrey Chaucer drew heavily from the *Teseida;* he used portions of the story to end his *Troilus and Criseyde* and parts of the plot as a foundation for his "Knight's Tale," from the *Canterbury Tales.* Chaucer also adapted a lengthy description of the temple of Venus for his *Parlement of Foules.*

Adulthood

Around age twenty-eight, Boccaccio returned to Florence with his father. It was during the next ten to twelve years, spent in and around Florence, that Boccaccio reached full maturity as a writer. From 1341 to 1345, he prepared *Il ninfale d'Ameto* (Ameto's Story of the Nymphs). During this period he also produced *L'amorosa visione* (The Amorous Vision; 1342–1343), a work in terza rima; the prose work *Elegia di Madonna Fiammetta* (1343–1344); and *Il ninfale fiesolano* (Tale of the Fiesole Nymph), a poem in ottava rima, probably from 1344 to 1345.

Boccaccio traveled during the middle and late 1340s. For some time in 1345 and 1346 he was in Ravenna, and in 1347 he was in Forli. Boccaccio was in Florence during 1348, when the Black Death, a catastrophic outbreak of bubonic plague, was devastating the city, and he was also in the city sometime during 1349. Like so many others, Boccaccio's worldview was profoundly affected by the plague, and his experiences during this time would inspire the *Decameron*—widely held to be his greatest work.

▲ *This heavily decorated manuscript page, which includes an illustration of four courtiers, is from a version of* Il Filocolo *created in 1460.*

▲ *Sandro Botticelli painted four scenes from the story of Nastagio degli Onesti, one of the tales of the* Decameron. *In the scene above, noble guests at a picnic are horrified to witness a phantom scene: a girl being torn apart by hounds at the orders of a knight. Both have been condemned to hell—he for suicide, she for driving him to it. The figure at the center of the scene, with his back to the viewer, is Nastagio degli Onesti, who has been rejected by his own cruel beloved (the woman in white, third from the left). Having witnessed the phantom murder, however, she finally agrees to marry Nastagio.*

The *Decameron*

The *Decameron* ("ten days' work") retells the stories of ten individuals who flee Florence during 1348 while the plague is running its course in the city. The seven women and three men spend a fortnight together at a distant, peaceful countryside location. They spend ten days gathering and telling stories (at one story each a day, the number of stories totals one hundred). Each day is given a loose theme, and each member of the party is given one day to act as king or queen over the group and thus to direct the day's activities. The stories encompass comic and tragic themes and tones; Boccaccio captures the desperations as well as the joys of life, and the storytellers also impart a good deal of moral and social wisdom. From the impropriety of an older man's marriage to a young woman to the need for good people to keep good company, Boccaccio covers a vast range of everyday topics. Although it contains somber moments, the overall tone of the *Decameron* is lively, and recreation seems to be the main purpose of the group's activities. Their retreat is presented in contrast to the gloom and despair of the plague that drove them out of the city. The *Decameron,* a magnificent piece of Italian prose in the classical style, also contains passages of stirring verse. Boccaccio moves from the most somber to the most upbeat of tones with a deftness of touch that sets the *Decameron* apart not only among his other works but also among poetry of the early Renaissance. Indeed, the influence of the work reverberates throughout Renaissance literature.

Later Years

In 1350 Boccaccio first met Petrarch, whose works the former had studied during his education in Florence. This meeting and the friendship that resulted had a tremendous impact on Boccaccio's style. When he finished the *Decameron,* Boccaccio gave up writing in Italian almost completely. Apart from *Il corbaccio* (The Old Crow; 1354–1355) and some writings on Dante later in life, he otherwise wrote in Latin. During this time Boccaccio focused his efforts on humanistic scholarship. It was most likely during 1350 that he began his work on the *Genealogia deorum gentilium* (Genealogy of the Gods of the Gentiles), the study begun by his friend from Naples Paolo de Perugia. From 1351

The tone of the fourth day of the *Decameron*, which is filled with stories of love lost, is somber. The following passage completes a story on the fifth day, when each speaker is told to banish the somberness of the preceding day by delivering a tale that ends with love prevailing.

. . . the variance ended in love and peace, and afterward they lived lovingly together, till old age made them as honorable, as their true and mutual affection formerly had done.

***Decameron*, day 5, novel 3**

to 1366, he worked on *Bucolicum carmen* (Bucolic Song), a compilation of several short poems related to contemporary events. Then, from 1355 to 1374, he produced *De casibus virorum illustrium* (On the Fates of Famous Men), and from 1360 to 1374, a collection of biographies called *De claris mulieribus* (Concerning Famous Women). These latter two works bear a direct relationship to similar pieces written by Petrarch. From 1355 to 1374, Boccaccio worked on a dictionary of classical geographical names (in translation the full Latin title of the dictionary means "on mountains, forests, springs, lakes, rivers, swamps or marshes, and on the names of the sea").

Boccaccio may have suffered some failed romance or another emotional challenge around the time of his meeting with Petrarch. With the writing of *Corbaccio,* a satirical portrait of a deceitful widow, Boccaccio seemed to renounce his romantic portrayals of women. It is also apparent that some religious experience affected Boccaccio during this time. According to Petrarch, Boccaccio at one point decided to burn his own writings and sell off his library, a course from which Petrarch deterred him.

In 1362 Boccaccio was excited to receive an invitation to return to Naples; however, disappointed by what he interpreted as a cool reception upon his arrival, he quickly returned to Florence. In 1363 he retired and moved to Certaldo. He did not remain in his ancestral home very long, however; he was named ambassador to the court of Pope Urban V in 1365 in Avignon and then in 1367 in Rome. In 1370 Boccaccio returned to Naples a second time but left the city again in 1371 after experiencing another chilly reception.

Around 1371 Boccaccio was given a commission by the commune of Certaldo to lecture on Dante, an author for whom he had great respect, and in 1373 he began delivering the readings in Florence. Old age, failing health, the death of his friend Petrarch in 1374, and scholarly disapproval of his public lectures for the multitudes disheartened Boccaccio greatly. He was forced by his health to discontinue his public lectures in early 1374, and he died the following year in Certaldo.

◀ *In this unattributed illustration from a sixteenth-century French manuscript of Boccaccio's* De casibus virorum illustrium, *invaders capture a town and behead its defeated inhabitants.*

FURTHER READING

Bergin, Thomas G. *Boccaccio.* New York, 1981.

Branca, Vittore. *Boccaccio: The Man and His Works.* Translated by Richard Monges. New York, 1976.

Grendler, Paul F., ed. "Boccaccio, Giovanni." In *Encyclopedia of the Renaissance.* New York, 1999.

Daniel Horace Fernald
Zachary C. Parmley

SEE ALSO

• Chaucer, Geoffrey • Florence
• Humanism and Learning • Literature • Petrarch

Bohemia

THE CENTRAL EUROPEAN STATE OF BOHEMIA, WHICH OCCUPIED ROUGHLY THE AREA OF THE MODERN CZECH REPUBLIC, WAS THE SCENE OF ETHNIC TENSIONS, POLITICAL EXPERIMENTS, AND RELIGIOUS REFORM AND UPHEAVAL DURING THE RENAISSANCE AND THE REFORMATION.

The state commonly known as Bohemia was actually a conglomerate of formerly independent regions drawn together in the course of the fourteenth century. To the core land of Bohemia, rulers of the Luxembourg dynasty added Moravia, Silesia, and Lusatia. The composite nature of the state added to the problem of creating a national identity, a problem that has dominated Bohemian history. The difficulties that beset Bohemia during the Renaissance and Reformation as it strove to become a single political entity are encapsulated in the country's very name. Bohemia, the German word for the region, derives ultimately from a Latin name for an early Celtic tribe, the Boii. The people of Bohemia, however, always understood themselves to be Czechs; the Czech word for the land during the period was Čechy. General use of the name Bohemia in the early modern period reflects a constant German presence in Czech government and economic life—a presence that often amounted to a degree of dominance that the Czech people deeply resented. The struggle for control of Czech resources, religion, and power repeatedly threatened to tear the country apart, a problem exacerbated by a long line of absentee foreign rulers. Bohemia, lying in almost the exact center of Europe, seemed very distant to most western Europeans, but its internal difficulties gave the state a surprisingly large role in shaping the course of European events.

The Beginning of Foreign Rule

In 1306 the last ruler of the native Přemyslid dynasty, Wenceslas (in Czech, Václav) III, died. The Přemyslids had built up a strong state; under

▶ The territory of Bohemia around the year 1450. By this time the civil wars that had been sparked by the 1415 execution of Jan Hus were over, but social and political conflict were common for the rest of the century.

their rule, Bohemia, though independent, was still part of the Holy Roman Empire, and the king of Bohemia served as one of the electors who chose the emperor. However, by 1306 foreign influence was already creating difficulties. The thirteenth-century kings had taken the initiative in creating towns and, hoping for rapid economic development, had stocked these new settlements with mostly German craftsmen and merchants. (As early as 1315, the Czech nobles complained about favoritism toward foreigners and the draining away of money from their country.)

The three daughters of Wenceslas III each claimed the throne, but the Bohemian diet, dominated by the great noble families, rejected all three. Instead they bowed to imperial pressure and elected Rudolf, the son of the Hapsburg Holy Roman emperor Albert I. The new king died within the year, and a bitter civil war ensued over the question of who should rule. The essential division within Bohemia was between German townsmen and Czech nobles. The conflict was resolved in 1310, when John of Luxembourg married the Přemyslid princess Elizabeth; the diet was able to stave off Hapsburg ambitions by electing John king of Bohemia. His Luxembourg dynasty ruled from 1310 to 1439.

Unfortunately for Bohemia, most kings of the house of Luxembourg showed little interest in their kingdom. King John had an illustrious career as a latter-day knight errant; he involved himself in nearly every European conflict until his death fighting the English alongside the French at the Battle of Crécy (1346). John's indifference to Bohemian affairs allowed a vast accumulation of noble power. In the Domzlice Agreement of 1318, the king dismissed all his foreign advisers and officials and swore not to bring foreign troops into the kingdom. The agreement was a significant step toward making the kings mere figureheads and leaving real power in the hands of the Czech nobles.

Prague's Golden Age

John of Luxembourg's son, King Charles I (reigned 1347–1378), became Holy Roman emperor as Charles IV in 1355. Charles was devoted to his Přemyslid mother's Czech cultural heritage. He had been raised mostly abroad and had forgotten the Czech language; that he relearned it when he became king sets Charles apart from other Bohemian rulers of the period. Indeed, Charles was intensely pro-Bohemian. He gave the kingdom political stability and economic prosperity and made Prague the capital

The crown of Saint Wenceslas, crafted in 1376, has been used in the coronation of twenty-two Czech kings.

THE CROWN OF SAINT WENCESLAS

The Czech crown was made by order of the Holy Roman emperor Charles IV. It is a precious monument to the high esteem in which Charles held his Bohemian territories. Crafted of 22-carat gold and weighing almost five-and-a-half pounds (2.5 kg), it includes twenty pearls and ninety-six precious stones. Six of its sapphires are among the ten largest in the world. This splendid work of fourteenth-century craftsmanship is known as Saint Wenceslas's crown because Charles IV "gave" the crown to the tenth-century saint and ordered that it be placed on the saint's skull in Prague's cathedral on feast days. Bohemian kings used the crown only at their coronation.

The association of the Bohemian monarchy with the patron saint of Bohemia was clearly intended to lend an air of sanctity to royal rule—to present the king as both protector of Christianity and beneficiary of the protection of Saint Wenceslas. The association was also an important compliment to the Czech people, since it affirmed that the foreign king esteemed the Czech patron saint.

city of the Holy Roman Empire. He also won both political and ecclesiastical independence for the Czechs. In 1344, when his father was still alive, Charles succeeded in having the bishopric of Prague raised to archiepiscopal status, and in 1366 he proclaimed Bohemia's judicial independence from the empire.

Also a great sponsor of building projects, Charles IV lavished his attention on Prague with monasteries, churches, and bridges. His most significant and longest-lasting contribution in this field was the foundation of the University of Prague in 1348. The university grew rapidly and soon became a focal point of nationalist aspiration and agitation, in this sense reflecting Charles's own love of the Czech language and culture.

▶ *Proud of his direct descent from the Přemyslids, the Holy Roman emperor Charles IV had this shrine to Saint Wenceslas built in Saint Vitus's Cathedral in Prague. Housed in the magnificent Chapel of Saint Wenceslas (completed in 1367), the gilded shrine, framed by walls studded with jasper, amethyst, and chalcedony, is an elaborate expression of Charles IV's devotion to the saint.*

Reform, Ethnic Tension, and the Decline of the Bohemian State

Wenceslas IV (1378–1419) proved to be an incompetent and bloodthirsty ruler. Legend has it that he once roasted a bad cook on the cook's own spit; he was certainly an alcoholic and subject to fits of rage. Wenceslas IV drew the hatred of Czech nobles by relying on German advisers and favoring wealthy German townsmen and miners. The nobles rebelled several times and won important concessions. During Wenceslas's reign the wealthy Bohemian church suffered a serious decline and fell prey to rapacious papal demands and an influx of foreign preachers. Decentralization, deeply resented foreign influence, and religious decline combined with an important lay spiritual movement to create a crisis of epic proportions.

The catalyst for this crisis was Jan Hus (c. 1370–1415), an important forerunner of the German Reformer Martin Luther (1483–1546). After leaving the University of Prague, Hus was installed in 1402 as preacher at the Bethlehem Chapel in Prague, founded in 1391 to promote sermons in Czech. He became rector of the university in 1409. Hus's preaching was increasingly radical; he argued for an increase in lay responsibility in matters of religion, sought to curb the privileges of the clergy, and ultimately urged the creation of what amounted to a national church, one that would use a Czech Bible and liturgy. The archbishop of Prague, a German, excommunicated Hus, but Hus kept preaching.

HUSSITES AND HUMANISM

To a great extent, the Hussite movement halted the spread of humanist learning (particularly the study of ancient Latin and Greek texts) in Bohemia, as foreign scholars vanished from the University of Prague. Yet Jan Hus himself played an important role in certain humanist endeavors, notably by helping Bohemia become a pioneer of the use of the vernacular. Hus standardized written Czech through sermons that were circulated widely throughout the country. He also encouraged an important branch of Hussite literature, the devotional hymn. Prague's Bethlehem Chapel was the center for a spiritual movement focused on the laity that included congregational singing of hymns. Hus composed several Czech hymns, and his disciples produced many more. The Hussite movement also encouraged a large body of polemical writing, in Czech as well as in Latin. When the first mechanized printing press in Bohemia was established at Plzeň in 1468, it was devoted mostly to printing materials written in Czech.

The university was torn apart by the Hus controversy. Czech faculty members and students sided with Hus, not only because of his religious message but also in protest at the privileges given to German professors. The conflict culminated in a mass exodus of Germans from the university, a situation that, in the long term, isolated Bohemia from the rest of the scholarly world.

The Hus uproar also made the divisions within Bohemia more apparent, as Czech nobles and commoners protested the presence of foreign friars, absentee German churchmen, and wealthy Germans in general. The matter came to a head when Hus was summoned to answer charges before the Council of Constance in 1414. Despite a safe-conduct (a guarantee of protection) from Emperor Sigismund (Wenceslas IV's brother), Hus was arrested after his arrival at the council and was burned as a heretic on July 6, 1415. No fewer than 452 nobles of Bohemia and Moravia protested the council's act as a national insult. Nevertheless, the king bowed to papal pressure to condemn Hus's followers as heretics. Civil war broke out on July 30, 1419, with the first so-called Defenestration of Prague, when a mob stormed the Prague Town Hall and threw the royal councillors from the window—the councillors were then slaughtered by the people below. The protesters went on to attack monasteries, churches, and the homes of German citizens. Wenceslas IV died of a stroke when he heard the news, but matters were only worsened when his brother Sigismund claimed the throne of Bohemia.

For over a decade Bohemia was devastated by civil war and by several crusades called by Emperor Sigismund against those he deemed to be heretics. The Hussites won a number of victories, but soon they too split into radical and moderate branches. Finally, the moderates and the Catholics allied to defeat the radicals in 1434. Sigismund was affirmed as king, the Hussites were allowed a Czech liturgy, and the laity was permitted to receive the Eucharist in the forms of both bread and wine (according to traditional Catholic practice, the chalice was witheld from the laity; to the Hussites this practice reinforced the inequality between lay worshipers and churchmen). Those who gained most from the situation were the nobles, who absorbed much church land and were able to weaken royal authority still further.

This illustration from a fifteenth-century chronicle by Ulrich von Richental depicts Jan Hus's arrest at the Council of Constance.

▲ Founded as part of the Klementinum and built between 1578 and 1601, the Church of the Redeemer, on Prague's Krízovnicka Square, was the first Jesuit church in Bohemia.

Bohemia remained in a state of anarchy until the reign of George of Podebrady (reigned 1458–1471), who had served as regent for the boy king Ladislav (also László V of Hungary) before being elected king himself. However, the pope and Bohemian Catholics alike opposed the moderate George, and after his death more wars of religion followed. George was succeeded by rulers of the Polish Jagiellon dynasty, who rarely visited their Bohemian kingdom. In their absence a small number of prominent families were able to exercise power almost unchecked. Two developments show the power of the nobility during this period: first, when Vladislav the Jagiellonian (also Ulászló II of Hungary) was elected king of Bohemia in 1471, he was forced to swear that he would confirm and increase the nobility's privileges and would not introduce any major administrative change without the consent of the diet, which the nobles controlled; second, beginning in the late fifteenth century, serfdom was gradually reintroduced to Bohemia, as nobles consolidated their rights over peasant tenants.

Hapsburg Ambitions

In 1526 the Bohemian diet elected as king the Hapsburg Ferdinand I (1526–1564), the brother of Holy Roman Emperor Charles V. Seeking to recover lost royal power in Bohemia, Ferdinand dissolved regional assemblies, subordinated city administrations to the crown, and, after twenty years of lobbying, won from the diet the right to hereditary Hapsburg succession. The choice of Ferdinand seems to have been inspired by the diet's desire to end the anarchy; furthermore, Ferdinand was a popular figure throughout Europe owing to his strong stand against the Turks. A devout Catholic, Ferdinand nonetheless swore to protect both Catholic and moderate Hussite churches, although he persecuted other Protestant groups. By this time, Bohemia had become a haven for many Protestant sects, since the king had no authority to intervene on noble estates and the nobles were rapidly converting to Protestantism.

Ferdinand always looked for opportunities to increase his power and Catholic control in Bohemia. Thus, after Charles V defeated the

NOBLES VERSUS KINGS

Rudolf II—Holy Roman emperor, king of Hungary, and ruler of Austria, as well as king of Bohemia—was a man singularly unsuited to rule. He sponsored artistic and intellectual endeavors but took no interest in governance, instead leaving the business of state to his chancellor. In 1599 a new chancellor upset the careful religious balance in Bohemia by favoring the Catholics. By this time Rudolf was ill, apparently suffering from bouts of insanity, and he did nothing to redress the crisis caused by his chancellor. A faction of Bohemian nobles finally allied with Rudolf's brother Matthias, king of Hungary, and forced Rudolf to abdicate in 1611, shortly before his death.

The heart of the difficulty for Bohemia was that it had to have a king, or else the country would fall prey to land-hungry rulers of surrounding lands. However, except for George of Podebrady (reigned 1458–1471), the Bohemian diet proved unwilling to elect a native Czech noble; rivalry was too strong among the magnate families. Thus, the nobles' only option was to invite another central European king to rule them, preferably one with sufficient personal resources to fight off other claimants but still willing to be little more than a figurehead in Bohemia. In an age of rule by divine right, this attempted restriction of the royal office was an impractical dream. Every competent king immediately took steps to increase his power, to which end he played religious factions off against one another and usually relied on German officials to act as a counterbalance to native Czechs.

Schmalkaldic League (an alliance of Protestant territories) in 1547, Ferdinand executed some Bohemian Protestants and confiscated the lands of others. Enjoying greater resources and status after his election as emperor in 1556, Ferdinand took cautious steps to stamp out what he saw as heresy. For example, in 1561, at Ferdinand's request, the pope's appointment of Anton Brus as archbishop of Prague ended a 140-year vacancy in the see. In 1562 Ferdinand also established the Klementinum, a Jesuit college in Prague that won university status in 1616.

Ferdinand's successors, Maximilian II (reigned 1564–1576) and Rudolf II (reigned 1576–1611), also combined the offices of king of Bohemia and Holy Roman emperor. Rudolf beautified Prague and made it the capital of the empire. He also sponsored leading intellectuals, including the Danish astronomer Tycho Brahe (1546–1601) and the German astronomer Johannes Kepler (1571–1630). However, very little of this cultural renaissance was Czech. The court was largely German, and many Germans came to take advantage of Rudolf's generosity. Maximilian and Rudolf continued to accede to the Bohemian nobility's demands for religious tolerance; the Czech Confession of 1575 and the Confessio Bohemica of 1609 were accorded legal status. Both were moderate statements of Protestant theology that provided for toleration of most Christian denominations.

The Ruin of the Czech State

The rising of the Czech Estates (nobles and townsmen) in 1618 triggered the Thirty Years War. Tensions between king and nobles, Germans and Czechs, and Catholics and Protestants had finally reached a breaking point with the threat that the Hapsburg Ferdinand II, a strong ruler and zealous Catholic, would succeed Matthias as king. Hostilities began on May 23, 1618, with a second Defenestration of Prague: a mob hurled three Catholic imperial officials from the windows of the town hall in a

▲ *An oil portrait of Rudolf II, painted by Alonso Sánchez Coello (c. 1531–1588). A man with little appetite or talent for rule, Rudolf had a lively interest in scholarship and science.*

CZECH NATIONALISM IN AND OUT OF EXILE

After 1620 Czech nationalism found expression primarily in literature. Czech Protestants in exile continued to write and print books in Czech. Particularly moving are works by members of the Bohemian Brethren, a religious group that originated in the Hussite movement. In the mid-seventeenth century Adam Samuel Hartmann published a history of the persecution the Brethren had suffered at the hands of King Ferdinand II. In histories of Bohemia, hymnals, and other works, numerous writers attempted to win European sympathy for the cause of devastated Bohemia.

Catholic Counter-Reformation authors within Bohemia also continued to foster a national consciousness, despite the continuation of foreign rule. They discovered that traditional Catholic ideas reached a wider audience when published in Czech. Organizations were also founded to preserve the purity of the Czech language in the face of foreign incursions. Despite these efforts, however, the language picked up ever more German elements, and public life in general was deeply Germanized.

▲ The unknown author of this contemporary printed broadsheet, which reports the second Defenestration of Prague in 1618, expresses horror at the uprising.

move that imitated the opening of the Hussite war (although in 1618 the officials survived, their fall cushioned by a large dung heap). In 1619 the Czech diet repudiated the Hapsburg succession and offered the throne to Frederick, the elector of the Palatinate and hero of the Protestant cause.

Frederick, who is often called the Winter King because of the brevity of his reign, proved to be a broken reed. During his short rule he antagonized many of the Czech nobles by attempting to force Calvinism on them. Meanwhile, Ferdinand moved to end what he perceived to be a rebellion against his lawful rule and met Frederick's troops at the Battle of White Mountain, near Prague, on November 8, 1620. The battle was decisive; the rebellion was crushed, and Frederick fled in ignominious panic.

Ferdinand's victory at White Mountain shaped Bohemia's history for centuries to come. He exacted a brutal revenge on the Czech nobles by executing noble leaders and carrying out a policy of mass confiscations—it is estimated that over three-quarters of noble land changed hands in the 1620s. A new, largely foreign aristocracy was created. In 1624 Ferdinand declared Roman Catholicism to be the only legal religion in Bohemia, and in 1627 he ordered Protestants to convert or leave. One-fifth of the surviving Czech and Moravian nobles and one-quarter of the burghers of Bohemia chose exile.

By 1648 war and exile had halved the population of Bohemia. The economy was in ruins, as was Czech intellectual life. The king's power, though nearly absolute, was exercised from afar, for later kings visited Bohemia only occasionally.

FURTHER READING

Bradley, J. F. N. *Czechoslovakia: A Short History.* Edinburgh, 1971.

Dvornik, Francis. *The Slavs in European History and Civilization.* New Brunswick, NJ, 1962.

Evans, R. J. W. *The Making of the Habsburg Monarchy, 1550–1700: An Interpretation.* New York, 1984.

Fudge, Thomas A. *The Magnificent Ride: The First Reformation in Hussite Bohemia.* Brookfield, VT, 1998.

Phyllis G. Jestice

SEE ALSO

• Hapsburg Empire • Heresy • Holy Roman Empire • Monarchy • Nationalism • Reformation • Thirty Years War • Universities

Borgia, Lucrezia

ALTHOUGH SHE IS REGARDED AS ONE OF THE MOST NOTORIOUS WOMEN OF THE RENAISSANCE, LUCREZIA BORGIA (1480–1519) WAS AT ONCE THE PAWN OF HER POWERFUL FATHER AND BROTHER AND AN ASTUTE POLITICAL ACTOR IN HER OWN RIGHT.

On April 18, 1480, in the fortress of Subiaco, near Rome, Lucrezia Borgia was born to Cardinal Rodrigo Borgia (the future Pope Alexander VI) and his mistress Vannozza Cattanei. While Alexander VI had several other illegitimate children, the three born to Vannozza—Cesare, Juan, and Lucrezia—were the most highly favored by their father. Lucrezia lived with her mother and brothers until age three, when Vannozza married.

The subject of Bartolomeo da Venezia's Portrait of a Woman *(c. 1510), an alluring young woman with flowing blond locks, is believed by many to be Lucrezia Borgia. The artist spent three years working for Lucrezia at Ferrara.*

At this time Lucrezia was placed in the care of Adriana de Mila, Alexander VI's cousin. Lucrezia was probably educated at the Dominican convent of San Sisto, on the Appian Way (the ancient Roman road that led to the south). This convent later became a place of refuge for Lucrezia when personal and political pressures overwhelmed her. Lucrezia received an education in languages, including Italian, French, and Latin and was capable of writing poetry in these languages and in Catalan, the language spoken at the papal court of Alexander VI (Catalan was spoken in eastern Spain, the original homeland of the Borgias). Lucrezia was acquainted with ancient Greek and had training in rhetoric (the art of persuasive public speaking), a skill that would prove invaluable in the public life she was to lead.

This public life began early. Lucrezia's father began arranging her marriage when she was barely twelve. Initially a Spanish nobleman named Juan Cherubin de Centelles was chosen; when this match fell through, Lucrezia was engaged to another Spanish noble, Gasparo de Procida. This engagement, too, came to nothing. Almost immediately after Rodrigo Borgia began his reign as Alexander VI in 1492, he negotiated a marriage between Lucrezia and Giovanni Sforza, lord of Pesaro.

This marriage, which took place in 1493, was designed as both a reward for Cardinal Ascanio Sforza's support in the papal election and a strategic affront to the Sforzas' enemy the powerful Ferdinand I (also known as Ferrante), king of Naples. Yet the temporary nature of the political situation the marriage addressed—Alexander's desire to ally himself with the Milanese Sforzas against the Aragonese rulers of Naples—condemned the marriage to be just as short-lived. Despite a genial affection between the spouses, Alexander VI's political ambitions prompted him to switch sides to Naples, and on December 20, 1597, Lucrezia's marriage to Giovanni Sforza was annulled on the grounds of Sforza's impotency—an act of political expediency that somewhat overlooked the fact that Sforza's first wife had died in childbirth.

CHRONOLOGY

1480
Lucrezia Borgia is born near Rome.

1493
Marries Giovanni Sforza.

1498
Marries Alfonso of Aragon, duke of Bisceglie.

1499
Gives birth to a son, Rodrigo; is made governor of Spoleto.

1501
Marries Alfonso d'Este.

1505
Ercole d'Este dies; Lucrezia becomes duchess of Ferrara.

1508
Her son Ercole (later Ercole II) is born.

1509
Another son, Ippolito (later Ippolito II, cardinal d'Este and archbishop of Milan), is born.

1511
Her son Rodrigo dies.

1515
Lucrezia gives birth to a daughter, Eleonora, later a nun of the convent Corpus Domini.

1516
Gives birth to a son, Francesco, who later becomes the marchese of Massalombarda.

1519
Isabella Maria, a daughter, is born but dies in infancy; Lucrezia dies.

Almost immediately Alexander VI arranged a new marriage for Lucrezia—to Ferdinand I's grandson, the eighteen-year-old Alfonso of Aragon, duke of Bisceglie. The couple married on June 20, 1498, amid great celebration. After the marriage Alexander placed Lucrezia in positions of authority—in August 1499 she was appointed governor of Spoleto, a central Italian town within the papl territories. In the meantime, political machinations throughout Europe began to threaten this second marriage. Scheming to conquer Naples, King Louis XII of France aligned himself with Alexander VI. Lucrezia's husband, a member of Naples's royal family, fled Rome in fear of his life. However, when Lucrezia returned to Rome, Alfonso felt secure enough in her affection to return to her. This mistake cost him his life. On July 15, 1500, on the steps of Saint Peter's Basilica, he was attacked by unknown assailants. Gravely wounded, he was taken to Lucrezia's apartments, where his wife was reportedly distraught. On August 18 Lucrezia's brother Cesare, the perpetrator of the attack, arrived at Lucrezia's rooms, sent the women away, and ordered that Alfonso be smothered. While this murder was primarily a political act, its effect on Lucrezia was devastating. She retreated to the citadel of Nepi, north of Rome, and remained in exile there for two months.

Duchess of Ferrara

The daughter of Pope Alexander VI was not allowed the luxury of mourning for long. By November, Lucrezia had been recalled to Rome to serve as regent of the Papal States during the absence of her father and Cesare, who were involved in yet another military campaign. Alexander was still intent on extending his influence, not only through military strategies but also through a magnificent new marriage for Lucrezia. This time Alexander chose Alfonso d'Este (1486–1534), son and heir to Ercole I, duke of Ferrara, a province of northern Italy. Lucrezia soon showed enthusiasm for the marriage, which would make her duchess of an important Italian state and, by providing her with a powerful base of her own, would free her from the political machinations of her father and brother. Alfonso was initially reluctant to marry Lucrezia. The very fact that her first marriage had ended in annulment and her second in the murder of her second husband understandably made marriage with her a rather unsettling

Lucrezia Borgia's bedroom at Sermoneta, pictured here, has been preserved as a museum exhibit. The room is rather sparsely decorated given the status of its occupant; Lucrezia used it during her short stay in Sermoneta, where she served as duchess and governor of the castle in 1500.

One observer in Ferrara—a servant doubling as a spy for Isabella d'Este, the marchioness of Mantua and Lucrezia's sister-in-law— was struck by Lucrezia's intellectual capabilities:

Every day she makes a better impression on me; she is a lady with a very good mind, astute, you have to keep your wits about you with her. To sum up, I hold her to be a wise lady, and this is not only my opinion but that of all this company.

Il Prete, letter to Isabella d'Este, January 19, 1502

The Disputation of Saint Catherine of Alexandria *(1492–1494), a fresco painted by Pinturicchio (c. 1454–1513) at the Hall of the Saints in the Borgia apartments at the Vatican. The artist is generally believed to have used the young Lucrezia as the model for Saint Catherine (the kneeling figure).*

proposition. However, politics again dictated the marriage. Ercole d'Este, finding himself under pressure from all sides, including from the king of France, agreed to the marriage, which was lavishly celebrated in Ferrara in 1501.

Lucrezia left Rome, never to return, on January 6, 1502. Among the records concerning her move to Ferrara is a list of books in her own private library. The list offers an insight into Lucrezia's interests. It includes a book of the Gospels in Italian; a printed romance of chivalry, *L'àquila volante* by Leonardo Bruni; a Latin world history, the *Supplementum chronicarum;* a Spanish *Life of Christ* by Ludolphus of Saxonia; a manuscript of Petrarch's poems; and many other books of a religious or philosophical nature.

After a journey filled with fine hospitality and great display, Lucrezia finally joined her husband in Ferrara. She quickly impressed the Ferrarese with her kindness, good sense, and political astuteness. She became a patron of the arts and entered into close friendships with several Italian poets, including Ludovico Ariosto (1474–1533), who composed a poem for her wedding and featured a portrait of Lucrezia in his masterpiece, *Orlando furioso* (1516). Lucrezia was also extremely fond of the poet Pietro Bembo. Other poets who sought patronage from Lucrezia included Tito and Ercole Strozzi and Antonio Tebaldeo. The celebrated humanist Gian Giorgio Trissino (1478–1550) was also frequently present at her court. These writers eulogized Lucrezia as the "most beautiful virgin" and helped her to promote an image very much at odds with her turbulent past.

As duchess Lucrezia fulfilled the many roles required of her. She maintained a magnificent and cultured court and governed Ferrara in the absence of her husband. Indeed, from 1509 to 1512, she was the de facto ruler in Ferrara owing to the incessant wars and political intrigues that occupied her husband. She also provided moral leadership during periods when Ferrara was in danger of being taken by its enemies.

THE REPUTATION OF LUCREZIA BORGIA

The name Lucrezia Borgia has often been synonymous with female treachery. Her detractors accused her of murder, sexual promiscuity, and even incest with her father and brother. These myths emerged during the early years of Lucrezia's life, when the Borgias were at their most powerful and ruthless. The cavalier way in which Lucrezia was married, divorced, remarried, and widowed certainly led anti-Borgia parties—of whom there were many—to write disparagingly of the beautiful daughter of a politically rapacious father and brother who were also well known for their sexual appetites. In Ferrara, at some distance from her family, Lucrezia had the opportunity to develop her own identity. She was clearly seen by most in a positive light, for numerous letters, poems, and works of art express great admiration for her.

After Lucrezia's death and the decline of Ferrara, her earlier reputation reasserted itself in the popular imagination—with the help of chroniclers hostile to the Borgias. It is this reputation that fired the imagination of such later writers as the English poet Lord Byron (1788–1824) and the French novelists Alexandre Dumas (1802–1870) and Victor Hugo (1802–1885). It is primarily through the works of these and other more recent writers that Lucrezia's reputation for immorality has been bequeathed to the present day.

This eighteenth-century copper engraving was copied from a painting attributed to Titian. The contemporary portrait captures the mature and respected woman of Lucrezia's later years.

Later Life

Lucrezia, who grew increasingly religious as the years passed, became a lay sister of the third Franciscan order. In 1513 the Augustinian friar Antonio Meli da Crema dedicated his *Libro de vita contemplativa (Book of Contemplative Life)* to Lucrezia; he wrote that she was "fired by chaste divine love" and attested that she instructed her ladies in matters of religion. This portrait is far different from the one drawn by those enemies of the Borgia family who had portrayed Lucrezia in her youth as lascivious, murderous, and incestuous, whereas in reality she had simply served as her father's pawn.

In 1519 Lucrezia gave birth to a baby girl, but after a difficult labor, she weakened and died. After her death, in a letter to his nephew, Lucrezia's husband praised her in the following terms: "I cannot write this without tears, knowing myself to be deprived of such a sweet and dear companion. For such her exemplary conduct and the tender love which existed between us made her to me."

Further Reading

Bellonci, Maria. *The Life and Times of Lucrezia Borgia.* Translated by Bernard and Barbara Wall. London, 2000.

Bradford, Sarah. *Lucrezia Borgia: Life, Love and Death in Renaissance Italy*. New York, 2004.

Faunce, John. *Lucrezia Borgia: A Novel.* New York, 2003.

Mallett, Michael. *The Borgias: The Rise and Fall of a Renaissance Dynasty.* Chicago, 1987.

Jessica L. Malay

SEE ALSO

• Italian City-States • Papacy • Religious Orders • Rome • Women

Bosch, Hieronymus

ALTHOUGH HE WAS THE MOST ENIGMATIC, ORIGINAL, AND UNUSUAL ARTIST OF THE RENAISSANCE, THE DUTCH PAINTER HIERONYMUS BOSCH (C. 1450–1516) ENJOYED GREAT POPULARITY IN HIS OWN DAY.

Hieronymus Bosch remains largely a mystery. What written records of his life remain shed little light on what prompted him to create his strikingly original paintings—and what those paintings were meant to convey. The forty extant works attributed to him, puzzling though they are, are the main source material for those seeking to understand Bosch. In some ways his paintings mark the end of the medieval style in art, especially in their use of delicate colors and their freely flowing style. However, a simple progression from a medieval to a Renaissance style is not in evidence; indeed, in his later works Bosch turns away from the clarity and realism of the Renaissance to the crowded canvases of the international Gothic style. In conceptual terms Bosch's paintings give a similarly mixed message. Bosch was startlingly modern in his critique of organized religion and in the demands he placed on the intellect of the viewer, but his paintings also reflect a pessimistic view of human life and a disdain for the material world that was informed by *contemptus mundi* literature, a genre of late medieval religious writing that voiced contempt for the world. Hieronymus Bosch was a remarkable figure; his style was unique, and while elements of his work were imitated, no other artist has duplicated his vision of the world.

Life

Hieronymus Bosch was born Jeroen van Aeken in 1450 in 's Hertogenbosch, in northern Brabant (in the present-day Netherlands). He was one of six children. Bosch's family had been established as artists in 's Hertogenbosch since his grandfather, a painter, moved there from Aachen, in Germany, around 1400. Anthonis van Aeken, Bosch's father, was also a painter, as were two of Bosch's uncles and two of his brothers. While 's Hertogenbosch was a prosperous commercial town—the fact that a fire during Bosch's youth destroyed four thousand houses suggests a substantial population for the late fifteenth century—it had few cultural pretensions. Although Bosch became famous in his lifetime, he never moved to a more significant cultural center. This relative isolation certainly helps account for his idiosyncratic style.

The theme of The Conjurer *(c. 1475–1480)—indeed, the dominant theme of all Bosch's work—is human greed and folly. The conjurer, a con man, makes frogs spring from a man's mouth while his accomplice quietly cuts the victim's purse. The victim, whose credulity has made the fraud possible, is equally to blame for his predicament.*

CHRONOLOGY

c. 1450
Hieronymus Bosch is born in 's Hertogenbosch.

c. 1470
His early period begins.

1475–1480
Bosch paints *The Cure of Folly* and *The Conjurer.*

c. 1480
His middle period begins.

c. 1490
Bosch paints *Death and the Miser.*

1490–1500
Paints *The Ship of Fools.*

c. 1500
Paints *The Garden of Earthly Delights.*

c. 1500–1502
Paints *The Haywain.*

c. 1505–1506
Paints *The Temptation of Saint Anthony.*

1510
His late period begins.

c. 1515–1516
Christ Carrying the Cross is executed.

1516
Bosch dies.

◀ *This detail from the central panel of* The Temptation of Saint Anthony *(c. 1505–1506) is a good example of Bosch's use of animals to suggest subversion and evil. A closer examination of what at first glance appears to be simply a rat reading a book reveals a ghastly wound on the animal's side; the whole is a dark parody of a priest saying Mass.*

Bosch's brother Goossen apparently succeeded as head of his father's painting workshop. Hieronymus clearly chose a different path: in signing his name Jheronimus Bosch rather than using the family name of van Aeken ("from Aachen"), he employed a shortened form of the name of his hometown. As a young man, Hieronymus married a wealthy patrician woman, Aleyt van der Mervenne. This marriage made Bosch financially independent and indeed wealthy; he was assessed in 's Hertogenbosch's highest tax bracket. Bosch and his wife lived in her small castle nearby.

Little further information about Bosch's life remains. What is certain is that in 1488 he joined a religious confraternity, the Brotherhood of Our Lady. This group, comprising around forty influential citizens of 's Hertogenbosch, was deeply conservative in its practices and beliefs. Bosch undertook a number of commissions for the brotherhood and was a member in good standing until his death. This fact makes it unlikely that Bosch was a heretic, as some scholars have suggested. Rather, his artistic output makes most sense when viewed as an expression of late medieval morality, which emphasized the futility and transience of worldly concerns and the torments that sinners endured in hell.

Style

Bosch's style owes little to his predecessors in the northern Renaissance—such Flemish painters as

MONEY AND ARTISTIC LIBERTY

One of the many mysteries surrounding Bosch's career concerns the surprisingly small fees he was paid for some of his works even though he was in considerable demand as an artist. The most likely explanation is that Bosch, who was financially secure, merely asked for token payments from some of his patrons—perhaps just enough to cover the cost of his artistic supplies.

Bosch's financial independence put him in an enviable position among artists of the Renaissance, for he did not have to cater to wealthy patrons whose tastes were likely to be conventional. Instead, it seems likely that Bosch painted what he wanted to, and the person who had commissioned the work could take it or leave it. Bosch's wealth is probably an important clue to the extraordinary originality of his compositions.

Jan van Eyck (c. 1395–1441) and Rogier van der Weyden (c. 1399–1464), for example. In contrast to the highly worked, flat, smooth surfaces of those artists' paintings, Bosch's works are rough to the touch. In general his technique is much less complicated than that of his contemporaries. He simply painted a panel white, drew on it, and then applied paint directly on top.

In the way he organized his works, too, Bosch ignored the fashions of his time. He rejected the contemporary tendency to have a few large-scale figures dominate a panel and instead produced often-confusing masses of figures against large backgrounds. He never painted a portrait, even though portraiture dominates the production of most artists of the northern Renaissance. Bosch also appears to have been indifferent to the anatomical studies of his era; his human figures, angular and usually not very graceful, bear a closer resemblance to fourteenth-century Gothic patterns than to the Italianate realism of his own time.

Artistic Development

Although none of his works have been firmly dated, Bosch's productive life can be roughly divided into early, middle, and late phases. Art historians are in general agreement about the broad phases of his work, but more precise dating is a matter of debate.

Paintings attributed to the early period (up to around 1480), in which Bosch's originality is already in evidence, include *The Conjurer, The Seven Deadly Sins, The Cure of Folly,* and several more conventional works on religious themes, including the *Marriage at Cana* and *Ecce Homo.*

◀ The Haywain *(c. 1500–1502) illustrates a Flemish proverb: "The world is a haystack and each man plucks from it what he can." However, by putting the haystack on wheels, Bosch propels the whole central panel toward its ultimate destination—hell. The central panel is a panorama of human vice, the people oblivious to the fact that the hay wagon is being drawn by demonic animals. Looking down from heaven, the solitary figure of Christ forms a striking contrast to the vast crowd of self-absorbed people below.*

Often called "The Musician's Hell," the right wing of *The Garden of Earthly Delights* (c. 1500), a study of the consequences of sin, specifically expresses Bosch's disapproval of contemporary music: tormented souls are racked in the strings of a harp and trapped inside a monstrous hurdy-gurdy.

In the *Cure of Folly* a surgeon is shown cutting open a man's head. At first glance this work is a relatively straightforward depiction of the horrors of fifteenth-century medicine. However, a funnel (representing wisdom) perched on the surgeon's head adds an element of absurdity to the painting. The viewer is left to wonder whether the title refers to folly that is being cut out of the patient's brain or to the folly of the surgeon himself—and if the latter, whether the painting should be read as a commentary on the folly of all worldly healing. In its original language the title supports either interpretation.

In his middle period, which lasted from around 1480 to 1510, Bosch freed himself from a number of traditional artistic practices. Works from this period include the *Crucifixion, Christ Carrying the Cross,* and *Crowning with Thorns*, all of which are dark, indeed near-demonic, treatments of traditional religious scenes. *Death and the Miser* and other small panels also treat a straightforward theme in a dark and unsettling way. In the aforementioned work, a miser on his deathbed is torn between an image of the crucified Christ and a demon proffering a moneybag; other demonic animals crawl around the room like enormous rats, and Death edges around the door. However, Bosch's most fascinating work lies in the three great allegorical triptychs (three-paneled works) of his middle period, usually called *The Garden of Earthly Delights, The Temptation of Saint Anthony,* and *The Haywain.*

Bosch's late works depict fewer and larger figures, in a manner more reminiscent of other Netherlandish artists. These works include the *Prodigal Son, Christ before Pilate,* and another *Christ Carrying the Cross.* This last painting, a harsh indictment of human evil, is now thought to be Bosch's last work. Nineteen heads are crushed tightly together. Most are nightmarish images, contorted and beastlike. Besides Jesus, only the good thief and Saint Veronica retain human features. Their passive expressions separate them from the hate that rages around them.

In *Christ Carrying the Cross* (c. 1515–1516), perhaps the artist's last work, Bosch lays bare the bestiality of humankind. Overwhelmed by a horde of tormentors, Christ shuts his eyes to the horrors around him.

The Impact of Hieronymus Bosch

For all his eccentricity, Bosch was appreciated by his contemporaries and for several generations afterward. In the mid-sixteenth century engravings of Bosch's paintings were made by Alart du Hameel, and other artists produced many copies of his works. King Philip I of Spain and his sister Margaret of Austria both collected Bosch's paintings. King Philip II also passionately admired Bosch; during the long Dutch war for independence from Spain, he carried off a large selection of Bosch's paintings to Spain, where they remain to this day. The impact of Bosch's style can be seen in both northern and Spanish art, most notably in the work of Pieter Bruegel the Elder (c. 1525–1569) and El Greco (c. 1541–1614). Bosch's work was then largely forgotten until the late nineteenth century, but in the twentieth century it is said to have inspired the surrealists.

THE GARDEN OF EARTHLY DELIGHTS

The Bosch triptych usually called *The Garden of Earthly Delights* is a large work—the central panel measures seven feet two inches by six feet four inches (220 x 195 cm). Its meaning has been endlessly debated. Certainly, Bosch included elements that were less obscure to contemporary viewers than they are to modern ones, such as astrological references and elaborate wordplay. There is general agreement, however, that the three panels represent, first, the Garden of Eden, second, human folly and sexual indulgence after the Fall, and third, an extraordinary hell in which musical instruments have become instruments of torture. When the side panels are closed, an exterior painting in grisaille (gray tones) shows God creating the world.

The central panel is the most enigmatic. Although the many naked figures look like innocent lovers, there is much to suggest a moral lesson condemning sexual freedom. First, the general temper of all of Bosch's works, which denounce human vanity and folly, makes it unlikely that he would turn to a springtime idyll in this work. Second, the layout of this triptych is identical to that of *The Haywain*, with a state of innocence depicted on the left panel and hell on the right; the implication is that here, as in *The Haywain*, the central scene must represent some sort of corruption that will lead humankind from paradise to hell. Third, closer examination of the painting itself reveals several clues to its darker message. Figures in a state of nudity are rarely seen in northern paintings of this age outside of images of the Last Judgment. Many seem also to be in a state of complete abandon, and some are drinking. The scene is filled with a large number of wild animals—which in Bosch's paintings tend to be suggestive of immorality or demonism.

Part of the confusion in interpreting this painting has been the assumption that it was intended for the altar of a church. Yet it seems likely that *The Garden of Earthly Delights* was made for a secular patron. Certainly in the year 1517 it was in the Brussels palace of the nobleman Henry III of Nassau. It remained in the possession of the Orange-Nassau family until 1568, when it was looted by Spanish troops and taken to Madrid. It has been suggested that Bosch painted the work to commemorate a noble wedding, an unusual commission but less shocking than if its intended home had been an altar.

BOSCH'S ANIMALS

One of the most distinctive features of Bosch's panels is his frequent use of wild animals in unusual contexts. A conjurer makes frogs spring from a person's mouth; people ride on robins and inside enormous oysters; and monstrous fish fly through the air. Such depictions, variously interpreted either as "cute" images or as examples of Bosch's anticipatation of surrealism, are far from the affirmation of nature that some modern viewers assume them to be.

Most of Bosch's animals and half animals are in fact clearly demons, as is clear from those that appear in his *Last Judgment* panels or in the hell panels of the great triptychs. Viewed in light of those obviously demonic depictions, Bosch's more neutral creatures take on a sinister tint. Whether specifically demons or not, the animals in Bosch's paintings suggest a very negative view of the natural world. Painted in an age that put a high value on human reason, Bosch's beasts are the irrational run rampant. That humans associate freely with these wild beasts suggests that the people involved are also untamed; unable to bridle their lustfulness, they give in to every impulse.

▼ *A work of Bosch's middle period,* The Ship of Fools *(c. 1490–1500) embodies the artist's view of the human condition. The figures represent humanity journeying across the sea of life, so occupied with eating, drinking, and games that the ship is allowed to float aimlessly.*

How can Bosch's popularity be explained? The esteem in which his paintings were held in northern Europe and Spain, especially among those most likely to have an understanding of art, suggests that educated tastes in these regions were not restricted to the realism of mainstream Renaissance art. Bosch's popularity, along with the large number of devotional works produced by northern European and Spanish presses, also bears eloquent testimony to continuing medieval concerns in religion, such as a profound sense of the consequences of the Fall and of human helplessness without God's aid. An examination of Bosch's paintings provides a salutary reminder that the Renaissance consisted of much more than the luminous secularism of Italian art.

FURTHER READING

Gibson, Walter S. *Hieronymus Bosch.* New York, 1973.

Harbison, Craig. *The Mirror of the Artist: Northern Renaissance Art in Its Historical Context.* New York, 1995.

Koldeweij, Jos, Paul Vandenbroeck, and Bernard Vermet. *Hieronymus Bosch: The Complete Paintings and Drawings.* New York, 2001.

Snyder, James. *Northern Renaissance Art: Painting, Sculpture, the Graphic Arts from 1350 to 1575.* Upper Saddle River, NJ, 2005.

Phyllis G. Jestice

SEE ALSO

• Bruegel, Pieter • Eyck, Jan van

• Painting and Sculpture • Philip II

Botticelli, Sandro

SANDRO BOTTICELLI (1445–1510), ONE OF THE MOST IMPORTANT FLORENTINE PAINTERS OF THE FIFTEENTH CENTURY, IS BEST KNOWN FOR HIS MYTHOLOGICAL PAINTINGS AND STRIKINGLY LIFELIKE PORTRAITS.

Alessandro di Mariano di Vanni Filipepi, nicknamed Botticelli, was born in Florence in 1445. He was the son of a tanner, and as was customary for young Florentine men from artisanal backgrounds, he became an apprentice in his early teens, first to a goldsmith and then to a painter. While it was unusual to undertake two apprenticeships, other Renaissance artists also trained with a goldsmith before becoming sculptors or painters.

Artistic Training and Style

Botticelli's apprenticeship to Filippo Lippi, one of the most famous and influential painters of mid-fifteenth-century Florence, was crucial to his artistic development. In 1461 or 1462 Botticelli joined the older master's workshop and spent a number of years there during a period when Lippi produced some of his finest paintings. Lippi taught Botticelli the key techniques of contemporary Florentine painting, the most significant being linear perspective, the technique whereby figures and structures painted on a two-dimensional surface—the canvas—appear to occupy three-dimensional space. In Botticelli's early paintings the placement of figures and the treatment of clothing also reveal Lippi's influence.

By 1470, the year after Lippi's death, Botticelli, now a rising talent, had opened his own workshop in Florence. The paintings from this period reflect his interest in the use of light and shadow to create figures both more three-dimensional and more expressive—an innovative technique among the artists of his day. Using this technique, along with those he learned from Lippi, Botticelli arrived at his own distinctive style, which may be seen in *Fortitude* (1470), the painting that firmly established his reputation in Florence.

Fortitude, one of a series representing the seven cardinal virtues, had been commissioned by a tribunal of judges who dealt with disputes between merchants. When Piero del Pollaiuolo, a noted Florentine painter who had originally received the commission, failed to finish on time, the judges asked the young Botticelli to paint *Fortitude.* While Botticelli's methods were those of his era, in skill and subtlety he far surpassed his contemporaries, including Pollaiuolo. *Fortitude,* while clearly representative of late-fifteenth-century Florentine painting, also defines Botticelli's individual manner.

Growing Fame

In the 1470s and early 1480s, a period when portraiture became more widespread (a reflection of the increasing importance of the individual in the Renaissance outlook), Botticelli became one of Florence's leading portrait painters. His most famous portrait, *Man Holding a Medallion of Cosimo de' Medici* (1475), exemplifies both his debt to contemporary artistic developments and his own contributions to portraiture. Although the young man's pose is typical of its time, Botticelli characteristically captures a sense of the sitter's character, as he had done in *Fortitude* five years earlier, through the subtle use of light and shade to define facial features. Later artists—such as Leonardo da Vinci in his *Mona Lisa*—continued to develop the expressive use of light and shade, and this technique became a defining feature of Renaissance portraiture.

During this period, as his fame spread beyond Florence, Botticelli produced several outstanding paintings on religious subjects. In 1481 Pope Sixtus IV, who had become aware of Botticelli's reputation, summoned him to Rome, along with several other leading painters of the age, to adorn the walls of the newly rebuilt chapel in the Vatican (which came to be called the Sistine Chapel in the pope's honor). This commission confirmed Botticelli's growing stature. Working in the Sistine Chapel from July 1481 to June 1482, Botticelli completed three scenes drawn from the lives of Moses and Jesus. (Popes were among the leading patrons of the Italian

BOTTICELLI'S STYLE

Fortitude provides an excellent vehicle to analyze Botticelli's style. The painting's commissioners required Botticelli to adhere to the same dimensions and the same general composition—a single figure seated on a throne—that Piero del Pollaiuolo had used for the other six virtues. Despite these restrictions and the two painters' use of the same Renaissance techniques, Botticelli was far more successful than Pollaiuolo in both design and execution. A close comparison of the two painters' work can be illuminating.

Both painters employ linear perspective to create the illusion of three dimensions. Pollaiuolo uses the technique to place Temperance in the background, whereas Botticelli brings Fortitude to the foreground and, in various subtle ways, makes her the center of attention. He allows, for example, the placement of her feet to extend beyond the throne. This placement keeps the architectural background from dominating the composition and reveals a characteristic aspect of Botticelli's style: an emphasis on figures over setting.

The detail of Fortitude's clothing is also noteworthy. Its careful modeling creates a vibrant and engaging figure, in contrast with Pollaiuolo's unimaginative and flat rendering of Temperance's clothing. The folds of Fortitude's drapery reveal Botticelli's debt to Lippi, his teacher, but the student's detailed rendering of Fortitude's metal breastplate may reflect his training as a goldsmith.

Both Botticelli and Pollaiuolo use shadows rather than sharp lines to bring the facial features of their virtues to life, but Botticelli again reveals the greater sensitivity. The face of Fortitude radiates the calm strength and self-assurance associated with this virtue. Overall, in *Fortitude*, Botticelli surpasses his older rival in creating a more lifelike figure that engages the viewer and dominates the composition.

Piero del Pollaiuolo's Temperance *(1469–1470) and Botticelli's* Fortitude *(1470) were part of the same series of pictorial depictions of the seven cardinal virtues. In Pollaiuolo's painting (left) Temperance dilutes wine with water as a symbolic representation of her virtue.* Fortitude *(right) signals the emergence of Botticelli's distinctive style. Fortitude sits on a throne holding a military staff of office, a traditional symbolic attribute of her virtue.*

Renaissance and employed many of its greatest artists, including Raphael and Michelangelo, who within thirty years would paint the ceiling of the Sistine Chapel and, twenty years later, the wall behind the altar.)

Mythological Paintings

Botticelli returned to Florence after completing the Sistine commission and soon began the first of a series of canvases with mythological subjects. These paintings—among which are *Primavera* (c. 1482), *Pallas and the Centaur* (c. 1482), *Venus and Mars* (c. 1483), and *The Birth of Venus* (c. 1485)—are now considered his most remarkable works. The paintings, which take the nature of love as their subject, were probably commissioned as wedding pictures. Though their precise meaning remains in dispute, the key to their interpretation is an understanding of the social and intellectual world of Florence during the early 1480s.

Botticelli painted the most important of these works for the Medicis (the ruling family of Florence) and families associated with them.

CHRONOLOGY

1445
Sandro Botticelli is born in Florence.

1459/1460
Is apprenticed to a goldsmith.

1461/1462
Is apprenticed to the painter Filippo Lippi.

c. 1465
Completes his first independent paintings under Lippi's supervision.

1470
Sets up his own workshop and completes his first masterpiece, *Fortitude.*

1475
Members of the Medici family commission works from Botticelli. Around this year Botticelli completes *Man Holding a Medallion of Cosimo de' Medici* and *Adoration of the Magi*.

1481
In Rome, helps paint the Sistine Chapel.

1482–1485
Executes a series of mythological paintings: *Primavera, Pallas and the Centaur, Venus and Mars*, and *The Birth of Venus*.

1490
Begins to devote himself almost exclusively to religious topics.

1510
Dies on May 17.

Man Holding a Medallion of Cosimo de' Medici *(1475). This portrait is one of several painted by Botticelli during the 1470s. The skillful use of light and shade conveys a sense of the personality of the unidentified young man.*

▶ *Primavera (c. 1482), outwardly concerning the arrival of spring, has as its true subject the two natures of love. It was probably executed for the wedding of Lorenzo di Pierfrancesco de' Medici, a distant cousin of the ruling Medicis of Florence.*

DECIPHERING *PRIMAVERA*

As is true of any work of art, the "meaning" of *Primavera* has changed with the passage of time, and a modern viewer may well wonder what the painting's original audience saw in it. The members of the Florentine aristocracy knew well both the philosophical ideas about love that Botticelli took as his subject and the ancient Greek and Roman stories that he used to explain them. For instance, an educated Florentine would have known that the title *Primavera* (Italian for "spring") referred to an ode to the fruitfulness of springtime written by the Roman philosopher Lucretius (c. 96–c. 55 BCE). Moreover, the Florentine would recognize that the real subject of *Primavera* is love because the central figure, with Cupid hovering above her, is clearly Venus, the Roman goddess of love.

For most of the last 1,500 years, virtually all Western art, both sacred and secular, employed a large number of widely used visual cues, symbols, and figures drawn largely from classical literature, Christian tradition, and the Bible. Their purpose was to communicate, in a fashion akin to shorthand, a lot of information in a little space. As a rule, artists could count on their observers' understanding of this system of symbols. Thus, the educated Florentine could have been expected to see that *Primavera* is sending a complex message about the two natures of love.

On the right-hand side of the painting, Botticelli examines physical or sensual love. He depicts the story recounted by Ovid (43 BCE–c. 17 CE) of the lustful pursuit of Chloris, a nymph, by Zephyrus, the god of the west wind (the blue-green winged figure bursting onto the scene). In the story Zephyrus ultimately feels remorse for allowing his passions to get the better of him; he shows his regret by transforming Chloris into the goddess of flowers. Thus, the two female figures on the right are really one and represent Chloris's transformation into a goddess (the flowers appearing from the mouth of the fleeing nymph provide a clue to this transformation). Botticelli uses Ovid's story to show how succumbing to unbridled lust and physical love leads to regret.

On the left-hand side Botticelli explores pure spiritual love. A viewer familiar with classical Greek myths would identify the three female figures as the three Graces, Venus's traditional companions, and the male figure with winged boots as Mercury, the messenger god. The key figure in this more tranquil and ordered portion of the painting is the Grace (with her back to the viewer) who looks toward Mercury and is the target of the blindfolded Cupid. She is unaware of Zephyrus's disorderly entrance to her right and instead focuses on the tranquil figure of Mercury, whose arm draws her view upward to otherworldly concerns. Likewise, Botticelli draws attention to the platonic love central to the philosophical thought of Florence in the 1480s.

These paintings reflect the Florentine aristocracy's interest in ancient Roman and Greek history, literature, poetry, and myth. The paintings also embody ideas taken from Neoplatonism—a philosophy that combined the teachings of the ancient Greek philosopher Plato with Christian beliefs. The Medicis and their allies sponsored a number of Neoplatonic philosophers, one of whose key ideas was that love had two natures: the one sensual and physical, the other spiritual and intellectual. These two forms represented opposing forces. Followers of Neoplatonism sought to control love's base sensual aspects in order to reach its ideal intellectual and spiritual form. This ideal form came to be called platonic love, a term still widely used.

A Shift in Focus

Around 1490 Botticelli's style changed considerably, and his subject matter shifted almost exclusively to religious topics. Florentine society had increasingly come under the sway of a religious movement that opposed the perceived worldliness accompanying the city's growing wealth. The leading figure in this movement was Girolamo Savonarola, a Dominican monk and fiery preacher who called on people, poor and wealthy alike, to do penance for their sins and prepare for God's judgment. The strength of the new religious fervor was revealed when the crisis created by the French invasion of Italy in 1494 led to the overthrow of the Medici regime and its replacement by Savonarola and his followers, who ruled Florence until 1498. In that year a popular election returned the Medici party to power, and Savonarola, who had lost most of his popular support and also been excommunicated by the pope, was tried on charges of sedition and heresy and executed.

Botticelli, like many of his contemporaries, was deeply influenced by Savonarola's message. Whether Botticelli was a committed follower of Savonarola remains uncertain, but the profound change in his style, which persisted until his death in May 1510, reveals heightened religious concerns. Botticelli partly abandoned the Renaissance ideal of using perspective to create lifelike figures and scenes and returned to the medieval practice of portraying figures in a size relative to their importance (note, for example, the oversized figure of the Virgin Mary in *The Mystical Nativity* [c. 1500]). The change in style, clashing as it did with current trends, may suggest that Botticelli was seeking to stress the picture's content over its form, its message over its manner.

The Mystical Nativity, like many other paintings from the same period, adopts an apocalyptic tone (that is to say, it is concerned with the end of the world and the second coming of Christ). On the surface *The Mystical Nativity* looks normal enough. However, in the lower portion of the panel, Botticelli has painted three angels

At first glance The Mystical Nativity *(c. 1500) seems a conventional depiction of the familiar scene. However, the figures in the foreground indicate that it reflected Botticelli's hope that the powers of heaven would soon overcome the powers of the devil on earth.*

PLEASING THE PATRONS

Patrons had a great deal of influence over the subject and composition of Renaissance art. As the custom of the time dictated, Botticelli frequently includes his patrons in his canvases—in *The Adoration of the Magi* (c. 1475), for example. This painting was commissioned by Guaspare di Zenobio del Lama, a wealthy Florentine businessman, who appears in the painting as the figure at the upper left gazing out toward the viewer. Del Lama also insisted on the depiction of many of his associates, including three leading members of the ruling Medici family, flatteringly portrayed as the three Magi. Botticelli may have placed himself among these prominent Florentines. He is believed to be the figure at the far right who is looking straight at the viewer.

◀ The Adoration of the Magi, *also known as the* Del Lama Adoration *(c. 1475). Best known for its depiction of important Florentines, including several of the Medicis and the artist himself, this painting was a high point of Botticelli's early output. The figures are arranged on ground that slopes gently upward to ensure that nearly all the individuals are clearly visible. The placement of figures tends to unify the scene and make the Virgin Mary the central focus.*

embracing three men and a series of devils attached to poles. These figures play no role in a conventional nativity scene. Their meaning becomes apparent only when one reads the Greek inscription at the top, where Botticelli explains that he is referring to the world he lives in, a world in which the devil and his minions run amok. The promises in the New Testament book of Revelation—that the devil will ultimately be cast down in chains with his supporters and a period of peace will reign on earth—come to mind. Like Savonarola, Botticelli may have believed that the end of the world was imminent and that the casting out of the devil and his supporters promised in the Bible was at hand.

Posthumous Acclaim

In the decades after his death, Botticelli's reputation and legacy remained quite modest. Few among his students earned even a measure of renown. Until the late eighteenth century Botticelli was not counted among the great artists of the Renaissance and was remembered primarily as a contributor to the painting of the Sistine Chapel. Only in the nineteenth century did his mythological paintings, now considered his greatest achievements, receive wide acclaim, thanks largely to the admiration of the Pre-Raphaelite Brotherhood, a movement of artists devoted to Renaissance ideals. Since that time the brilliance and importance of Botticelli's work have been fully appreciated.

FURTHER READING

Deimling, Barbara. *Botticelli.* Cologne, 2000.

Lightbown, Ronald. *Sandro Botticelli: Life and Work.* 2nd ed. New York, 1989.

Santi, Bruno. *Botticelli.* Florence, 1976.

Zeri, Federico. *Botticelli: The Allegory of Spring.* Translated by Susan Scott. Richmond Hill, ON, 2000.

Eric Nelson

SEE ALSO

- Florence • Humanism and Learning
- Leonardo da Vinci • Medicis, The • Michelangelo
- Papacy • Platonism • Raphael • Rome

Bramante, Donato

DONATO BRAMANTE (1444–1514) BROUGHT THE ANCIENT ROMAN STYLE OF ARCHITECTURE TO PREEMINENCE IN THE HIGH RENAISSANCE. ACCLAIMED IN THEIR OWN DAY, BRAMANTE'S BUILDINGS, NOTABLY THE FAMOUS TEMPIETTO, GREATLY INFLUENCED LATER ARCHITECTS WORKING IN CLASSICAL STYLES.

Bramante took to architecture late in life; he was already in his fifties when his rebuilding of Santa Maria delle Grazie was completed. Note the ornateness of the dome in comparison with his later work in Rome.

Donato Bramante came from a humble farming family in a village near Urbino, in central Italy. He first emerges as a painter in the ducal court of Federigo Montefeltro at Urbino. Here and in the surrounding cities, Bramante would have first seen Renaissance buildings and met and learned from the famous artists and architects of his day, including Piero della Francesca (c. 1420–1492) and Andrea Mantegna (1431–1506). Bramante appears to have left Urbino in 1472 and spent several years undertaking small commissions as an artist and possibly as an architect in the cities of Lombardy, in northern Italy. In the late 1470s he finally settled in Milan and, under the patronage of the duke, Ludovico Sforza, turned to architecture.

Bramante's first major commission in Milan, documented from 1482, was the pilgrim church of Santa Maria presso Santo Satiro. He appears to have drawn on such churches as Filippo Brunelleschi's Santo Spirito, in Florence (built 1434–1487), and Leon Battista Alberti's San Andrea, in Mantua (1470), in his use of a Latin cross with an aisled nave and monumental barrel vaults. However, challenged by a lack of space in the chancel (the part of the church containing the altar and choir), Bramante created an astonishing trompe l'oeil of a barrel vault. The first known example of such an optical illusion, this feature reflects Bramante's early training in the art of perspective. His other major church in Milan was Santa Maria delle Grazie, begun in 1492 as a mausoleum for the duke. The design, in which a monumental interior consists of a dome surrounded by projecting semicircular apses, shows Bramante's growing fascination with apses and appears to have been influenced by his close relationship with Leonardo da Vinci, who was also working in Milan and whose architectural drawings show similar designs. Leonardo's influence reappears in Bramante's plans for the rebuilding of Pavia's cathedral. Bramante also won commissions to design courtyards, including one for the monastery of San Ambrogio in Milan, and a monumental square, the Piazza Ducale, in the town of Vigevano, near Milan.

CHRONOLOGY

1444
Donato Bramante is born at Monte Asdrualdo, near Urbino.

1472
Begins taking commissions in the cities of Lombardy.

c. 1479–1499
Is based in Milan.

1499
Moves to Rome.

1502
Is commissioned to build the Tempietto.

1504
Completes his first major commission in Rome, the cloisters of Santa Maria della Pace.

1504
Begins work on the Cortile del Belvedere in the Vatican.

1505
Rebuilding of Saint Peter's to Bramante's design begins.

April 11, 1514
Bramante dies in Rome and is buried in Saint Peter's.

Cardinal Oliviero Carafa (1430–1511), a Neapolitan cardinal, made his name by leading a papal fleet against the Turks. In later years he became a patron of architectue; this cloister in the Church of Santa Maria della Pace was commissioned from Bramante in 1500 after the architect's arrival in Rome. Bramante is already using classical orders inventively (note how the columns of the upper row rise from the center of the arch below) but not yet with the confidence shown in the Tempietto and in his later work at the Vatican.

A MODEL OF ENDURING INFLUENCE

In creating the exquisite Tempietto, Bramante drew heavily on the ancient Roman models around him. Beside the Tiber River, near the old Roman fruit market, a circular temple to Hercules had recently been restored, and Bramante must also have visited the second-century-BCE circular temple to Vesta at Tivoli. The impact of the Tempietto was immediate. In his *Architettura* (1537–1545), the architectural historian Sebastiano Serlio reproduced the full plans of the building and praised Bramante's role in the revival of the ancient style, while the architect Andrea Palladio considered no other example of contemporary architecture—with the exception of his own buildings—worthy of inclusion in his *Quattro libri* (1570). Little wonder, then, that the Tempietto inspired later architects. In London, Christopher Wren used the model of a circle of columns surmounted by a dome for Saint Paul's Cathedral (1696–1708), while Nicholas Hawksmoor's mausoleum at Castle Howard in Yorkshire (1729) and James Gibbs's Radcliffe Camera in Oxford (1739–1740) exploit the same theme. The Capitol in Washington, DC (1793–1800), is similar in style, and this building in turn served as a model for countless capitols across the United States. Although the Tempietto remains the original inspiration, it is worth noting how flexibly the model can be used. The columns may be arranged at equal intervals or in pairs, and the dome can take on a variety of shapes.

Move to Rome and the Tempietto

In 1499 the Sforzas were driven out of Milan by French armies. Bramante was now in his mid-fifties, and with the fall of his patron, his career might have been considered over. However, he went to Rome and enjoyed what proved to be the most productive period of his life. He had already shown a deep interest in the architecture of ancient Rome, and his buildings had used classical domes, columns, and pilasters (embedded columns), although he clearly derived many of these features from contemporary rather than antique models. With a chance to study the original buildings, he developed a much more rigorous knowledge of how the different classical orders had been used alongside one another. In the cloister of the Church of Santa Maria della Pace, his first major commission in Rome, he showed a new confidence in his own understanding of how he could use the language of Roman architecture to suit his own ends. In the case of Santa Maria della Pace, completed in 1504, he did so in a square two-story courtyard.

In 1502 Bramante received his most famous commission, from the Spanish monarchs Ferdinand and Isabella. He was to design a small circular "temple" on the supposed site of the martyrdom of Saint Peter on the Janiculum Hill. Since martyrs' relics were often preserved in circular buildings, there were Christian precedents for the building, but Bramante preferred to draw on Roman models he had seen. He relied heavily on the rules laid down by the first-century-BCE Roman architect Vitruvius to create a beautifully harmonious building wherein a colonnade of Doric columns runs around a core on which is placed a small dome. (Bramante's original dome was replaced in the early seventeenth century.) The building was planned to be set within a larger circular colonnade, but this larger colonnade was never built. Nevertheless, the Tempietto was immediately seen as a supreme example of the best of Roman architecture translated into a Christian context.

▲ *The Venetian architect Andrea Palladio said of Bramante that he was "the first to bring to light good and beautiful architecture which from the time of the ancients to his day had been forgotten." Certainly in the Tempietto (above), Bramante was the first Renaissance architect to place simplicity and harmony at the core of his work.*

Pope Julius II and the Plans for Saint Peter's

Julius II, who was pope from 1503 to 1513, was a man of iron will and boundless ambition. He was determined to proclaim and enhance the authority of the papacy, not least through the restoration of Rome and the glorification of the Vatican City. In Bramante, Julius found an architect with the power and imagination to help him realize his vision. Theirs was an extraordinary relationship in which the ambitions of two aging men culminated in the fulfillment of a vast building program. In Rome itself Julius employed Bramante to help create new streets, such as the Via Giulia, and a number of churches and palaces.

▶ In his sixties but given new energy by Pope Julius II, Bramante embarked on the redesign of Saint Peter's (he was nicknamed Il Ruinante for the vigor with which he pulled down the old building) and the linking of the Vatican palaces. This extraordinary staircase was built by Bramante to connect the two floors of the Belvedere Pavilion at the northern end of the Vatican Hill. At each turn of the staircase Bramante used a different architectural order, from Tuscan at the bottom through to Corinthian at the top.

Bramante's most important commissions were two projects in the Vatican, where two papal palaces stood—that of Pope Nicholas V and the Villa del Belvedere, which was about 330 yards (300 m) farther up the Vatican Hill. To connect the two, Bramante designed a vast courtyard, the Cortile del Belvedere, with three terraces ascending to the villa. Nothing of its magnitude had been attempted since antiquity, and its significance as a tribute to Roman architecture was enhanced by the pope's housing of his antique statues in a sculpture court. Alongside the Villa del Belvedere, Bramante designed a staircase ramp, again using classical columns in an original design. He exploited the perspective in such a way that, upon entering the staircase, one can look up through the columns to the top. The whole complex stands as a stunning example of Bramante's ability to innovate within traditional classical forms.

By this time Julius had also embarked on a complete reconstruction of the Basilica of Saint Peter. Bramante designed a plan based on a Greek cross (one whose arms are of equal length). The arms were to end in apses; each corner of the building would have a tower, and the towers and apses would be connected by arched passageways. The whole building was to be surmounted by a massive dome apparently modeled on that of the Pantheon, and there would have been additional domes at each diagonal. For this design Bramante seems to have been inspired by the ruins of monumental Roman baths. Yet the project was far too ambitious for two elderly men, and in fact, the new Saint Peter's would take the reigns of twenty-two popes to complete. The central crossing of the existing building is constructed according to Bramante's original plan, but most of the rest, including the dome, which was designed by Michelangelo, is the work of later architects.

Another of Bramante's influential buildings in Rome was the two-story Palazzo Caprini (1510), which Bramante's friend and colleague Raphael later bought. The ground level, which originally housed shops, has simple arched openings set in rusticated stonework, a form of rough-surfaced masonry. The upper story, which housed the grand rooms of the palace, was austerely classical but altogether more refined. This combination, entirely new, was copied in palaces throughout Italy in the next century.

Personality and Achievement

Bramante was always an outsider, both socially and intellectually. He never married and appears to have lacked strong roots. Accounts of his personality suggest that he was usually lively,

Tradition has it that an ill-tempered rivalry persisted between Bramante and Michelangelo. However, by the time he wrote the following accolade, over thirty years after Bramante's death, Michelangelo had apparently mellowed:

It cannot be denied that Bramante was as worthy in architecture as any other man from the ancients until today. He laid the first stone of Saint Peter's, not full of confusion but clear and uncluttered and luminous, and free-standing . . . and it was held to be a beautiful thing, as is still obvious: in such a way that anyone who departed from the design which Bramante had laid down, departed from the truth.

Soon afterward, in an anecdotal biography of Bramante first published in *Lives of the Artists* (1550), Giorgio Vasari gave his own assessment:

Of very great advantage to architecture, in truth was the new method of Filippo Brunelleschi, who imitated and restored to the light, after many ages, the noble works of the most learned and marvellous ancients. But no less useful to our age was Bramante, in following the footsteps of Filippo, and making the path of his profession of architecture secure for all who came after him, by means of his courage, boldness, intellect, and science in that art, wherein he had the mastery not of theory only, but of supreme skill and practice.

Quoted in Arnaldo Bruschi, *Bramante*

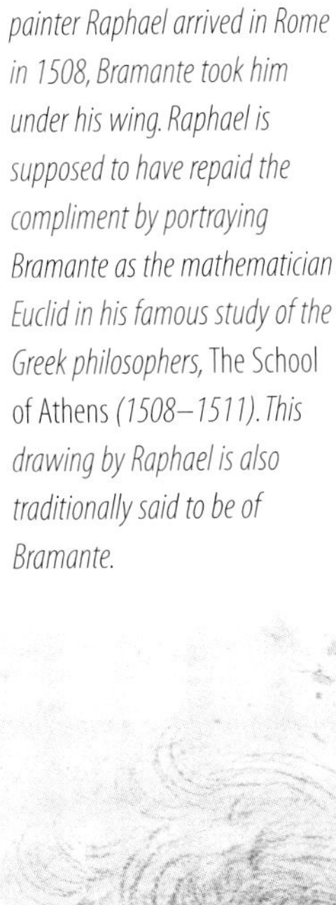

▼ *When the brilliant young painter Raphael arrived in Rome in 1508, Bramante took him under his wing. Raphael is supposed to have repaid the compliment by portraying Bramante as the mathematician Euclid in his famous study of the Greek philosophers,* The School of Athens *(1508–1511). This drawing by Raphael is also traditionally said to be of Bramante.*

friendly, and quick to pick up new ideas, but a far more introspective and insecure side of his character emerges in the sonnets he wrote. In later years he seems to have reveled in the wealth his papal contacts brought him. His energy was concentrated on his work, and he combined immense technical ability with an almost obsessive desire to find the rules that underlay Roman architecture. In the opinion of his contemporaries and many architects who followed him, he succeeded. No architect before him had integrated Roman styles so accurately and so imaginatively into such a wide range of buildings.

Further Reading

Bruschi, Arnaldo. *Bramante.* Translated by Peter Murray. London, 1977.

Summerson, John N. *The Classical Language of Architecture.* London, 1980.

Vasari, Giorgio. *The Lives of the Artists.* Translated by Julia Conaway Bondanella and Peter Bondanella. New York, 1998.

Charles Freeman

SEE ALSO

- Architecture • Brunelleschi, Filippo
- Renaissance • Rome

Bruegel, Pieter

THE FLEMISH ARTIST PIETER BRUEGEL THE ELDER (C. 1525–1569) IS REMEMBERED CHIEFLY FOR HIS DEPICTIONS OF PEASANT LIFE AND FOR HIS REVOLUTIONARY APPROACH TO LANDSCAPE PAINTING.

Most painters became masters in their early twenties; given that Pieter Bruegel's name appears on the Antwerp guild lists of 1551, it is likely that he was born sometime between 1525 and 1530. Though some scholars have argued that Bruegel came from the Belgian village of Brogel, he was probably born near the city of Breda, in the duchy of Brabant, an area of cultural and commercial importance in present-day southern Netherlands and central and northern Belgium. His surname, which he spelled Brueghel until 1559, may be a toponym (an indication of his birthplace) or a patronymic (a derivation of his father's name). His sons, the painters Jan and Pieter the Younger, along with their descendants, always included the *h* in the spelling of the name.

Training and Formative Influences

The principal source for information about Bruegel's training and early life is *Het Schilderboeck (The Painter's Book),* written by the Dutch scholar Carel van Mander and published in 1604. Van Mander claims that Bruegel was apprenticed to the artist Pieter Coeck van Aelst (1502–1550), who ran studios in Brussels and Antwerp. This assertion may be true—indeed, Bruegel married Coeck's daughter Mayken in 1563. Nevertheless, no influence of Coeck's heavily Italianized style of painting is found in Bruegel's works. Even Bruegel's lengthy stay in Italy (1552–1554) does not appear to have given him a taste for the Italianate style popular among many of his northern European contemporaries. Bruegel eschewed classical subject matter altogether, and the carefully ordered, monumental figural compositions that define the painting of the Italian Renaissance appear only in Bruegel's later works. Bruegel's travels in Italy did, however, influence his artistic sensibilities. The Italian countryside, particularly its alpine regions, imprinted themselves on Bruegel's mind and inspired the artist's mature style.

The busy composition and numerous fantastic creatures of The Fall of the Rebel Angels *(1562) demonstrate the influence of the painter Hieronymus Bosch on the young Pieter Bruegel. Saint Michael, resplendent in golden armor, leads the angels in their attempt to vanquish the monsters let loose upon the earth.*

ITALIANISM IN NORTHERN PAINTING

Numerous northern European artists of the sixteenth century traveled to Italy—and in particular, Rome—in order to visit the newly rediscovered classical ruins and to witness the revolutionary technical advances being made by the painters of the High Renaissance. A certain degree of transalpine cultural exchange already existed during the Middle Ages, but as a result of an increase in international trade, improvements in roads, and greater political stability, from the sixteenth century it was much easier for artists to travel throughout the Italian peninsula.

Techniques developed by late medieval Italian painters, notably Giotto di Bondone (1267–1337), appear with increasing regularity in northern art from the early fourteenth century. Such techniques include the experimental use of illusory perspective—that is, the illustration of three-dimensional space on the flat surface of a painting—and the use of modeling (subtle shading) to indicate the volume of a figure (as opposed to the more linear techniques that were traditionally employed in medieval art).

In Flanders in the early sixteenth century, there was great demand for paintings in the Italianate style. Artists who worked in this style, called Romanists, included the Flemish painters Jan Gossaert (known as Mabuse; c. 1478–c. 1532), Bernard van Orley (c. 1492–1542), and Pieter Coeck van Aelst. By drawing upon ancient mythology for their subject matter, Romanists were able to explore a new range of subjects and compositions while meeting the demands of their classically educated humanist patrons. Romanists also borrowed visual elements from Italian paintings and, at times, from the Italian landscape—for instance, by setting their religious paintings among classical ruins rather than in the bourgeois homes found in northern cities and by populating them not with the slim, rather attenuated figures traditionally used but with solid, monumental figures arranged in classical poses and dressed in flowing ancient garments. Recently developed in Italy, the eye-level viewpoint (which gives the viewer the sense of standing within the painted space) begins to replace the more extreme view from above or below that was formerly favored by the painters of northern Europe.

Back in Antwerp, Bruegel designed engravings for the Four Winds publishing house, which was owned by the Antwerp engraver Hieronymus Cock (1510–1570). Cock, a scholar, art dealer, and artist in his own right, sold works in a variety of styles, including the new classicism imported from Italy and numerous indigenous northern styles. There was a particular demand in mid-fifteenth-century Flanders for works inspired by the Dutch painter Hieronymus Bosch (1450–1516). Many of the engravings drawn by Bruegel for Cock, like most of Breugel's own early paintings, bear the influence of Bosch, whose complex schematized compositions teem with countless figures in a variety of (frequently grotesque) postures. Several of Bruegel's early commissions—*Big Fish Eat Little Fish* (1556), for example—were made into engravings and wrongly attributed to Bosch. Bruegel's *Fall of the Rebel Angels* and *The Triumph of Death* (both dated 1562) provide clear proof that he continued to imitate Bosch into the early 1560s.

This panel, painted by the Flemish artist Jan Gossaert around 1520, depicts Saint Luke, the patron saint of artists, at work on a sketch of the Virgin Mary and the infant Jesus (the Madonna and Child). The strongly classicized architectural details were no doubt inspired by the High Renaissance interiors that Gossaert would have seen during his visit to Rome in 1508.

CHRONOLOGY

c. 1525–1530
Pieter Bruegel is born in the duchy of Brabant.

1551
Appears as a free master painter on the guild list of Antwerp.

1555–1563
Designs fifty prints to be sold through the publishing house of the Antwerp engraver Hieronymus Cock.

c. 1560
Begins to focus on painting.

1563
Marries Mayken, the daughter of Pieter Coeck van Aelst, and settles with her in Brussels.

1564 or 1565
Is commissioned by Nicolaes Jonghelinck, an Antwerp merchant, to make a series of paintings (of which only five survive) of the changing seasons.

1569
Dies in Brussels sometime between September 5 and 9.

Bruegel's Peasants

While the busy compositions and occasionally perverse activities of Bruegel's early depictions of peasant life may have been influenced by Bosch, Bruegel was no mere imitator of the earlier master. In such paintings as *Carnival and Lent* (1559) and *Children's Games* (1560), numerous figures are involved in a range of activities related to the central theme. The figures exhibit minimal individuality; instead, Bruegel emphasizes the collective hustle and bustle of the crowd.

Artists traditionally represented members of the lower classes as simple, rowdy, and earthy, and Bruegel was no exception. Yet in Bruegel's work there is a greater profundity that stems from the artist's ability to empathize with his subjects. Carel van Mander states that Bruegel and his friends often dressed as peasants and attended weddings and festivals with the local folk. Bruegel's works exhibit an understanding of peasant life that, although shot through with humor, displays an affectionate respect for lowly people and their way of life. Bruegel intended his viewers to smile or even to laugh out loud but never to mock or ridicule.

Bruegel's later peasant paintings, though profoundly different, are also gently satirical works of social commentary. The busy figures that abound in the earlier works are replaced by fewer, larger figures conceived on a more monumental scale. The later figures are placed closer to the frontal plane and are seen almost at eye level rather than from far above. The sense of noise and activity remains, but instead of numerous frantic participants, Bruegel captures figures at a precise moment within a given activity. This new technique, in which the essence of movement is conveyed without the scenes appearing staged, has been likened to modern candid photography. Bruegel's later compositions were no less carefully planned than his earlier ones, however, and their candid appearance is belied by numerous carefully placed clues that allow the informed spectator to interpret the artist's hidden meanings.

Altering the Landscape

Bruegel's sketches of Italian landscapes proved popular among his patrons, who gave him numerous commissions for engravings and paintings. Primarily interested in mountain views, Bruegel conceived a landscape almost as an animate being; his landscapes convey the same sense of movement found in his earlier figural compositions. Although people and animals

Children's Games *(1560) includes depictions of over eighty popular games, many of which are still played. Note Bruegel's accomplished use of perspective in the landscape and the street scene in the upper corners of the painting.*

▲ *In* Peasant Dance *(c. 1567), Bruegel faithfully captures the jollity of a village festival. However, this work contains numerous clues suggesting that such joviality is not without its darker side.*

INTERPRETING BRUEGEL'S *PEASANT DANCE*

The large figures in Bruegel's *Peasant Dance* (c. 1567) contrast greatly with the tiny figures that appear in his earlier works, such as those in *Children's Games*. The spectator's viewpoint has also changed; the figures in *Peasant Dance* are seen from slightly above eye level, as if the viewer, walking downhill toward a village, has suddenly arrived on the scene. Each figure is caught in the midst of a specific motion within a riotous country dance, and there is a tremendous sense of movement to the composition as a whole. The figures at the left engage in particular actions—the blowing of a pipe, the exchange of a kiss—that further help to invoke the sounds, sights, and smells of such a gathering.

Bruegel no doubt intended to convey far more to his patrons than an image of peasants enjoying themselves. Ever the social commentator, Bruegel laced his work with numerous elements that hint at deeper meanings. Bruegel and his contemporaries believed that peasants, who lived close to the land and lacked both the advantages and the restrictions of polite society and education, experienced the vicissitudes of life more directly than the gentry or city dwellers did. In *Peasant Dance* local people are depicted enjoying themselves but not in quite the harmless way that might initially be assumed. The occasion is a *Kermess*, a saint's feast, but in Bruegel's painting nobody is paying attention to the small image of the Virgin Mary on the tree at the far right, and not one of the figures actually faces the church at the far end of the marketplace. At the left one couple embraces, and another argues at the door of the local hostelry, while the men seated at the table, clearly having drunk too much, appear on the verge of a fight. Music and dancing (in which even the children take part) might be innocent recreation—but they might also be seen as means by which the devil incites the peasants to yield to their baser instincts.

Hunters in the Snow (1565). *This view from the edge of a northern village onto an alpine landscape is obviously a flight of fancy on Bruegel's part. His landscape is rendered extremely sensitively, however, and the subtle use of a limited palette and of lines of trees to emphasize spatial depth is remarkable.*

often appear in his landscapes, such figures—typically shown from the back and executed with minimal detail—pale into insignificance alongside their majestic natural surroundings. Many art historians maintain that Bruegel's profound understanding and appreciation of nature in its own right remains unrivaled by any painter before or since.

Carel van Mander 1548–1606

The Dutch poet, painter, and humanist scholar Carel van Mander is best remembered for his work on art history, *Het Schilderboeck* (The Book of Painters), published in Haarlem in 1604. An important source of information about the life and times of many early northern European painters, *Het Schilderboeck* is a useful companion to the Tuscan painter Giorgio Vasari's *Lives of the Artists* (1550), a series of biographies of the most influential Italian artists up to Vasari's day.

Though written nearly fifty years after Bruegel's death, *Het Schilderboeck* provides the fullest available picture of Bruegel; owing to the lack of documentation about Bruegel's life and career, scholars have relied heavily on van Mander's work. Van Mander affirms that Bruegel was heavily influenced by the style and subject matter of Hieronymus Bosch. He also notes that Bruegel painted many exceptionally amusing scenes and for this reason earned the nickname Pier den Droll (Pieter the Joker).

Bruegel's Legacy

Pieter Bruegel the Elder died, while in his forties, in September 1569. In the years before his death, he was living and working in Brussels. Although nothing is known about his political leanings, there is evidence that he destroyed some of his final works in the fear that they commented too openly on the conflicts between local inhabitants and the Catholic Spanish regime in the Netherlands. Already popular during his lifetime, Bruegel has enjoyed continued and broadening popularity up to the present day.

FURTHER READING

Friedländer, Max J. *From Van Eyck to Bruegel.* Translated by Marguerite Kay. 3rd ed. Ithaca, NY, 1981.

Orenstein, Nadine M., et al. *Pieter Bruegel the Elder: Drawings and Prints.* New York, 2001.

Roberts-Jones, Philippe, and Françoise Roberts Jones. *Pieter Bruegel.* New York, 2002.

Caroline S. Hull

SEE ALSO

• Bosch, Hieronymus • Giotto
• Humanism and Learning • Painting and Sculpture
• Popular Culture

Brunelleschi, Filippo

The Florentine architect Filippo Brunelleschi (1377–1446) constructed the dome of the cathedral of Florence, arguably the greatest architectural achievement of the fifteenth century.

Filippo Brunelleschi was born in Florence in 1377. His zest for craftsmanship was so apparent that his father apprenticed him to the guild of silk workers, whose members also included goldsmiths. It was as a goldsmith that Brunelleschi was accepted as a master craftsman in July 1404.

This sculpture of Brunelleschi was made in Florence by Luigi Pampaloni (1791–1847). In the 1830s Pampaloni completed several commemorative statues of great Renaissance Florentines.

By this time Brunelleschi's talent was already widely recognized. In 1401 he had been invited to enter the competition to provide panels for the east door of the baptistery of Florence's cathedral. The competition was won by the sculptor Lorenzo Ghiberti (c. 1378–1455); the two men's lives were to be entwined—although unhappily—in years to come.

According to his first biographer, Antonio Manetti, Brunelleschi then left Florence with the sculptor Donatello to study ancient buildings in Rome. Brunelleschi was fascinated not only by the style and proportion of the ancient buildings but also by the principles of their construction. He continued his studies in Tuscany, the region surrounding Florence, and by 1404 was being consulted on architectural works in Florence, where an enormous number of building projects were under way. The city authorities were responsible for a new cathedral, the wealthy guilds were sponsoring their own buildings, and the great merchant families were constructing palaces and churches.

The Cathedral Dome

By 1412 the authorities in Florence were preoccupied with the problem of how to complete the dome of the city's great cathedral. With typical confidence the Florentines had already laid an octagonal base of unprecedented dimensions; it measured 131 feet (40 m) across and was topped with a drum that rose some 148 feet (45 m) above the ground. The usual method of constructing a dome was to place a central beam across the drum, build a timber framework around the beam, and construct the dome around the frame. However, there were no timbers long enough to span such a breadth, and the weight of any frame would probably have been too great for the walls of the base to bear. The problem might have been solved if buttresses could have been added to the outer walls, but no space had been left. In any case, the Florentines despised buttresses as unnecessary decorations. The Florentines were desperate: if construction was halted or, even worse, a structure collapsed while it was being built, Florence would be the laughingstock of Italy.

CHRONOLOGY

1377
Filippo Brunelleschi is born in Florence.

1404
Matriculates as a master craftsman; joins an advisory committee on the building of Florence's cathedral.

1420
With Ghiberti, is given joint responsibility for the construction of the dome.

1423
Is described as the "inventor and governor" of the dome project.

1425
Ghiberti withdraws from the dome project.

1436
Main structure of the dome is completed; work begins on the lantern.

1446
Brunelleschi dies.

Brunelleschi explained his plans for the dome of the cathedral to the city overseers as follows:

The difficulties of this erection being well considered, magnificent signors and wardens, I find it cannot be made a perfect circle because the huge span could not bear the weight of the lantern. I propose to build for eternity. I have therefore determined to use pointed arches springing from the eight angles of the walls. When loaded with the lantern, each will help to stabilize the other. The thickness of the base of the vault must be seven feet and it will diminish like a pyramid towards the top where it must be two feet thick. A second [outer] vault must be built as a protective roof for the first. The parts of this shell, lighter than the dome, must meet the inner vault at the top, where it will be two-thirds as thick as the base.... The first and second courses from the base must be strengthened everywhere by long plates of hard stone laid crosswise in such a way that both inner and outer vaults rest on these stones. Throughout the whole height, at every seventeenth foot, small arches shall be constructed between the buttresses [i.e., the ribs], with strong clamps of oak, to bind and strengthen the buttresses. These are to be built of hard stone, and the walls are to be solid hard stone bound to the buttresses to the height of forty-six feet. Above that the walls should be constructed of brick or some light stone.

Giorgio Vasari, *Lives of the Artists*

This view of the dome of Florence's Cathedral of Santa Maria del Fiore from above demonstrates the extraordinary challenge faced by Brunelleschi in erecting such a complex structure so high above the ground. The outer dome conceals an inner one; the two were built up together, layer by layer.

Brunelleschi's beautiful, light Ospedale degli Innocenti, which provided a home for abandoned children, is one of the first Renaissance buildings. The medallions over the columns, created by Andrea della Robbia in 1487, show babies in swaddling clothes. Babies left at the Ospedale were placed in a box, at the left end of the portico, which was then rotated to bring the baby inside the building. The Ospedale remained an orphanage until the year 2000.

A model of how the dome might look had been agreed upon as early as 1367. Guild regulations required that the dome be constructed according to the model. In 1417 Brunelleschi submitted more detailed drawings based on the model. First Brunelleschi and later Ghiberti were asked to translate these drawings into wood. Their work was accepted, and in 1420 the *Operai,* the city's overseers of the project, appointed the two men joint supervisors of the works. Thus began the real challenge—constructing the dome. Counter to all received opinion, Brunelleschi claimed that he could build the dome without a central timber frame.

Brunelleschi's solution was ingenious. From each of the eight corners of the octagon, he would build up stone ribs layer by layer. In between each pair of ribs would be two smaller ones. All twenty-four ribs would be linked horizontally by brickwork and iron chains. The eight larger ribs would show through the outer masonry. The dome would be completed one layer at a time in such a way that each layer was supported by the layer beneath it and then locked into place when each circle of brick and stone was completed. Brunelleschi had also decided that he would build the first-ever dome to have two shells. The outer shell, he claimed, would keep the damp out and make the whole look more magnificent. In order to prevent the stonework from falling inward, the pitch of the dome had to be steep—much steeper, for instance, than the original model of 1367. The lower layers were the easiest to complete, as they hardly leaned inward, but by 1425, when Brunelleschi was a third of the way up, he had to begin to close the circle. The work became very precarious as the angle of the elevation decreased. Brick was substituted for stone to keep the upper layers light. At this difficult stage of the project, Ghiberti resigned. The two men had fallen out, partly because Brunelleschi, perhaps unfairly, had always openly doubted Ghiberti's building skills.

The Ospedale degli Innocenti

From 1418, as his fame increased, Brunelleschi was consulted on or asked to construct a wide variety of buildings. One of his first commissions was awarded in 1419 by his own guild of silk merchants, who wished to build an orphanage in Florence. Brunelleschi's main contribution was the facade of the building, which still overlooks the Piazza Santa Annunziata. Brunelleschi's work influenced the design of the later buildings that surround it; the square is one of Florence's most beautiful.

▲ This photograph shows the harmonious interior of the Old Sacristy of the Church of San Lorenzo. In the pendentive the coat of arms of the Medici family is topped by a design of the Four Evangelists made by the celebrated sculptor Donatello. The dome of the altar chapel is decorated with an image of the signs of the zodiac as they appeared in the sky in July 1349, when leading figures of the Eastern and Western churches gathered at an ecclesiastical council in Florence.

For the first time Brunelleschi was free to depart from the traditional Gothic style of the previous century and create a design truly his own. Instead of building pointed arches, for example, he returned to the semicircular ones that characterized the buildings of antiquity. Each arch rests on a slender classical column topped by a Corinthian capital (column head). Beyond each arch is a dome that comes to rest on corbels (projecting supports) on the back wall of the facade. On a Gothic building this dome would have been ribbed, and the inner lines of the arches would have been triangular. On the Ospedale degli Innocenti, they are archivolts—that is, they are completely flat. Classical styles inform the whole structure. It has, with very good reason, been called the first truly Renaissance building.

The Old Sacristy of San Lorenzo

In 1419 Brunelleschi also received a commission from Giovanni di Averardo de' Medici to work on the Church of San Lorenzo (Brunelleschi's first church). The first structure to be built was the sacristy, the room where sacred vessels and vestments are kept. Now known as the Old Sacristy, the structure was to rise independently of the main body of the church. Brunelleschi saw an opportunity to create a building whose proportions were mathematically harmonious. The floor plan is a square with the walls rising to an entablature that is supported by columns embedded in the walls (pilasters).The height of the walls measures the same as the sides of the square to form a cube. From each of the upper corners a pendentive (spherical triangle) sweeps upward and joins with the others to form the base for a dome. The dome itself is an umbrella dome—that is, it has ribs inside it. The symmetry of the building is broken by an altar room on one wall. Entered under an arch, the altar room itself has a hemispherical dome.

Brunelleschi's sacristy inspired the design of the rest of the church, which was still under the patronage of Giovanni de' Medici. The extent of Brunelleschi's day-to-day involvement in the construction of the rest of the church is unclear, but he can certainly be credited with bringing mathematical proportion to the traditional shape of a Christian basilica (which was itself based on Roman models). The basis of the floor plan is a central square. The square is repeated to form a choir in front and a transept at either side. On the fourth side the nave extends back the length of four further squares of the same size. Therefore, the shape of the church is essentially a cross, six squares long and three squares wide. Either side of the nave is an aisle half the width of the original central square. Spaced regularly along each aisle are columns at intervals that, again, are half the width of the basic square. Thus, each divided section of the aisle is a quarter of the area of the basic square.

Although the roof of the church is flat, each section of the aisles is topped with a small dome. Despite the elegance of the church's proportions, the interior as a whole is not as harmonious as Brunelleschi's next large basilica, Santo Spirito.

THE PAZZI CHAPEL: QUINTESSENTIAL RENAISSANCE BUILDING

Although Manetti makes no mention of the Pazzi Chapel in his *Life* and although it was built mostly after Brunelleschi's death, its similarity to the Old Sacristy is undeniable. The chapel's origins may lie in a design of the 1420s. Andrea di Guglielmo Pazzi (1372–1445) commissioned the chapel to fill a space in a cloister of the Church of Santa Croce that had been left after a fire. He hoped that his own body would rest there; in fact, he died long before it was completed in 1478 and was buried next door in Santa Croce.

The key to the beauty of the Pazzi Chapel is proportion. As with the San Lorenzo sacristy, Brunelleschi based the plan on a central square, to either side of which he added a rectangle half the square's width. An umbrella dome—another feature shared with the sacristy—rises over the central square. Within the base of the dome are windows that throw light down into the center of the building. A delightful addition to the building is its portico (colonnaded entrance), which has a central archway and columns that associate it with the adjoining cloister. The decoration of the chapel, with grey pilasters against white walls, is not as heavy as that of the Old Sacristy. It is considered altogether a beautifully light and fascinating building.

The exterior of the Pazzi Chapel typifies the deceptive simplicity of Brunelleschi's style. The whole is harmonious in itself but also fits well with the surrounding cloister. The portico may in fact have been designed by Giuliano di Maiano (1432–1490), who was also responsible for the carved wooden entrance doors.

▲ *Inside the Pazzi Chapel the gray* pietra serena *stone (quarried in the hills to the north of Florence) contrasts well with the white background. The roundels, created by Luca della Robbia from 1442 to 1452, show the Twelve Apostles. Donatello may have designed the evangelists that appear on each of the four pendentives.*

Santo Spirito

At Santo Spirito, an Augustinian church that lies south of the Arno River, Brunelleschi had another chance to design a basilica that was wholly satisfying in the harmony of its proportions. The basic cross of the floor plan is the same as that of the Church of San Lorenzo—six bays long by three wide. In addition, the main interior area is surrounded by identical chapels, each (as with the aisle sections of San Lorenzo) a quarter of the area of the central square. Each chapel is backed by a semicircular niche, and each niche is connected to the next by a half column that echoes the freestanding columns in the nave. The height of the building from nave to roof is exactly twice the height of the arcade that runs over the top of the columns. This feature of its design, more than any other, gives Santo Spirito a greater feeling of harmony than even San Lorenzo possesses. Moreover, the windows of Santo Spirito are arranged so as to spread light evenly throughout the interior. Brunelleschi's design for Santo Spirito, executed between 1434 and 1487, was to prove immensely influential to later Renaissance architects.

Completing the Dome

By 1436 the dome of Florence's cathedral was almost complete. In 1434 Leon Battista Alberti, who achieved in architectural theory what Brunelleschi achieved in architectural practice, had been overwhelmed when he visited Florence. He described the dome as "a structure so great, rising above the skies, large enough to shelter all the people of Tuscany in its shadow . . . of a craftsmanship which perhaps not even the ancients knew or understood." All that remained for Brunelleschi was to insert into the finished circle a lantern that would provide the weight to keep the whole structure firmly in place. Brunelleschi produced an octagonal turret with a pilaster at each of the eight corners. To fix it in place, he linked the eight great ribs to buttresses that supported the sides of the lantern. Although the concept was a Gothic one, Brunelleschi was determined to make his own mark, and so he gave the buttresses a unique Renaissance styling by adding classically inspired volutes (ornaments in the shaped of a rolled scroll).

Before his death, Brunelleschi also designed this graceful new cloister (known as the Second, or Greater, Cloister) for the Church of Santa Croce; it was eventually built by the architect Bernardo Rossellini (1409–1464). Rossellini also adopted the style of Brunelleschi for the tomb of the Florentine humanist Leonardo Bruno, a celebrated piece of work that is in the church itself.

Antonio di Tuccio Manetti's lively biography of Brunelleschi was probably written in the 1480s, some forty years after Brunelleschi's death. That Manetti (who met Brunelleschi in the 1440s) considered the architect a hero is clearly reflected in the biography.

He longed for distinction in whatever he undertook. From childhood he had a natural interest in drawing and painting. For that reason he elected to become a goldsmith . . . and he quickly became very proficient in a profession in which he displayed himself most wonderfully. Within a brief period he became a complete master in niello, enamel, and ornamental architectural reliefs, as well as cutting, mounting and polishing all kinds of precious stones. It was in general the same in everything he dedicated himself to. . . . [After the Baptistery competition] he went to Rome where at that time one could see beautiful works in public places. . . . In studying the sculpture as one with a good eye, intelligent and alert, would do, he observed the method and the symmetry of the ancients' way of building. He seemed to recognise very clearly certain arrangement of members and structure just as if God had enlightened him about such matters. . . . He decided to rediscover the fine and highly skilled method of building and the harmonious proportions of the ancients and how they might, without defects, be employed with convenience and economy. . . . He repeated constantly that [the dome of Florence Cathedral] could be vaulted without centering. After many days of standing firm—he in his opinion and they [his opponents] in theirs—he was angrily carried out [of the hall] by the servants of the Operai *and the Wool Merchants' Guild, the consuls and many others present, as if he were reasoning foolishly and his words were laughable . . . he had the feeling that behind his back they were saying: look at that mad man who utters such nonsense. However, he persevered in his judgment with great prudence, caution and incredible patience.*

Antonio Manetti, *Life of Filippo Brunelleschi*

BRUNELLESCHI'S INVENTIONS

Brunelleschi designed a hoist to raise the large and heavy building materials from the ground up to the dome of Florence's cathedral. In compexity and ingenuity the hoist was well ahead of its time, and it became almost as popular a spectacle as the dome itself.

The hoist was operated by oxen driving a shaft that engaged with cogwheels. Those cogwheels in turn rotated three other shafts (the heavier the weight to be lifted, the smaller the diameter of the shaft chosen for that particular task). The hoist had a reversible gear so that the oxen could continue in the same direction, regardless of whether a load was to be lifted or lowered.

Once the stone had been lifted, it was transferred to a crane that was perched on the wall of the dome, its beam balanced with a counterweight. Holding a piece of stone that could weigh up to a thousand pounds (454 kg), the beam swung across the void to the exact place where the stone was needed.

Nearly six hundred years after Brunelleschi accepted the commission, the dome of Florence's cathedral still dominates the city. To the left, the tall and graceful campanile (bell tower), which was designed by Giotto, and the smaller dome of the cathedral baptistery are also at the core of a city whose identity is dominated by the Renaissance.

Among Florence's other surviving Brunelleschi buildings are the unfinished circular Church of Santa Maria degli Angeli and the assembly hall of the headquarters of the city's Guelf faction (those who were loyal to the papacy in its struggles with the Holy Roman Empire). Brunelleschi's name was associated with many other projects besides. He was a man of extraordinary confidence and ingenuity, and insofar as he adapted classical styles of architecture to new uses, he deserves his place as the founding architect of the Renaissance. "He was sent by heaven," wrote Giorgio Vasari in the next century, "to invest architecture with new forms after it had wandered astray for many centuries." The dome of the cathedral must be considered his crowning achievement, and it is fitting that he is commemorated in a roundel in the cathedral itself.

FURTHER READING

Battisti, Eugenio. *Filippo Brunelleschi.* Translated by Robert Erich Wolf. Milan, 2002.

King, Ross. *Brunelleschi's Dome: How a Renaissance Genius Reinvented Architecture.* New York, 2001.

Klotz, Heinrich. *Filippo Brunelleschi: The Early Works and the Medieval Tradition.* Translated by Hugh Keith. New York, 1990.

Manetti, Antonio. *The Life of Filippo Brunelleschi.* Translated by Catherine Enggass and edited by Howard Saalman. University Park, PA, 1970.

Charles Freeman

SEE ALSO

• Architecture • Florence • Medicis, The • Renaissance • Science and Technology

Burgundy

UNDER THE VALOIS DUKES BURGUNDY WAS ONE OF THE RICHEST AND MOST POWERFUL EUROPEAN PRINCIPALITIES OF THE FIFTEENTH CENTURY.

Burgundy, now a region of central France, takes its name from the Burgundians, a Germanic people who invaded Gaul, a province of the declining Roman Empire, in the fifth century. In 534 the Franks, another Germanic people, conquered the Burgundians and absorbed them into the Frankish empire. After the Frankish empire broke up at the end of the ninth century, western Burgundy became a duchy, or dukedom, of the kingdom of France. Eastern Burgundy, united with the southern kingdom of Provence and parts of the Alps, became a subkingdom of the Holy Roman Empire, which was dominated by the Germans. This subkingdom was broken up in the eleventh century, and eastern Burgundy was reduced to the status of a county by the name of Franche-Comté.

▼ *An anonymous sixteenth-century portrait of Philip the Bold, the first Valois duke of Burgundy. A younger son of King John the Good of France, Philip was given Burgundy as a reward for his valor at the Battle of Poitiers in 1356.*

Origins of Valois Burgundy

In 1363 King John the Good of France (reigned 1350–1364), a member of the Valois dynasty, decided to appoint his younger son, Philip (1342–1404), duke of Burgundy. The appointment was a reward for Philip's courage during the battle of Poitiers in 1356. Since the time of the battle, when Philip was only fourteen years old, he has been known as Philip the Bold.

Philip's fortune was truly made by his elder brother, Charles V, who became king of France in 1364. In 1369 Charles arranged for Philip to marry Margaret of Flanders, the only child and heir of Louis II de Male, the powerful count of Flanders. Owing to its flourishing cloth industry, Flanders (part of present-day Belgium) was one of the wealthiest regions of northern Europe. Though officially part of France, the monarchy had never had much authority there, and Charles saw the marriage as a way of bringing Flanders under royal control. Apart from Flanders, Louis also ruled the French counties of Artois, Rethel, and Nevers as well as Franche-Comté (then still part of the Holy Roman Empire). In 1379 the people of Flanders rebelled against Louis, and he was forced to ask Charles V for help. The king sent Philip, who enhanced his reputation as a military leader when he crushed the rebels at the battle of Roosebeke in 1382. Two years later Louis died. Philip inherited all his lands and thus became one of the richest princes of Europe.

Philip the Bold's principality consisted of two widely separated parts. The two Burgundies and Nevers formed the southern part; Flanders, Artois—also a rich cloth-making area—and Rethel formed the northern part. The southern territory was administered from Dijon, the northern, from Lille.

THE CRUSADE OF NICOPOLIS

In 1354 the crusading movement was reinvigorated when the Muslim Ottoman Turks invaded Europe and began to advance into the Balkans and threaten the strategic Christian city of Constantinople (present-day Istanbul). The crusade of Nicopolis was called in 1396 to try to force the Turks to lift a two-year blockade of Constantinople. The crusade attracted ten thousand Christian knights from all over western Europe; the largest contingents were the Hungarians, under King Sigismund, and the French and Burgundians, under John the Fearless. As had been hoped, the Ottomans lifted their blockade of Constantinople and headed north to confront the crusaders, who had laid siege to Nicopolis (modern-day Nikopol, in Bulgaria) on the Danube River. The disaster that unfolded was due almost entirely to the pride and ill discipline of the French and Burgundians, who demanded the honor of leading the attack. As they did so often during the Hundred Years War, the French and their Burgundian comrades simply charged headlong at the enemy. Turkish horse archers showered the crusaders with arrows, all the time leading them on toward a hidden belt of sharpened stakes, which brought many of their horses down. Many other knights were thrown by their panicked horses. The crusaders continued their attack on foot but were surrounded by the spahis, the elite Ottoman heavy cavalry. Seeing that their situation was hopeless, the crusaders surrendered en masse. Most were later ransomed and returned home to a hero's welcome. The blockade of Constantinople was resumed. No further major crusading expeditions were launched after Constantinople finally fell to the Turks in 1453, and the movement died out in the sixteenth century.

▲ *This image, from the fifteenth-century* Chronicle of Ulrich von Richental, *depicts a knight pledging loyalty to King Sigismund of Hungary. A leading supporter of the crusading movement, Sigismund fought bravely at Nicopolis in support of the French and Burgundians.*

The main ambition of Philip and his successors was to unite the two parts of their principality by winning possession of the lands in between, either by diplomacy or war. It was to the dukes' advantage that they held lands in both France and the Holy Roman Empire. This situation allowed them to play the two rulers off against each other. It was also to the dukes' advantage that France and England were locked in the Hundred Years War. French kings were willing to pay a high price to ensure the loyalty of the Valois dukes. The dukes also had a powerful means of influencing the English: Flanders was the most important market for wool, England's chief export. English kings were therefore keen to maintain good relations with the Valois dukes. Thus, the Valois dukes could act as if they were independent rulers, even if in law they were not.

John the Fearless

Philip's ambitions received a helping hand when his nephew, King Charles VI (reigned 1380–1422), went mad in 1392. Philip became the effective ruler of France and ruthlessly used crown revenues to his own advantage. These revenues helped Philip finance a crusade against the Muslim Turks in 1396. The crusade, which was led by his son John the Fearless (1371–1419), ended in a disastrous defeat at the Battle of Nicopolis. John was taken prisoner and ransomed for a huge sum. Yet the failure of the crusade did no harm to the reputations of either John or Philip. The mere fact that they had lived up to chivalric ideals and had been prepared to defend Christendom when other princes had failed to act greatly enhanced their prestige.

When Philip the Bold died in 1404, he was succeeded as duke by John the Fearless. John tried to maintain his father's control over King Charles VI and the royal finances, but he was outmaneuvered by the king's brother, Duke Louis of Orléans, who had a greater right to act as regent. Realizing that he was about to be shut out of power and influence, John hired a gang of thugs, who ambushed Louis in a Paris street one night in 1407 and brutally hacked him to death. The consequences of the murder dominated the next thirty years of French history.

John tried to justify his action by claiming that Louis had been misusing royal revenues. The charges against Louis were true, but nobody was under any doubt as to John's real motives, and the French reacted to the murder with shock and outrage. Though John regained control of the government, a league of French princes was formed under the leadership of Bernard, count of Armagnac, to oppose the Burgundian domination. An intermittent civil war broke out between the Burgundians and their Armagnac opponents. John lost control of the government once again in 1413, when a popular uprising forced him to flee Paris. He was not able to return until 1418 and then only with an army behind him. By this time John had begun to contemplate an alliance with England; he had remained neutral during King Henry V's successful Agincourt campaign against the French in 1415. In September 1419 the dauphin, the future king Charles VII, invited John to a parley on a bridge at Montereau. As John knelt to greet the dauphin, he was murdered by the royal guards.

This depiction of the 1419 assassination of Duke John the Fearless is taken from a manuscript by Enguerrand de Monstrelet, who chronicled the latter stages of the Hundred Years War. The duke's murder on the bridge of Montereau by royal guards forced his son Philip the Good into an alliance with England.

Philip the Good

The circumstances of John the Fearless's death left his successor, his son Philip the Good (1396–1467), with little choice but to seek a full alliance with England. Philip's defection to the English swung the course of the Hundred Years War strongly in England's favor. In 1420 Henry V of England concluded the Treaty of Troyes with Charles VI of France. This treaty gave England control of northern France, including Paris, and disinherited the dauphin by making Henry heir to the French throne. The treaty was repudiated by the dauphin, and so the war continued. Even after the death of both Henry V and Charles VI in 1422, the English continued to make territorial gains. Concerned that the balance of power was shifting too greatly toward England, Philip gave his allies little active support. After Joan of Arc revived French resistance, Philip began to seek a reconciliation with the new French king, Charles VII. By the Treaty of Arras in 1435, Philip abandoned his alliance with England in return for territorial concessions. This treaty was the turning point of the Hundred Years War. Within twenty years the English were expelled from France.

While the war continued, Philip the Good was actively expanding his territories in the Holy Roman Empire. By 1451 he controlled most of the Low Countries (present-day Belgium and the Netherlands) and Luxembourg and was trying to unite them into a single principality under a centralized government. Resistance by the independent-minded cities of Ghent and Bruges was brutally put down. However, Philip enjoyed only limited success, and at the time of his death, Valois Burgundy still lacked administrative cohesion. Every county and city still had its own laws and customs.

Owing to their ambition to control the French crown, the first two Valois dukes had spent more of their time living in France than in

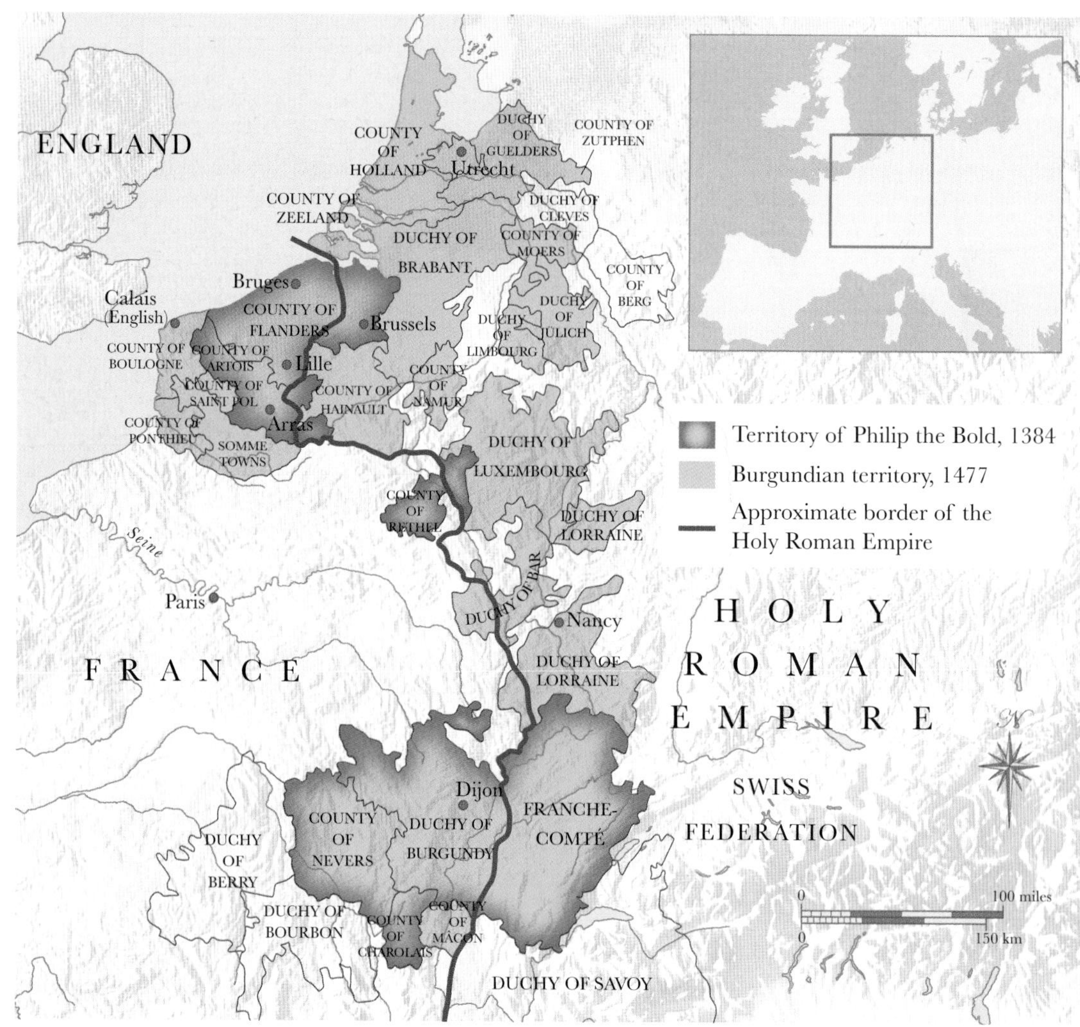

The Valois dukes of Burgundy controlled territories whose location between the lands of the king of France and those of the Holy Roman emperor gave Burgundy supreme strategic importance and made the dukes key players in European politics.

THE ORDER OF THE GOLDEN FLEECE

Burgundy under Duke Philip the Good was a wealthy principality, but it had no natural political, cultural, or geographical unity. The counties, duchies, and towns that made up Philip's dominions had their own customs and laws; some belonged to France, others to the Holy Roman Empire. Philip's subjects included speakers of French, German, and Netherlandish who had no sense of common identity. The nobility, politically the most important class, had no tradition of working together for a common goal and had never been united in loyalty to a common ruler. Philip tried to remedy this weakness in his principality by founding the exclusive chivalric Order of the Golden Fleece *(Toison d'Or)*. In doing so, Philip was emulating other late medieval rulers, such as King Edward III of England, who founded orders of chivalry as a form of elite club to create a sense of corporate identity among the nobles and strengthen their relationship with the crown.

Membership in the Order of the Golden Fleece brought valuable privileges: a member also automatically became a member of the Council of State, and he could be tried in court only by the duke and fellow members of the order. At first, the order was limited to only twenty-four members, but membership was later increased to thirty-one. In return for their privileges, members swore allegiance to the duke and promised to defend his lands and join him if he went on crusade. In public, members always had to wear the insignia (official emblem) of the order. This emblem combined a golden fleece with the ducal symbol of the flint and steel striking sparks. The incorporation of the ducal insignia was a clear statement that the duke was head of the order and that those who wore the insignia were his men. New members were given a copy of the laws of the order and were expected to set high standards of behavior. Those who fell short of these standards could be suspended while their behavior was investigated. The punishment for the three most serious offenses—treason, heresy, and cowardice in battle—was expulsion from the order and public disgrace.

their own principality. Philip the Good had no such opportunities and instead emphasized his independence by spending little time in France. There was talk that the Holy Roman emperor Frederick III had offered Philip a crown in 1447. Accepting this offer would have been tantamount to a declaration of independence; the offer came to nothing, however. Because they were the wealthiest part of his principality, Philip spent most of his time in the Low Countries, and by the 1450s Brussels had emerged as the effective capital of Valois Burgundy. The wealth of the Low Countries was such that Philip's income of 900,000 ducats in 1455 was equal to that of the Republic of Venice and twice that of the papacy.

Chivalry in Action

Although the armored knight no longer dominated the battlefield in the fifteenth century, chivalry remained the code of conduct most admired by the nobility. Philip the Good's founding of the exclusive Order of the Golden Fleece, to which only the most favored of his nobles were admitted, was intended to enhance his image as a chivalric ruler.

In this painting by the Flemish Renaissance artist Rogier van der Weyden, Duke Philip the Good wears the insignia of the chivalric Order of the Golden Fleece.

▲ *Knights in the tourney yard at a tournament, from a fifteenth-century Flemish book of chivalric tales. The dukes of Burgundy held spectacular tournaments in order to increase the glamour and prestige of their court.*

Philip was a lavish sponsor of tournaments. In peacetime tournaments were a great opportunity for young ambitious knights to show off their skills in the hope that they might be recruited into the service of a wealthy lord. Knights from all over Europe flocked to Philip's tournaments; the Burgundian court possessed a cosmopolitan glamor that no European ruler could match. Philip continued the family tradition of commitment to the crusading movement by paying for the upkeep of warships in the Mediterranean to oppose the Ottoman Turks.

The final defeat of England (in 1453) in the Hundred Years War changed relations between France and Burgundy. Burgundy could now be seen for what it was—a challenge to the territorial integrity of the French kingdom. The reconciliation effected by the Treaty of Arras had never been a very sincere one, at least as far as Charles VII was concerned. Charles continued to see Burgundy as a threat to the monarchy. He never fulfilled the terms of the treaty; he even broke his promise to bring the murderers of John the Fearless to justice. Relations became even more strained when Philip gave refuge to Charles VII's son, the future Louis XI, after Louis rebelled against his father's authority. Relations continued to deteriorate after Louis became king in 1461. In 1465 Philip joined other powerful French nobles in the so-called War of the Common Weal, an unsuccessful attempt to limit the growing power of the monarchy.

Charles the Rash and the Fall of Valois Burgundy

When Philip the Good died in 1467, his son Charles (1433–1477) succeeded him. Charles, an impetuous man who fully deserved his nickname—the Rash—enlarged Valois Burgundy to its greatest extent but was also responsible for its downfall. Charles was even more vigorous in asserting Burgundy's independence than his father had been. His ambition was probably to turn Burgundy into an independent kingdom stretching from the North Sea to the Mediterranean. To do so, he needed to conquer Lorraine, which separated the two Burgundies from the Low Countries, and to regain the former Burgundian territories in Provence and the Alps. Charles also needed to persuade the Holy Roman emperor Frederick III to recognize Burgundy as a kingdom. Even the most powerful feudal principality was ultimately merely a collection of estates and rights that could easily be broken up if its ruler died without a male heir. As an independent sovereign state, Burgundy would have a much better chance of long-term survival. Unfortunately for Charles, Frederick refused him a crown.

Charles's ambitious plans made him numerous enemies abroad and alienated his own subjects, who were being taxed very heavily to pay for them. This was a situation Louis XI—whose scheming earned him the nickname the Universal Spider—could all too easily exploit. Louis persuaded Charles's most able advisers, notably Philippe de Commynes, to change sides and then exploited their knowledge of the duke's character. When Charles allied with Edward IV of England, Louis simply paid the invading English army a great deal of money to go home. Although Charles was left without major allies, he recklessly continued to pursue his territorial ambitions. Louis continued to undermine Charles by giving money to the duke of Lorraine and the Swiss, enemies of the Valois who were threatened by Charles's territorial ambitions. The Swiss, reputed to be the toughest infantry soldiers in Europe, defeated Charles twice in 1476. With a demoralized and much depleted army, Charles faced the Swiss again at Nancy in January 1477. His officers advised him to withdraw and wait for reinforcements, but true to his nickname, he would not listen. In the battle that followed, the Burgundian army was routed, and Charles was killed.

Court and Culture

In their effort to appear the equals of the monarchs of Europe, Philip the Good and Charles the Rash were both lavish patrons of the arts. They commissioned writers to glorify the great deeds of the dukes in immensely popular chivalric tales. Master illuminators produced lavishly illustrated Books of Hours and other devotional books. The walls of the ducal courts and banqueting halls were decorated with beautiful tapestries. One of the most famous depicted the ancient legend of Jason and the Argonauts, whose quest for the golden fleece had inspired the founding of the order of that name. The court at Dijon was famous for its choral music. Jan van Eyck, Rogier van der Weyden, and many other Flemish painters enjoyed the patronage of the dukes. Splendid Gothic palaces and chapels were built at Dijon, Brussels, and Bruges (they have not survived). The dukes also liked to impress with their lavish hospitality and extravagantly expensive clothing.

The Fate of Burgundy

Charles the Rash left as his only heir his nineteen-year-old daughter Mary. Louis XI hoped to force Mary into marriage with his son and heir the

▲ An unattributed seventeenth-century portrait of Charles the Rash, the last Valois duke of Burgundy. A reckless general, Charles was killed fighting the Swiss at Nancy in 1477.

In 1498 a Burgundian courtier and confidant of Charles the Rash who defected to the French rues the demise of the Valois, whom the wheel of fortune raised up and then brought crashing down:
Our Lord in one fell swoop caused the overthrow of this great and magnificent edifice; this powerful house which has produced and maintained so many fine gentlemen and which was so renowned both far and wide for so many more great victories and good fortune and God's favor for a hundred and twenty years whilst all its neighbors like France, England and Spain were suffering. And all of them had on some occasion to come to seek help from Burgundy. . . . On all sides I have seen this family honored and then suddenly overthrown and turned upside down and its prince and people more desolated and defeated than any of its neighbors.

Philippe de Commynes, *Memoires*

▲ *This Crucifixion scene forms part of a book of hours (a devotional prayer book) made in Utrecht, in the present-day Netherlands, for Yolande de Lalaing, the wife of a leading Burgundian courtier.*

future Charles VIII and thereby bring all the Burgundian lands into the French kingdom. However, Louis mishandled the affair, and Mary managed to preserve most of her inheritance intact by marrying Maximilian of Austria, the eldest son of the Hapsburg emperor Frederick III. Louis had to be content with conquering the duchy of Burgundy and Artois and leaving the wealthy Low Countries as part of the Hapsburg empire. Louis's failure had serious consequences for France. When the Spanish throne passed to the Hapsburgs in 1516, France faced the threat of encirclement by the Hapsburgs.

Valois Burgundy came into existence at a time of weak French royal authority. While royal authority remained weak, Burgundy prospered, but as soon as the French monarchy began to recover under Charles VIII and Louis XI, Burgundy's fortunes began to wane. Even had Charles the Rash not gotten himself killed fighting an unnecessary battle, Valois Burgundy was probably living on borrowed time by 1477. The main historical significance of Valois Burgundy was that it united the many feudal lordships of the Low Countries into a single political unit for the first time. It is from this achievement that the origins of the modern kingdoms of Belgium and the Netherlands can be traced.

Philippe de Commynes 1447–1511

The most important source of information about the fall of Valois Burgundy is Philippe de Commynes's *Memoires*. Commynes was one of a new breed of courtiers who owed his influence to the quality of his political advice rather than military ability or high birth. Commynes had little respect for the code of chivalry. For his ruthlessly realistic attitude to politics, he has often been compared with his near contemporary, the Italian statesman Niccolò Machiavelli (1469–1527).

The son of a knight of the Golden Fleece, Commynes was born in Flanders and brought up at the Burgundian court. In 1464 he became squire to Charles the Rash and took part in Charles's early military campaigns. When Charles became duke in 1467, Commynes became a trusted counselor and went on embassies to Spain, Brittany, and England. In 1468 Commynes negotiated an agreement between Charles and King Louis XI. Impressed by Commynes's diplomatic skills, Louis persuaded him to change sides in 1472. In Louis's service, Commynes used his inside knowledge against his former employer. After Louis's death, Commynes fell from favor and was jailed for several months for plotting against the government. Restored to favor by king Charles VIII in 1489, Commynes became ambassador to Venice. He wrote his memoirs in 1498, and they quickly became a best seller.

Further Reading

Commynes, Philippe de. *Memoirs: The Reign of Louis XI, 1461–83.* Translated by Michael Jones. Harmondsworth, UK, 1972.

Vale, M. G. A. *War and Chivalry: Warfare and Aristocratic Culture in England, France, and Burgundy at the End of the Middle Ages.* Athens, GA, 1981.

Vaughan, Richard. *Philip the Bold: The Formation of the Burgundian State.* Rochester, NY, 2002.

———. *Valois Burgundy.* Hamden, CT, 1975.

John Haywood

SEE ALSO

• Agincourt, Battle of • Chivalry • Eyck, Jan van • France • Holy Roman Empire • Hundred Years War • Switzerland

Byzantium

LOCATED AT THE MEETING POINT OF EUROPE AND ASIA AND OF THE MEDITERRANEAN AND BLACK SEAS, THE ANCIENT CITY OF BYZANTIUM BEQUEATHED A SIGNIFICANT CULTURAL LEGACY TO THE RENAISSANCE.

The city of Byzantium stood in the ancient region of Thrace on the western shore of the Bosporus, the narrow channel that runs south from the Black Sea via the Sea of Marmara, the Dardanelles, and the Aegean Sea to the Mediterranean Sea. (The site is occupied by the present-day Turkish city of Istanbul.) From the eighth century BCE, Greeks began to migrate into Thrace from the south and establish colonies on the Thracian coasts. One of these colonies was Byzantium, founded in 660 BCE.

From around 200 BCE the region fell under the control of the Roman Empire. At first Byzantium enjoyed relative freedom under the Romans, but over the years Roman imperial control tightened. In 324 CE, after a series of civil wars, Constantine I defeated his rivals and became sole emperor of the entire Roman Empire. In 330 he chose the site of Byzantium for his new capital. He named the city New Rome, but the people came to call it Constantine's City, or Constantinople. The largest and perhaps most splendid city of the Middle Ages, Constantinople shared the glories of the Byzantine (Eastern Roman) Empire until 1453, by which time the shrunken empire consisted of little more than the city itself. In that year the Ottoman Turks conquered and secured Constantinople. It was officially renamed Istanbul in 1930.

Byzantine Culture

Owing to its supreme geographical location, the city was a crossroads of European and Asian cultures for centuries. Whoever controlled the city also controlled the passage of ships between the Black and Aegean seas. This responsibility placed the city and its leaders under almost perpetual strain. Byzantium's location also greatly influenced the cultural development of the region's peoples, who influenced one another culturally as they interacted in trade and war. The civilization that developed around Byzantium was a remarkable admixture of great cultural traditions. Many historians contend that the unique Byzantine culture that emerged under the Hellenic Greeks, which was established as the dominant culture of the region by around 400 BCE, remains the region's dominant culture in the present day.

After the fall of the Roman Empire in the West in 476 CE, the cultural significance of Constantinople increased yet further. Not only the heir and preserver of the ancient Greco-Roman cultural tradition, Constantinople was

▼ The artist who drew this picture imagined Constantinople as an English walled city with a church, alehouses, and musicians emerging from its gates. The image appears in the psalter produced for the English landowner Geoffrey Luttrell around 1340.

At the center of this mosaic is Emperor Justinian (483–565); other figures include General Belisarius (the bearded man to the right of Justinian) and Archbishop Maximian (to the right of Belisarius). The mosaic reflects the idea that the emperor is a political leader (he is adorned with a jeweled crown) and a religious leader (the golden bowl he is holding represents the body of Jesus Christ).

also the headquarters of Eastern Christianity. Constantine had legalized Christianity in 313; within seventy years it was the official religion of the Roman Empire. The forms practiced in Constantinople and Rome—the two chief cities of Christendom—soon began to diverge. The differences between East and West became irreconcilable, and in the Great Schism of 1054, Constantinople split from Rome.

When the Muslim Ottoman Turks defeated Constantinople in 1453, many in the West feared that the Muslims had achieved their goal of ending Eastern (Orthodox) Christianity. However, the Muslims gave little consideration to Russia, the final remnant of Greek Orthodoxy. In the eleventh century Orthodox monks had entered Moscow in a bid to convert the Slavs. Before long, Orthodox Christianity became so integral a part of Russian culture that the Romanov dynasty even adopted the double-headed eagle of the Greek house of Palaeologus as part of the family crest.

The fall of Constantinople in 1453 marked the end of the political entity known as the Byzantine Empire. What did not vanish was the cultural influence of the Byzantine civilization that had thrived at the entrance to the Black Sea for almost two millennia. The culture that had symbolized first Byzantium and then Constantinople for such a long time continued to influence the residents of the city even after the Ottoman Turks sacked it. Orthodox Christians, though subject to the sultan, still constituted a sizable portion of the population.

The reason for the continuation of Byzantine culture is perhaps best summed up in the writing of the English historian Arnold Toynbee, who contended that Byzantine culture extended far beyond the political boundaries of the Byzantine Empire. Despite the fact that the conquering of Constantinople in 1453 marked a paradigm shift for the city, it did not necessarily result in the same type of shift for the conquered populations, who retained a cultural identity that went all the way back to the Hellenes of ancient Greece.

Philosophy in the Greek-Speaking World

The democratic form of government and the absence of a strong priesthood in Greek city-states combined to create an atmosphere of intellectual freedom. Additionally, Greek trade and colonization put the Greeks into contact with civilized peoples and barbarian tribes throughout the Mediterranean basin and the Black Sea. This experience allowed the Greeks to develop a com-

HISTORICAL HELLENISM

Scholars studying Byzantium are concerned with two meanings of the term *Hellenism.* The first describes a connection between medieval and modern Greeks and ancient Greek civilization and culture. The second refers to a historical period beginning around 1200 BCE and ending in 338 BCE, the year that marks the conquest of Greek territory by the Macedonian king Philip II and his son Alexander the Great. However, Hellenic culture remained vibrant long after the supposed end date of the Hellenic period. Hellenic culture greatly influenced the Romans during their conquest of the Mediterranean region. Indeed, Hellenic culture continued to influence the peoples of the Balkan Peninsula and the eastern Mediterranean for over a thousand years. Hellenic culture even continued to influence Constantinople after the Muslim Ottoman Turks conquered the city in 1453.

Hellenism usually refers primarily to the culture, ideals, and pattern of life of Athens and the cities it controlled during the age of Pericles (a statesman who lived during the fifth century BCE). The term is also applied to the ideals of later writers and thinkers who drew their inspiration from ancient Greece. When used in contrast with *Hebraism* (a word that describes the pattern of life that predominated among the monotheistic ancient Hebrews), *Hellenism* denotes pagan exuberance, freedom, and love of life as opposed to the austere morality of the Old Testament.

The Greek polis, the city-state, unified the people who lived within its limits. The inhabitants of the polis were not kinsmen—as are the members of a tribal clan, for example—but were united as *politai,* or citizens. Athens led the way in establishing an open and democratic form of government. Unlike previous civilizations, the Greeks did not have a godlike ruler who demanded unswerving allegiance (Greek city-states certainly had strong secular leaders, however).

The primary function of the city-state was to promote the development of goodness *(Arete)* and wisdom *(Sophia)* within each citizen. Security from outside invasion, which prevailed through much of the Hellenistic era, gave people the freedom to strive toward these goals. The Greeks made huge advances in the fields of science, mathematics, philosophy, art, and literature; their intellectual achievements underpin much of mankind's subsequent progress in knowledge of the world.

In other ways, however, the Greeks were less advanced. Within a day's journey of Athens, Greek peoples could be found engaging in primitive rituals. Even within Athens ordinary citizens did not tend to travel around unarmed. The Greeks never established a central government strong enough to unify and secure the many city-states that they colonized or conquered. They did not establish a network of military roads, as the Persians did, or an elaborate drainage system, as the Romans did. Although ancient Greece often conjures up images of extravagant temples, its buildings did not compare with those of many Eastern civilizations.

parative approach in their attempts to discover the essential nature of things and man's purpose and place in the universe. They failed to reach definitive conclusions—but such is the nature of philosophy. The scope and intensity of their philosophical enquiry was so far-reaching that it totally dominated Western thought for nineteen centuries. Ancient Greek philosophy continues to be the basis for European philosophy. Greek philosophy dismantled the polytheistic Greek religion and paved the way for acceptance among the peoples of the Mediterranean of a monotheistic religion—Christianity.

This first-century Roman mosaic depicts the school of philosophy of the great ancient Greek philosopher Plato (428–348 BCE). The Greek-speaking world remained a cultural and intellectual center under the rule of the Romans, the Byzantines, and the Ottoman Turks.

This fifteenth-century Russian icon depicts (from left to right) Saint John Climacus, known as the Scholastic, a hermit who lived at Mount Sinai, in present-day Egypt; Saint John of Damascus, the last father of the Eastern church and one of its greatest poets; and Saint Arsenius, known as the Teacher of the Kings, who was first hired as a tutor by Emperor Theodosius in 383 CE.

Byzantine Philosophers

The Greek theologian John of Damascus (c. 675–749) offered five possible definitions of *philosophy:* knowledge of divine and human matters; assimilation to God; preparation for death; the art of arts and the science of sciences; and the love of wisdom. Early philosophy in the Hellenistic tradition is thought by many to have been essentially pagan because of its tendency to challenge an automatic belief in supernatural beings or forces. (Many philosophers throughout history have considered belief in supernatural beings an obstacle to effective thought.) Christians living in Byzantium, however, described the Christian faith as the true philosophy. John of Damascus divided philosophy into two branches, theoretic (dealing with knowledge) and practical (concerned with virtues).

The Byzantine philosopher and theologian Michael Constantine Psellus (1018–c. 1078) founded a school of philosophy in the eleventh century as part of the new University of Constantinople. He headed the school and, by teaching all branches of philosophy, attained a mastery of his subject that was unequaled by any other philosopher in Byzantium. In 1204 Constantinople was sacked during the Fourth Crusade as a result of political differences with Venice. At the crusaders' temporary capital of Nicaea, the court preserved philosophical thought and study by refusing to break the Byzantine tradition of learning.

The antagonism between philosophy and Christianity was an enduring feature of intellectual life in Constantinople. Church leaders did, however, begin to use philosophy as a means of strengthening the faith of the individual. Furthermore, the link between higher education and philosophy made it difficult in later centuries to dispense with philosophy altogether.

When the Ottoman Turks, led by Mehmed II, conquered Constantinople in 1453, the city entered a dark age of philosophical study. Philosophy and higher education had been closely linked in Constantinople. After the Turkish conquest many Byzantine philosophers moved to Italian universities. Among them was Johannes Argyropoulos (1415–1487), who in 1438 had traveled to the Council of Florence (at which bishops of the Eastern and Western churches met together) as a companion of John VIII Palaeologus, ruler of the Byzantine Empire. Argyropoulos remained in Italy for about five years—during which time he learned Latin—before returning to Constantinople. When the city was sacked in 1453, he fled. He spent a few years in Greece serving at the court of Thomas Palaeologus before returning to Italy in 1456 as an ambassador to the papal, French, and English courts. While Argyropoulos was on this mission, Cosimo de' Medici invited him to join the University of Florence. His teaching there revitalized interest in Greek studies. Argyropoulos spent the mornings lecturing on Aristotle and the afternoons giving private lessons to some of Florence's most prominent intellectuals. He became popular and was granted Florentine citizenship in 1466.

In spite of the reputation he earned while in Florence, Argyropoulos moved to Rome in 1471 for reasons that are unclear. In Rome he delivered public lectures in the Vatican on Greek philosophy and literature and continued to translate Greek texts into Latin. He died there on June 26, 1487. A fresco of him created by Domenico Ghirlandaio adorns the walls of the Sistine Chapel, a reminder of the high status that the Byzantine philosopher attained in Italy.

A sixteenth-century Ottoman depiction of Mehmed II, who, though known as the Conqueror, was instrumental in helping preserve Byzantine culture in Constantinople.

Mehmed II **1432–1481**

Mehmed II, also called the Conqueror, was born in 1432. He became the seventh sultan of the Ottoman dynasty and extended the empire's control west to the Danube River in Europe and east as far as the Euphrates River in Asia Minor. He ascended the throne in 1451 upon the death of his father, Murad II. One of his principal objectives was to establish a global empire similar to that of the Romans. He conquered the Byzantine capital of Constantinople in 1453 and rebuilt it into the prosperous capital of the Ottoman Empire. Mehmed authorized local administrators to give his subjects, especially those of Christian faith, religious freedom. The purpose of this policy was to gain the support of religious leaders. Mehmed was just launching a campaign to extend his empire into southern Italy when he died suddenly in 1481

▶ *This ornate Byzantine crucifix from the great monastery at Mount Athos, in present-day Greece, dates from the twelfth century.*

Christianity in Ottoman Constantinople

The last patriarch of Constantinople, the head of the Eastern Orthodox Church, had been forced to flee to Italy in 1451 because of his unpopular belief that the Orthodox Church should unite with the Catholic Church in Rome. An Aristotelian scholar named Gennadius II Scholarios (c. 1405–c. 1473) was chosen by Mehmed II to be the new patriarch. The two men signed an agreement that granted religious freedom to the Greeks. The patriarchate would maintain authority over the *rum milleti,* the Orthodox nation, but would still answer to the sultan. In exchange for this religious freedom, the patriarch had to maintain order and ensure that the Greeks remained subservient.

Byzantine culture continued to influence both Christians and Muslims in Constantinople. The survival of Hellenism after 1453 can be accredited largely to Mehmed II and Gennadius. While some of their successors were not as diplomatic and perhaps not as enlightened, their work allowed Byzantine culture to persist and further diffuse throughout the Ottoman Empire.

The Orthodox Church maintained the flame of Byzantine tradition under the sultans, but the culture was not bound by the city limits of Constantinople. The Hellenic tradition had diffused through the Aegean watershed, some of the Mediterranean basin, and much of the Black Sea basin as well. After 1453 it would continue to diffuse and influence the development of many other European cultures that trace their cultural lineage to the ancient Hellenes. Among them are the Balkan peoples of Bulgaria, Serbia, Rumania, and Albania. The task of examining Hellenistic culture in the post-Byzantine period is made extremely complex by the variety of languages that a historian must understand in order to utilize the primary-source material available. In addition to classical Greek and Roman, a historian needs knowledge of the modern languages of the peoples identified above and of Turkish, Arabic, and even Persian. One historian contends that the student must become a classicist first and then a Slavist, Orientalist, and neo-Hellenist in order to reach an understanding of the Byzantine legacy in the formal culture of the Balkan peoples.

For the Byzantine Christians art and architecture were primarily a function of religious needs. Because Christians were allowed to maintain religious freedom under the sultans, Byzantine art and architecture continued to influence the city and the region and even developed after the fall of Constantinople.

Many of the southern Slavs who migrated to the Balkan Peninsula around the first century CE from an area of eastern Europe known as Pripet Marsh embraced Greek Orthodox Christianity. Under Turkish rule the Orthodox Church played a vital role as the representative of the Slavs and other Christian peoples living throughout the Ottoman Empire. The church also greatly influenced Byzantine culture via its internal administrative network of clergymen.

The Ottoman Turks began converting many of the Christian churches into mosques after the sack of Constantinople. Beyond the city borders

In the aftermath of the sack of Constantinople, the diplomatic relationship between Sultan Mehmed II and the patriarchate of Constantinople proved invaluable to the survival of Hellenistic culture.

Mehmed was a remarkable young man. He was able and farsighted beyond his years, self-reliant, secretive and devious, trusting no one, and utterly merciless when it suited him. But at the same time, he had a respect for culture, an interest in philosophy and the arts, and a genuine concern for the general welfare of his subjects. He should not be regarded as a savage oriental tyrant but should, rather, be compared with the Italian princes of the time or with monarchs such as Henry VIII of England. He was not unfriendly to the Greeks. He had grown up at a time when Constantinople, decayed though it was politically, was still a renowned cultural center. He almost certainly spoke and read Greek; and he was interested in Greek philosophy. With the great city in his power he saw himself as the heir to the emperors. He ruthlessly eliminated any Greek layman of prominence. But once that was done he was ready to give his Greek subjects guaranteed legal status.

Steven Runciman, *The Byzantine Tradition after the Fall of Constantinople*

the monasteries experienced greater autonomy because of their distance from the city and its administrative leaders. Consequently, they were able to build larger structures that served as the model of Byzantine architecture in the Ottoman Empire. Many of these monasteries became self-sufficient and even flourished under Ottoman rule because they were officially under the domain of the patriarchate. One of the most prominent churches of this period was built at Mount Athos, in northeastern Greece. Inside Constantinople the patriarch was subject to special Ottoman regulations that ensured that the Christian churches were comparably less extravagant than the mosques.

Hagia Sophia

The Orthodox Church of Hagia Sophia in Constantinople, commissioned by Emperor Justinian I in 531, is a masterpiece of Byzantine architecture. An outstanding testimony to Roman construction methods, the building is further enriched by colorful materials and ornamentation that exemplify newer aesthetic theories. The church is filled with beautiful figure mosaics, and all interior surfaces are sheathed with polychrome marbles and gold mosaic encrusted upon the brick core of the structure. The exterior has broad, smooth stucco walls with vaults and domes that soar skyward. Many of the city's great Turkish mosques were modeled after the church.

The magnificent Church of Hagia Sophia (Holy Wisdom), originally constructed during the rule of Justinian I.

POST-BYZANTINE INFLUENCES UNDER THE OTTOMAN SULTANS

When the Ottoman Turks sacked the city of Constantinople in May 1453, the Palaeologus family had ruled for almost two hundred years. While the empire's military might was dwindling in the latter generations, it continued to develop the Hellenic cultural heritage that dated to its founding by the ancient Greeks. By means of diplomacy, the Hellenic tradition was able to thrive under Ottoman control and even to diffuse with Turkish culture. Soon after the fall of the city, the once great Christian churches were converted into mosques, and church bell towers were replaced with minarets. Nevertheless, the Byzantine culture that had dominated the development of the city and the region for so long served as the unifying factor for the Orthodox Christians who remained in the city as subjects of the sultan.

An important challenge facing any historian studying cultures and civilizations is to identify the point at which one culture is replaced by another. The origin of the Byzantine Empire as a political entity can be dated to 330, when Emperor Constantine rebuilt the city of Byzantium and called it New Rome. The Byzantine Empire ceased to exist in 1453, when Mehmed II led the Ottomans into the city. Thenceforth, Byzantine culture merged with that of the occupying Turks, and the two diffused. Which cultural tradition was the stronger influence is hotly debated. What is more important, though, is the fact that the Byzantine cultural tradition did not die along with the political entity that was Byzantium.

▶ *Inside Hagia Sophia, which the Ottoman Turks converted into a mosque in 1453, all Christian inscriptions and figures have been covered with plaster and replaced with passages from the Koran. The building was again converted in 1935, this time into a museum.*

The first church to stand on the site of Hagia Sophia was built under the order of Emperor Constantius II in 360, allegedly on the site of a pagan temple, although there are no artifacts to support this claim. It was first named Megale Ekklesia ("great church"). The structure was either partially or entirely destroyed and reconstructed on several occasions. Emperor Justinian ordered it to be rebuilt following the Nike Revolt. It was Justinian's construction that far surpassed all other churches in its magnificent splendor. During the dedication ceremony, Justinian put aside formalities of ceremony and law and entered the church to say a prayer.

When the Turks conquered Constantinople in 1453, Hagia Sophia was converted into a mosque. In subsequent years the interior frescoes and mosaics that exemplified Byzantine artistic style were covered with plaster because Islamic code forbids figural representations. In 1926 the Republic of Turkey appointed a commission to examine the architectural strength of the building. The investigation determined that the building rested solidly on a rock foundation. In 1935 it was converted into a museum.

Further Reading

Gerstel, Sharon E. J., and Julie A. Lauffenburger, eds. *A Lost Art Rediscovered: The Architectural Ceramics of Byzantium.* University Park, PA, 2001.

Hadas, Moses. *Hellenistic Culture: Fusion and Diffusion.* New York, 1959.

Murray, Gilbert. *Hellenism and the Modern World.* Boston, 1954.

Walbank, F. W. *The Hellenistic World.* Rev. ed. Cambridge, MA, 1993.

Yiannias, John J., ed. *The Byzantine Tradition after the Fall of Constantinople.* Charlottesville, VA, 1991.

Brian A. Carriere

SEE ALSO

• Architecture • Established Churches
• Florence, Council of • Iconoclasm • Islam

Calendars

In the sixteenth century religious authorities, both Catholic and Protestant, initiated calendar revision based on scriptural and astronomical information for a variety of spiritual, political, and practical reasons.

For thousands of years, people based measurements of time on observations of solar and lunar cycles and celestial phenomena. The ebb and flow of days, months, and seasons gave reference points for the planting of fields, the conducting of trade, and the holding of festivals and provided some degree of structure and unity for communities all over the world.

▼ *This elaborate illumination of the month of August, made around 1450, is from the duchess of Burgundy's Book of Hours (a prayer book). This page is typical of the calendars owned by nobles. The most important feast days are in red.*

At the dawn of the Renaissance, the principal use of calendars in Europe was liturgical; a calendar made plain, for clergy and laity alike, the dates of religious feasts and fasts. Liturgical calendars were commonly included in missals (books containing the words of the Mass), breviaries (books containing the psalms, hymns and Biblical lessons to be used in church services), and popular devotional books called books of hours. Also popular among laypeople were symbolic calendars of the kind known in seventeenth-century England as clog calendars. Commonly carved on pieces of wood, clog calendars used symbols to indicate the different days of the year. The symbols were often related to activities that were appropriate to that time of year. For example, the feast of Saint Barnabas (June 11) was indicated by a hay rake because this was the time of year to begin hay making. Calendars were calculated from tables of astronomical data known as almanacs.

The spread of printing technology from the late fifteenth century on made calendars more widely available than ever before. Cheaply produced pocket-sized almanacs became very popular in the sixteenth century. As well as giving solar, lunar, and other astronomical data for each day of the year, they also included dates of religious festivals and fasts and such other useful information as the dates of trade fairs, law terms, and high tides and chronologies of historical events. By the seventeenth century it had also become common for almanacs to include astrological forecasts, though predictions were usually couched in the most general terms to save the writer from ridicule if they failed to come true.

Early Calendars

Although there is evidence that many prehistoric peoples had calendrical knowledge, the earliest recorded calendars date from the third millennium BCE. These calendars, developed by the Egyptians and the Sumerians (a people who lived in the southern part of present-day Iraq), were based on observations of the moon.

The modern international calendar (known as the Gregorian calendar) ultimately descends from the ancient Roman calendar. The Roman calendar was originally based on a lunar year of

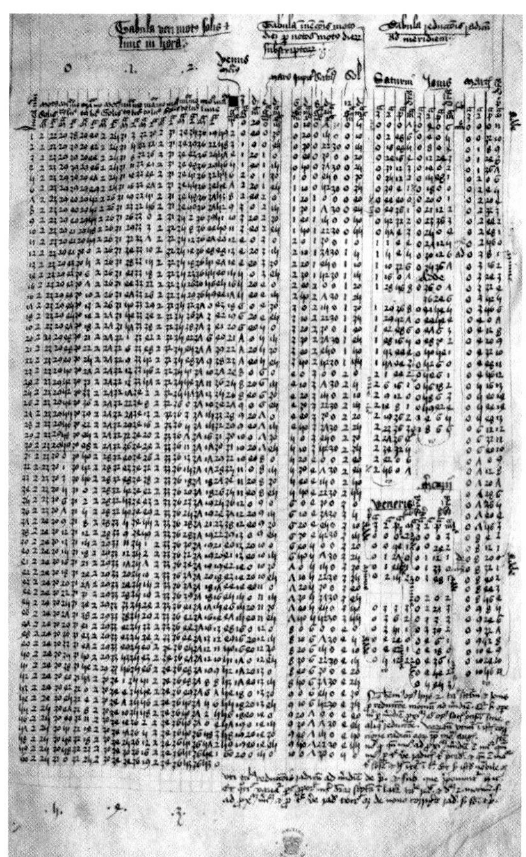

► *This astronomical table, compiled by John Killingworth, provided data for the entire fifteenth century. Scientific information, especially concerning solar and lunar patterns, influenced calendar reform but was often ignored.*

355 days divided into 12 months. Because a lunar year is over ten days shorter than a solar year (that is, the time the earth takes to complete one orbit of the sun), periodic adjustments were needed to keep the calendar in step with the seasons. Every two years an extra month was added to the calendar, and extra (or intercalary) days were also supposed to be added on an irregular basis to make finer adjustments when necessary. However, because these intercalary days were considered to be unlucky, they were usually omitted in times of war. As a result, the calendar was three months ahead of the seasons by the middle of the first century BCE.

Recognizing the need for a reliable calendar, Julius Caesar enacted calendar reforms in 46 and 45 BCE. The new Julian calendar was based on a year of 365 days divided into 12 months; each month had the same number of days that it currently has. No attempt was made to relate the months to observations of the moon. Roman astronomers had calculated the true length of a solar year to be 365.25 days, and so it was decided to designate every fourth year a leap year and add an extra day to the month of February.

In fact, the Romans had overestimated the length of the solar year by eleven minutes and fourteen seconds. Because of this miscalculation, the Julian calendar contained 3 leap years too many for every 385-year period. The net result was that the calendar dates of the seasons regressed by almost one day per century. By the mid-1500s the discrepancy had accumulated to ten days.

Dating Easter

The inadequacies of the Julian calendar were a source of increasing concern for the Catholic Church. The timing of many religious holidays was tied to Easter—the most important Christian festival—so it was a desire to calculate the date of Easter more accurately that spurred calendar reform.

In 325 the Council of Nicaea had determined that Christians should celebrate Easter on the first Sunday after the first full moon after the vernal equinox (the two annual equinoxes are the dates on which the sun crosses the equator and day and night are of equal length). Disregarding natural lunar and solar cycles, however, the Julian calendar had artificially set the vernal equinox on March 25 (which remained New Year's Day until the seventeenth century). The vernal equinox gradually began occurring earlier in the calendar year, and the dates associated with Easter and other feasts became inaccurate. Medieval scientists, including Johannes de Sacrobosco (also known as John of Holywood) and Roger Bacon, declared that the date of the equinox was premature and should be adjusted.

Pope Clement VI hosted astronomers at a fourteenth-century conference. By the next century, astronomers and mathematicians had recorded calendar mistakes and urged church officials to correct them. Scientifically knowledgeable cardinals reiterated the need for calendar reform at the councils of Constance (1414–1418) and Basel (1431), but the need to heal schisms in the church took priority, and nothing was done. In 1472 the German astronomer Johann Müller, known in Latin as Regiomontanus, prepared an almanac that gave what he believed were more accurate dates for Easter than those derived from the Julian calendar. Impressed by Müller's astronomical expertise, Pope Sixtus IV asked him to reform the Julian calendar in 1474. However, little progress had been made by the time of Müller's death in 1476, and it took another century to achieve calendar reform.

The Reformation and the Gregorian Calendar

Although Martin Luther observed in 1538 that the Julian calendar was causing problems calculating the date of Easter, he considered calendar reform a matter for the secular authorities as it was not itself a matter of faith. Following his lead, other Protestant Reformers took little interest in the matter. Although the Catholic Church was more concerned about calendar reform, it saw combating the spread of Protestantism as a more pressing problem. There was no mention of calendar reform at the Council of Trent, which closed in 1563, but the call to reform the breviary and the missal implicitly required reform of the calendar on which they were based.

It was Gregory XIII (pope from 1572 to 1585) who finally ordered reform. A new calendar, compiled by Luigi Lilio and Christoph Clavius, was introduced by papal decree in 1582.

MATHEMATICS AND THE GREGORIAN CALENDAR

The mathematical skill of two men, the Italian physician Luigi Lilio (also known as Aloysius Lilius) and the Bavarian Jesuit mathematician Christoph Clavius, was crucial to the 1582 Gregorian calendar. Lilius, a professor from Naples, was a talented mathematician and astronomer. He envisioned ways to improve the Julian calendar but died before he could share them with Catholic officials. His brother, Antonio Lilius, presented Luigi's ideas to Pope Gregory XIII's calendar commission, and the historian Pedro Chacón summarized them in his *Compendium*.

Clavius, who was the commission's leading mathematician, elaborated Lilius's proposals and endeavored to coordinate religious and astronomical cycles. He calculated feast dates until 5000 CE. Clavius incorporated Lilius's recommendations and realized ten days needed to be removed from the calendar in order to adjust celestial and ecclesiastical events. His explanations convinced the commission to approve the majority of those reforms. The first day in the reformed calendar, October 15, 1582 (which followed October 4, 1582), was designated Lilian Date.

This unattributed painting depicts Pope Gregory XIII presiding over deliberations at a calendar commission meeting. Egnatio Danti, who had served on the papal calendar commission, built the Tower of the Four Winds at the Vatican to celebrate Gregory's calendar reform.

To bring the calendar back into line with the seasons, ten days had to be omitted; thus, October 15 that year followed October 4. To prevent the calendar from falling out of step with the seasons again, the system of leap years was reformed. A centenary year would now count as a leap year only if it was divisible by four hundred (rather than by four, as had been the case previously). In this way 1600 and 2000 remained leap years, but 1700, 1800, and 1900 did not. The Gregorian calendar, as it became known, was criticized by some scholars for fixing the date of the vernal equinox on March 21; in reality, the vernal equinox can fall one day either side of this date.

Acceptance of the Reformed Calendar

Owing to a variety of religious and political issues, acceptance of the Gregorian calendar across the whole of Europe took over three hundred years. In such strongly Catholic countries as Spain, Portugal, and Italy, the new calendar was accepted at once. France—which, though strongly Catholic, endeavored to assert its independence of the papacy—introduced the Gregorian calendar in December 1582, but only after it had been debated and approved in the national parliament. The last Catholic country to accept the new calendar, Transylvania, in eastern Europe, did so in 1590.

FRANCISCVS

▼ *Decisions made at the Council of Trent (1545–1563), which Gregory XIII had attended before he became pope, could not be fully implemented without calendar reform. It was by signing the document pictured here that Gregory, as pope, ordered the reform of the Julian calendar in 1582.*

Acceptance of the Gregorian calendar in Protestant countries was retarded by anti-Catholic sentiments. Only in the Protestant Dutch provinces of Holland and Zeeland was the change accepted immediately. Their early adoption of the new calendar is all the more surprising given that the Dutch were embroiled at the time in a bitter war of independence with Catholic Spain. Other Protestant Dutch states refused to accept the reforms, and when the Spanish-held city of Groningen came under Protestant control in 1594, it reverted to the Julian calendar. In Germany, which was divided between Catholic and Lutheran states, the Gregorian and Julian calendars continued in use side by side. To avoid confusion, official documents were dated using both systems. The widening gap between the two calendars eventually forced Protestants to accept the need for reform. In 1700 most of the Protestant states of continental Europe officially adopted what they called the Improved Julian Calendar, in which the date of Easter was supposedly calculated from the astronomical equinox. In fact, the Protestants were merely saving face: the Gregorian Easter was observed.

England's Protestant queen Elizabeth I (reigned 1558–1603) saw the merits of the Gregorian calendar and was minded to accept it. The queen passed the papal decree to her astrologer John Dee for assessment. Dee recommended some modifications based on his own calculations, which he believed would make the Gregorian calendar more precise, and advised the queen to accept the new calendar. However, the English bishops were unwilling to accept a reform that came from the papacy, and, in the face of wider anti-Catholic sentiments, the queen quietly backed down. Only when popular anti-Catholicism went into decline in the eighteenth century did anyone again dare to propose calendar reform. Finally, in 1750 an Act of Parliament required Great Britain and its colonies to accept the Gregorian calendar. Adjustments began when September 3, 1752, became September 14,

John Dee inferred from contemporary astronomical evidence that the Julian calendar should be adjusted by eleven days instead of the ten days the Catholic calendar commission had endorsed: ***The Romanists have done verie imperfectly, in chosing and preferring the time of Nicene Councell, to be the principal marke, and foundation of reforming the Kalendar.... Christians should regard his [Christ's] birth as the "Radix of Time."***

John Dee, *A Playne Discourse*

1752, and the New Year started on January 1 rather than on March 25.

In Orthodox Christian countries, where hostility to the papacy was even more deeply rooted than in Protestant ones, the Gregorian calendar was not accepted until the twentieth century; Russia, for example, adopted it in 1918, Greece in 1924, and Bulgaria not until 1968. The demands of commerce, communications, and air travel have made the Gregorian calendar the international standard, but other systems—the Islamic lunar calendar, for example—remain widely used for religious or cultural reasons.

Popular Attitudes to Calendar Reform

There was little popular enthusiasm for calendar reform. Many people believed that the date of their death had been divinely preordained. Therefore, some people feared that dropping ten days from the calendar might have shortened their life by the same amount. Others apparently believed that the Day of Judgment had been brought that much nearer. A great deal of cherished popular weather lore was linked to the Julian calendar, and farmers especially were unhappy that it had been rendered obsolete. Opposition to calendar reform was often expressed in satirical terms. In "The Women's War against the Pope for Stealing Ten Days from the Calendar," a German poet refers to the tradition that a wife ought not to prevent her husband from visiting the tavern during Holy Week. In the poem, the wives complain that, owing to the coexistence of Julian and Gregorian calendars in Germany, their husbands have now gained an extra week of freedom by celebrating Holy Week twice. However, despite occasional violent disturbances, notably in England, discontent with the new calendar was usually short lived.

▲ *The enigmatic John Dee (shown here in an unattributed contemporary portrait) consulted other scholars and his own private library in order to develop an English calendar that he believed would measure time more accurately than any other. His mysterious behavior alienated many possible supporters, who misinterpreted his secretiveness.*

FURTHER READING

Blackburn, Bonnie, and Leofranc Holford-Strevens. *The Oxford Companion to the Year: An Exploration of Calendar Customs and Time-Reckoning.* New York, 1999.

Courtright, Nicola. *The Papacy and the Art of Reform in Sixteenth-Century Rome: Gregory XIII's Tower of the Winds in the Vatican.* New York, 2003.

Cressy, David. *Bonfires and Bells: National Memory and the Protestant Calendar in Elizabethan and Stuart England.* Berkeley, CA, 1989.

Richards, E. G. *Mapping Time: The Calendar and Its History.* New York, 1999.

John Haywood
Elizabeth D. Schafer

SEE ALSO

• Astrology • Copernicus, Nicolaus • Exploration • Galilei, Galileo • Leo X • Mathematics • Papacy • Reformation • Trent, Council of

Calvinism

Starting around 1534, John Calvin undertook the reform of his inherited Catholicism and became, through his preaching and writing, the founder of the Reformed tradition in Germany, Switzerland, and the Netherlands, of Presbyterianism in Britain, and of Congregationalism in New England.

▼ *In this engraving by Georg Vischer (1629–1658), John Calvin is depicted reading his* Institutes, *the founding document of the Reformed tradition.*

Calvinism was the last of the great reforming movements that changed the face of European Christianity in the early 1500s. Martin Luther had begun the Protestant Reformation in Germany in 1517, when he posted his Ninety-five Theses on the door of the university chapel in Wittenberg. Huldrych Zwingli began the Reformation in Switzerland in 1519 with his sermons on the New Testament. Soon after, the Anabaptists (led by Thomas Münzer), who rebaptized adults in the belief that infant baptism was invalid, were active in Germany and the Low Countries. Between 1532 and 1536, King Henry VIII of England began a series of reforms that culminated in the creation of the Church of England. When John Calvin began to preach the doctrines that would later bear the collective name of Calvinism around 1534, Reform was already in the air.

While none of the great Reformers agreed completely with one another, they shared certain common principles. Among these principles were a reliance on the Bible, widely available in new printed editions, rather than church tradition; a rejection of the doctrine that Christ and his sacrifice were present during the Mass; and a belief in a single life-changing religious experience through which a Christian was justified, that is, made worthy of salvation. These ideas became the foundation for Calvin's new doctrine. Within his lifetime Calvinism, sometimes called simply the Reformed church, would become important across Europe.

Medieval Catholicism

John Calvin was born into a world in which the practice of traditional Catholicism held sway. The sacraments of the Catholic Church, especially the Eucharist, the blessing and offering of bread and wine in remembrance of the death and resurrection of Jesus Christ, were at the heart of everyday life. The church in which the Mass (the celebration of the Eucharist) was held was at the heart of every village, and the cathedral, the bishop's church, was at the heart of every city. God and the Virgin Mary were always nearby, and the saints were familiar friends. Images of Christ and the saints were in the streets and on the walls of houses. The pope of Rome governed the church; while kings and barons held sway in the worldly realm, priests held sway in the spiritual.

John Calvin 1509–1564

John Calvin was born at Noyon, in Picardy, in northern France, on July 27, 1509. His father, Gerard, was secretary to the bishop of Noyon. Calvin was educated in the household of a noble family, the Montmors, whom he would later thank for his upbringing and his introduction to studies. In 1521 he was given his first benefice, a church appointment that required no duties but produced income for the holder of the office.

Sometime between 1521 and 1523, Calvin accompanied the Montmors to Paris, where he studied first in the Collège de la Marche and then in the Collège de Montaigu. He attended the lectures of Mathurin Cordier and perfected his Latin. He also knew the great Greek scholar Guillaume Budé. Around 1528, having obtained his Master of Arts, Calvin moved to Orléans, where he began legal studies. He attended the lectures of the controversial Italian humanist Andrea Alciati and was taught by Pierre de l'Estoile, the most distinguished French lawyer of the period. At Orléans, Calvin began to function as a member of the faculty (he was presented with a doctor's degree on his departure for Bourges). He also met Melchior Wolmar, who taught him Greek and perhaps introduced him to Lutheran ideas.

Upon the death of his father in 1531, Calvin returned to Paris. Sometime before 1534 he experienced what he later (in 1557) called a sudden conversion. At that moment Calvin became (and remained) an avowed reformer of the Catholic tradition in which he had been reared.

In 1535 Calvin went to Basel, where his *Institutes of the Christian Religion* was published in 1536. In his efforts to establish the religion laid down in the *Institutes,* Calvin was a tireless traveler and a convincing apologist who displayed great courage throughout his career. His involvement with Geneva began in 1536 when Guillaume Farel (1489–1565) persuaded him to stay in the city and help establish the Reformed faith. Calvin's first stay in Geneva was stormy; the citizens resisted the form of church government he wished to impose and his use of excommunication to enforce discipline. Calvin fled to Strasbourg, where he served as pastor of the French congregation and published the second Latin edition of the *Institutes* (1539) and the first French edition (1541). He also published a commentary on Saint Paul's Letter to the Romans and entered into controversy with the Catholic humanist bishop Jacopo Sadoleto.

In 1540 Calvin married the widow Idelette de Bure, who died in 1549 (their only son died shortly thereafter). In 1541, at the invitation of the city council, Calvin returned to Geneva. There was some resistance to his authority, and in 1548 an anti-Calvin party held power briefly, but after 1555 Calvin's theology was unopposed.

Among the reformers Calvin was the great scholar. The French version of the *Institutes* helped shape the development of the French language.

The Paris Calvin knew, pictured here in a map engraved by Sébastien Munster around 1530, was the heart of France, a city of palaces, churches, and colleges built around the island on which stood the great Gothic Cathedral of Notre-Dame ("Our Lady").

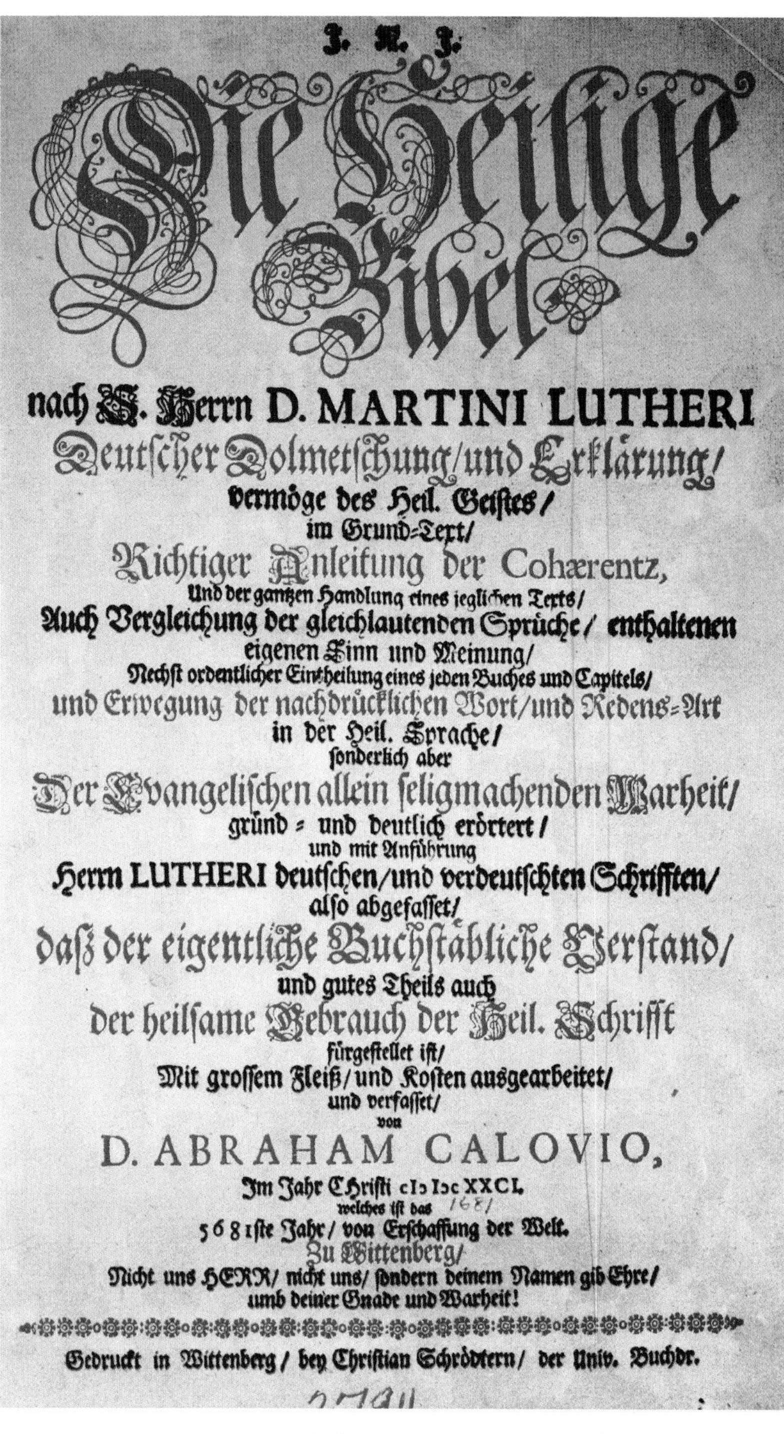
J. N. J.

Die Heilige Bibel

nach S. Herrn D. MARTINI LUTHERI
Deutscher Dolmetschung/und Erklärung/
vermöge des Heil. Geistes/
im Grund-Text/
Richtiger Anleitung der Cohærentz,
Und der gantzen Handlung eines jeglichen Texts/
Auch Vergleichung der gleichlautenden Sprüche/ enthaltenen
eigenen Sinn und Meinung/
Nechst ordentlicher Eintheilung eines jeden Buches und Capitels/
und Erwegung der nachdrücklichen Wort/und Redens-Art
in der Heil. Sprache/
sonderlich aber
Der Evangelischen allein seligmachenden Warheit/
gründ- und deutlich erörtert/
und mit Anführung
Herrn LUTHERI deutschen/und verdeutschten Schrifften/
also abgefasset/
daß der eigentliche Buchstäbliche Verstand/
und gutes Theils auch
der heilsame Gebrauch der Heil. Schrifft
fürgestellet ist/
Mit grossem Fleiß/und Kosten ausgearbeitet/
und verfasset/
von
D. ABRAHAM CALOVIO,
Im Jahr Christi CIↃ IↃC XXCI.
welches ist das
5681ste Jahr/ von Erschaffung der Welt.
Zu Wittenberg/
Nicht uns HERR/ nicht uns/ sondern deinem Namen gib Ehre/
umb deiner Gnade und Warheit!

Gedruckt in Wittenberg/ bey Christian Schrödtern/ der Univ. Buchdr.

▲ Luther's German New Testament, available by 1522, provided the inspiration for the French translations on which the spread of Calvinism depended.

Salvation was a process of becoming holy through developing a love for God that inspired good actions. Christians often failed in their quest for salvation, but their failures and sins could be forgiven by a priest. The sinner also had a duty to make up for having offended God's justice by doing good works. Good Christians might commit sins for which they had been forgiven but for which they had not done penance during their lifetime. Most would therefore spend some time in purgatory and make up in suffering there for suffering not undertaken voluntarily during life on earth.

Indulgences were granted by the church as a means of commuting periods of penance—including the penance undergone in purgatory by the souls of departed sinners. A Christian still living could secure an indulgence on behalf of a relatives or loved one suffering in purgatory, if not by good deeds, then by donating money—toward the costs of refitting a church, for example. By offering Mass for departed relatives, a priest might shorten the time those relatives would spend in purgatory. Thus, in an age when eternal salvation was the goal of life, the church was the most important institution and also the wealthiest.

Changing World

In common with members of any wealthy, dominant institution, the temptation of servants of the church to abuse their power and abandon their ideals was ever present. Most clergymen, bishops, and priests were holy men. Some, however, used the church for their own ends. In 1511 the Dutch humanist Desiderius Erasmus published a best seller entitled *The Praise of Folly,* an enormously popular book in which he poked fun at monks, priests, and bishops.

By 1500 the Christian empire founded by Charlemagne in 800 was breaking apart. The notion of European Christendom was losing ground against the new nationalism of such kingdoms as England and France, which sought a political identity based on the nation-state, with one language and unified territory. Tension between the pope and the princes was high. The rulers of England, France, and other powerful nation-states came increasingly to resent the pope's claim to the right to collect church taxes and appoint bishops.

By the time of Calvin, printing was almost a century old, and books were easily available. The printed Bible made workable the Lutheran doctrine that scripture alone, not the traditional teaching of the church, was the authority for Christians. Printing also facilitated the controversial and apologetic literature of the Reformation, the many confessions of faith and articles in which theologians advanced their

CALVINISM AND HUMANISM

During his studies in Paris in the early 1520s, Calvin first encountered humanist ideas, which dominated work in the liberal arts faculties. He also knew the work of his distant relation Pierre-Robert Olivétan, who exemplifed both Reformation and humanist ideals by translating the Old Testament from Hebrew into French.

Humanists looked back to ancient Greece and Rome as the pinnacle of civilization and sought to reinvigorate intellectual life in Europe by recovering the texts of the ancients. The general tendency of humanism was to elevate mankind's position in the scheme of the universe and to take the labors and pleasures of everyday life as the chief concern of the intellectual. Thus, humanism undermined the late-medieval Catholic belief that man's life on earth was geared entirely toward the the reward of eternal life in heaven.

Renaissance humanists preferred the texts and the learning of ancient Rome and Greece to the Scholastic philosophy of the theological schools that had dominated the late Middle Ages. The humanists' interest in original texts included the text of the Bible. However, humanists studied the Bible not in light of the theological commentaries built up over centuries but with direct reference to the text. In 1516 the Dutch humanist Desiderius Erasmus published his Greek New Testament. In the writings of the early fathers of the church, the Reformers found primitive faith and practice, free from the corruptions of contemporary popular religion.

Calvin embraced humanism to a certain extent. In 1532 he wrote a commentary on a work by the first-century Roman philosopher Seneca titled *On Mercy*. Calvin's interest in the Roman and Greek classics would never fade. Toward the end of his life, in 1559, he founded a school in which Reformed religion and classical studies were studied together. Calvin's ideal of Christian classicism would become the pattern for the hundreds of classical academies and colleges sponsored by Congregationalists and Presbyterians in the eighteenth century.

Nevertheless, Calvin's theology was in part a rejection of humanism. For humanists this present life was the ultimate concern of man. For John Calvin the glory of God would be the purpose of life, and in Calvinism, at least with regard to matters of salvation, God would be everything, man nothing.

ideas. There was also interest in a new kind of history, written by scholars who set aside traditional subjective accounts in order to pay careful attention to factual evidence and chronology—the order in which events had really occurred.

On the one hand, the inherited idea that every person's first duty was to God and the salvation of his or her soul still dominated the popular imagination. This concern was shared alike by the great figures of the Reformation—Zwingli, Luther, and Calvin—and their Catholic opponents. However, Zwingli, in Zurich in 1525, abolished the Mass in favor of a symbolic Lord's Supper, and in Germany the Lutheran revolution had succeeded in spite of papal condemnation. In the field of philosophy, the balance of power was also shifting. The authority of the ancient Greek philosopher Aristotle, whose logical method had governed the Scholasticism of the thirteenth century, was giving way to nominalism, a philosophy proposed by William of Ockham (c. 1285–c. 1349) in the fourteenth century, and to a renewed interest in another ancient Greek philosopher, Plato.

The scholarly Erasmus, painted by Hans Holbein the Younger in 1523, offered a critical view of the church and the priesthood that underpinned Calvin's arguments for reform.

▲ This painting of Saint Augustine teaching was made by Defendente Ferrari in the sixteenth century, when the writings of Augustine (354–430), which emphasized the inability of fallen humanity to achieve any state of goodness without God's grace, had been popularized by Calvinist theologians.

Nominalism and Calvinism

In his battle against superstition, Calvin would come to rely, consciously or unconsciously, on the new philosophy of nominalism. It is possible that Calvin was first introduced to nominalism by the Scottish theologian John Major in Paris. Nominalists rejected the existence of secondary causes in philosophy, and this stance became the model for Calvin's rejection of such secondary causes in theology. In philosophy the prime example of a secondary cause was the idea, or form, a true pattern for every category of created thing in the world (just as there are many trees and many things that are beautiful, for example, so there is an idea of a tree and an idea of beauty). The ideas—as understood, albeit with some differences, by Plato (c. 428–c. 348 BCE), Saint Augustine (345–430 CE), and Thomas Aquinas (1225–1274)—were traditionally thought to exist in God himself. The nominalist philosophers, on the other hand, argued that these ideas were merely products of human imagination, merely names (*nomen* means "name" in Latin), and that in any event, whatever God could create through ideas, he could create without them.

In traditional theology the secondary causes were the sacraments that helped make people holy; the priesthood, whose members mediated between God and man; and the efforts people made, when aided by grace, to do good works. Calvin's denial of the reality of any of these secondary causes was borne out of his conviction that God caused all human actions and all events immediately without recourse to any intervening secondary cause.

For Calvinism the sacraments, sacred images, and any other secondary causes that interceded between the Christian and his salvation were considered unnecessary and potentially idolatrous. The priesthood was likewise seen as an unnecessary intermediary between God and man; the authority that the confessional gave the priest was rejected in the Reformed faith in the belief that every Christian could speak for himself or herself before God.

Nominalism had other implications. If the ideas (or forms) accepted by medieval philosophers and theologians as secondary causes did not exist, beings or creatures did not participate, or share, in common natures. Humans did not share in humanity; trees did not share in treeness. Christians, who were supposedly baptized into Christ, did not really share in Christ. The world consisted of individuals, each related to God by his all powerful will, none related to another except by a kind of similarity of action. It followed that if this one-to-one relationship between God and his creatures described the world, any hierarchy, any arrangement of things or persons according to degrees of quality, was merely conventional or arbitrary. A pauper was indeed as good as a prince, and a layman as good as a priest or a pope. When the forms or ideas are destroyed, what remains for Calvinism is the unqualified and unmediated power of God.

THE CONSEQUENCES OF RELIGIOUS CONTROVERSY

One of the results of religious controversy was that the hold of each of the disputants over the would-be believer weakened. There was of course a core of fervent believers in each of the contending religious bodies, but the ongoing polemics tended to teach many that religion was merely a matter of opinion. As late as the Thirty Years War (1618–1648), fought mainly in Germany and principally on religious grounds, many seemed willing to die for the sake of religion, but after that bloody and exhausting fray, political zeal on behalf of religion was limited to British and American fear of French and Spanish Catholicism. The bitter disputes that raged among the three protagonists—Calvin, Luther, and the pope—left many believers turning away from all three and uttering instead the words of the Twenty-third Psalm: "The Lord is my shepherd."

Encouraged by Calvinist preaching against images, mobs destroy windows and paintings in a Catholic church in the Netherlands in this 1566 engraving by Franz Hogenberg.

Pure Doctrine and Superstition

One way of understanding Calvinism is by considering the contrast between pure religion and superstition. For Calvin pure religion was a religion based on the Bible alone. Calvinism was a religion of words; in Calvin's view the Catholicism he was seeking to replace was a religion of images and sacraments. Calvin saw pure worship as preaching and prayer and nothing else, and although the Lord's Supper was celebrated in Calvin's church, it was understood that this celebration was entirely distinct from the Mass. Calvinists viewed the Mass with horror because it seemed to make God subservient to a priest, who through his words caused Jesus to be present on the altar.

For Calvinists the belief that any human action was effective in salvation was mere superstition. Thus, pilgrimages, penances, and fasting were seen by Calvinists as useless. The reverence Catholics paid to images was seen as especially impure and superstitious. In the Calvinist argument against superstition, there was perhaps a reluctance to accept the consequences of the Incarnation. Christians had always believed that the defining doctrine of Christianity was the belief that God had become man in the person of Jesus Christ. According to the traditional Catholicism against which Calvin set himself, Christ, who had entered history fifteen centuries earlier, remained present in the sacraments of the church, especially in the Mass. For Calvin, Christ was in heaven. The great truth upon which Calvinism rested was that of the supreme majesty and sovereignty of God. Calvin would build his whole system on this theme.

▲ As religious unity dissolved in France, Protestants and Catholics alike took up arms: what came to be called the wars of religion were fought from 1562 to 1598. This engraving by Franz Hogenberg depicts a Protestant attack on the city of Bourges in 1569.

The Lord's Supper, Not the Mass

The Mass had been the center of worship and indeed of Christian life across Europe. Although in his teaching on baptism and the Eucharist Calvin always seemed anxious to avoid the bare symbolism taught by his fellow Reformer Zwingli—the idea that the presence of Christ in the Eucharist depends on the faith of the believer—Calvin seemed equally anxious not to fall into Roman error. The doctrine of transubstantiation held by the medieval Catholic Church taught that Christ is personally present in the bread and wine of the Mass, the substance of bread and wine having been changed, or transformed, into the substance of the body and blood of Christ. (The term *substance* in this context is used in its Aristotelian sense of the underlying essence of a thing.) Since Calvin did not accept the core notion that substances underlie all worldly phenomena, transubstantiation was an idea he could not readily accept. Furthermore, in nominalist philosophy, which insisted upon the radical individuality of every being and lacked any notion that creatures might participate in a common form or substance, Jesus Christ could not be in two places at once. If Christ was in heaven, it was impossible for him to be present in the Mass, and any attempt to represent him as being so was idolatrous.

Calvin's rejection of transubstantiation inspired not only the abolition of the Mass but also iconoclasm, the destruction of icons—sacred images of Christ and the saints traditionally thought to possess miraculous powers. Statues, stained glass windows, and paintings, once thought to aid piety in the worshiper and now seen as idolatrous, were destroyed or defaced. For Calvin claims that the act of breaking bread and pouring wine represented the death of Christ on the cross and that the Eucharist served to mediate between God and man were idolatrous. He considered the abolition of the Mass the necessary sign of the triumph of pure religion.

In a work of 1537, Calvin set down the principle that God exercises his absolute sovereignty in choosing or electing some for salvation, others for ruin.

Only let us have this resolved in ourselves that the dispensation of the Lord, although hidden from us, is nevertheless holy and just. For, if he willed to ruin all mankind, he has the right to do it, and in those whom he rescues from perdition one can contemplate nothing but his sovereign goodness. We acknowledge the elect to be recipients of his mercy (as truly they are) and the rejected to be recipients of his wrath, a wrath, however, which is nothing but just.

Instruction in Faith

Predestination

Calvinism swept away the Mass, sacred images, and the priesthood as at best unnecessary and at worst blasphemous. Such intermediaries, or secondary causes, somehow limited the sovereignty of God, whose every action, in the Calvinist view, was immediate, effective, and unaffected by any kind of human effort. The ideas that Calvin developed from his reflections on God's unmediated sovereignty and absolute power—a power not governed by any form of reason that humans could comprehend—included unconditional election by God, who saved whom he would without regard to merit or desire. Thus, the good effects of the atoning sacrifice of Christ on the cross were limited to those who would in fact be saved. In the Calvinist view to teach otherwise would be to render God's will ineffective. If man could resist grace, God's power would be limited by the human will, so God's grace must be irresistible and unchangeable. It followed that those elected by God for salvation, the recipients of divine grace, would persevere throughout life and attain heaven.

To the idea that the absolute power of God was the direct cause of every human action was joined the idea that humans were unable to take any good action that might affect their salvation. The term Calvinism used to describe man's ineffectuality was "total depravity." Man's intellect and will had been so damaged by the rebellion of Adam and Eve in the Garden of Eden that the first steps toward salvation were impossible without the gift of grace. This conclusion was influenced in part by a pessimistic view of human powers derived from late medieval piety, especially the works of such mystical writers as Johannes Tauler (1300–1361) and Thomas à Kempis (c. 1379–1471).

▲ *In Protestant churches the altar was displaced by the pulpit, as this drawing of the Lyon Temple by Jean Perrissin (1536–1611) shows.*

Justification by Faith Alone

Although Calvin shared with Martin Luther the belief that mankind was justified (made worthy of salvation) by faith alone and not through any human effort, the Calvinist doctrine differed from the Lutheran in important respects. For Calvinists and Lutherans alike, Christ alone was perfectly righteous; his righteousness was a quality imputed, or attributed, to sinful men. For Luther man was always a sinner; perfection was not something within human reach. According to Calvin, on the other hand, the elect were destined to achieve holiness (although a person's attainment of holiness would be the work of God entirely).

In the following passage from his seminal work, published in 1536, Calvin sets out his view of justification:

It is entirely by the intervention of Christ's righteousness that we obtain justification before God. This is equivalent to saying that man is not just in himself, but that the righteousness of Christ is imputed to him, while he is strictly deserving of punishment. Thus vanishes the absurd doctrine that man is justified by faith, inasmuch as it brings him under the influence of the Spirit of God by whom he is rendered righteous.

***Institutes* II:XI:23**

▲ The Council of Trent, depicted here by Nicolo Dorigati (1692–1748), was convened in 1545 to renew the Catholic Church and answer the Protestant challenge.

The Council of Trent, a meeting of bishops held in northern Italy from 1545 to 1563, would insist while Calvin was still alive that believers are justified by the gift of the Holy Spirit. Although the Trent doctrine insisted upon the efficacy of good works, the efforts made by the faithful to achieve righteousness are not unaided but are the product of God's enabling grace. Nevertheless, for Calvin the Trent doctrine seemed to collapse too easily into a theology of salvation by human effort and to attribute to man a goodness that belonged only to God. For Catholics human cooperation with grace is essential. For Calvinists human cooperation is an impossibility.

In the sixteenth century it would have been understood that Calvin was citing and condemning as absurd the standard Catholic doctrine that would be ratified at the sixth session of the Council of Trent in 1547. According to that doctrine, if Christians were justified because the Holy Spirit made them so, the Christian life required the pursuit of Christian perfection, or holiness. On the journey toward holiness, the Christian was aided by repentance, penances, sacraments, and absolving priests—indeed, the whole Catholic system of intermediaries that Calvin sought to replace. Calvin rejected the Catholic doctrine that to become holy required good works that were pleasing to God. If Calvin was right, mankind could be justified simply by believing in the efficacy of the atonement wrought by Christ's sacrifice on the cross, a belief that implied no anxious confessions and uncomfortable penances. According to Catholic doctrine, the process by which God's grace makes believers holy is one in which the human will must cooperate. According to Calvin's teaching, God is the sole cause of the believer's justification.

Calvinism and the Civil Order

In September 1541 Calvin returned to Geneva. During the next fourteen years he established his Reformed religion and the theocracy (religious government) it implied. His *Ecclesiastical Ordinances,* published in the same year, empowered the consistory, a committee of lay (unordained) elders and pastors, whose purpose it was to maintain orthodoxy and to punish sinners with excommunication. The line between the punishment of sin by the consistory of the church and the punishment of crime by the city council was necessarily imprecise. The civil power resisted the consistory's claims that the consistory and not the city fathers should exercise the power of excommunication. After Calvin's death the consistory gradually lost its religious purpose.

Whereas the Anabaptists denied that Christians should take any role in political life, civil government played an important role in Calvinism. According to Calvin, the first task of civil government was to foster and defend the church and sound doctrine. Calvinists believed that Christians had a duty to remake the present world, insofar as might be possible, into the image of the heavenly city. The means of this remaking was to be the discipline exercised by church elders over the congregation. With this doctrine in mind, Calvin tried to make Geneva a theocracy, a city in which God governed through the church. A century after Calvin's death, the Puritans (strict Calvinists) would teach that each person's citizenship in the earthly kingdom required citizenship in the church. Calvin was a man of his time in his conviction, shared by Protestants and Catholics alike, that every kingdom was at the same time a religious community and that dissent from the common religion was not only sinful but also a political danger. This belief, called confessionalism, would not fade until the eighteenth century.

The Burning of Michael Servetus

Many in the sixteenth century viewed erroneous ideas as diseases of the soul. Heretics were poisoners of the mind who by teaching error might divert souls from the path of salvation. Capital punishment of heretics was almost universally accepted. In 1553 Michael Servetus, a Spanish physician and theologian with heretical views on baptism, the Trinity, and the role of church and state, was arrested in Geneva. Calvin played a prominent role in the trial and the death sentence imposed on Servetus, who was burned alive on October 27.

During the age in which Calvin lived, the Roman Inquisition executed heretics; German Catholics executed radicalized peasants en masse at the close of the Peasants' War (1524–1525); there were violent reprisals against papal loyalists at the conclusion of the short-lived Pilgrimage of Grace, the 1536 challenge to Henry VIII; the Catholic English queen Mary Tudor earned the name Bloody Mary by executing Protestant dissenters; and Mary's half-sister Elizabeth I inflicted gruesome punishments upon Catholics. That Servetus was the only person burned for heresy in John Calvin's Geneva attests, if anything, to restraint.

In an age when national religion might change at the whim of the ruler, Hugh Latimer and Nicholas Ridley, bishops who had served the English king Henry VIII and his Protestant son Edward VI, were burned at the stake in 1555 by the Catholic queen Mary Tudor. Their execution is depicted in this image from John Foxe's Acts and Monuments of the Church *(1563).*

▶ Geneva, Switzerland, the subject of this 1597 illustration, was the scene of John Calvin's experiment in godly government in the 1550s.

An International Religion

Although Calvinism took the Netherlands by storm, its influence in its continental heartland was never dominant. As the sixteenth century wore on, some Swiss cities became Calvinist, others adhered to Catholicism. Even Geneva after 1600 was not securely Protestant, owing in part to the work of the Catholic bishop Saint Francis of Sales.

Calvin, hoping for the conversion of his native land, had dedicated the *Institutes* to King Francis I. In France, Calvinists were called Huguenots (possibly a French corruption of the German word that means "confederates"). Formally organized in 1536, the Huguenots were tolerated under the terms of the Colloquy of Poissy (1561). This toleration ended on Saint Bartholomew's Day, 1572, when, with the complicity of the French government, the Huguenots were murdered. Huguenot Calvinism was never subsequently a major force in French national life although the Huguenots remained the party of resistance to royal absolutism (the investment of absolute power over all matters in a king or queen who claims a divine right to rule).

Calvinism's greatest successes came in the British Isles and their linguistic and cultural dependencies. Calvin had corresponded with the lord protector Somerset during the reign of Edward VI (1547–1563), and Calvinist ideas influenced the writing of the founding documents of the Church of England, the Book of Common Prayer and the Thirty-nine Articles. When Queen Mary Tudor restored England to papal obedience in 1553, Protestant divines fled to the Swiss and German cities of Geneva, Emden, Strasbourg, Zurich, and Basel. At Mary's death they returned to establish in England, especially in East Anglia, Puritanism, a distinctively English variety of Calvinism. Puritanism encouraged within the Church of England a low church piety (that is, with a minimal emphasis on the power of the priesthood and on ceremony in worship). Puritans sought reform along Calvinist lines; splinter groups became Congregationalists (who emphasized the autonomy of each local congregation) and Presbyterians (who invested ecclesiastical bodies called presbyters with considerable powers). The Puritans, fearing that the regime of kings and bishops was a return to the hierarchically ordered world they so disliked, sowed the seeds of resistance to the royal absolutism of Elizabeth and the Stuarts who followed her.

The northern colonies of British North America were settled in the 1620s, often by immigrants from Calvinist parts of England. The founders of Massachusetts and Connecticut were Congregationalists of Puritan bent, and their religion would find support from the state in one form or another until the 1820s.

Calvinism came to Scotland and the north of England through the efforts of John Knox (1513–1572). The Reformed tradition in Scotland took the form of Presbyterianism. In 1607 the Catholic king James VI of Scotland (also James I of England), determined to secure a loyal population, encouraged numerous Scotch Protestants to emigrate to northern Ireland. They took their religion with them. In the eighteenth century large numbers of Scots and Scotch-Irish emigrated to British North America, especially to Pennsylvania, whence they moved down the Valley of Virginia. Thus, Presbyterianism became the religion of the frontier. Presbyterians were the chief sponsors of education. They founded hundreds of academies and many colleges, including Princeton and Washington College. In this regard they imitated their northern coreligionists, who had founded Harvard and Yale in the seventeenth century. Taken together, Massachusetts Congregationalism and southern Presbyterianism, reinforced by Huguenot immigration to the southern colonies, made Calvin's Reformed faith the religion of the American founding.

Calvinism and Capitalism

Calvinism was the religious engine of Anglo-American economic success in the late sixteenth and early seventeenth centuries, although opinions vary as to why. According to some theorists, belief in the immediacy of God's government over Christian souls tended to undercut royal claims to divine authority and to make Presbyterians and Congregationalists defenders of individual liberties—and even revolutionaries, as was the case in England in the 1640s and America in 1776. According to another view, Calvinists, for whom God was the immediate cause of all human events, tended to the belief that those whom God had elected he caused to

John Knox 1513–1572

Little is known of John Knox's life before 1545, when he met George Wishart, a Scottish Reformation leader and one of the first Protestant martyrs (he was burned for heresy in 1546). A convert to the Reformed faith, Knox served briefly as chaplain in the court of the Protestant king Edward VI, where he was influential in the creation of the decidedly Protestant *Second Prayer Book* of 1551.

On Mary Tudor's accession to the English throne, Knox joined the flight to Geneva, where he met John Calvin. Knox was the moving spirit behind *The Book of Common Order* (1556–1564) and the *First Book of Discipline* (1560). After 1560 Knox preached in Scotland. Around that time he drew up the Scottish Confession, which called for the abolition of the Mass (which Knox considered idolatrous) and of papal authority in Scotland. After Mary Stuart returned to Scotland from France in 1561, Knox agitated against her Catholicism. In 1567 Knox preached against the queen daily. After Mary Stuart abdicated in favor of her infant son, James, in 1567, Knox was influential with the regent, the Earl of Moray. John Knox was the principal founder of Presbyterianism in Scotland.

This woodcut illustrates the attack launched by the Scottish Calvinist John Knox (also known as Goodman Knokes) against both Mary, Queen of Scots (left), and Elizabeth I of England (right) in his book The First Blast of the Trumpet against the Monstrous Regiment of Women *(1558).*

CALVINISM AND THE MAX WEBER THESIS

In his book *The Protestant Ethic and the Spirit of Capitalism,* the German sociologist Max Weber (1864–1920) argued that Calvinism made it morally acceptable to pay attention to this world, to accumulate capital through enterprise, and to pass that capital on to heirs who would continue the enterprise. In this sense Calvinism departed from the medieval habit of leaving wealth to the church.

The raison d'être of medieval Catholicism, the performing of good works for the salvation of the soul, was rejected by Calvinist theology. During the fifteenth century the almshouses and hospitals erected by repentant sinners disappeared as quickly as the townhouses of the Calvinist upper middle class grew sumptuous.

Clearly there is some relation between Calvinism and economic activity, for a map of 1600 would show that the areas of greatest economic activity were also areas in which Calvinism was the dominant religion. However, neither Weber nor any of his successors have explained this relation exhaustively.

▲ *In the late sixteenth century Calvinism rallied much of the population of the Low Countries against the region's Catholic Spanish rulers. The brutal retaliation against Protestants, which was led by the Spanish governor, the duke of Alba, is the subject of this 1573 engraving.*

prosper. (Interestingly, a religion that denied the usefulness of good works in matters of salvation encouraged labor directed toward improving one's position in this world.)

Perhaps the best explanation for the connection between the Anglo-American economic success of the late sixteenth and early seventeenth centuries and a widespread adherence to Calvinist principles is to be found in the humanist aspect of Calvinism. Before Luther and Calvin, Erasmus and other humanists encouraged men to forgo pilgrimages and to "watch the shop"—that is, to turn their attention to things of this world. Calvinists distrusted leisure and considered activity the means by which man might best glorify God. Nothing is calculated more to improve the economic lot of men and women than hard work and plain, pure living.

The Arminian Challenge

By the end of the century in which Calvin was born, his system was under attack in the Netherlands. The theologian Jacob Harmensen (known by the Latin form of his name, Jacobus Arminius; 1560–1609) found error in Calvinist determinism (that is, the belief that men are entirely impotent in the appointment of the elect). By 1750 the Arminian impulse had begotten within Presbyterianism the New Divinity, which denied at least some of the tenets of Old Calvinism and insisted that Christ had died for all men. The intellectual descendants of both Old Calvinism and the New Divinity are still represented in the Netherlands, the United States, Canada, and Scotland, where Presbyterianism is the legally established religion.

Further Reading

Breen, Quirinus. *John Calvin: A Study in French Humanism.* Hamden, CT, 1968.

Kendall, R. T. *The Influence of Calvin and Calvinism upon the American Heritage.* London, 1976.

McKim, Donald K., ed. *Major Themes in the Reformed Tradition.* Grand Rapids, MI, 1992.

McNeil, John Thomas. *The History and Character of Calvinism.* New York, 1954.

James A. Patrick

SEE ALSO

• Church of England • Elizabeth I
• Established Churches • Henry VIII
• Humanism and Learning • Lutheranism • Papacy
• Reformation • Stuarts, The • Trent, Council of

Caravaggio

CARAVAGGIO (1571–1610) IS FAMOUS FOR THE STRIKING NATURALISM OF HIS PAINTINGS AND HIS DRAMATIC USE OF LIGHT AND SHADE, AS WELL AS FOR A TEMPESTUOUS CHARACTER AND EXTRAVAGANT LIFESTYLE.

Michelangelo Merisi, nicknamed Caravaggio after the town of his birth, was born in 1571. In 1584 he was apprenticed for four years to a minor Milanese painter, Simone Peterzano. Although he acquired a range of skills and techniques, in his earliest work, which owes nothing to his master, he broke with existing conventions.

Caravaggio's *Bacchus*, a depiction of the Roman god of wine, is typical of the paintings the artist created during the early part of his career in Rome. Caravaggio emphasizes his subject's well-developed muscles and red hands rather than create a standard portrait of a classical god (compare, for example, the depiction by Annibale Carracci in his own fresco the *Triumph of Bacchus and Ariadne* [see page 195]). The glass filled with red wine, the carafe, the bowl of fruit, and the vine and grapes in Bacchus's hair are painted with striking naturalism.

Caravaggio moved to Rome around 1593. He struggled initially before attracting the attention of his first major patron, Cardinal Francesco Maria del Monte (1549–1626). In response to charges leveled by religious reformers that the church was institutionally corrupt, most cardinals had adopted a lifestyle marked by austerity and spirituality. Del Monte—whose lifestyle was famously lavish—was an exception.

The vivid and immediate drama of Caravaggio's early paintings marks a significant departure from the work of many of his contemporaries, whose chief virtue lay in their studied concern for decorum and tradition. Caravaggio examined his own dramatic facial expressions in a mirror and re-created them in paintings of himself as a boy—recoiling with surprise when bitten by a lizard and as a sickly Bacchus, the god of wine. In the *Cardsharps* (c. 1596), a middle-aged man, peering over the shoulder of an oblivious young card player, indicates to his younger accomplice across the table which cards are about to be played.

Del Monte bought the *Cardsharps* and gave Caravaggio board and lodging in his palace. In return, Caravaggio gave del Monte the *Concert of Youths* (c. 1595), another fine example of Caravaggio's early style. In *Lives of the Artists* (1642), which contains one of the earliest biographies of Caravaggio, Giovanni Baglione (1573–1644) wrote that "because of his interest in painting Cardinal Del Monte took Caravaggio into his house, where, having a place and provisions, Caravaggio took heart and made for the cardinal a music piece of some youths painted from nature in half length." The enclosed setting of the *Concert of Youths,* the neutral background, and the strong light all serve to emphasize the

CHRONOLOGY

1571
Michelangelo Merisi is born in Caravaggio, in Lombardy, in northern Italy.

c. 1595
Moves into the palace of Cardinal Francesco del Monte.

1599–1606
Completes major commissions for churches in Rome. By this time his paintings are much sought after by important private collectors.

May 28, 1606
Kills Ranuccio Tomassoni after a tennis match and flees Rome.

1606–1610
Moves to Naples, Malta, and Sicily; returns to Naples.

1610
Dies on July 18 on his way back to Rome to receive a pardon.

youths' physical presence. Their heads, costumes, and musical instruments and the bare shoulder of the boy on the right are painted with a striking realism. On the other hand, the loose white shirts the youths wear were not worn in Rome at the end of the sixteenth century. Del Monte must have been pleased with the gift, since he collected nine further paintings by Caravaggio. Although the subject matter of most of these early works was secular, by 1599 Caravaggio had begun to concentrate on religious subjects.

Growing Fame and Controversy

The exceptionally well connected del Monte was able to further Caravaggio's career. During the remainder of his time in Rome (1599–1606), Caravaggio received commissions for paintings in six churches. The first was for the *Calling of Saint Matthew* and the *Martyrdom of Saint Matthew* in the Contarelli chapel in the Church of San Luigi dei Francesi (1599–1601). The church was near del Monte's palace, and the cardinal ensured that the commission, which had been planned as early as 1565, went to Caravaggio. Although Caravaggio had to work to a detailed program, his paintings were highly original.

Saint Matthew had been a moneylender before his conversion. In the *Calling of Saint Matthew,* he is depicted seated behind a table counting money with three elegant young companions and an older man. Matthew looks up at Christ, who has just entered the room. Christ's right hand is outstretched; he is summoning Matthew, who responds by pointing at himself in surprise. Caravaggio eschews the formulas that were traditionally used by painters when depicting scenes of the Christian saints in favor of an

► *Caravaggio's* Calling of Saint Matthew *(pictured here) is on the left-hand wall of the Contarelli chapel in the Church of San Luigi dei Francesi. (The* Martyrdom of Saint Matthew *is on the right-hand wall and the slightly later* Inspiration of Saint Matthew *appears above the main altar.) Much of the drama and underlying meaning of this scene is conveyed through the dynamic contrasts of light and shade.*

earthy sense of drama and an almost homely scale. The painting's sharp contrasts of light and dark are innovative, and there is a profusion of fine detail in the clothing: the elegant striped sleeves of the young men at the table are juxtaposed with the ragged costume of Saint Peter, who accompanies Christ.

Caravaggio's work in San Luigi dei Francesi secured his success. Later in 1600 the contract for the Cerasi chapel, in the Church of Santa Maria del Popolo, referred to Caravaggio as "the famous painter in the city." During the extraordinary burst of activity that followed, Caravaggio produced the *Entombment* for the Church of Santa Maria in Vallicella (1602–1603), the *Madonna di Loreto* for the Church of Sant'Agostino (1603–1606), the *Madonna and Child with Saint Anne* for Saint Peter's Basilica, and the *Death of the Virgin* for the Church of Santa Maria della Scala. Caravaggio also produced a number of pictures for distinguished private patrons. Among these works were *Love Triumphant, Doubting Thomas,* a painting of a young boy holding a ram—probably intended as a *Saint John*—and a *Sacrifice of Isaac.*

Following the Reformation, church authorities were concerned that newly commissioned paintings should accurately reflect Catholic doctrine. Altarpieces created by Caravaggio and a number of his Roman contemporaries were rejected as unsuitable. Private collectors were

▲ *Caravaggio's* Conversion of Saint Paul *was commissioned for the Cerasi chapel in the Church of Santa Maria del Popolo in 1600. Caravaggio flouted traditional depictions of the scene by dramatically foreshortening the central figure and having him nearly trampled by his mount.*

THE CERASI COMMISSSION

Owing to his wealth and social standing, Tiberio Cerasi could afford a chapel in the Church of Santa Maria del Popolo and, furthermore, could commission the two leading artists of the day, Caravaggio and Annibale Carracci (1560–1609), to produce works for the chapel. Caravaggio painted the side pictures, the *Martyrdom of Saint Peter* and the *Conversion of Saint Paul*, while Carracci painted the altarpiece, the *Assumption of the Virgin*. The Assumption (in which the Virgin Mary is taken into heaven) was a popular subject in Renaissance art, and Carracci depicted the scene in the traditional manner. The emotions of the apostles, who are gathered at the Virgin Mary's tomb, are expressed through the direction in which they look and the gestures they make with their hands.

According to the Acts of the Apostles, the New Testament book that follows the Gospels, Saint Paul was on his way to Lystra to continue his persecution of the Christians when he was converted by a great voice and a blinding light. The subject had been painted many times before, but Caravaggio's *Conversion of Saint Paul* differs from any earlier version. Saint Paul's armor, that of a Roman soldier, is the only concession to tradition. Caravaggio was the first artist to set the scene at night. By doing so, he was able to intensify the light, which picks out the flank of the horse, the knees of the attendant leading it, and the saint's upraised arms. His head almost presses out of the painting in a new, dramatically foreshortened pose that contrasts with the restrained gestures of the apostles in Carracci's altarpiece.

▲ *Caravaggio's* Death of the Virgin *was commissioned for the Church of Santa Maria della Scala. The picture was rejected owing to Caravaggio's depiction of a barefoot Virgin who was dead rather than dying.*

eager to buy any rejected pictures. When the first version of Caravaggio's Contarelli altarpiece, *Saint Matthew and the Angel,* was rejected, it was acquired by one of Rome's major collectors, Marchese Vincenzo Giustiniani.

Caravaggio's second version, known as the *Inspiration of Saint Matthew*—which must have been produced nearly simultaneously in 1601—remains on the altar. The first two side pictures for the Cerasi chapel were rejected by the patron but bought by a prominent cardinal. *The Death of the Virgin* was rejected because it showed the Virgin Mary dead rather than dying. (The replacement, painted by Carlo Saraceni, depicted the Virgin dying, as was customary.) By 1607 Caravaggio's work was up for sale. It was acquired by the dukes of Mantua on the advice of their court painter, Peter Paul Rubens (1577–1640), who was then in Rome. When the *Madonna and Child with Saint Anne* was rejected, the confraternity responsible for the commission sold the painting to one of Rome's most significant private collectors.

Flight from Rome

Caravaggio's success went to his head. He eschewed the traditional role of the artist as courtier and acted as a swaggering bully, ready to fight on any pretext. In 1600 he was accused of assault. In 1603 Giovanni Baglione brought a libel suit against him. He was imprisoned for throwing stones in 1604 and for three separate offenses—including carrying an illegal weapon—in 1605. On May 28, 1606, Caravaggio killed the friend with whom he had been playing tennis and had to leave Rome.

Constantly on the move from the moment he left Rome, Caravaggio continued to produce large altarpieces and a few private pictures. All were rapidly painted, with none of the attention to surface detail and none of the rich color of his Roman works. By late 1606 he was in Naples, where he painted the *Seven Works of Mercy* and the *Flagellation of Christ.* From there Caravaggio went to Malta, where he produced his largest altarpiece, the *Beheading of Saint John the Baptist* (1608), for an oratory in the cathedral in Valletta. He became, briefly, a knight of the Order of Malta, an honor granted in recognition of his portrait of the grand master of the order, Alof de Wignancourt. Following further quarrels Caravaggio was thrown into prison, escaped, and was expelled from the order. He moved to Syracuse, in Sicily, where he produced the *Burial of Saint Lucy.* Later in 1608 Caravaggio moved north from Syracuse to Messina, where he painted his last three altarpieces, the *Raising of Lazarus,* the *Adoration of the Shepherds,* and the *Adoration of the Shepherds with Saints Lawrence and Francis.*

Annibale Carracci 1560–1609

The Carracci family of artists trained and worked in Bologna, in northeastern Italy. Annibale and his older brother, Agostino (1557–1602), were probably trained by their older cousin, Ludovico (1555–1619). Some of Annibale's aims as an artist were similar to Caravaggio's. In a series of altarpieces he created for Bologna and neighboring cities, Carracci developed an expressive and naturalistic style. The Carraccis are credited with the invention of caricature, a humorous representation of a person in which certain physical characteristics are distorted or exaggerated to a ludicrous extent.

In contrast with Caravaggio, the Carraccis also worked in fresco (the technique of painting on plaster while it is still wet). Owing to their success in palace decoration in Bologna, they received a commission from Cardinal Farnese to work at the Palazzo Farnese in Rome from 1595 onward. Annibale began with a relatively small room, where canvases were placed in a frescoed frame. He went on to fresco the vault of the Farnese Gallery with an exuberant series of mock paintings, set in a brilliantly realized feigned marble architectural frame, celebrating the loves of the gods. After the vault was finished in 1600, Carracci began work in the Cerasi chapel. He died apparently broken by Cardinal Farnese's failure to appreciate his outstanding achievement.

Death and Posthumous Fame

Caravaggio returned once more to Naples, where in October 1609 he was attacked and left badly wounded. By the following year his supporters in Rome had persuaded the pope to grant him a pardon. He set out from Naples by boat and landed at Port'Ercole, in Tuscany, where he was mistakenly arrested for two days. Caravaggio died of fever on July 18, 1610, while looking for the boat that contained his possessions.

Caravaggio's art had a huge impact among distinguished collectors and both Italian and northern artists. Gian Lorenzo Bernini (1598–1680) imitated Caravaggio's dramatic facial expressions in his early sculpture. Other painters imitated his dark backgrounds, elegant

▼ *In 1600 Annibale Carracci completed the* Loves of the Gods, *a series of frescoes in the Palazzo Farnese, with the* Triumph of Bacchus and Ariadne, *in which the two gods celebrate their marriage.*

In this 1672 excerpt an outstanding historian and critic of Italian seventeenth-century art paints a vivid picture of Caravaggio's attitudes and behavior:

Caravaggio began to paint according to his own inclinations; not only ignoring but even despising the superb statuary of antiquity and the famous paintings of Raphael, he considered nature to be the only subject fit for his brush. When shown the most famous ancient statues, his only answer was to point to a crowd of people, saying that nature had given him an abundance of masters. . . . Caravaggio's preoccupation with painting did not calm his restless nature. After having painted for a few hours in the day he used to go out on the town with his sword at his side like a professional swordsman, seeming to do any thing but paint. During a tennis match with a young friend of his they began hitting each other with their rackets. At the end Caravaggio drew his sword, killed the young man and was wounded himself.

Giovanni Pietro Bellori, *Lives of the Modern Painters, Sculptors and Architects*

Caravaggio painted this Flagellation of Christ, *a version of his 1607 altarpiece on the same subject in the Church of San Domenico in Naples, for a private patron. He worked quickly, as he did on all of his later paintings. The emotional drama and somber atmosphere of the scene are emphasized by the dark background and sharp light.*

costumes, intense lighting, and choice of subjects. By the mid-1620s, however, Caravaggio was no longer a major influence; his former followers developed styles and subjects more appropriate for their careers at the courts of Europe. Northern artists rationalized Caravaggio's system of lighting by introducing candlelight into their scenes. Even though Rembrandt (1606–1669) had never visited Italy, he was influenced by Caravaggio's use of candlelight as well as by the practice of studying facial expressions in a mirror. Caravaggio's paintings fell out of fashion in the eighteenth century and were largely overlooked until the early years of the twentieth.

Further Reading

Christiansen, Keith, ed. *The Age of Caravaggio.* New York, 1985.

Hibbard, Howard. *Caravaggio.* New York, 1983.

Puglisi, Catherine R. *Caravaggio.* London, 1998.

Spear, Richard E. *Caravaggio and His Followers.* New York, 1975.

Richard Cocke

SEE ALSO

• Bernini, Gian Lorenzo • Gentileschi, Artemisia • Reformation • Rembrandt • Rome • Rubens, Peter Paul

Catherine de Médicis

CATHERINE DE MÉDICIS (1519–1589) EXERTED CONSIDERABLE INFLUENCE ON FRENCH POLITICS DURING THE REIGN OF HER HUSBAND, KING HENRY II OF FRANCE, AND THOSE OF HER THREE SONS, FRANCIS II, CHARLES IX, AND HENRY III.

Catherine de Médicis was born Caterina de' Medici in Florence in 1519. Her father was Lorenzo de' Medici, duke of Urbino, and her mother was Madeleine de la Tour de Auvergne. Within a few months of her birth, both Catherine's parents died. She was given into the care of her grandmother Alfonsina Orsini and her cousin Giulio de' Medici (later Pope Clement VII) and taken to Rome at the request of her uncle, Pope Leo X (Giovanni de' Medici).

In the 1520s Catherine returned to Florence in the care of her aunt Clarissa Strozzi. Her privileged life in Florence did not last long. When she was eight years old, the Medici palace in Florence was attacked by anti-Medici forces. For three years the new government of Florence kept Catherine prisoner. She was first placed in the convent of Santa Lucia. Later she moved between a number of convents. Ever at the mercy of the fluid political situation, her life was frequently in danger. Finally, in 1530 Catherine was freed and allowed to leave Florence. Her cousin Giulio, by now Pope Clement VII, brought her to Rome once again, where she lived in the Palazzo Medici under his guardianship. She continued her education and mastered Latin, Greek, and French.

This portrayal of the marriage of Catherine de Médicis and Henry, duke of Orléans, presided over by Pope Clement VII, was painted by Jacopo Chimenti Empoli (1551–1640).

Marriage

Catherine's status as an eligible heiress involved her in Clement VII's international policy. Potential suitors included the duke of Richmond (Henry VIII's illegitimate son) and King James V of Scotland. In 1531 Clement VII finally decided to marry Catherine to Henry, duke of Orléans, the second son of King Francis I of France. After protracted negotiations, the marriage took place on October 27, 1533.

Catherine spent the next fourteen years at the court of Francis I. She admired her father-in-law and later held up his method of government as a model for her children. She, together with many of the court ladies, accompanied Francis I on his many excursions. Yet she soon found her position in the French court to be a difficult one. The death of Pope Clement VII less than a year after the marriage of Catherine and Henry nullified the political advantages Francis I had hoped to gain by the marriage. The death in 1536 of Francis I's first son, the dauphin (prince) François, further complicated matters, since Catherine's husband was now heir to the French throne. Catherine's Italian ancestry and her inability to produce children in the first years of her marriage made her something of a political liability. A move to have the marriage annulled began shortly after the death of the dauphin. However, Catherine managed to avoid this calamity, and after taking advice from a doctor named Jean Fernel, she finally became pregnant. Catherine gave birth to a son, Francis (the future

CHRONOLOGY

1519
Caterina de' Medici is born.

1544
Catherine's first child, the future king Francis II, is born on January 19.

1545
Catherine's daughter Elisabeth, the future queen of Phillip II of Spain, is born on April 7.

1547
Catherine's daughter Claude, the future duchess of Lorraine, is born on November 12.

1550
Catherine's son Charles-Maximelien, the future king Charles IX, is born on June 27.

1551
Catherine's son Edouard-Alexandre, the future Henry III, is born on September 20.

1553
Catherine's daughter Marguerite, the future queen of Navarre, is born on May 14.

1555
Catherine's son Hercule, later François, duke of Alençon and duke of Anjou, also a suitor to Queen Elizabeth I of England, is born on March 18.

1558
Catherine's son Francis marries Mary, Queen of Scots.

1584
Catherine's youngest son, François, dies.

1589
Catherine dies on January 5.

THE GUISE FAMILY

The Guise family began its rise to power under King Francis I (reigned 1515–1547). Claude de Guise, who formed a close friendship with Francis I, was an able military leader who routed the Germans in Champagne (1522–1523). Francis made Claude duke of Guise after he successfully suppressed a peasant revolt in Lorraine (1527). Claude's marriage to Antoinette de Bourbon was politically advantageous, as Antoinette was the daughter of François de Bourbon, comte de Vendôme, and sister to the king of Navarre. Claude and Antoinette produced a large family, including Marie de Guise, who became the wife of James V of Scotland and mother of Mary, Queen of Scots. Claude's son, François de Lorraine, the second duke of Guise (1519–1563) increased in influence and power during the reign of Henry II (Catherine's husband) owing to his military acumen. In 1557 Henry II made François de Lorraine lieutenant general throughout France. At this time Henry II also made Guise's brother, Charles de Guise (1525–1574), cardinal of Lorraine—a position that gave him responsibility for domestic and foreign affairs.

The culmination of the Guise family's rise to power came on the death of Henry II in the palace coup engineered by François de Lorraine in 1559. Even after Catherine reestablished her political authority, the Guise family continued to exert a great deal of political influence for the remainder of the sixteenth century. Conflicts between the Guises, who championed the Catholic religion, and the Protestant Huguenot nobles became a major cause of the wars of religion in France that lasted from 1562 until the Edict of Nantes in 1598.

King Francis II) in 1544. During her marriage she had nine further children: Elisabeth (the future queen of Philip II of Spain), Claude (the future duchess of Lorraine), Charles (the future Charles IX), Edouard-Alexandre (the future Henry III), Marguerite (the future queen of Navarre), Hercule (later François, duke of Alençon and duke of Anjou), and three others who died in infancy.

This miniature of Catherine de Médicis (c. 1589) is attributed to François Clouet (1510–c. 1572), who served as court painter under the French kings Francis I, Henry II, Francis II, and Charles IX.

Queen of France

In 1547 Francis I died, and Catherine's husband became King Henry II of France. Though queen of France, Catherine was able to exert little political power owing to the influence of Henry II's mistress, Diane de Poitiers. In 1559 Catherine's husband was wounded in a tournament accident when a shard of wood pierced his eye and embedded in his brain. Ten days after the accident he died, and Catherine's eldest son ascended the throne as King Francis II. Francis, whose queen was Mary Stuart, queen of Scotland (usually known as Mary, Queen of Scots), ruled for only seventeen months. His reign is most notable for the rise of the powerful Guise family.

Regent of France

Catherine's second son, Charles IX, came to the throne in 1560, at the age of ten. Catherine was chosen to rule the country on behalf of her son as queen regent of France. Even after Charles IX reached the age of majority (fourteen), Catherine exerted great political influence. The greatest threat to the Valois monarchy during this period was the power of the Guise family. Exploiting the religious tensions between the Catholic majority and the Huguenot (Protestant) minority, the Guises fomented conflicts that threatened to undermine the power of the French monarchy. Catherine's overriding goal was to preserve the position of her son.

This unattributed portrait of Catherine in a magnificent regal dress captures its subject in all her power and majesty.

The tensions ultimately broke out into the wars of religion. Initially, Catherine attempted to negotiate a settlement between the Catholic nobles (especially the Guises) and the Huguenot nobles, who were led by Antoine de Bourbon, king of Navarre; Louis de Bourbon-Vendôme, prince of Condé; and Gaspard de Coligny, admiral of France. Unfortunately, Catherine's policies did not bring about peace and security. Instead, a meeting between Catherine and her daughter Elisabeth Valois sparked fears among Huguenots of an imminent Spanish invasion to destroy the Huguenots. (Elisabeth had married Philip II, the Catholic king of Spain, in 1559.)

SAINT BARTHOLOMEW'S DAY MASSACRE

According to several sources, what ended up as a massacre was initially planned as only the assassination of Gaspard de Coligny, a powerful Huguenot leader. It appears that when the plot went awry, a new plan developed to massacre all the Huguenot nobles in Paris. The motivation behind this massacre was the perceived threat that the Huguenots, who were well armed, were preparing to enter the war against Spain in the Netherlands. Doing so threatened to provoke a war between France and Spain. Another motivation for the massacre could have been the opportunity it presented to rid France of several Huguenot leaders at one time. Catherine was certainly involved in the decision to murder the Huguenot leaders, but it is unlikely that she or her son Charles IX anticipated the carnage that would spread across France between August and October of 1572. Approximately 70,000 people died during this period of terrible unrest.

▲ A detail from the depiction of the Saint Bartholomew's Day Massacre by François Dubois (1529-1584), who was an eyewitness. The violence of this graphic portrayal is consistent with printed and manuscript accounts of the brutality and wholesale slaughter that occurred in the days following the marriage of Marguerite de Valois and Henri de Bourbon.

The Huguenots formed a plan to capture Catherine, together with Charles IX, at Meaux, a town south of Paris (this plan came to be known as the *Surprise de Meaux*). Catherine and Charles were forced to flee to Paris. For a while, Catherine abandoned attempts to mediate between the Huguenots and the Catholics. She told the Venetian ambassador, Giovanni Michieli, "there are circumstances . . . which oblige one to turn upon oneself and to submit to what one did not want in order to avoid greater ills." Catherine negotiated the Peace of Saint-Germain, a treaty favorable to the Huguenots, and also the marriage of the Protestant Henry of Navarre to her daughter Marguerite de Valois. However, her distrust of the Huguenots finally involved her in one of the most infamous events in French history, the Saint Bartholomew's Day massacre.

Adviser to Henry III

In 1573 Catherine negotiated for her son Edouard-Alexandre, duke of Anjou, to become king of Poland (the Polish throne had been left vacant when Sigismund-August II died without an heir). The Polish electors voted to make Anjou their king, and he left for Poland. He did not remain there long. On May 30, 1574, King Charles IX died, and Anjou was recalled from Poland immediately. Catherine was chosen to serve as regent until Anjou, now Henry III, returned in September.

During the reign of Henry III, Catherine continued to exert influence. She served tirelessly as adviser, negotiator, and mediator. Although Henry often chose to ignore his mother's advice, he did employ her for certain important and sensitive negotiations. One of her most important commissions was yet another negotiation with the Huguenot nobles. Her efforts resulted in the Treaty of Nérac (1580). Henry III also relied on Catherine to divert his brother François from involvement in the ongoing wars in the Netherlands and from his association with the Protestant Henry of Navarre (later Henry IV of France). At one point Catherine even attempted

▲ *In this painting by François Dubois (1529–1584), Henry III and Catherine de Médicis are depicted attending a ball to celebrate the marriage of the duc de Joyeuse to Marguerite de Lorraine-Vaudémont in 1581. Henry looks confidently out at the viewer, whereas Catherine's worried gaze is turned upon her son. The painting is strangely prophetic of the tragic end of this particular king of France.*

to arrange a marriage between François and Elizabeth I of England, though her efforts came to nothing.

Final Years

In her final years Catherine had very little influence over Henry III's actions and policies. In September 1588 Henry dismissed all his ministers and replaced them with others who owed Catherine nothing. Later that year he made the disastrous decision to murder Henry, third duke of Guise, together with Guise's brother. The murders took place on December 23 and 24. Upon hearing the news, Catherine is reported to have exclaimed, "Oh! wretched man! What has he done? . . . I see him rushing towards his ruin. I am afraid he may lose his body, soul and Kingdom."

Catherine died shortly after this episode, on January 5, 1589. The forty-two years since the death of her husband in 1559 had been fraught with political and religious unrest. Catherine worked relentlessly to secure and promote the rights of her children, the stability of France, and the survival of the Valois monarchy. She arranged marriages for her daughters that were designed to protect and increase the power of the French throne. She mediated between the many contentious factions within France and negotiated several edicts and treaties. She served as regent of France on numerous occasions and was an astute political adviser to her sons. For several years she promoted a policy of religious tolerance and conciliation. However, at times, most infamously during the Saint Bartholomew's Day massacre, she approved persecution and murder as a means of achieving her desired ends.

On August 1, 1589, Henry III was murdered by a Guise assassin. Henry of Navarre, who became King Henry VI of France, summed up the life of his most powerful adversary by asking, "What could the poor woman do, with five children in her arms after the death of her husband and with two families in France, ours and the Guise, attempting to encroach on the throne? Was she not forced to play strange parts . . . to protect her children?" In the "strange parts" she played, Catherine's role was always determined if not always admirable.

Further Reading

Frieda, Leonie. *Catherine de Medici.* London, 2003.

Knecht, R. J. *Catherine de' Medici.* New York, 1998.

Ross Williamson, Hugh. *Catherine de' Medici.* New York, 1973.

Whitelaw, Nancy. *Catherine de' Medici and the Protestant Reformation.* Greensboro, NC, 2005.

Jessica L. Malay

SEE ALSO

• Elizabeth I • France • Francis I • French Civil Wars • Henry IV • Machiavelli, Niccolò • Medicis, The • Paris

Cervantes, Miguel de

THE SPANISH NOVELIST MIGUEL DE CERVANTES (1547–1616) WROTE ONE OF THE MOST INFLUENTIAL PIECES OF RENAISSANCE LITERATURE—*DON QUIXOTE,* A SATIRICAL PORTRAIT OF A MAN DRIVEN MAD BY TALES OF ROMANCE.

On October 9, 1547, Miguel de Cervantes Saavedra was baptized in the Church of Saint Mary the Great in the town of Alcalá de Henares, east of Madrid, in central Spain. His father, Rodrigo de Cervantes, was a surgeon who claimed noble ancestry, and the family of his mother, Leonor de Cortinas, owned a small amount of land near Madrid.

Education and Early Career

The circumstances of Cervantes's early education are uncertain. When he was four years old, his family moved north to Valladolid. Cervantes's father was soon imprisoned for debts, and all the family's possessions were confiscated. The pattern of this experience was repeated again and again. Cervantes's youth was itinerant; his family moved from city to city and suffered varying degrees of poverty.

In 1570, at age twenty-three, Cervantes entered the employment of Cardinal Guilio Acquaviva y Aragon and moved to Rome. In the same year four of his poems were included in a collection of student work honoring Queen Elisabeth de Valois of Spain. The collection was published by Cervantes's former teacher, the humanist López de Hoyos.

Cervantes's service to the cardinal lasted only a matter of months. By late 1570 Cervantes, together with his younger brother Rodrigo, enlisted in the army to fight against the Turks of the Ottoman Empire. Both brothers fought at the Battle of Lepanto (1571), where Cervantes's left hand was shattered by gunshot. Despite this injury he also took part in Juan of Austria's campaigns in Navarino, Corfu, and Tunis. During the return voyage to Spain in 1575, Cervantes and his brother were captured by Arnaute Mami, an Algerian corsair (pirate), and taken to Algiers. Cervantes wrote of this capture, "For in the galley Sol, whose luster fell / by my ill fortune, I was doomed to see / my comrades' ruin and mine own as well" (*Journey to Parnassus;* 1614).

Algerian Captivity

Cervantes remained captive for almost five years. His family in Spain solicited first the Council of Castile and then the Royal Council for help in raising the ransom needed to secure his release. When the Royal Council proved unwilling to provide the funds, the Cervantes family turned to the Council of the Cruzada, an organization that administered funds given to Spain by the pope. Cervantes's mother made the appeal and succeeded in securing a small grant toward her sons' release. In 1577 Rodrigo Cervantes was ransomed and returned to Spain.

This portrait of Cervantes, painted by Juan de Jáuregui y Aguilar around 1600 (when its subject was fifty-three), reveals a middle-aged man who is confident and reflective.

THE SATIRE OF *DON QUIXOTE*

Don Quixote is a finely crafted novel that mocks the literary fashion of Cervantes's times. The tale concerns the adventures of the country gentleman Alonso Quixana. After reading too many popular novels containing stories of chivalry, heroes in battle, magicians, beasts, and fair maidens, "his brain dried up and he lost his wits." In his madness Quixana decides to ride out into the world to seek adventure, to set right injustice, and to win the love of the fair maiden Dulcinea. His adventures include numerous episodes that are at once ludicrous and touching, the most famous of which is his assault upon a windmill. This episode is the origin of the phrase "tilting at windmills," which describes a struggle against adversities that are entirely imaginary.

Though the novel is humorous, satirical, and openly comedic, at the same time it engages the reader's sympathy. Cervantes's ability to ridicule much of what he saw in the society around him while at the same time conveying his affectionate attachment for that society and for humanity in general has made *Don Quixote* popular for almost four hundred years. Although Don Quixote seems mad, the purpose of his quest is serious. His actions reveal the highest human aspirations of fidelity, service to humanity, justice, truth, and love.

CHRONOLOGY

1547
Miguel de Cervantes Saavedra is born in Alcalá de Henares.

1566
Publishes a sonnet in honor of the birth of Princess Catalina Micaela, the second daughter of Philip II and Elizabeth of Valois.

1572
After suffering several wounds at the Battle of Lepanto, rejoins the army in the regiment of Don Lope de Figueroa.

1592
Is imprisoned in the Castro del Río jail; is contracted to write six plays.

1593
Cervantes's mother dies; Cervantes composes several poems, including the *Invincible Armada.*

1594
Is sent to jail once again.

1597
Is imprisoned in Seville for an unpaid debt; begins *Don Quixote.*

1614
Viaje del Parnaso (Journey to Parnassus) is published; César Oudin translates *Don Quixote* into French.

1616
Cervantes dies.

1617
Cervantes's wife, Catalina, publishes *The Trials of Persiles and Sigismunda.*

Cervantes served on one of the ships that make up the vast tangled fleet in Guarino Veronese's 1572 depiction of the Battle of Lepanto. The upper half of the painting is an allegorical depiction of the victory of the Christian Europeans over the Muslim Turks.

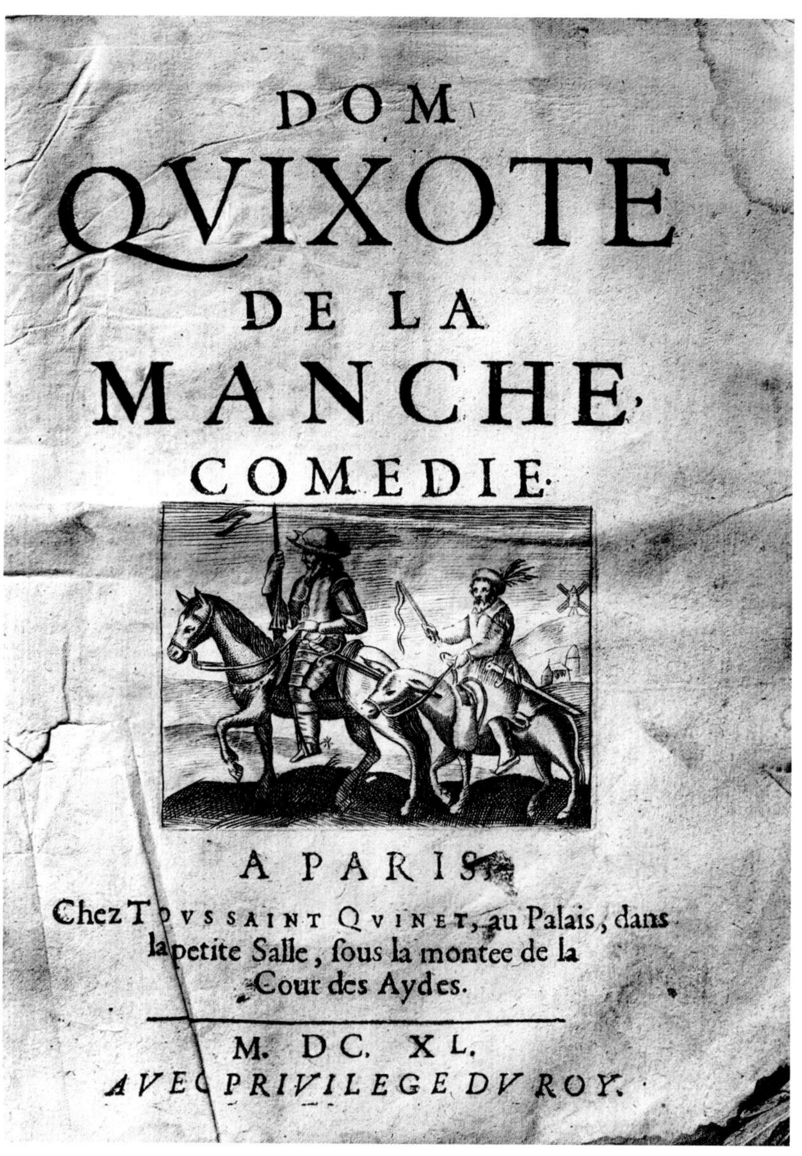
DOM
QVIXOTE
DE LA
MANCHE,
COMEDIE.
A PARIS,
Chez TOVSSAINT QVINET, au Palais, dans la petite Salle, sous la montee de la Cour des Aydes.
M. DC. XL.
AVEC PRIVILEGE DV ROY.

▲ *This title page from Guérin de Bouscal's 1640 French translation of* Don Quixote *includes a depiction of the intrepid hero followed by the faithful Sancho Panza.*

Continuing to collect money, the family drained all its financial resources, including the dowries of the two Cervantes daughters, and contracted large debts that brought it to the brink of financial ruin. Despite these efforts the family was unable to negotiate Cervantes's release. Increasingly desperate, Cervantes made four daring but unsuccessful escape attempts. Each resulted in increasingly harsh treatment by his captors. Cervantes was finally returned to Spain in 1580 through the efforts of the Trinitarians, a Catholic missionary order.

Literary Beginnings

Cervantes had hoped to secure a lucrative government position through the influence of Don Antonio de Toledo, one of his fellow former captives, but these hopes were dashed when Toledo died. In 1581 Cervantes received one minor government commission, an obscure assignment to Oran, a seaport in northwestern Algeria. He subsequently spent several years as a poorly paid government administrator. During his period of service to the government, Cervantes was bankrupted and imprisoned at least twice. His difficulties are generally attributed to the antagonism of the people from whom he was required to purchase goods for the government at low prices as well as to an antiquated accounting system that created irregularities in his accounts. It is believed that Cervantes pursued his assignments honestly but was the victim of unpopular government policies and practices.

Despite his constantly strained financial position, the 1580s saw the beginning of Cervantes's literary career. In Madrid he began moving in literary circles and met important writers of his day, including Francisco de Figueroa, Luis de Vargas Manrique, and Lope de Vega. In 1585 Juan Gracián in Alcalá de Henares published Cervantes's first novel, the pastoral romance *La Galatea.* At this time Cervantes also wrote several plays for the Madrid public theaters (which were known as *coralles*). Only two plays, *El trato de Argel* and *La Numancia,* survive.

Shortly before the publication of *La Galatea,* Cervantes was involved in two romances of his own. One was with Ana de Villafranca, or Ana Franca de Rojas, a tavern owner. The result of this relationship was Cervantes's only known child, Isabel de Saavedra. Around the same time, in 1584 he met and married Catalina de Salazar y Palacios, the daughter of prosperous peasants. Catalina was eighteen years Cervantes's junior, and the marriage was not a success. He soon left her and spent the next two decades living a nomadic existence and carrying out his assignments as a government commissioner. Among his undertakings was an ill-fated assignment as commissioner of supplies for the Armada, the armed Spanish naval fleet, under the supervision of Antonio de Guevara.

The Writing of *Don Quixote*

The disastrous defeat of the Armada by the English navy inspired Cervantes to write odes to this doomed adventure. He also continued to

Every man has something of Don Quixote in his Humor, some darling Dulcinea of his Thoughts, that sets him very often upon mad Adventures. What Quixotes does not every Age produce in Politics and Religion, who fancying themselves to be in the right of something, which all the World tells them is wrong, make very good sport to the Public, and show that they themselves need the chiefest Amendment.

Peter Motteux, Translator's Preface to *Don Quixote* (1700)

write plays and ballads. By 1598 he was almost certainly working on *Don Quixote* along with some of the novellas later published as *Novelas ejemplares (Exemplary Stories).* Cervantes's whereabouts during the period 1598 to 1602 have been the subject of a great deal of conjecture. Some historians assert that he spent much of this time in prison, while others believe he continued with the itinerant life he had settled into. Certainly by 1604 Cervantes had followed his sister and other members of his family to Valladolid, the new location of the Spanish court.

By this time the manuscript copy of the first part of *Don Quixote* was complete. Early in 1605 *El ingenioso hidalgo Don Quijote de la Mancha,* dedicated to the duke of Béjar, was being printed and sold by the bookseller Francisco de Robles. The tremendous success of the book transformed Cervantes into one of Spain's most famous men. Yet while the reception of the book among ordinary readers was overwhelmingly positive, the literary community of Spain was mixed in its critical opinion. Lope de Vega openly dismissed the book, and Vicente Espinel ridiculed it. Others, however, recognized the book's value. In *Los cigarrales de Toledo,* Tirso de Molina called Cervantes "our Spanish Boccaccio." (Boccaccio was the revered Italian writer of the *Decameron,* a collection of one hundred stories that greatly influenced European literature). The rapid appearance of pirated editions of *Don Quixote* in Lisbon (in Portugal) and Valencia (in Spain) prompted Robles to put out a second edition. The translation of the first edition of *Don Quixote,* part 1, into English was completed by Thomas Shelton in 1607 and published in 1612.

Later Life and *Don Quixote,* Part 2

Despite the success of *Don Quixote,* part 1, soon Cervantes was again mired in financial and personal problems. On June 27, 1605, a man named Gaspar de Ezpeleta was mortally wounded in front of Cervantes's house. Cervantes brought the wounded man into his house, where he was cared for by Cervantes's sisters and a surgeon. Ezpeleta died two days later, and Cervantes was arrested together with his sisters, his daughter, and other members of the household. Within twenty-four hours those arrested were sent home, and by July 18 the case had been dropped. This incident was not the end of Cervantes's domestic problems. In March 1607 his daughter, Isabel, became pregnant and was married to Juan de Urbina. Urbina died in 1608, and Isabel's quick remarriage, to Luis de Molina, plunged the family into conflicts over her dowry. The same year also saw the death of several of Cervantes's family members.

▲ *This atmospheric nineteenth-century illustration by the Frenchman Gustave Doré captures the foolhardy madness of Don Quixote as he battles a giant windmill, whose sail has snagged both him and his horse, Rosinante.*

In this excerpt Cervantes looks back to his participation in the Battle of Lepanto and the wounds he received there:

My wounds... shall be esteemed at least in the judgment of such as know how they were gotten. A soldier had rather be dead in battle than free by running away. And so it is with me.... I should rather have desired to have been in that prodigious action; than now to be whole skin, free from my scars, for not having been in it.... The scars which a soldier shows in his face and breast are stars which lead others to the Heaven of Honor and to the desire of just praise.

Preface to *Don Quixote*, part 2

► *In his painting* Don Quijote and Sancho Panza *(1855), Honoré Daumier contrasts the eccentric activity of Don Quixote, who lowers his lance to battle some unseen enemy, with Sancho Panza's relaxed position on his mule. Panza seems completely unconcerned with the actions of his knight.*

Despite these domestic challenges, Cervantes continued to write. He penned several plays during the period from 1608 to 1615. He also continued to work on *Exemplary Stories* (published in 1613). When Alonso Fernández de Avellaneda published his own sequel to *Don Quixote,* the *Second Volume of the Ingenious Don Quixote of La Mancha,* Cervantes was galvanized to complete his own part 2—which was published in the fall of 1615. Cervantes also published *Eight Plays and Eight Interludes, New and Never Performed* in 1615 and finished *Los trabaios de Persiles y Sigismunda (The Trials of Persiles and Sigismunda).*

At the end of this flurry of creative production, Cervantes chose to take final monastic vows in the Tertiary Order of Saint Francis, which he had joined three years before as a novice. By this time extremely ill, he remained in his home. The exact date of Cervantes's death is unknown but is generally believed to have fallen between April 22 and April 24, 1616. He was buried in his Franciscan habit at the Convent of the Barefoot Trinitarians, on Cantarranas Street (now Lope de Vega Street), in Valladolid.

Further Reading

Byron, William. *Cervantes: A Biography.* New York, 1988.

McCrory, Donald. *No Ordinary Man: The Life and Times of Miguel de Cervantes.* Chester Springs, PA, 2002.

Marlowe, Stephen. *The Death and Life of Miguel de Cervantes.* New York, 1996.

Jessica L. Malay

SEE ALSO

• Armada, Spanish • Lepanto, Battle of • Literature • Religious Orders • Spain

Charles V

Holy Roman emperor Charles V was the most powerful monarch of Renaissance Europe.

Charles was born in Ghent, in present-day Belgium, in 1500. In 1506 he inherited the Netherlands from his father, Philip, duke of Burgundy. His mother, Juana, the daughter and heiress of Ferdinand of Aragon and Isabella of Castile, was mentally unstable. Isabella died in 1504, and although Juana lived until 1555, on the death of Ferdinand in 1516, Charles proclaimed himself King Charles I of Castile and Aragon (a territory that encompassed the greater part of Spain). With the kingdom of Aragon, Charles inherited the islands of Sardinia and Sicily, off the coast of Italy, and the kingdom of Naples. With Castile he inherited lands being conquered and colonized by Spanish conquistadores in the Caribbean and South America. From Philip's father, the Hapsburg Holy Roman emperor Maximilian I, who died in 1519, he inherited lands in Austria. With a combination of diplomacy and bribery, he secured his own election as Charles V, Holy Roman emperor.

▼ *A portrait of Charles at age sixteen by Bernard van Orley (1492–1542). Charles, who has the distinctive Hapsburg facial features, is wearing the collar of the Burgundian chivalric Order of the Golden Fleece, of which he was the head.*

Childhood and Youth

Charles scarcely knew his parents. After Philip's death in 1506, Juana was confined in Spain, and Charles was brought up by his aunt Margaret in the Netherlands. Although as a boy he was more interested in hunting than in books, throughout his life Charles took pleasure in the arts, especially music. As a youth he appeared solemn and reserved; he matured into a conscientious and hardworking ruler. Contemporaries respected his abilities at the same time as they feared his power.

Taking Control of the Spanish Inheritance

In 1515 Charles took over direct rule of the Netherlands territories he inherited from his father. In 1517 he traveled to Spain to take control there. He did not speak Spanish, and the arrogance and greed of the Flemish courtiers he brought with him angered his Spanish subjects. The Spanish, who wanted a king of their own, were not impressed by Charles's becoming emperor in 1519. Indeed, dissatisfaction with Charles as a ruler was one of the major causes of the rebellion of important Castilian towns that broke out in 1520, just after Charles left Spain to travel to Germany. By the time of his return in 1522, the rebellion had been defeated. Charles learned from his mistakes and appointed Spaniards to the councils that governed the kingdom. He mastered Spanish, which became the language of his court, and no longer seemed an alien king to his subjects. The Spanish kingdoms, particularly Castile, became the most solid foundation of his power.

Rivalry with France

Charles's rivalry with the king of France was his main preoccupation throughout his reign. Charles's domains encircled France, and with them he inherited long-standing territorial disputes. To Charles the most personally significant was the dispute over the duchy of Burgundy itself, which had been lost to France in 1477. For much of his life, he dreamed of recovering this territory. There was also an element of personal rivalry between Charles and Francis I. Francis tried hard to be elected emperor in 1519 and continued to seek alliances with German princes in order to counter Charles's power. Francis also cooperated with Charles's other major external enemies, the Ottoman Turks and the Muslim corsairs of the Barbary coast of North Africa. Charles was at war with Francis and then with Francis's son and successor, Henry II (reigned 1547–1559), for much of his reign. Much of the fighting took place in Italy as well as on the borders of France.

The most dramatic episode of Charles's conflict with France was the capture of Francis by imperial troops at the Battle of Pavia in February 1525. Francis had been attempting to reconquer the duchy of Milan, to which he laid claim. He was sent to Spain, where he was held captive for a year. His marriage to Charles's sister Eleanor in 1530 did nothing to reconcile the two monarchs.

Charles V and Italy

The Battle of Pavia confirmed Charles's dominance in Italy. He controlled the kingdoms of Naples and Sicily and the island of Sardinia. Technically, the duchy of Milan was part of the Holy Roman Empire, and as emperor, Charles could determine the fate of the duchy after the last Sforza duke, Francesco II, died in 1535. Charles took Milan under his own rule, although he transferred the title to the duchy to his son, Philip, in the 1540s. Charles also determined the fate of Florence: when the siege of the city by imperial troops brought the downfall of the last republican government in 1530, he supported the Medicis in their bid to become lords of Florence. By using his authority as emperor to reinforce Spanish power in Italy, Charles established the hegemony of Spain over Italy that would have such a profound effect on Italian culture, society, and politics.

▼ The coronation of Charles V as Holy Roman emperor by Pope Clement VII in Bologna in 1530—the subject of this painting by Juan de la Orte (1597–1660)—was the last occasion on which a pope crowned an emperor.

CHARLES AS EMPEROR

Even if he had not been elected emperor, Charles V would still have been one of the most powerful rulers in Europe—indeed, being Holy Roman emperor did not in itself confer a great deal of power. The Holy Roman emperor did not rule the territory of the empire directly, except for those of his own family lands that fell within its borders. In 1522 Charles ceded the hereditary lands of the Hapsburgs in Austria to his brother, Ferdinand. Each of his territories outside the empire kept its own administration, its own laws, and its own political institutions, and being emperor gave him no additional power over them.

As emperor, Charles could claim to be the lay leader of Christendom, and as such, it was his responsibility to promote peace and concord among Christian states. Some historians have argued that Charles was inspired by this ideal vision of the Christian emperor, particularly under the influence of his chancellor, Mercurino da Gattinara. At times, Charles claimed that as emperor he had a particular duty to defend Christendom against the forces of Islam, to combat heresy, and to urge the pope to call the ecumenical council needed to confront divisions within the church.

In practice, however, the need to devise effective solutions to the relentless succession of problems that pressed upon him left little scope for pursuing grandiose visions. While some of his councillors spoke of the ideals of empire, others, equally influential, urged him to heed his overstretched resources—in particular, his perpetual shortage of money—and to make peace for the good of his subjects. Far from bringing peace among Christian states, Charles spent much of his reign at war, mostly against Christians. He was forced to accept compromises with the Protestants of Germany, at times he found himself at war with the pope, and his troops were responsible for the shocking sack of Rome. If the interests of the empire conflicted with the interests of his family, the latter took precedence.

In this portrait, by Parmigianino, Charles V is portrayed at the height of his power (around 1529 or 1530); victory hovers above his head. Although the lands Charles ruled in the Americas as king of Castile were not part of the Holy Roman Empire, his possession of them contributed to the popular image of Charles as an emperor who dominated the world.

CHRONOLOGY

1500
Charles is born in Ghent on February 29.

1521
Wars with France—which would continue intermittently for the rest of Charles's reign—begin.

1526
Charles marries Isabella of Portugal.

1530
After being crowned emperor by Clement VII in Bologna, returns to Germany.

1532
Defends Vienna against the Turks.

1535
Conquers Tunis.

1539
Empress Isabella dies.

1539–1540
Charles travels through France on the way to suppressing a rebellion in Ghent.

1541
Leads an unsuccessful expedition against Algiers; attends the Diet of Regensburg.

1544
Invades France and makes the Peace of Crépy with Francis I.

1551–1552
Faced with the rebellion of German princes, forms an alliance with Henry II of France. Refuses terms for the recognition of religious divisions in Germany.

1554
Arranges marriage of his son Philip to Mary Tudor of England.

1558
Dies at Yuste, Spain, on September 21.

Relations with the Papacy

In his capacity as emperor with a duty to defend the Christian faith, Charles pressed upon the popes the urgent need to summon a council of the church to meet the calls for reform and to deal with the challenge of the Protestants. The popes, determined that the decision to summon a council should be theirs alone, did not agree that the emperor had a special role to play.

Another source of tension between empire and papacy was the popes' traditional unwillingness to have the ruler of the kingdom of Naples, to the south of the Papal States, also dominant in the north of Italy—especially if that ruler was the Holy Roman emperor. Pope Clement VII joined Francis I of France and the rulers of Venice in the League of Cognac (1526), which was directed against Charles. The sack of Rome by imperial troops in 1527 and the subsequent virtual captivity of the pope in his own fortress sat ill with the emperor's role as defender of the church. Charles, though genuinely shocked and aggrieved by the brutality of the sacking of Rome, was nevertheless ready to extract diplomatic advantages from his power over the pope. Clement abandoned the league, and in 1530 he crowned Charles emperor in Bologna.

None of the popes who reigned while Charles was emperor gave Charles the support against the king of France that he felt was his due. Even Pope Adrian VI (reigned 1522–1523), who had been Charles's tutor in the Netherlands, saw it as his duty to be neutral. Clement's successor, Paul III (reigned 1534–1549), would not commit himself to supporting Charles against France, despite Francis's alliance with the Ottoman sultan Süleyman I (reigned 1520–1566) and the marriage of Charles's daughter Margaret to Paul's grandson, Ottavio Farnese. Differences between Charles and Paul over when and where a council of the church should be summoned, who should attend, and what should be discussed there were never resolved satisfactorily.

Charles in Germany

Charles was faced with three major problems within the empire: Protestantism, the attacks of the Ottoman Turks in the east, and the attempts by France to form alliances with the German princes against him. He was repeatedly forced to make compromises in one field or another so that he could deal more effectively with whichever problem was greatest. In 1521 the diet (deliberative assembly) of the Holy Roman

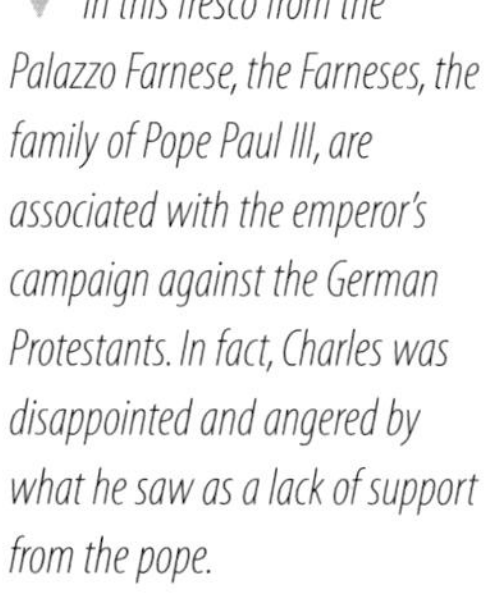

▼ *In this fresco from the Palazzo Farnese, the Farneses, the family of Pope Paul III, are associated with the emperor's campaign against the German Protestants. In fact, Charles was disappointed and angered by what he saw as a lack of support from the pope.*

In a memorandum of January 1548 Charles advised his son, Philip, on how Philip should rule the dominions he would soon inherit.

You should above all strive to maintain and defend our holy faith, in general and in particular matters, in all the states and dominions you will inherit from us [and] to repress by all possible means, according to law and equity, the heresies and sects contrary to our venerable religion.... After all the effort and expense I have endured to bring back to the bosom of the true Church the dissidents of Germany, I have clearly recognized that the only way to achieve this end is to hold a council.

Quoted in Salvador de Madariaga, ed., *Charles Quint*

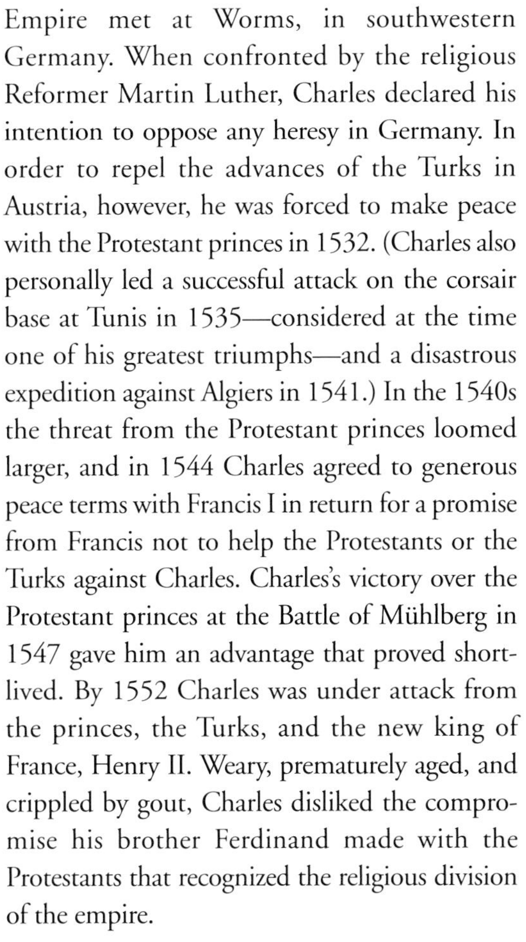

Empire met at Worms, in southwestern Germany. When confronted by the religious Reformer Martin Luther, Charles declared his intention to oppose any heresy in Germany. In order to repel the advances of the Turks in Austria, however, he was forced to make peace with the Protestant princes in 1532. (Charles also personally led a successful attack on the corsair base at Tunis in 1535—considered at the time one of his greatest triumphs—and a disastrous expedition against Algiers in 1541.) In the 1540s the threat from the Protestant princes loomed larger, and in 1544 Charles agreed to generous peace terms with Francis I in return for a promise from Francis not to help the Protestants or the Turks against Charles. Charles's victory over the Protestant princes at the Battle of Mühlberg in 1547 gave him an advantage that proved short-lived. By 1552 Charles was under attack from the princes, the Turks, and the new king of France, Henry II. Weary, prematurely aged, and crippled by gout, Charles disliked the compromise his brother Ferdinand made with the Protestants that recognized the religious division of the empire.

Resignation from Power

In October 1555 Charles handed over the Netherlands to his son, Philip, and the following year he also resigned the kingdoms of Castile and Aragon to his son. His resignation as emperor was not accepted by the electors until 1558. Charles retired to Yuste, in Spain, where he had had a small villa built for him next to a remote monastery. There he enjoyed his books and music and his collection of clocks, as well as fishing and overeating. He died at Yuste on September 21, 1558.

▲ *Charles's son, Philip, who was in the Netherlands when he heard the news of his father's death, ordered elaborate mourning ceremonies to be held in Brussels. This engraving by Franz Hogenberg demonstrates the prominent role played by the regalia of the Order of the Golden Fleece in the funeral procession.*

FURTHER READING

Brandi, Karl. *The Emperor Charles V: The Growth and Destiny of a Man and a World-Empire.* Translated by C. V. Wedgwood. London, 1980.

Fernández Álvarez, Manuel. *Charles V: Elected Emperor and Hereditary Ruler.* Translated by J. A. Lalaguna. London, 1975.

Rodríguez Salgado, M. J. *The Changing Face of Empire: Charles V, Philip II, and Habsburg Authority, 1551–1559.* New York, 1988.

Christine Shaw

SEE ALSO

• Burgundy • Clement VII • Ferdinand and Isabella • Francis I • Hapsburg Empire • Holy Roman Empire • Islam • Italian Wars • Leo X • Lombardy • Lutheranism • Maximilian I • Philip II • Reformation • Rome • Spain • Trent, Council of

Chaucer, Geoffrey

TRADITIONALLY CONSIDERED THE FATHER OF ENGLISH LITERATURE, GEOFFREY CHAUCER (C. 1340–1400) HELPED REESTABLISH ENGLISH AS A LITERARY LANGUAGE.

Geoffrey Chaucer was born in the early 1340s, probably in London. He grew up on Thames Street in Vintry, a wealthy district at the heart of London where many wine merchants (of which Chaucer's father was one) lived and worked. He may have learned Latin at one of the three schools near his comfortable boyhood home; one of those schools, the Almonry School of Saint Paul's Cathedral, has preserved an inventory of books from 1358 that includes Latin poetic classics, grammars, encyclopedias, and theological treatises. As a boy Chaucer probably also began to learn Italian through contact with the Italian shipmen, merchants, and financiers who dealt with his father.

This illumination of Chaucer is from the so-called Ellesmere *Canterbury Tales*, a manuscript that was produced within five years or so of the writer's death. Chaucer included himself as one of the pilgrims and even told his own stories—"The Tale of Sir Thopas" and "The Tale of Melibee."

Page to the Countess of Ulster

The social prominence of Chaucer's family made it possible for him to serve the household of the countess of Ulster as a page, perhaps in his early teens. Young sons of such wealthy commoners as Chaucer's father often lived and served as pages in noble households as a first step toward securing the patronage necessary for a career in public service.

As a page Chaucer acquired a thorough acquaintance with the world of fourteenth-century English nobility, including court etiquette and dress. He presumably accompanied the countess on at least some of her regularly occurring travels and attended royal feasts, jousts, and hunting parties. He would also have taken part in the daily routine of service at meals and in other menial chores, in addition to such physical activities as riding, swordsmanship, and the sport of handball.

Chaucer may have received informal schooling in Latin from a household clerk, and he would have learned to speak French, the language of polite discourse used by a ruling class that shuttled regularly back and forth among holdings and relatives in England, France, and elsewhere in Europe. By Chaucer's time Anglo-Norman, the hybrid of English and Norman French spoken by English nobles and courtiers of previous generations, had given

Though recognizable to a speaker of modern English, the Middle English spoken during Chaucer's time differs substantially from its present-day counterpart. In the following excerpt Chaucer complains of the errors his scriveyn (scribe) makes when copying such works as Chaucer's translation of Boethius or his *Troilus and Criseyde*. The "scalle" that Chaucer wishes on his scribe if he does not write more accurately is a scaly eruption of the scalp.

Adam scriveyn, if ever it thee bifalle
Boece or Troylus for to wryten newe,
Under thy long lokkes thou most have the scalle,
But after my making thow wryte more trewe;
So ofte adaye I mot thy werk renewe,
It to correcte and eke to rubbe and scrape,
And al is thorugh thy negligence and rape.

Chaucer's Wordes unto Adam, His Owne Scriveyn

CHRONOLOGY

c. 1340
Chaucer is born, probably in London.

c. 1378–1381
Writes *Hous of Fame*, *Anelida and Arcite*, *Parlement of Foules*, and *Palamon and Arcite* (later "The Knight's Tale").

c. 1381–1386
Translates Boethius's *Consolation of Philosophy* and writes *Troilus and Criseyde*.

1385–1389
Writes *The Legend of Good Women* and begins writing *The Canterbury Tales*.

c. 1391
Writes *A Treatise on the Astrolabe*.

1400
Dies in London on October 25.

▲ *This manuscript page includes the opening of "The Knight's Tale" and a depiction of the knight himself.*

way to a more international form of French. In the countess's household Chaucer would have had access to French romances, dream visions, and books of religious instruction, in addition to English romances.

Royal Esquire

Chaucer apparently left the countess's household in order to enter the retinue of Prince Lionel, the countess's husband. In September 1359 Lionel was part of an unsuccessful invasion of France led by King Edward III, who intended to have himself crowned king of France at Reims. Chaucer was captured by the French, briefly held hostage, and then ransomed by the English king in March 1360. In October 1360 Lionel paid Chaucer to carry letters from Calais to England during peace negotiations at Calais. This journey was the first of many Chaucer was commissioned to make by members of the royalty.

Chaucer served the English royal household as a yeoman or esquire in the 1360s. He joined about forty other young commoners, whose service sometimes included military expeditions and other journeys abroad. During these years of service to the king, Chaucer may also have acquired some knowledge of the law at the Inner Temple, one of London's Inns of Court (law schools), but he received nothing resembling a formal university education. He traveled to Navarre, in Spain, in 1366, possibly on a pilgrimage or on some kind of secret diplomatic mission. A three-month journey in 1368 may have taken him only as far as Flanders or France, but it is possible that he traveled as far as Milan on a mission that was connected with the marriage of Prince Lionel to a daughter of the powerful Visconti family.

In 1366 Chaucer married Philippa, apparently the daughter of Gilles de Roet, a knight

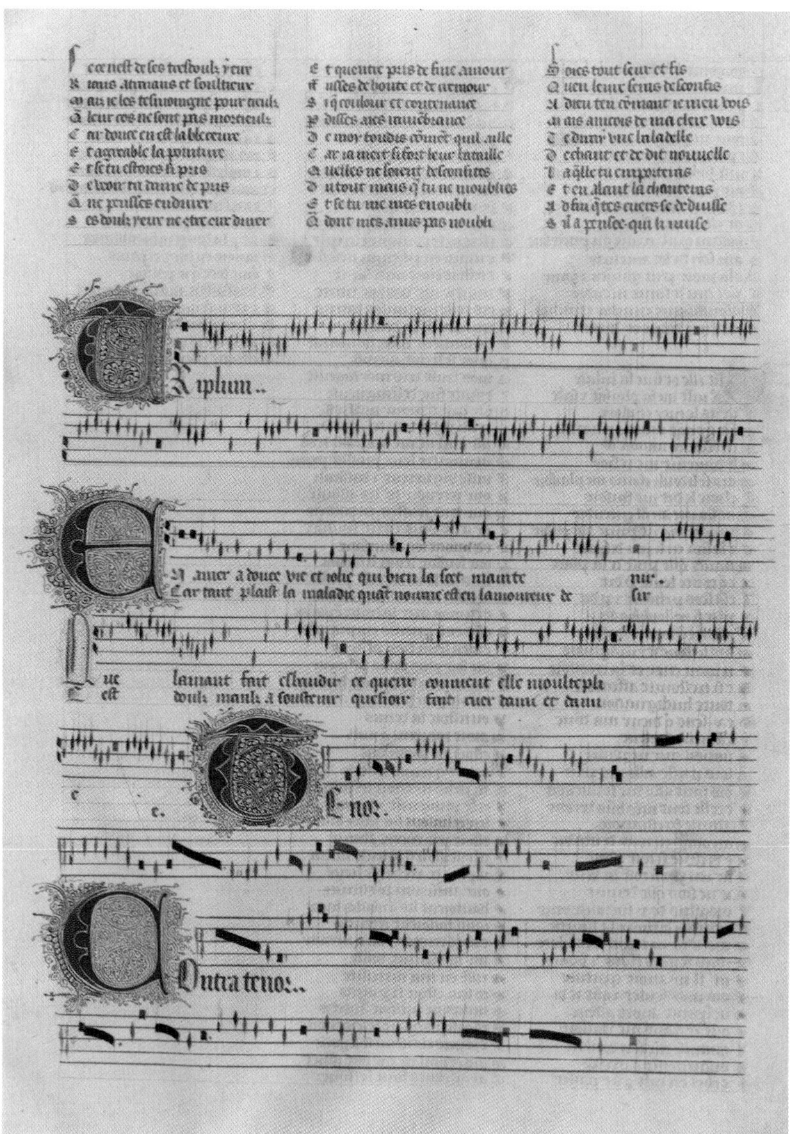

▲ *This musical score, a work by the medieval French poet and composer Guillaume de Machaut, was handwritten during the fourteenth century. Chaucer's exposure to the poetry and music of France inspired him to match—and surpass—in the English language the achievements of the French poets in their language.*

of Hainaut, in the Low Countries. Gilles de Roet had accompanied Queen Philippa to England when she married Edward III. Catherine Swynford, another daughter of Gilles, was the mistress of John of Gaunt for over twenty years. (John of Gaunt, the fourth son of Edward and Philippa and the richest and most powerful man in England, eventually married Catherine in 1396.) As did her husband, Philippa Chaucer served the royal court; she attended the queen and two daughters-in-law of the king (one of whom was Constance of Castile, John of Gaunt's second wife). Both Geoffrey and Philippa Chaucer received annual payments and other gifts from the king and John of Gaunt in return for service to the court. In 1369 Chaucer accompanied the latter on a military expedition to Picardy, in northern France.

Apprentice to French Poets

During his period of royal service, Chaucer produced the first English translation of the most influential poem of the Middle Ages, the French *Roman de la rose,* which was begun by Guillaume de Lorris around 1230 and completed by Jean de Meun in the 1280s. During this period Chaucer also wrote *The Book of the Duchess* (c. 1369).

Old English literature—work produced by the Anglo-Saxons between the 600s and 1066—was unknown to Chaucer. Prior to the fourteenth century, few literary works of merit had been produced in the form of English Chaucer and his contemporaries spoke—what is now called Middle English. Middle English literature amounted to little more than poorly written romances, legendary tales of knightly adventure and love that often involved supernatural elements. Middle English was considered a backward and inferior language, one in which it would be impossible to write great poetry. From 1066, the year of the Norman Conquest, to the mid-1300s, French language and culture was so dominant that most surviving literature produced in England is in French, Anglo-Norman, or Latin. Indeed, French was the most important of all European vernaculars (the spoken languages that came to replace Latin).

Because little literature in English was available, Chaucer began this early phase of literary experimentation as a kind of poetic apprentice to the established French models. The troubadours and trouvères, wandering poets and minstrels of noble birth, had established French as the language of love songs in the twelfth and thirteenth centuries. Romances and fabliaux (short, humorous, and usually obscene stories of cunning deceptions and marital triangles) became popular in the thirteenth century. In his portion of the *Roman de la rose,* Guillaume de Lorris assimilates elements of troubadour, trouvère, and romance literature by turning song into narrative. The first part of *Roman,* a dream vision narrated in the first person (in the manner of a love song), describes an adventure that takes place entirely in the narrator's imagination. Jean de Meun draws on the fabliau for the comic portraits in his later continuation of *Roman.* The *dits amoureux* (love narratives) and most of the lyric poems of Guillaume de Machaut and Jean Froissart continue the tradition of song turned into narrative. By translating part of *Roman* into English, Chaucer made this repository of French literature more accessible to English readers and also took the poem as a foundation for his own work. In 1385 the French poet Eustache Deschamps sent Chaucer a ballad in which he praised Chaucer for his translation.

The Book of the Duchess, a dream vision in close imitation of the *dits amoureux,* represents the next stage of Chaucer's poetic apprenticeship to French tradition. The poem was almost certainly composed shortly after the death of Blanche, the first wife of John of Gaunt. The middle-class narrator dreams that he meets a grieving Black Knight (identified with John); Chaucer's interest in the juxtaposition of members of different tiers of society is already evident. Rather than translate a specific French poem, in *The Book of the Duchess,* Chaucer produces a pastiche that echoes a great number of Latin poems and many French poems, including the *Roman de la rose* and three poems by Machaut. Indeed, such was the success of *The Book of the Duchess* that Froissart appears to imitate it in one of his own *dits amoreux.*

Guillaume de Machaut c. 1300–1377

The most important French poet and composer of the fourteenth century, Guillaume de Machaut wrote 420 lyric poems, of which he set about 140 to music, and composed a mass and 23 motets (choral compositions). He also wrote eight long *dits amoureux* and four shorter *dits.* Most subsequent French *dits amoureux* are modeled on Machaut's, and the influence of his music and poetry reached many other parts of Europe. Among his *dits amoureux* that influenced Chaucer are *Le jugement du roy de Behaigne (The Judgment of the King of Bohemia)* and *Le remède de fortune (The Remedy of Fortune),* both written around 1340.

Machaut appears to have been born to middle-class parents near Reims, in the Champagne region. After completing a university master of arts degree, he traveled from 1323 through the 1330s as the personal secretary to Jean of Luxembourg, the king of Bohemia. In gratitude, Jean had Machaut appointed canon at Reims, where he spent the rest of his life and did most of his writing. From Reims he traveled occasionally to visit his many other noble patrons. Machaut's prominence brought new status to vernacular poets, none of whom is referred to in French as *poète* before the fourteenth century.

In this illustration to a 1584 edition of the works of Guillaume de Machaut, the poet receives the personification of Nature, who introduces him to emotion, rhetoric, and music.

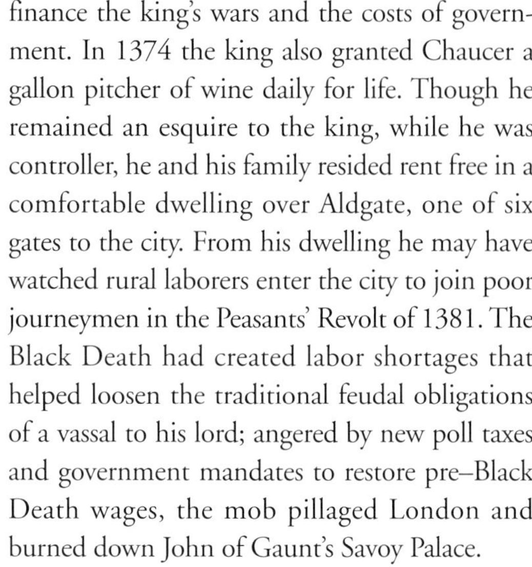

▼ *This fresco of Dante Alighieri was painted by Andrea del Castagno (1421–1457). The works of Dante, especially the* Divine Comedy, *were an extremely important influence on Chaucer.*

Controller of Customs and Envoy

In 1374 Edward III appointed Chaucer controller of customs in the port of London, a position he held for twelve years. As controller Chaucer recorded payments of the export tax on wool, sheepskins, and leather. Taxes collected on wool, England's principal export, helped to finance the king's wars and the costs of government. In 1374 the king also granted Chaucer a gallon pitcher of wine daily for life. Though he remained an esquire to the king, while he was controller, he and his family resided rent free in a comfortable dwelling over Aldgate, one of six gates to the city. From his dwelling he may have watched rural laborers enter the city to join poor journeymen in the Peasants' Revolt of 1381. The Black Death had created labor shortages that helped loosen the traditional feudal obligations of a vassal to his lord; angered by new poll taxes and government mandates to restore pre–Black Death wages, the mob pillaged London and burned down John of Gaunt's Savoy Palace.

During this period the king sent Chaucer on several missions abroad. Chaucer's first recorded contact with Italy was a royal commission (1372–1373) to negotiate the use of an English port with the doge and people of Genoa. On that trip Chaucer also visited Florence on the king's business. The king sent him to Genoa again soon after. In 1376 and 1377 Chaucer made several trips to France "on secret business of the king." According to Froissart, Chaucer took part in a mission to discuss a marriage between the new English king, Richard II, and a French princess (the marriage did not take place). In 1378 Chaucer returned to Lombardy, in northern Italy, to meet with Bernabò Visconti to discuss "certain business concerning the king's war."

Apprentice to Italian Poets

At the time of Chaucer's visit to Florence, Francesco Petrarca (Petrarch) and Giovanni Boccaccio were already distinguished poets; they probably also lived nearby. Whether or not Chaucer met them, he must have heard much about them and about Dante Alighieri, whom Florentines still held in high regard five decades after his death in exile. Chaucer's later visit with Visconti, whose family members were patrons of Petrarch and who owned extensive libraries, surely helped Chaucer broaden his familiarity with Italian literature. On his return from these trips, Chaucer may have brought back to England manuscripts of these poets' works.

In the first few years after his visit with Visconti, Chaucer produced four poems, all

Dante Alighieri 1265–1321

Dante Alighieri, the author of the *Divine Comedy,* established Italian as a literary language by transforming earlier poetic genres into what he called new poetry. A surviving Italian translation of the *Roman de la rose* may have been written by Dante. *Il fiore* (*The Flower*), composed in the 1280s, comprises sonnets adapted from the *Roman de la rose*. From the same period, *Il detto d'amore* (its title is the Italian equivalent of the French *dit amoureux*) reveals influences from *Roman* and from poetry written in Provençal, a Latinate language spoken in southeastern France. In *La vita nuova* (*The New Life;* c. 1294), the story of Dante's poetic apprenticeship, the poet attempts to transcend traditional Provençal poetic conventions in order to tell the story of his love for Beatrice. *De vulgari eloquentia* (*On the Eloquence of Vernacular;* written in Latin around 1307) finds in vernacular Italian the foundation of Italian law, theology, and poetry. In it Dante urges writers in vernacular languages to imitate the Latin classics. In the *Divine Comedy,* different poetic genres are associated with the three regions Dante visits—hell, purgatory, and paradise. In *De monarchia* (*On Monarchy;* written around 1313 in Latin), Dante argues for a separation of church and state. Born into a prominent local family, Dante served as one of seven priors of Florence before being exiled for political reasons in 1302. In Dante's conceptions of vernacular language, law, and the church lie many seeds of the European Renaissance and Reformation.

A sixteenth-century portrait of Giovanni Boccaccio, a pioneer of vernacular literature and, through works in which he played down the role of divine intervention in human affairs, one of the founders of humanism.

clearly influenced by Italian poetry: *Hous of Fame, Parlement of Foules, Anelida and Arcite,* and *Palamon and Arcite,* probably in that order. The first two were modeled on a French-derived dream framework. However, Dante's influence is also evident in *Hous of Fame,* which focuses on the difficulty faced by a poet in trying to relate his work to antecedent poetic traditions. The golden eagle that carries Chaucer to the heavens in *Hous of Fame* imitates the eagle that carried Dante in the *Divina commedia* (*Divine Comedy;* c. 1321). The *Parlement of Foules,* in which birds of different social classes attempt to interact and communicate, echoes the language of Boccaccio's *Teseida* (1341) and various Latin sources. The *Parlement of Foules* probably alludes to the negotiations for Richard II's marriage to Anne of Bohemia. Rhyme royal, the verse form Chaucer employs in *Parlement* (and later in *Troilus and Criseyde;* c. 1386) derives partly from the ottava rima verse form of Boccaccio's *Filostrato* (c. 1339) and *Teseida.* Chaucer drew on Boccaccio's *Teseida* to begin his experimental *Anelida and Arcite,* a poem that he left unfinished. *Palamon and Arcite,* the romance Chaucer later incorporates into *The Canterbury Tales* as "The Knight's Tale," is primarily based on Boccaccio's *Teseida.*

During his last years as controller of customs, Chaucer translated the *Consolation of Philosophy,* a Latin dream vision written around 524 by Anicius Manlius Severinus Boethius that strongly influenced "The Knight's Tale." He also wrote *Troilus and Criseyde,* a story of ill-fated lovers set during the ancient siege of Troy and based primarily on Boccaccio's *Filostrato* (with influences from Boethius). *Troilus* also draws from earlier accounts of the Troy legend in French and Latin. Like *Filostrato, Troilus* remains under the spell of the *Roman de la rose* and Dante's

▶ *Canterbury Cathedral, the destination of the pilgrims of* The Canterbury Tales, *has been England's ecclesiastical headquarters since the seventh century. Part of the present-day building dates from the eleventh and twelfth centuries, part from the sixteenth. The pilgrims' aim was to visit the tomb of Thomas Becket, the "turbulent priest" who opposed King Henry II's reforms and was murdered by Henry's henchmen (who may have acted without Henry's knowledge) on December 29, 1170.*

Divine Comedy. With *Troilus,* Chaucer succeeds in creating a vernacular masterwork in English that bears comparison with the *Roman de la rose,* the *Divine Comedy,* and Boccaccio's *Decameron* (c. 1358), all of which assimilate the greatest works of older genres into new languages. With *Troilus,* Chaucer demonstrated that the English language was capable of sustaining a poetic masterpiece.

Later Years

In 1385, as the French threatened to invade the south of England, Chaucer was appointed justice for the Kentish peace commission. In 1386 he represented Kent as a knight of the shire (member of the House of Commons). In 1389 King Richard appointed Chaucer clerk of the king's works; in this capacity Chaucer oversaw maintenance and construction at ten royal residences and at the Tower of London and managed hunting lodges in royal forests. In 1391 Chaucer was appointed subforester of the royal forest at North Petherton, Somerset, in southwestern England. After Henry IV was crowned king of England in 1399, he increased the annual payments Chaucer had received under Richard II (Chaucer had composed *The Book of the Duchess* in memory of Henry's mother). The date of Chaucer's death inscribed on his tomb at Westminster Abbey is October 25, 1400. He was buried in the abbey because he was a royal servant who had resided on abbey grounds during his last year, not because of his poetic achievement. Nevertheless, his tomb was the first in what came to be Poets' Corner.

The Canterbury Tales

Chaucer appears to have begun work on his best-known masterpiece, *The Canterbury Tales,* shortly after he resigned from the customs house. At his death the work remained unfinished. A series of tales is contained within a frame narrative about a group of travelers who take turns telling stories during a pilgrimage from Southwark to Canterbury. The tomb of Thomas Becket (c. 1118–1170) in Canterbury Cathedral was the most important pilgrimage destination in England, and the route from London to Canterbury was a well-trodden one. Chaucer probably wrote *The Legend of Good Women* (c. 1395), an unfinished initial attempt at a collection of tales in the style of Boccaccio's

The opening lines of *The Canterbury Tales* offer an elaborate description, typical of medieval literary prologues, of the way in which spring weather (the sweet showers of April) affects different creatures in the hierarchy of nature.

Whan that Aprill with his shoures soote
The droghte of March hath perced to the roote,
And bathed every veyne in swich licour
Of which vertu engendred is the flour;
Whan Zephirus eek with his sweete breeth
Inspired hath in every holt and heeth
The tendre croppes, and the yonge sonne
Hath in the Ram his half cours yronne,
And smale foweles maken melodye,
That slepen al the nyght with open ye
(So priketh hem Nature in hir corages),
Thanne longen folk to goon on pilgrimages,
And palmeres for to seken straunge strondes,
To ferne halwes, kowthe in sondry londes;
And specially from every shires ende
Of Engelond to Caunterbury they wende,
The hooly blisful martir for to seke,
That hem hath holpen whan that they were seeke.

General Prologue of *The Canterbury Tales*

Decameron, before he began writing *The Canterbury Tales.* In addition to the French genres of romance and fabliau, *Tales* bears the influence of such Latin genres as the sermon, the hagiography (saint's life), and the hymn. In common with the *Decameron,* Chaucer's tales include coarse and earthy narratives. However, the ten young nobles who narrate the stories of the *Decameron* represent a much narrower social spectrum than do the pilgrims who narrate *The Canterbury Tales.* Among Chaucer's pilgrims are a knight, a squire, a prioress, a monk, a friar, a merchant, and a parson, in addition to a summoner (one who serves processes for an ecclesiastical court), a pardoner (an itinerant salesman of indulgences, pardons for sin), the prosperous Wife of Bath, and many others. Chaucer's framing device thus enables him to present a great variety both of genres and of points of view. In *The Canterbury Tales* Chaucer established the expressive range of English, much as Boccaccio, Dante, and the writers of the *Roman de la rose* had done for Italian and French.

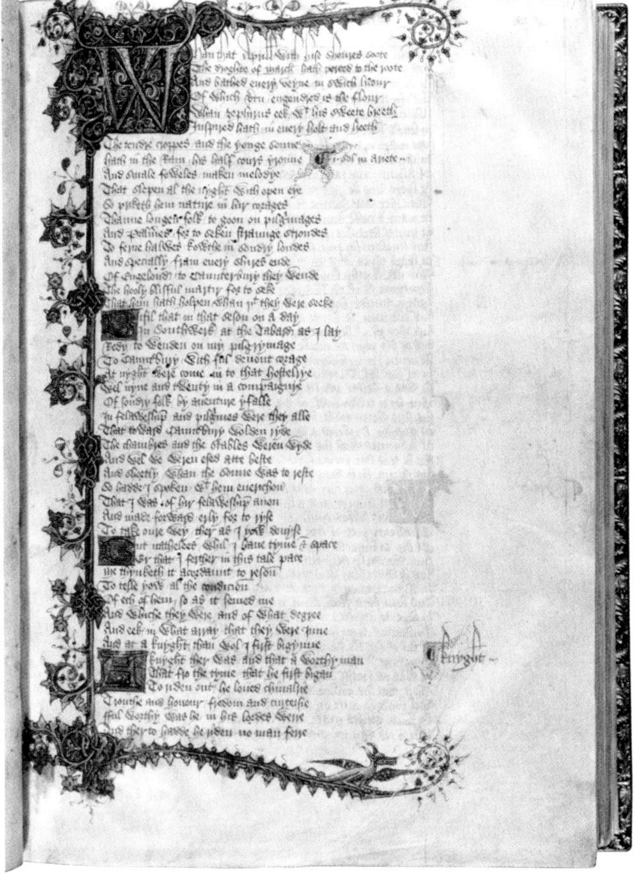

The opening page of the Ellesemere Canterbury Tales *(c. 1405), currently in the possession of the Huntington Library and Art Gallery in San Marino, California.*

Father of English Literature

Chaucer had the good fortune to live at a time when spoken and written English, though beginning to replace French in official and commercial spheres, was still fluid and highly susceptible to influence. The infusion of Latin, French, and Italian material in *Troilus* and *The Canterbury Tales* established a solid foundation for a vernacular poetic tradition in English. Chaucer was also fortunate to be born into a reputable family of merchants at a time of great opportunities for upward mobility. Thus, the literary foundation he established reflects not only a changing English language but also a rapidly evolving European society. In the first century after Chaucer's death, he remained such a dominant figure that many English poets felt constrained to produce rather stilted imitations of his style.

CHAUCER, WILLIAM LANGLAND, AND THE PEARL POET

haucer's writings exhibit little or no influence from the two other great English poets of the late fourteenth century, the Pearl Poet (also known as the Gawain Poet) and William Langland. Little is known about the life of either poet, and their writings show little or no converse influence from Chaucer. It is not known whether Chaucer met either of them or read any of their poetry, though he must have known Langland by reputation. Langland's *Piers Plowman* (completed around 1385) is a lengthy, densely theological dream vision that attacks political and ecclesiastical corruption.

The Pearl Poet is the author of four poems discovered in a single manuscript in the nineteenth century: *Pearl, Cleanness, Patience,* and *Sir Gawain and the Green Knight,* all probably written in the last two or three decades of the fourteenth century. The poet's knowledge of theology and of literature in French and Latin suggests that he was a cleric in minor orders. The style of *Sir Gawain and the Green Knight,* a romance with fabliau elements, suggests that its author was especially familiar with French romance. *Pearl,* a dream vision, bears the influence of French love narratives and the *Divine Comedy. Cleanness* and *Patience* are biblical paraphrases that draw on wide knowledge of the Bible and the church liturgy.

Langland and the Pearl Poet are the chief exponents of the late-fourteenth-century alliterative revival. (Unrhymed alliterative verse, in which the repetition of initial sounds in neighboring words is the principal structural and rhythmic device, had been the hallmark of Old English poetry). Both poets wrote in the dialect of the northern Midlands rather than that of London. The Pearl Poet had no significant influence until his rediscovery in the nineteenth century, and Langland's alliterative style quickly lost its appeal to English readers. Because of the immediate and lasting popularity of Chaucer's London dialect and continental rhyme schemes, the roots of English literature will always lie in Chaucer's work.

▼ *Chaucer's tomb, in the enclave of London's Westminster Abbey known as Poets' Corner.*

FURTHER READING

Chaucer, Geoffrey. *The Riverside Chaucer.* Edited by Larry D. Benson. Boston, 1987.

Boitani, Piero, and Jill Mann. *The Cambridge Companion to Chaucer.* New York, 2003.

Howard, Donald Roy. *Chaucer: His Life, His Works, His World.* New York, 1987.

Pearsall, Derek Albert. *The Life of Geoffrey Chaucer: A Critical Biography.* Cambridge, MA, 1992.

Kevin Marti

SEE ALSO

- Boccaccio, Giovanni • England • Henry IV
- Languages, Vernacular • Literature • London
- Peasants' Revolts • Petrarch • Pilgrimage
- Viscontis, The

Chivalry

ORIGINALLY THE CODE OF BEHAVIOR ASSOCIATED WITH KNIGHTS, CHIVALRY BECAME THE MOST PERVASIVE LAY ETHICAL AND CULTURAL CODE OF THE MIDDLE AGES AND THE RENAISSANCE.

Chivalry had its origins in the ethical code and culture of cavalrymen (those who fought on horseback), specifically with the elite cavalrymen who were known as knights (in French, chevaliers). The high cost of a horse and the equipment a knight needed tended to restrict knighthood to those of elevated social status. The church, in an attempt to instill in the knights its own code of ethics, insisted that the primary duty of a knight was to defend the church and the clergy and also to protect the weak and defenseless. Although these religious values had some influence on the knightly ethos, they never displaced the secular values of the warrior elite—courage, honor, loyalty, and prowess—or the brutal realities of a life dedicated to jousting and war.

The Burgundian courtier depicted in this portrait by Rogier van der Weyden (1400–1464) is wearing the collar of the Order of the Golden Fleece. The arrow he is holding apparently identifies him as a tournament judge; the arrow would be thrown as a signal to the combatants to stop fighting.

The secular culture of chivalry was also heavily influenced by the notion that a knight should serve a lady. Although the ideal of courtly love (according to which a knight was to show a lady unflinching loyalty and a reverence bordering on worship) added an element of refinement to the chivalric code, courtly love was incorporated into the military ethic; fine words and good manners might help woo a lady, but the strongest foundation for her love, according to convention, would be admiration for the knight's prowess in fighting, either in war or at a tournament.

By 1300 the expense of a knight's equipment—arms and armor, several horses, squires, and servants—was so great that only the richer nobles and gentry could afford to have their sons formally dubbed knights. Through exceptional bravery and service in war, a soldier might also win knighthood; to be knighted on the battlefield was a great honor. During his attempt to recover Milan for France, King Francis I was said to have been knighted after the Battle of Marignano (1515) by Pierre de Bayart, who was known as the chevalier sans reproche (the knight without reproach). Bayart was regarded as exemplifying chivalric values and virtues: courage and skill in fighting, loyalty to one's lord and comrades, generosity, courtesy, and fidelity to one's given word. By the sixteenth century the army and the court of the king or prince was increasingly the main arena for the display of chivalric virtue. In the fourteenth century the idea of the knight-errant, who ventured forth in search of opportunities to win honor and renown, could still send men on long and dangerous journeys. On one such adventure, in 1392 Henry Bolingbroke (from 1399, King Henry IV of

▲ *This fifteenth-century illustration of a tournament involving the knights of the Round Table, watched by courtly ladies from the safety of the stands, is from a manuscript of a French Arthurian tale,* Le roman de Tristan.

England) went to Prussia to fight alongside the Teutonic Knights.

The Laws of War

With the acceptance of the chivalric code of conduct throughout Europe, internationally accepted conventions, known as the laws of war, arose. The laws of war regulated such matters as the treatment of prisoners, particularly concerning ransoms and the conditions under which the commander of a besieged fortress or town could surrender without loss of honor. The laws had little bearing on such matters as the treatment of civilians: excessive cruelty could be criticized but would not be prosecuted. Expeditions whose sole purpose was to devastate the territory of an enemy, a favored tactic in warfare, would not attract reproach. Massacring infantry would also not bring reproach, whereas killing a noble who had surrendered would be reproachable.

The laws of war were essentially concerned with nobles, knights, and those men who were of sufficient status to be accepted as the nobles' and knights' comrades-in-arms. While these laws may appear to be rules devised in order to make warfare less lethal for the elite, they did at least foster the idea of respect for the enemy and the notion of international law. Accusations of breaches of the laws of war could be brought and cases won in the law courts of the enemy.

Chivalric conventions also gave rise to episodes that had little bearing on the outcome of wars but to which great attention was paid. Challenges to one-on-one combat or to combat between small chosen groups of champions could be issued either during sieges or during a period of truce; taking part in such an action could win a man international renown. Even rulers would sometimes challenge their rivals to single combat—as was the case when the Holy Roman emperor Charles V challenged Francis I of France—although there was no prospect of such confrontations ever taking place.

Chivalry and Literature

Chivalry was a major theme of the literature of the Middle Ages and Renaissance throughout western Europe. The exploits of historic and legendary figures were recounted in epic poems known as chansons de geste, notably *Le chanson de Roland (The Song of Roland),* which celebrates the deeds of the Frankish emperor Charlemagne and his followers. The stories of King Arthur and the knights of the Round Table, an extremely popular subject of medieval romances (tales of legend, adventure, and chivalric love) were given their first great poetic treatment by Chrétien de Troyes in the twelfth century. Such literature filled the imagination of many men and women who were not part of chivalric society. For the nobles, as well as for the soldiers and their families and followers, who made up that society, the literature of chivalry provided a common culture, one that, under the guise of tales of heroic deeds, improbable adventures, and enchantments, embodied their values, aspirations, and ideal self-image.

In the fifteenth and sixteen centuries there was a revival of this literary genre. Some books developed and extended tales from the literature of the twelfth and thirteenth centuries. The prose romance *Amadís de Gaula (Amadis of*

CHIVALRIC ORDERS

Several military orders were formed during the Crusades, a series of Christian military expeditions, especially in the eleventh, twelfth, and thirteenth centuries, whose purpose was to regain the Holy Land from the Muslims. Military orders were organized groups of knights who had taken monastic vows of poverty, chastity, and obedience and who vowed to fight in defense of Christians. By the fourteenth century most military orders had lost their crusading zeal, although the Hospitalers of Saint John of Jerusalem continued to harass Muslim shipping from their base on the island of Rhodes (when that island fell to the Turks in 1522, the Hospitalers retreated to Malta). In Prussia (in northeastern Europe) the Teutonic Knights set up their own state and fought the pagan inhabitants of the Baltic states. At the Battle of Tannenberg in 1410, the Teutonic Knights suffered a crushing defeat at the hands of a combined force of Poles and Lithuanians.

In the fourteenth century significant lay chivalric orders began to be formed, usually by princes. The most important were the Order of the Garter, founded by King Edward III of England in 1348, and the Order of the Golden Fleece, founded by Duke Philip of Burgundy in 1430. Election to such princely orders was a much-coveted honor. Most orders had statutes governing admission and prescribing how members were expected to behave. At regular meetings (called chapters), members could be censured or praised. Most members would be subjects of the prince who presided over the order, but foreigners, even other rulers, could also be elected. Some historians have seen these orders as mere charades, opportunities for princes and nobles to play at being King Arthur and the knights of the Round Table. Others argue that they had a serious political purpose, intended as they were to bind prominent nobles to the prince by the ties of a chivalric oath.

▲ A 1576 depiction of a procession of the knights of the English Order of the Garter. The coat of arms of each knight is displayed above his head surrounded by the garter, the symbol of the order.

Gaul), for example, was so successful when published in Spain in 1508 that several sequels were hurriedly written and published; it also became very popular in France, Italy, and Germany. In England the stories in *Amadis* never challenged the popularity or influence of the Arthurian romances, especially *Le Morte d'Arthur* (The Death of Arthur), the version written by Thomas Malory in the fifteenth century and published by the first English printer, William Caxton, in 1485. Some of the major poems of the Italian Renaissance were also reworkings of tales of chivalry. Among the best known are Matteo Maria Boiardo's late-fifteenth-century retelling of the legends of Charlemagne's nephew, Roland, in *Orlando innamorato (Orlando in Love);* Ludovico Ariosto's *Orlando furioso (The Madness of Orlando),* first published in 1516; and Torquato Tasso's epic account of the First Crusade, *Gerusalemme liberata (Jerusalem Delivered),* published in 1581. Miguel Cervantes' novel *Don Quixote* (1605) was a parody of the tales of

► *This unfinished fresco of a tournament by Pisanello, which dates from the first half of the fifteenth century, was uncovered in the palace of the Gonzaga family (whose emblem appears in the frieze) only in the 1960s. It is believed that the Gonzagas and their courtiers watched tournaments in the courtyard below from the windows of this room.*

knights-errant; it is said to have put an end to the genre of chivalric romances.

While much chivalric literature was written primarily to entertain, some works, such as Malory's *Morte d'Arthur,* were also intended to offer their readers inspiring examples of chivalric conduct. In addition, numerous widely circulated treatises on chivalry described the duties of a Christian knight, for example, or offered practical information on the laws of war. One of the best known, the idealistic *Book of the Order of Chivalry*, written by the Catalan knight Ramon Lull in the late thirteenth century, was still being read in the sixteenth century.

Biographical accounts of famous knights, such as the early-fifteenth-century life of Jean II le Meingre Boucicaut, marshal of France, presented their subjects as exemplars of chivalry. Chronicles and histories were written in the same vein, the most celebrated being the *Chronicles* of Jean Froissart, who wrote of fourteenth-century political events, especially the wars in western Europe. On his extensive travels Froissart covered ground from Scotland to Italy in the service of his patrons (who included Queen Philippa, consort of Edward III of England) and in search of material for his chronicles. Although he himself was a priest, his book is a celebration of chivalric values, of "marvellous deeds and noble feats of arms," and above all of valor, without which, according to Froissart, no man of good birth could attain honor and glory. He wrote that he wanted his work to be a source of good examples that would inspire young men to valiant deeds and the pursuit of honor. Froissart's *Chronicles* was widely circulated. A lively, if sometimes inaccurate translation into English by John Bourchier, published in 1525, ensured the continued popularity of the work in England.

Images of Chivalry

Visual images of chivalry were everywhere. The archangel Michael, Saint George, Saint Maurice, and other holy figures were portrayed as knights in armor, as were heroes of antiquity, such as Alexander the Great. Paintings and tapestries depicting themes from the literature of chivalry decorated the castles and houses of nobles and princes. Household furniture, including painted chests and beds, everyday utensils such as cups and mirrors, and arms and armor might all bear similar chivalric decoration.

TOURNAMENTS

Tournaments, whose origin lay in large-scale mock battles that might last for days and range over several miles, were arranged to provide training, entertainment, and the opportunity to win glory—as well as to profit from ransoms and from captured horses and arms. By the fourteenth century tournaments had become much more formal affairs that took place in a designated space, often with stands constructed for spectators. Later tournaments were governed by elaborate rules, with points being awarded not only for victory but also for the style with which blows were delivered. A fight between groups of combatants, the melee, remained the main event, but jousts, in which mounted opponents charged at each other and tried to unseat each other with a long lance, were an important feature. Weapons came to be modified with blunted edges and points, and tournament armor was specially designed to give greater protection than could be provided by battle armor (which had to permit greater mobility). Nevertheless, serious injuries and deaths did occur at tournaments. Even when the combat was an elaborately staged reenactment of a historical or legendary battle or siege or the mock rescue of a damsel from a wooden castle, the fighting could be lethal.

In Germany tournaments were organized by groups of nobles. From the late fourteenth century anybody deemed to have breached the chivalric code of honor was punished by being beaten with wooden clubs during the tournament or (more shameful) being placed on the barriers around the tournament ground.

Tournaments became an important element in the culture of the princely courts, and princes, even kings, would take part in the fighting or act as judges. Henry VIII of England (reigned 1509–1547) was an enthusiastic participant, for example, and King Henry II of France was mortally wounded while jousting in a court tournament in 1559. By that time, historians have argued, the methods of combat in tournaments had so little to do with fighting on the battlefield that tournaments could no longer be seen as effective training for war; instead they had become merely elaborate and anachronistic cultural displays. Yet a display of martial skill at a tournament could still win a participant a good reputation and the favor of the prince, and as Henry II's death shows, the fighting was no mere charade.

Nevertheless, the cultural aspects of the tournament were becoming dominant in the sixteenth century. In England, for example, the Accession Day Tilts, jousts held every year from 1581 to celebrate the anniversary of Queen Elizabeth's accession to the throne, were elaborate pageants in which the chivalric ethic was blended with Protestant propaganda. In the seventeenth century mock battles at court festivities became mimes and ballets, theatrical entertainments rather than martial sports.

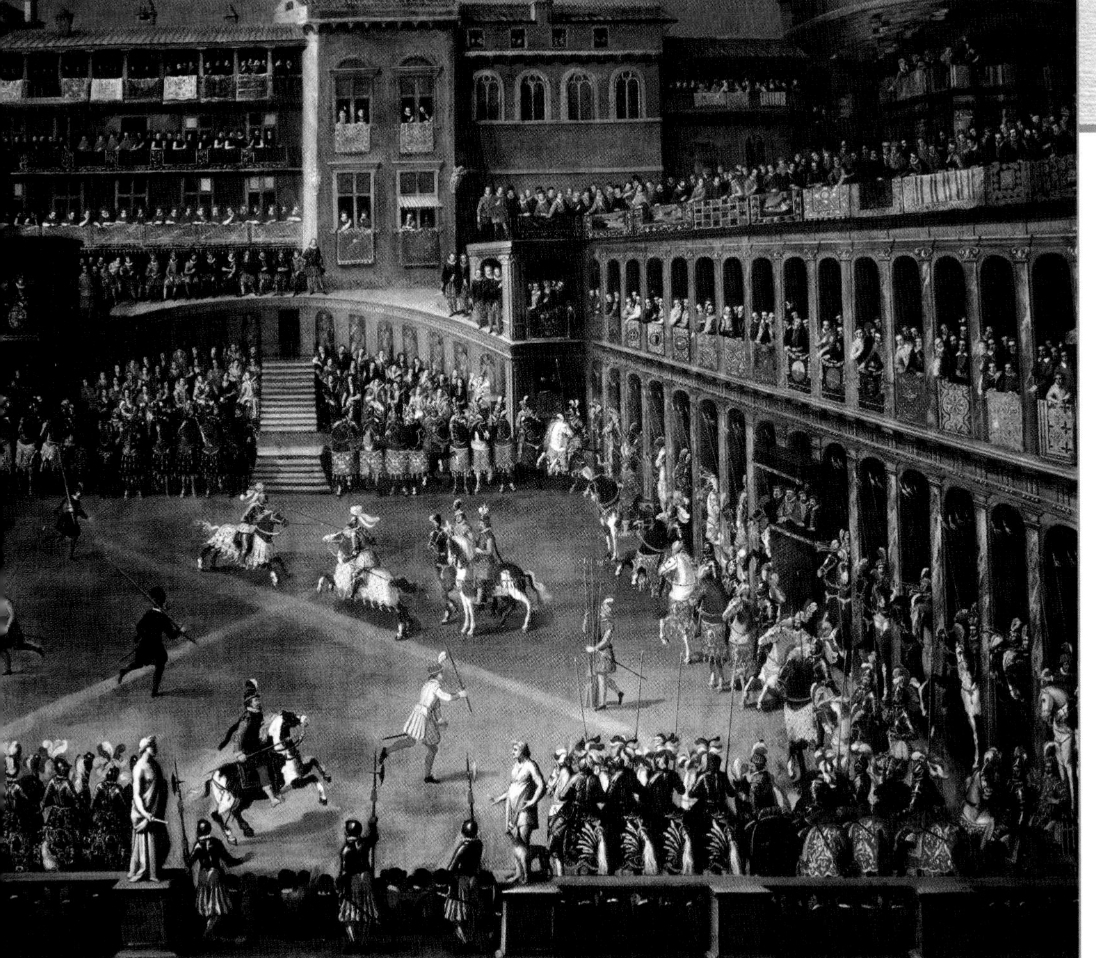

Tournaments were so much a part of court culture that they might be held even in the papal court of Counter-Reformation Rome, as this anonymous 1610 Italian painting demonstrates. The various teams of horsemen, distinguished by their different costumes and the trappings of their horses, are lined up around the courtyard.

SOLEMN VOWS

One of the most important elements in the chivalric code was the duty of a knight to keep his word: a formal verbal promise was as binding as any written contract. To enhance their reputation, some knights made solemn, sometimes extravagant vows. Men might die needlessly because they had sworn never to turn their back on an enemy. Groups of men might take an oath together, as at the spectacular Feast of the Pheasant in 1453, when Duke Philip of Burgundy and his courtiers swore to go crusading after Constantinople fell to the Turks. In imitation of the exploits of legendary knights, men might station themselves at a river crossing and swear to defend it against all comers. More commonly, men would swear to complete a particular task at a tournament; often such vows were taken to honor a lady.

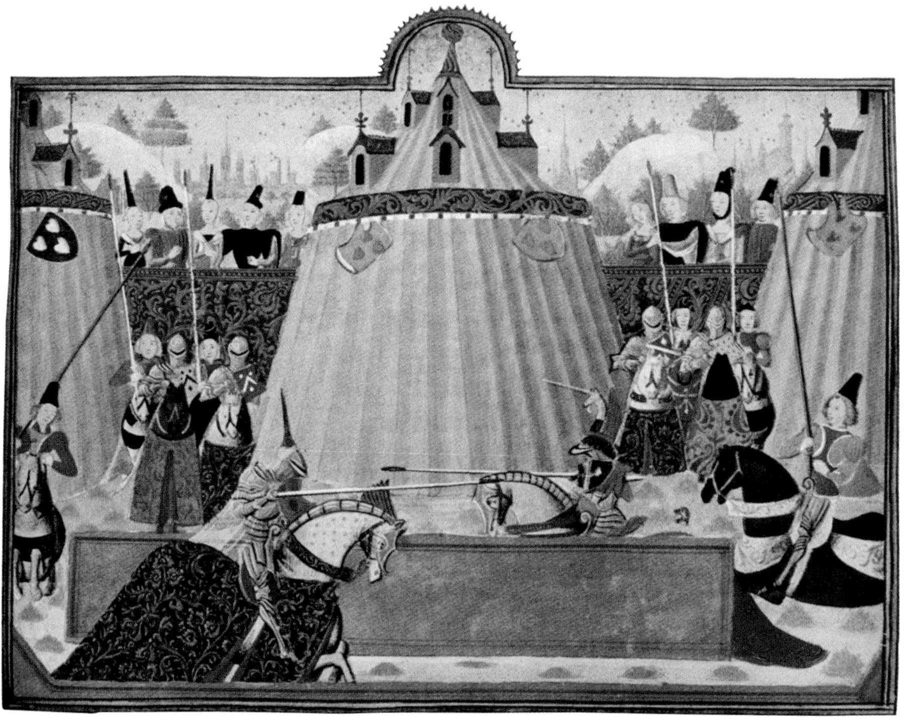

▲ *A manuscript illustration of the tournament at Saint-Inglevert, near Calais, France, held in 1390. Such elaborate tournaments might be organized by the knights themselves in order to prove their prowess in jousting.*

Visual display was an important aspect of chivalry. The coats of arms and devices (symbols) adopted by knightly families were a highly decorative means of identifying individuals encased in armor on the battlefield. Coats of arms became status symbols, prominently displayed on belongings, in houses, and on tombs. The visual trappings of chivalry—the sheer spectacle of a troop of horsemen in full armor, their weapons gleaming and their coats of arms prominently displayed on their clothing, horses, and banners—were an exhilarating sight for Froissart and others like him.

Endurance of Chivalric Values

Some critics complained that chivalric ideals were a false cover for a brutal and selfish reality; on the other hand, pessimists complained that chivalric values had degenerated. Such criticisms were still being made in the sixteenth century. Although the fashion for tournaments and chivalric literature persisted until the end of the century, the role of chivalry in the life of the military elite changed significantly. With the increasing domination of the battlefield by infantrymen and firearms, the heavily armed knight was no longer the decisive military unit. Those who wanted to make a career in the service of the prince needed the arts of the courtier or the craft of a lawyer; the skills of the knight were increasingly reserved for entertainment. Yet the military and cultural values of chivalry lived on in the code of gentlemanly behavior. Readiness to defend one's honor in a duel became the badge of a gentleman; the rapier replaced the jousting lance as the distinctive weapon of chivalry, and the etiquette of dueling replaced the laws of war.

Further Reading

Barber, Richard W. *The Knight and Chivalry.* Rochester, NY, 1995.

Keen, Maurice Hugh. *Chivalry.* New Haven, CT, 2005.

Vale, M. G. A. *War and Chivalry: Warfare and Aristocratic Culture in England, France and Burgundy at the End of the Middle Ages.* Athens, GA, 1981.

Christine Shaw

SEE ALSO

• Burgundy • Cervantes, Miguel de • Feudalism
• Hundred Years War • Literature
• Nobility and Rank • Spenser, Edmund • Warfare

Christina

DETERMINED AND INDEPENDENT, CHRISTINA VASA (1626–1689) RULED AS QUEEN OF SWEDEN FROM 1632 UNTIL HER VOLUNTARY ABDICATION IN 1654, WHEN SHE MOVED TO ROME AND BECAME AN INFLUENTIAL PATRON OF THE ARTS.

Born on December 8, 1626, Christina was the daughter of king Gustavus II Adolphus and his German wife, Maria Eleonora of Brandenburg. At the time of Christina's birth, Sweden was allied with the German Protestant princes, who were fighting the Thirty Years War against the Catholic Hapsburg-controlled Holy Roman Empire. Gustavus II Adolphus was often away campaigning, and in 1632, just a few weeks before Christina's sixth birthday, he was killed at the Battle of Lützen, in eastern Germany. Christina, as Gustavus's only child, was immediately named queen-elect. Because she was too young to rule the country herself, the government was entrusted to a council of five regents headed by the chancellor (prime minister) Axel Oxenstierna.

▼ A portrait of Queen Christina of Sweden by the French artist Sébastien Bourdon, who was her court painter from 1652 to 1654. With her plain dress and her shoulder-length hair (the style fashionable among men of her day), Christina cultivated a masculine image.

Christina's Education

Because women were not expected to play an active role in public life, it was unusual for girls to be educated as highly as boys in the seventeenth century. However, Gustavus II Adolphus had left instructions that Christina should be brought up in the manner of a prince. Bishop Johannes Matthiae, a prominent Lutheran theologian, was appointed as her tutor.

It soon became clear that Christina had a brilliant mind and a strong will. Philosophy and theology interested her the most, but she also learned to speak seven languages, including Latin and ancient Greek. The Riksdag (parliament) saw to it that Christina learned about Swedish history and cultural tradition, while Oxenstierna himself taught her about politics. From age fourteen she was allowed to attend the meetings of the regents' council, where she impressed everyone with her good sense. Aware that the world of politics was dominated by men, Christina was determined to be the equal of men in everything. She learned to ride, shoot, and sword-fight and deliberately made no effort to learn what she called "women's work and occupations."

Queen of Sweden

In 1644, when she was eighteen, Christina was formally crowned queen of Sweden. The problem the young queen faced—how to command the same loyalty and obedience that a male monarch would—was similar to the one faced by the young queen Elizabeth I of England when she came to the throne in 1558. While Elizabeth had exploited her femininity to the full, Christina did the opposite by creating a masculine image for herself. Christina was not an attractive woman—she had a bad complexion and a slightly deformed right shoulder—and she deliberately spoke with a low, masculine voice. She dressed in plain gray skirts and men's jackets and wore her hair shoulder length, as was the fashion for men at that time.

CHRONOLOGY

1626
Christina is born in Stockholm, Sweden, on December 8.

1644
Is crowned queen of Sweden.

1654
Abdicates in favor of her cousin Charles Gustav.

1655
Arrives in Rome after publicly converting to Catholicism.

1671
Opens the Tordinona opera house, the first public opera house in Rome.

1689
Dies in Rome.

Although Christina's image convinced her subjects that she was the equal of her warlike father, they still hoped that she would marry and have children to secure the succession. In the seventeenth century it was expected that even a queen would submit to her husband's authority, but Christina wanted more than anything to remain independent. Despite being put under pressure to marry her cousin Charles Gustav, Christina stubbornly refused. Another reason for her unwillingness to marry was her fear of childbirth—unsurprising, perhaps, in an age when as many as one-third of women died during their twenties as a result of complications during labor.

Soon after her coronation, Christina began to lose trust in Oxenstierna. She suspected that he favored the aristocracy and even that he planned to set up a republic. Although Oxenstierna was a good soldier, Christina was critical of his conduct of the war. She became one of the main supporters of the Treaty of Westphalia, which finally brought the Thirty Years War to an end in 1648. Although the treaty gave new lands in Germany and Poland to Sweden, peace brought other problems. There were growing tensions between the aristocracy, who had gained from the war, and the common people, who had paid for it in high taxes. Many peasant freehold farmers, ruined by the taxes, had lost their land as a result. The war had been very expensive, and Christina made things even worse by her extravagant spending on luxuries and lavish grants of crown lands to noble families. Despite her reservations about Oxenstierna, she had to call on him to solve the country's financial problems.

As a child Christina had been, in her words, "enchanted to see all these people at my feet, kissing my hand." As an adult, however, she did not enjoy the responsibility of being a ruler. Preferring instead to continue her studies, she became friends with many of the leading scholars of the day, including the French philosopher René Descartes (1596–1650). Descartes died while staying at the Swedish court, apparently worn out by the queen's frequent demands that he meet her for philosophical discussions at five o'clock on freezing winter mornings. Christina wrote plays and operas for performance in the royal theater, set up Sweden's first nationwide school system, and encouraged innovation and endeavor in the fields of science, literature, and architecture. The first Swedish newspaper was published during her reign.

Queen Christina was one of the most learned women of her day. In this copy of a painting by Louis-Michel Dumesnil (1680–c. 1746), she is shown in discussion with the French philosopher René Descartes, who was a guest at her court.

The following eyewitness account of Christina's abdication was written by a Swedish nobleman:

The queen came out of her chamber with the crown upon her head, the orb and scepter in her hand, dressed in her coronation robes and otherwise wearing a simple white garment, and began her oration. . . . Thereafter, Her Majesty laid down one royal emblem after another, stepped down from her throne, addressed the hereditary prince [Charles Gustav], who would soon be crowned king, recommending to him the good of the fatherland. The queen stood and spoke so beautifully and movingly, occasionally one sensed she was close to tears.

Per Brahe

After her abdication in 1654 and conversion to Catholicism, Christina was treated as a celebrity in Catholic Italy and France, where she received a rapturous welcome on her visit to Paris in 1657.

The Abdication

Christina's refusal to marry was a constant source of friction with her subjects. Queen Elizabeth I of England, every bit as wary of marriage as Christina was, was careful never to say never. Elizabeth was able to use the uncertainty about her marriage plans to her political advantage by playing off one suitor against another. Christina had neither the patience nor perhaps the desire to pursue the same strategy.

In 1651 Christina sent shock waves throughout Europe by announcing her intention to abdicate in favor of Charles Gustav. She claimed that the burden of ruling was too heavy for a woman and that it was making her ill. In fact, the real reason was that she had secretly decided to convert to Roman Catholicism, which had been made illegal in Sweden during the Reformation. Christina's decision to convert probably resulted from her discussions with Descartes and a secret correspondence with the Jesuits. Part of the attraction of Catholicism over Protestantism for Christina may have been the more idealistic Catholic attitude toward celibacy.

Immediately after King Charles X Gustav was crowned on June 6, 1654, Christina left Sweden dressed in the clothes of a man with her hair cut short. She later wrote that she felt she had found freedom at last. Christina would return to Sweden only twice: in 1660, for the funeral of Charles Gustav, and in 1667, to see to the management of her estates. After traveling around Europe for eighteen months, in December 1655 she arrived in Rome, where she was given a lavish welcome by Pope Alexander VII. The pope hoped that this well-known convert would be

▲ The Riario (now the Corsini) palace, Christina's home in Rome. Owing to extravagant spending during her exile, Christina was always short of money.

useful in promoting the Catholic cause. He was soon disappointed. Christina, opposed to public displays of piety, would not cooperate. Christina's conversion was a matter of personal conviction, and she felt no hostility toward Protestantism. She would later publish letters calling on Catholics to be more tolerant of Protestants and to stop persecuting Jews.

Minerva of the North

Christina decided to settle in Rome, where she found no shortage of admirers who were charmed by her wit, intelligence, and energetic personality. Because of her learning, Christina became known as the Minerva of the North (Minerva was the ancient Roman goddess of wisdom). Although she had income from her private estates in Sweden and a papal pension, Christina was always short of money. She was well known for her lavish parties and her sponsorship of plays, operas, art, and music. Through her patronage Christina had an important influence on European culture. Under her direction the first public opera house in Rome was opened in 1671. She also built her own private theater and astronomical observatory. In 1674 she founded the Accademia dell'Arcadia (Arcadia Academy) for the study of philosophy and literature. Christina's palace, the Riario (in the present day called the Corsini), was a popular meeting place for writers and musicians. Christina was the first to recognize the talent of the early baroque composers Alessandro Scarlatti and Arcangelo Corelli, whom she patronized. One of Christina's close friends was the sculptor and architect Gian Lorenzo Bernini. To save Bernini's reputation at a time when his rivals were trying to discredit him, she commissioned the art historian Filippo Baldinucci to write his biography. At her palace Christina gathered the world's greatest collection of Venetian paintings and an enormous collection of books and medieval manuscripts, presently housed in the Vatican Library.

Having once been a ruler, Christina found that she could not easily give up her involvement in politics. Soon after arriving in Rome, she began plotting with the French foreign minister, Cardinal Mazarin, to seize the Spanish-ruled kingdom of Naples, in southern Italy. Christina planned to become queen of Naples and leave the throne to a French prince when she died. The plot collapsed while she was visiting France in 1657. Christina accused one of her retinue, the marquis Gian Rinaldo Monaldeschi, of treason and had him executed on the spot while she watched. The king of France and the pope were both appalled at her behavior, as were many of her friends in Rome. Christina tried to justify her action on the grounds that she was a monarch, but as far as most people in Europe were concerned, she had lost that status with her voluntary abdication.

Christina and the Cardinal

In 1666 Christina became involved in another plot, this time to seize the throne of Poland, which had become vacant following the abdication of King John II Casimir (who was Christina's cousin). This scheme came to nothing, however. By this time Christina had become active in papal politics. She played an influential role during the election of Pope Clement IX in 1667. She formed a close friendship with Decio Azzolino, the leader of a group of cardinals known as the Squadrone Volante ("flying squadron"), who wanted the papacy to adopt a policy of political neutrality. Though priests were supposed to be celibate, rumors flew around Rome that Christina and Azzolino had become lovers. The couple's letters, which were discovered in the nineteenth century, bore evidence of their passionate feelings for each other.

The principal source of information about Christina's life is the autobiography she wrote during her later years when living in Rome. Christina felt that she had been destined to be a nonconformist from the very beginning of her life:

I was born with a caul [an embryonic membrane] and only had the face, arms and legs free. My whole body was hairy and I had a coarse, strong voice. For this reason, the midwives who received me initially believed that I was a boy. They filled the palace with their false shouts of joy, which for a short time even deceived the king himself... but a profound embarrassment spread among the women when they realized they had been mistaken.... [My mother] could not abide me, for, she said, I was a girl and I was ugly. She was not entirely wrong in this judgment.

Autobiography

This contemporary painting by the Italians Filippo Gagliardi and Filippo Lauri depicts the colorful pageant held in honor of Christina at the Palazzo Barberini in Rome in February 1656. Pope Alexander VII gave Christina a lavish welcome because he hoped she would help him promote Catholicism.

After a long illness, Christina died in Rome on April 19, 1689, aged sixty-two. Azzolino ignored her request for a simple funeral, and after a splendid service she was buried in the crypt at Saint Peter's Basilica alongside the popes. Although Christina has been seen as a model of female independence, the life she chose for herself would not have been open to most of her contemporaries. Had it not been for her royal birth, it is unlikely that she would have become as influential as she was.

Further Reading

Buckley, Veronica. *Christina, Queen of Sweden: The Restless Life of a European Eccentric.* New York, 2004.

John Haywood

SEE ALSO

• Bernini, Gian Lorenzo • Descartes, René • Education • Rome • Sweden • Thirty Years War • Women

Church of England

In the 1530s the English church split from the Catholic Church in Rome under the combined pressure of widespread desire for theological reform and royal ambitions that were at odds with the wishes of the pope.

When Henry VIII came to the throne in 1509, the Catholic Church in England was wealthy and apparently secure. There were, however, signs of discontent. Around 1360 John Wycliffe (c. 1330–1384), an Oxford philosopher, had begun to teach that the Bible was the only source of doctrine. Wycliffe also argued that the power of the papacy was not well rooted in Scripture. Before long, people with economic as well as religious grievances began to gravitate toward groups of Wycliffe's followers, who were known as Lollards.

Lollardy persisted into the sixteenth century, when it became the background for the teaching of William Tyndale (c. 1494–1536). Tyndale proposed many of the themes that would come to characterize the Protestant Reformation. He declared that the Bible alone (and not the papacy) was the sole source of Christian doctrine, that a Christian was justified (made worthy of salvation) by faith in Christ and not by doing good works, and that the pope in Rome was wicked (by now, Reformers were often calling the pope the Antichrist).

By 1520 the writings of Martin Luther were available in London. In 1511 Bishop Fitzjames of London had rounded up fifty heretics. Between 1527 and 1532, more than two hundred were arrested (this figure may be merely the token of a far larger number). Some of those arrested were priests. Thus, the idea of religious change was in the air when the matter of the king's divorce came up around 1527.

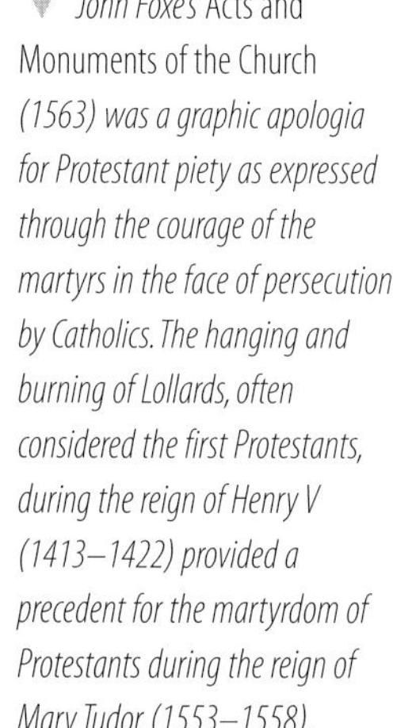

▼ *John Foxe's* Acts and Monuments of the Church *(1563) was a graphic apologia for Protestant piety as expressed through the courage of the martyrs in the face of persecution by Catholics. The hanging and burning of Lollards, often considered the first Protestants, during the reign of Henry V (1413–1422) provided a precedent for the martyrdom of Protestants during the reign of Mary Tudor (1553–1558).*

The King's Divorce

The occasion for the creation of a national church in England was not any deliberate plan for reform but the personal circumstances of the king. In 1509, the year of his accession to the throne, Henry VIII married Catherine of Aragon, the widow of his deceased brother, Prince Arthur. At that time Henry was a staunch defender of the papacy. He had been granted the title Defender of the Faith by the pope for his *Defense of the Seven Sacraments* (1521), a reply to Martin Luther's treatise entitled *The Babylonian Captivity of the Church* (1520).

In 1527 the king declared his desire to have the pope annul his marriage to Catherine. Henry knew if the pope could find some impediment that had existed when the marriage took place, the union of Henry and Catherine would never in fact have been a rightful marriage. Henry wanted to be free to marry again while remaining in the good graces of the church.

Henry had been married to Catherine in the first place under the authority of a dispensation granted by Pope Julius II in 1503. The papal dispensation allowed an exception to the rule that it was wrong for a man to marry his sister-in-law. Whether Julius II had had the authority to grant such a dispensation was later contested, but the very fact that Henry and Catherine had been married under a papal dispensation was the crucial factor.

WHY A MALE HEIR MATTERED

It is easy to be cynical about the reasons for Henry's demand for a divorce, but the previous generation had seen a great many reversals of fortune, and the Tudor dynasty was as yet extremely insecure. The first Tudor was Henry's father, Henry VII. With his slaying of the Yorkist Richard III at the Battle of Bosworth, Henry VII had put an end to the Wars of the Roses, thirty years of turbulence, bloodshed, and civil strife. However, Henry VII's reign was beleaguered by the threat of Yorkist plots to regain the crown. In the 1490s Henry VII conducted a small war against a pretender named Perkin Warbeck on the basis of a rumor that Warbeck might be the Yorkist heir. If Henry VIII were to die childless or with a female heir who might easily be put aside, the crown could once again be rolling in the dust of Bosworth Field.

The king desired the divorce for a number of reasons. After twenty years of marriage, Catherine had produced no male heir to take the English throne after Henry's death. The only surviving child of her marriage to Henry was a girl, Mary. Henry, who wanted a son, may have feared that, in the absence of a male heir, the kingdom would be vulnerable to a repetition of the tumultuous dynastic wars that had brought his own father, Henry VII, to power in 1485.

Henry was also in love with Anne Boleyn. Anne's sister had been Henry's mistress, and so Anne knew that Henry soon tired of his mistresses. She therefore refused Henry's advances until she was certain that he would make her queen. Determined to marry Anne, Henry needed some judgment that granted him his freedom. The king could also argue that putting away Catherine of Aragon was a matter of conscience. According to the Old Testament book of Leviticus, 20:21, a marriage with a brother's wife was destined to be childless. On the other hand, according to other texts, notably Deuteronomy 25:7–11, a man was required to take his deceased brother's wife. Nevertheless, Henry became convinced that his marriage to his brother's widow was sinful and that the pope had had no authority to allow the marriage. Throughout the lengthy matter Henry sometimes argued that, because the pope could not grant annulments against Scripture, Henry had never been married to Catherine; at other times he would plead that an annulment was required.

Catherine of Aragon, the subject of this unattributed portrait, was the daughter of Isabella of Castile and Ferdinand of Aragon. Catherine never admitted that any flaw existed in her marriage to Henry VIII and infuriated the king by refusing to agree to a divorce.

ANNE BOLEYN AT THE ENGLISH COURT

The daughter of the nobleman Thomas Boleyn, Anne spent her youth in the Netherlands and at the French court. After she came to the English court in 1521, she was the center of a circle of admirers that by 1526 included Henry VIII. Anne, a vivacious and strong-willed Protestant, put before Henry the writings of William Tyndale. Cardinal Reginald Pole, Henry's cousin, surmised that Anne herself had put the idea of the divorce in Henry's mind. She and Henry married in secret around January 25, 1533; the marriage was made public at Easter of the same year, and Henry's marriage to Catherine of Aragon was declared null on May 23. Anne's outspoken behavior won her few friends at court. Those who opposed her took advantage of Henry's loss of interest in her, which stemmed partly from her failure to produce a male heir. In May 1536 she was tried for adultery with various men, convicted, and beheaded.

The king's business, the question of the divorce, came to be the most pressing matter of state in the late 1520s. The chancellor of England and archbishop of Winchester, Cardinal Thomas Wolsey (c. 1475–1530), was made manager of the project to secure the divorce. His failure to do so was almost inevitable. Securing the divorce involved cajoling Pope Clement VII into granting an annulment in 1529 on the grounds of a condition that had been specifically dispensed by the Holy See in 1503. The pope had said in 1503 that Henry could marry Catherine despite the fact that she was his sister-in-law. It was problematic in 1529 for the successor of that pope to declare that the marriage was null on the same grounds. At the same time the pope, who wanted to do all in his power to accommodate the powerful king, was slow to say bluntly that no annulment would be forthcoming. The pope hoped that Catherine could be persuaded to go into a convent; Henry would thus be free to remarry. It was also suggested in Rome that Catherine's death would be a great relief. However, Catherine was defiant. Her uncle was the Holy Roman emperor Charles V. An annulment on any of the grounds proposed seemed dishonorable.

When Henry realized that the pope would never grant his divorce, he began taking steps to put Catherine aside and marry Anne on his own terms. In 1529 he removed Wolsey, whom he blamed for the failure to secure the divorce from Rome, from the office of chancellor. When the

Anne Boleyn, shown here in a painting by Frans Pourbus (1569–1622), insisted on being Henry's wife, not his mistress. When it proved impossible under church law to divorce Catherine, Henry defied the pope and established an English church competent to grant his divorce.

archbishop of Canterbury, William Warham, died in 1532, Henry appointed the Cambridge professor Thomas Cranmer (1489–1556). As early as 1529, Cranmer had been helpful to Henry by soliciting the opinions of European universities regarding the marriage. In May 1533 Archbishop Cranmer granted Henry his divorce in England and on English terms.

Birth of the Church of England

Having acted without the approval of the pope, Henry proceeded to remove England from papal obedience with a series of acts passed between 1532 and 1534. These acts forbade the clergy to make laws for the church without his consent, named Henry supreme head of the church on earth, and forbade paying certain taxes to Rome and making appeals to Roman courts. The Church of England was born.

Henry's chancellor from 1529 to 1532 was the London lawyer Thomas More, a man of great literary reputation known for his integrity. Because More would not sign an oath that implied the lawfulness of Henry's actions, More was beheaded on July 6, 1535. The only bishop who objected to Henry's actions, John Fisher of Rochester, was beheaded on June 22, 1535.

The English Church under Henry VIII

Henry VIII rejected the authority of the pope and tolerated and promoted clergy of Lutheran sympathies—Archbishop Thomas Cranmer, for example. He encouraged Thomas More's successor, Thomas Cromwell, to besiege the English religious houses with commissions of inquiry and finally to close the monasteries and convents. Whether the monasteries were guilty of the immorality of which they were accused has been questioned, but it is certain that Henry and Cromwell wanted the monasteries' wealth and property. The closing of the monasteries caused the only significant rebellion against Henry's policies. In 1536 men from Lincolnshire and Yorkshire rose against the king and began the Pilgrimage of Grace, an armed march toward London. Henry was able to get the pilgrims first to halt and then to negotiate. Finally, after some delay, Henry hanged Robert Aske and the other leaders of the pilgrimage.

▲ *This portrait of Thomas Cromwell (c. 1533) by Hans Holbein depicts the cool, determined character who as chancellor managed Henry VIII's affairs after Thomas More's execution in 1535. Serving Henry was dangerous work; Cromwell was made earl of Essex in April 1540 and executed for treason in the July following.*

There is little evidence that, once having secured his will in the matter of the divorce from Catherine of Aragon, Henry wished to reform the teaching of the English church. The principal change in religion authorized by Henry was the use of the litany, a lengthy prayer, in English, asking for the intercession of the saints. As late as 1539, in an act called the Six Articles, the king required the teaching of the Catholic doctrine of transubstantiation, according to which Christ is personally present in the bread and wine at the Eucharist. The Six Articles enshrined a number of other fundamental elements of Catholic doctrine, including the celibacy of the clergy and the necessity of confession to a priest.

▲ A contemporary portrait of Queen Mary Tudor (known as Bloody Mary), whose restoration of Catholicism was broadly popular but vehemently opposed by a clamorous Protestant minority. Insensitive to the claims of English nationalism, Mary renewed an unpopular alliance by marrying Philip II of Spain. Mary was no more "bloody" than any other Tudor, but the Elizabethans who wrote the history of that troubled period cast her as a persecuting fanatic.

When Henry died in 1547, the manner of worship followed by the parishes in English villages had not changed much. However, Henry's ecclesiastical policy already foreshadowed that of Elizabeth, his daughter by Anne Boleyn. He protected conservatives, such as Stephen Gardiner, bishop of Winchester, who valued the traditional theology, from the Reform-minded Cranmer; he also protected the Reformers from the conservatives. Henry sought a middle way.

The Protestant Prince

During the last years of Henry's reign, Protestant ideas were making some progress among the clergy. On Henry's death, when his only legitimate son, Edward VI (whose mother was Jane Seymour), came to the throne at the age of nine, the Protestant Reformation began in earnest. Archbishop Cranmer was free from the conservative restraint imposed by Henry VIII. The lord protector, Edward Seymour, a Calvinist, set in motion plans to suppress the Mass. In 1549 in a new prayer book, called the Book of Common Prayer, the sacrificial aspect of the Mass was subtly transformed into a Protestant service of communion. A second Book of Common Prayer, still more Protestant, was authorized in 1552. A rubric stating that the practice of kneeling to receive communion did not imply that Christ was personally present in the Eucharist was appended to the 1552 Book of Common Prayer.

The drift toward an unambiguously Protestant church was interrupted in 1553 by the death of Edward VI at the age of sixteen. Under the terms of Henry VIII's will, Mary Tudor was to succeed her half brother. After an unsuccessful attempt by the Protestants to make Lady Jane Grey queen, Mary Tudor began her brief reign in 1553.

Catholicism Restored

For five years, until Mary's death in 1558, the Church of England disappeared beneath the superficially restored Catholicism of Queen Mary. The true daughter of Catherine of Aragon, Mary returned the realm to Roman obedience and did her best to halt the spread of Protestant ideas. Cranmer and other prominent Protestants were executed for heresy. In 1554 Mary was married to King Philip II of Spain, but the marriage produced no heir and was unpopular with the English people. The queen was unable to secure the return to church authorities of the monastic lands distributed by Henry VIII to his followers. Mary died in November 1558, and the archbishop of Canterbury, her cousin Reginald Pole, died two months later. The Protestant-minded clergy who had left England when Mary came to the throne hurried back to England.

The Elizabethan Settlement

Elizabeth succeeded her half sister in 1558. On the morning of her first attendance at Mass in

Thomas Cranmer 1489–1556

One of the outstanding theologians of his time, Thomas Cranmer was the single person essential to Henry's plans. He appears to have been a persistent, quiet Protestant of cautious temperament who tended toward mildly Lutheran views. By 1525 he was praying for the abolition of papal power in England. In retrospect, his principle seems to have been never to defy the royal will. He was instrumental in the numerous annulments and two executions that marked Henry's marital career.

The crisis of Cranmer's life was his trial for heresy under the Catholic queen Mary Tudor in 1556. These proceedings tested his apparent conviction that the will of the monarch is law, for only a deep unwillingness to stand against his sovereign can explain his recantations at his trial of his long-held Protestant views—as well as his dramatic withdrawal of those recantations as he was about to be burned at the stake.

the chapel royal, Elizabeth instructed the priest not to elevate the host, the eucharistic bread. (The elevation of the host was associated with the Catholic belief in the presence of Christ at the Mass.) The priest disobeyed and was banished, but Elizabeth's intentions were soon clear: she would have no Mass and would establish a national church that owed no allegiance to Rome. The English church, while preserving decency in its ceremonies, would reflect the religious ideas of as many of her subjects as possible. Thus, Elizabeth hoped to keep within the Church of England not only a middle group who readily accepted its teaching and worship but also at least some of the Puritans and English Calvinists, as well as the Roman Catholics who were willing to conform to the changes in religious practice. When Queen Mary's bishops refused Elizabeth's request to ordain the moderate dean of Lincoln Matthew Parker to the archbishopric of Canterbury, Elizabeth used the bishops of Protestant mind who had fled to Germany in 1553. In doing so, she maintained continuity with the church of her father and of her brother, Edward.

During the long years of Elizabeth's reign (1559–1603), the character of the Church of England was established. The hierarchy of bishops, priests, and deacons was maintained, but bishops were appointed, as during the reign of Henry VIII, with the approval of the crown. English theologians maintained that the succession of bishops begun by the apostles themselves had continued down to the consecrators of Matthew Parker, Queen Elizabeth's archbishop. Therefore, they argued, apostolic succession was a mark of the Church of England.

As archbishop of Canterbury, Thomas Cranmer, the subject of this anonymous sixteenth-century portrait, nudged the English church in a Protestant direction after Henry VIII's break with Rome in 1534. Cranmer created the documents that came to characterize the Church of England—the second Book of Common Prayer (1552), the Forty-two Articles (1553), and the first Book of Homilies (c. 1548)—under the Protestant Edward VI.

▶ English Catholics hoped that the death of Elizabeth and the accession of James I would bring toleration of their religion; when these hopes were dashed, extremists attempted to bring down the government by blowing up king and parliament with gunpowder placed in the cellars underneath the houses of Parliament. The discovery of the so-called Gunpowder Plot before it could be carried out and execution of Guy Fawkes and his coconspirators (depicted in these contemporary engravings) stiffened opinion against Catholicism and inspired a new round of anti-Catholic laws.

The Church of England kept something of the appearance of the old religion through its dignified liturgy (rites of service) and its use of vestments (ceremonial clothing). The Book of Common Prayer, written in the elegant prose of the sixteenth century by Thomas Cranmer, formed the basis of an Elizabethan tradition of prayer and worship. The Church of England came to see itself as the representative of the early church fathers, the Christian teachers of the first centuries, and stood in opposition to the perceived corruptions of pure worship that had accrued in Rome. This self-image was defended by John Jewel in his *Apology for the Church of England* (1562). During Elizabeth's reign the English became a Bible-reading people. Such translations as the Geneva Bible, the Great Bible, and the Bishops' Bible were widely available.

CATHOLIC DISSENT IN THE AGE OF ELIZABETH

English Catholics were thought to pose the greatest political threat to the integrity of Elizabethan England. In 1570 Pope Pius V excommunicated Elizabeth and called for her deposition. This action clarified the position of Catholics, many of whom were becoming so-called church papists—that is, they maintained their old religion in secret while attending prayer services in the Church of England. The pope's action also caused Catholics generally to be viewed as disloyal.

While the majority of Catholics merely wanted the freedom to practice their religion in peace, a few were dedicated to the restoration of Catholicism by political means. In 1588 Philip II of Spain launched an attack on England with the Spanish armada, an armed naval fleet. The attack was motivated partly by Philip's desire to restore Catholicism in England and partly by a desire for retribution for English attacks on Spanish commerce at sea. The humiliating defeat of the armada was seen by Protestants as a divine intervention on behalf of England and Elizabeth.

In 1587 a plot to remove Elizabeth in favor of her Catholic cousin, Mary, Queen of Scots, was discovered, and Mary was executed. After the Jesuits undertook an effort to reinforce the dwindling Catholic community in England in the 1580s, Catholic priests, seen as traitors, were hunted down and executed.

The Elizabethan Settlement, as the queen's religious policy was called, was largely successful, strained though it was by the persistent dissent of both Protestants and Catholics. The realm had been modestly enthusiastic when Mary restored Catholicism in 1553, and a considerable body of Catholics remained loyal to the old faith. There was also a large body of Puritan opinion, often held most ardently by the exiles who had experienced the "pure" religion of continental Europe during the reign of Queen Mary.

▲ *Her surviving prayers suggest that Queen Elizabeth I was probably no more than conventionally pious, but it was important that as governor of the Church of England she be devout. This illustration from* Christian Prayers *(1569) shows the queen, hands folded in prayer, kneeling before a prayer book.*

Stuart Divine Right and the Caroline Divines

Elizabeth's successor in 1603 was James Stuart, King James I of England and James VI of Scotland. The new ruler continued to oppose and pursue Catholics, especially after the detection and failure of the Gunpowder Plot (November 1605), a Catholic-sponsored plan to blow up king and Parliament. Perhaps the greatest achievement of the Church of England during the reign of James I was the publication in 1611 of the Authorized Version, also called the King James Bible.

With the accession of the Stuarts, absolutism, a radical theory of kingship, was proposed. According to James's book, *The True Law of Free Monarchies* (1603), the king, the father of his people, ruled by divine right. Obedience to the king's commands was a religious duty. To bolster their absolutist claims, James I and his Stuart successors Charles I, Charles II, and James II formed an alliance with the bishops, who were for the first time in half a century admitted to the councils of state. The notion of divine right was naturally disliked by the Puritans, whose Calvinist leanings made them doubt the validity of any form of political hierarchy.

Upon the death of James I in 1625, his son Charles came to the throne. Charles also espoused the theory of the divine right of kings and made the defense of episcopacy, government of the Church of England by bishops, an important part of his policy. In 1637 Charles encouraged his archbishop, William Laud, to institute the Prayer Book and episcopacy in Scotland, a policy that failed after causing much resentment. Theology during Charles's reign was marked by a growing interest in non-Calvinistic themes that emphasized outward piety and the growth in holiness of the individual Christian. This new piety marked a great period in the Church of England. The theologians of this revival were called the Caroline divines, since most lived and wrote during the reigns of Charles I (1625–1649) and Charles II (1661–1685).

Clergy and lay people holding staunchly Protestant or Puritan opinions were kept out of positions of influence. When Charles I needed the authority of Parliament to raise money, the Protestants rallied behind Parliament in a single opposition to perceived monarchical overreaching. The struggle between the high Anglican, divine right monarch and the Parliament, whose ranks now included many disaffected Puritans and Calvinists, would continue until civil war broke out in 1642. Parliamentary forces, led by Oliver Cromwell, finally won in 1649. The king was beheaded, and for a dozen years England was a commonwealth dominated by Protestants of Puritan descent, Presbyterians, and independents. During this period, use of the Book of Common Prayer was discouraged, and ordination by a bishop was considered unnecessary.

CHRONOLOGY OF REFORM IN ENGLAND

1520	Lutheran ideas begin to filter into England.
1521	Henry VIII, having answered Luther with his *Defense,* is rewarded by Pope Leo X with the title Defender of the Faith.
1527	Henry VIII decides to cast aside Catherine of Aragon in order to marry Anne Boleyn.
1532	Having failed to obtain a divorce from the pope, Henry plans to be divorced in England by English authority. When William Warham, the archbishop of Canterbury, dies in August, Henry appoints Thomas Cranmer to the office.
1533	Henry and Anne Boleyn are married in January. Elizabeth, the future queen, is born in September.
1534	With acts that make it illegal to appeal to Roman courts, illegal to deny that Henry is supreme head of the church, and illegal for clergy to pass church laws without his consent, the withdrawal of the English church from papal authority is complete.
1539	Henry imposes the Six Articles, which maintain such traditional practices as confession to a priest.
1547	Henry VIII dies and is succeeded by Edward VI.
1549	The first English prayer book (The Book of Common Prayer) is published, and images are removed from churches.
1552	The second English prayer book is published.
1553	Edward VI dies, and Mary Tudor becomes queen. England is restored to Roman obedience.
1558	Elizabeth becomes queen.
1559	The Book of Common Prayer is revised and reinstated. The Mass is abolished in favor of the Holy Communion service (the Lord's Supper). Elizabeth's policy of inclusion makes the Church of England broad enough to contain both moderate Puritans and those who remember the Mass with nostalgia.

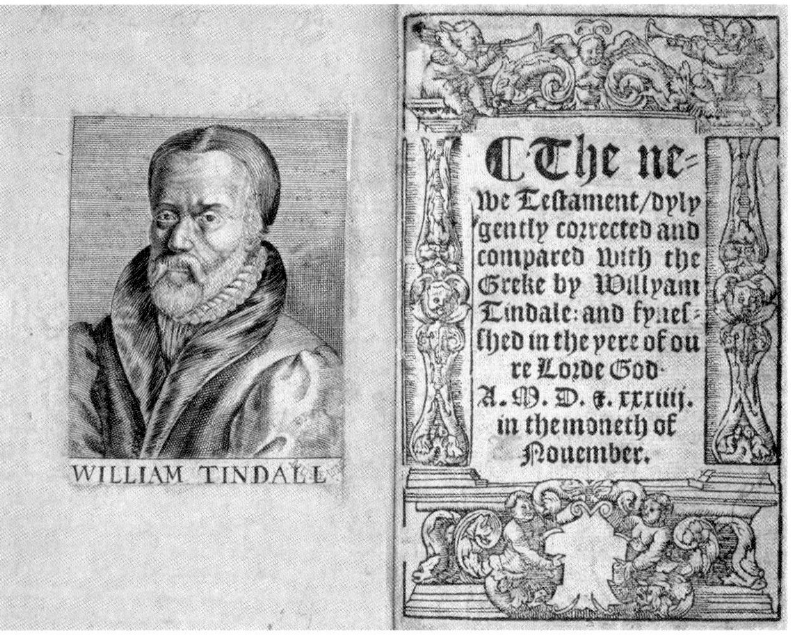

▲ *The English theologian William Tyndale (or Tindale) published his English translation of the New Testament in 1526; this revised version was published in Antwerp in 1534. Tyndale, whose Bible was the chief basis of the 1611 Authorized Version, also called the King James Bible, was executed for heresy in Vilvoorde, near Brussels, in 1536.*

Restoration

In 1660 Charles II was restored to the throne of his father, and laws enforcing the position of the Church of England were passed. The Corporation Act required members of public bodies to swear that they had received communion within the year. The Nonconformist Act of 1665 prohibited any nonconforming clergyman from preaching within five miles of any city unless he had taken an oath promising never to attempt to alter the government of church or state.

When Charles II died in 1685—having become a Catholic on his deathbed—the first great age of the Church of England was drawing to a close. The two forms of religious expresson that would mark its future course were in place. One was the dignified, liturgically rich, and somewhat diffident Protestantism of the Elizabethan age, with its emphasis on justification by faith alone and on Bible reading. The other was the high-church piety of the seventeenth century, with its emphasis on Holy Communion and the episcopacy.

Further Reading

Haugaard, William P. *Elizabeth and the English Reformation: The Struggle for a Stable Settlement of Religion.* London, 1968.

Kelly, Henry Ansgar. *The Matrimonial Trials of Henry VIII.* Stanford, CA, 1976.

Scarisbrick, J. J. *The Reformation and the English People.* Oxford, 1984.

Smyth, Charles Hugh Egerton. *Cranmer and the Reformation under Edward VI.* Cambridge, UK, 1926.

James A. Patrick

SEE ALSO

• Bibles • Calvinism • Elizabeth I • England • Established Churches • Henry VIII • Reformation

Clement VII

THE FLORENTINE GIULIO DE' MEDICI, WHO REIGNED AS POPE CLEMENT VII FROM 1523 TO 1534, WAS A MAJOR PATRON OF ARTISTS AND WRITERS. HE FOUGHT A LOSING BATTLE TO KEEP THE HOLY ROMAN EMPEROR CHARLES V FROM BECOMING DOMINANT ON THE ITALIAN PENINSULA.

Giulio de' Medici, the illegitimate son of Giuliano de' Medici (brother of Lorenzo the Magnificent), was born in Florence on May 26, 1478. One month before his birth, his father was assassinated in the so-called Pazzi conspiracy, a plot led by the rival Pazzi family to overthrow the Medicis. At age seven Giulio went to live at the house of his uncle Lorenzo, where, alongside his cousin Giovanni, he received a humanist education. When Giovanni went to Rome in March 1492 to assume his duties as a cardinal, Giulio accompanied him. Within a month Lorenzo de' Medici died, and then in 1494 the Medicis were expelled from Florence. Only in 1512, with the support of a Spanish army, did they return to power there.

Sebastiano del Piombo became Clement VII's favorite portraitist. In this 1525 image, painted early in his pontificate, Clement appears circumspect and poised for action. Austere and grave, the figure recalls earlier works of Michelangelo, a friend of both the painter and the pope.

Rise in the Church

In 1513 Giovanni de' Medici was elected pope; as Leo X he named his cousin Giulio archbishop of Florence and created him cardinal a few months later, on September 29. Giulio accumulated titles and benefices at a rate unusual even for the time. His responsibilities also grew: Leo entrusted him with several diplomatic missions, and in 1517 he became vice-chancellor of the Catholic Church. From 1519 to 1521, Giulio divided his time between Rome and Florence, where he bolstered Medici rule over what was still nominally a republic. In mid-November 1521, as Leo's legate, he helped lead a papal army allied with troops of Charles V (who was both Holy Roman emperor and king of Spain) that drove the French from Milan. Giulio's reputation for efficient administration and effective leadership grew to the point that some thought him the real power behind the papal throne.

Leo X died unexpectedly on December 1, 1521. Giulio, lacking sufficient support to gain the papacy for himself, engineered the election of Adrian VI, a reliable if elderly sympathizer with the Holy Roman Empire. Upon Adrian's death, Giulio received the emperor's firm support, and on November 19, 1523, Cardinal Medici became Pope Clement VII.

Cultural Ambitions

While Clement's elevation perpetuated the alliance between the papacy and Charles V that had been established in 1521, artists and humanists anticipated a return to Medicean largesse. The artist Michelangelo, rejoicing in Clement's election, wrote that "there will be a lot of art to be made." The Latin scholar Pietro Bembo even predicted that "Clement will be the greatest and wisest pope whom the Church has seen for centuries."

CHRONOLOGY

1478
Giulio de' Medici is born in Florence on May 26.

1513
Is named archbishop of Florence and created cardinal.

1523
Is elected pope and takes the name Clement VII.

1533
Orchestrates marriage of Catherine de Médicis to Henry of Orléans.

1534
Affirms validity of Henry VIII's marriage to Catherine of Aragon. Dies on September 25.

These hopes, though soon disappointed, were not baseless. As cardinal, Giulio de' Medici had been a discerning and generous patron; he had commissioned works that ranged from illuminated manuscripts and small objets d'art to paintings (Raphael's *Transfiguration,* for example) and architectural projects. Whereas Adrian VI had been parsimonious and austere, Clement initially spent freely. If he particularly favored Michelangelo, whom he had known since boyhood, he employed numerous outstanding artists, including Giulio Romano, Girolamo Mazzola (know as Parmigianino), and Giovanni Battista Rosso (known as Il Rosso Fiorentino). He also undertook urban construction and repairs. However, by the mid-1520s military expenses overwhelmed papal resources, and cultural patronage suffered accordingly.

Downward Spiral

Clement's alliance with Charles V had both a religious and a political basis. As emperor, Charles sought to contain the spread in Germany of the ideas of Martin Luther, whom Leo X had excommunicated in 1521. Initially, his military strength counterbalanced that of Francis I of France, but when Charles gained the upper hand in Italy, Clement feared Spanish hegemony, and so in 1524 he allied the papacy with France.

This alliance proved disastrous: in the Battle of Pavia (February 24, 1525), imperial troops won a decisive victory and took Francis I prisoner. Clement soon made peace with Charles V, who guaranteed protection of the Papal States (Italian territory under the political governance of the pope) and of Medici control in Florence. The following winter, with the Treaty of Madrid, Francis obtained his release in return for territorial concessions in Italy. Once freed, however, he reneged. Sensing an opportunity, Clement joined the papacy and Florence with France, Milan, and Venice in the League of Cognac (May 22, 1526), a move urged by several of his advisers, including Francesco Guicciardini.

Upon learning of Clement's latest betrayal, Charles V intensified his campaigns in Italy. In July his forces retook Milan. League troops suffered setbacks, and France provided no relief. In September the Turks, advancing westward in

Woven of costly materials, including not only wool but also silk, silver, and gold, tapestries gave epic proportion to the events they portrayed. Charles V's aunt Margaret commissioned Bernard van Orley, her court painter, to make the designs for a series of eight tapestries—of which this is one—commemorating the imperial army's victory at Pavia, which took place on Charles's twenty-fifth birthday.

THE SACK OF ROME

At 4:00 a.m. on May 6, 1527, an imperial army 40,000 strong besieged Rome. In addition to the French troops of Charles of Bourbon, who had rebelled against Francis I, the force comprised Spaniards, Germans, and even some Italians. It included not only Catholics but also Lutherans (including Sebastian Schertlin, who brought with him a silk rope with which to hang the pope). Bourbon fell in the first assault (the goldsmith Benvenuto Cellini later boasted of having fired the fatal shot), but by 7:00 a.m., aided by an unusually dense fog, the numerically superior invaders breached the walls of the city. Among the defenders discipline collapsed. Most ran for their lives across the bridges into the center of Rome. Pope Clement, who was saying Mass in Old Saint Peter's Basilica, fled at the last moment to the Castel Sant'Angelo.

By the following morning practically all resistance had ceased. Lacking a sure leader, the victors tortured citizens, priests, and nuns alike to extract ransoms; desecrated churches; and unearthed tombs in search of loot. Clement capitulated on June 7 and remained in the fortress under imperial guard for six months. The occupying army lived off the carcass of Rome, intermittently tormenting its remaining citizens, until the following February.

While it was not the only brutal siege of its time, the sack of Rome had special cultural and psychological repercussions owing to the city's unique significance: here, at the center of western Christendom, amid the ruins of ancient Rome, Renaissance culture had reached its apex. Humanists and artists who had previously heralded the dawn of a new golden age now had to lower their expectations.

At the beginning of the twentieth century, the German historian Ludwig von Pastor expressed the dominant view when he wrote that the sack of Rome marked "the end of the Renaissance." Present-day scholars view the event less as a turning point than as a traumatic interlude. Still, the event had a lasting impact not only on eyewitnesses but also on all who looked to Rome for religious and cultural leadership, as well as on critics of the papal court, who interpreted the sack as a divinely mandated punishment.

This idealized image, one of a series of engravings made by a Dutch engraver in 1555 and 1556, depicts Charles, the duke of Bourbon and commander of the imperial troops, falling from a ladder after being fatally wounded while leading the attack against Rome.

Hungary, won a major victory at Mohács. Closer to home, an imperial army led by Charles of Bourbon marched southward on the Italian peninsula, and by March 1527 it threatened Florence. Clement arranged an armistice with Charles de Lannoy, the imperial viceroy of Naples, but Bourbon and his troops ignored the armistice and went on to attack Rome on May 6. Pope Clement and a thousand others found refuge in Castel Sant'Angelo, but within a day the imperial army controlled the city. When news of the taking of Rome reached Florence, opponents of the Medicis had them exiled and established a new government. Clement did not escape until December 1527, and he returned to Rome only in the fall of 1528.

Accommodation to Spanish Hegemony

While in exile Clement explored options for regaining territory and political autonomy and also for returning his family to power in Florence. At first, he held out hope for French and Venetian support. By autumn 1528, however, it had become clear that the French would not take Naples and that Clement could not reach favorable terms with northern Italian powers. In practice, the pope's allies in his struggle against the emperor's armies had actually been fighting different wars: Venice consistently looked to its own interests in northern Italy but was reluctant to commit troops in the south, while France wanted only to conquer the kingdom of Naples.

A contemporary engraved portrait of the Florentine patrician Francesco Guicciardini (1483–1540), who served Clement VII in the mid-1520s as a political adviser and as lieutenant general of the papal contingent in the army of the ill-fated League of Cognac.

Relinquishing any hope that Spanish dominance over Italy could be avoided, in late 1528 Clement reopened negotiations with Charles V. In the fall of 1529, they met in Bologna, where on February 24, 1530—the fifth anniversary of the crucial imperial victory at Pavia—Clement officially crowned Charles Holy Roman emperor (Charles had been elected in 1519, but only with a papal coronation did the title become official). That summer an imperial army subdued Florence and restored it to the control of the Medicis, who now ruled under the aegis of Charles V.

Concerns of the Final Years

Until 1530 the paramount need for political survival and economic solvency had forced other concerns into the background. Now Clement could at last focus attention on arresting the fragmentation of Christendom, patronizing the arts, and providing for the future of his family.

After years of delay, in March 1534 he proclaimed that he would not annul Henry VIII's first marriage, to Catherine of Aragon (who was Charles V's aunt). Clement never called a general council of the church to initiate reform, in part because a council might challenge his legitimacy as a pretext for removing him from office. Unlike most Renaissance popes, he refused to sell cardinalates—except, that is, in 1527, when financial desperation compelled him to do so.

Military expenses significantly reduced Clement's patronage, first of humanist scholars and then also of artists. Many projects were left unfinished, and few were begun. Still, he remained a discerning patron. In his last years he commissioned Michelangelo to paint the Last Judgment on the altar wall in the Sistine Chapel, but he did not live to see the painting completed.

The legacy that most concerned Clement was his family. Upon falling gravely ill in early 1529, he elevated his young second cousin Ippolito de' Medici to the cardinalate despite Ippolito's own objections. The same year Clement also arranged the betrothal of Alessandro de' Medici—who may have been Clement's own natural son—to the emperor's illegitimate daughter, Margaret. In 1532 he had Alessandro installed in Florence with the heredi-

A Florentine statesman and historian who served Clement VII as a diplomat and adviser offers a searing indictment of the pope's character flaws:

And although he had a most capable intelligence and marvelous knowledge of world affairs, yet he lacked the corresponding resolution and execution. For he was impeded not only by his timidity of spirit, which was by no means small, and by a strong reluctance to spend, but also by a certain innate irresolution and perplexity, so that he remained almost always in suspension and ambiguous when he was faced with deciding those things which from afar he had many times foreseen, considered, and almost resolved. Whence, both in his deliberations and in executing what he had already decided upon, any small aspect newly revealing itself, any slight impediment that might cross his path, seemed sufficient to make him fall back into that confusion wherein he was before he had come to a decision, since it always seemed to him, once he had decided, that the counsel which he had rejected was better. For afterward, summoning up in his mind only those reasons which he had neglected, he did not recall those reasons which had motivated his choice: the conflict and comparison of which would have weakened the weight of the opposing reasons. And although he remembered having often been the prey to foolish fears, he had not learned the lesson not to permit himself to be overcome by fear. Thus, as a result of his complicated nature and confused way of proceeding, he often permitted himself to be led by his ministers and seemed directed rather than counseled by them.

Francesco Guicciardini, *The History of Italy*

tary title of duke. Finally, in October 1533 he oversaw the marriage of his niece Catherine de Médicis to Henry of Orléans, a member of the French royal family. Thus, from the political wreckage of his pontificate, he salvaged a promising future for the Medicis.

From Infamy to Partial Rehabilitation

Clement VII's contemporaries viewed his pontificate as disastrous. Francesco Vettori, a friend of the statesman Niccolò Machiavelli and a Medici partisan, marveled at how Clement "endured a great hardship to become, from a great and much-admired cardinal, a small and little-esteemed pope." Many, including the historian Guicciardini, faulted him above all for his indecisiveness and inconsistency.

That Clement often vacillated is beyond question, but modern historians tend to emphasize instead the insurmountable challenges that confronted him. Papal equivocation was not new: Leo X and Julius II before him had similarly sought to maintain political equilibrium among Italian territorial states and to carve out a space for family ambitions within that context. They, too, alternated between pro-Spanish and pro-French policies with a view to maintaining papal autonomy. Neither Leo nor Julius had done much to reform the church. Clement also resembled them in using the papacy's clout to advance

◀ During the Renaissance gold coins—such as this papal ten-ducat piece, stamped with an image of Clement VII—combined monetary value with political propaganda, their circulation among merchants and nobles ensuring the wide dissemination of the images and mottoes on them.

Lucrezia Salviati 1470–1553

Under Leo X and Clement VII, some women of the Medici family were politically active in the papal court—which had previously been an all-male preserve—provided that they were viewed as supporting their menfolk's interests. Among the most effective was Lucrezia de' Medici Salviati, the eldest daughter of Lorenzo the Magnificent and the only one of Leo X's siblings to outlive him.

Married in 1488 to Jacopo Salviati, scion of another powerful Florentine family, Lucrezia came to exert influence through him and through their son, Giovanni, whom Leo created cardinal in 1517. During Clement's pontificate Jacopo was among the pope's most trusted advisers. However, it was in managing the household of her son that Lucrezia had the greatest political impact. When Cardinal Giovanni Salviati served as papal legate to Bologna in 1524 and 1525, his mother managed his household affairs—no small task in a palace that was home to around 120 of his retainers—and even administered the ecclesiastical benefices upon which he relied for income. More generally, she looked after family interests and sought favors for Salviati relatives and clients by bringing them to the attention of Cardinal Giovanni and even of the pope himself, whom she could petition on behalf of her son as an act of maternal devotion.

The town of Orvieto, which sits atop an isolated rock in the central Italian province of Umbria, became a papal possession in 1448. Its cathedral, pictured at the center of this photograph, is a supreme example of Italian Gothic architecture. Clement VII spent several months in exile in Orvieto following the sack of Rome in 1527.

family interests. Finally, if his cultural legacy did not rival that of earlier Renaissance popes, the reason lay in financial constraints rather than in a lack of interest or taste on the part of Clement.

Ultimately, Clement VII may be perceived to have failed where his predecessors had succeeded less because of flaws in his character than because of changes in the circumstances surrounding the papacy. Goals that the popes had pursued with some success—such as maintaining papal revenues, keeping the Papal States intact, avoiding ecclesiastical changes that could abridge papal authority, and spending lavishly on the arts—were no longer tenable in the dawning age of the Reformation. Martin Luther's theological attack upon the papacy raised poignant questions about whether popes ought to pursue such goals at all.

Further Reading

Gouwens, Kenneth, and Sheryl E. Reiss, eds. *The Pontificate of Clement VII: History, Politics, Culture.* Burlington, VT, 2005.

Guicciardini, Francesco. *The History of Italy.* Translated by Sidney Alexander. Princeton, NJ, 1984.

Hook, Judith. *The Sack of Rome: 1527.* New York, 2004.

Tomas, Natalie. *The Medici Women: Gender and Power in Renaissance Florence.* Burlington, VT, 2003.

Kenneth Gouwens

SEE ALSO

• Catherine de Médicis • Charles V • Florence • Francis I • Henry VIII • Italian Wars • Leo X • Medicis, The • Michelangelo • Papacy • Rome • Warfare

Columbus, Christopher

IN 1492 THE EXPLORER CHRISTOPHER COLUMBUS (1451–1506) CHANGED THE COURSE OF HISTORY WHEN HIS THREE SHIPS CROSSED THE ATLANTIC OCEAN FROM SPAIN AND LANDED ON A SMALL CARIBBEAN ISLAND.

Christopher Columbus was born Cristoforo Colombo in 1451 in Genoa. Located on the Mediterranean coast of northwestern Italy, Genoa had a thriving tradition of trade with distant lands. Columbus's parents, Domenico Colombo and Susanna Fontanarossa, provided him with a comfortable childhood. Domenico, a weaver, manufactured and sold wool from a shop attached to the family home. Domenico also had important connections in the Genoese government.

Columbus's basic formal education was probably supplemented with hands-on training in the skills (technical, mathematical, and linguistic) that he would need to succeed as a merchant. Given Genoa's maritime status, it is unsurprising that Columbus decided to ply the family trade overseas. It is likely that he first went to sea as a merchant's assistant at age thirteen or fourteen. After a period of apprenticeship, he continued trading at sea and extended his father's business to international markets.

▼ *This portrait of Columbus in his forties is attributed to the Florentine artist Domenico di Tommaso Bigordi, known as Ghirlandaio (1449–1494).*

Columbus in Portugal

In the mid-1470s Columbus moved from the Mediterranean Sea to Portugal and its island possessions in the Atlantic Ocean. In 1479 he married Felipa Perestrello e Moniz, the daughter of a prominent Portuguese family. Through his marriage Columbus gained social acceptance in Portugal and the right to trade in any Portuguese-controlled port. He was soon sailing to western Africa and the Atlantic island chains of Cape Verde, Madeira, and the Azores. During these trips Columbus gained practical knowledge of the Atlantic winds and currents. This knowledge bolstered his belief that by traveling west, a ship could reach and return from the spice-rich Indies (the islands of Southeast Asia).

By 1484 Columbus was ready to present his proposal to King John II of Portugal. The Portuguese ruler, perhaps deterred by Columbus's demands for substantial financial and personal rewards, perhaps convinced that his own explorers would soon discover a route to the Indies by sailing around the southern tip of Africa (they did so in 1487), turned the offer down. Dejected, Columbus left for Spain.

Columbus in Spain

In 1485 Columbus moved to Cádiz, a Spanish port. Early in 1487 he met the so-styled Catholic monarchs, Ferdinand of Aragon (1452–1516) and Isabella of Castile (1451–1504), whose marriage in 1469 had unified Spain's two most powerful independent kingdoms. Ferdinand and Isabella appointed a royal council to thoroughly examine Columbus's proposal. However, a number of events—a royal wedding, the campaign to oust the Muslims from the Iberian Peninsula, and a trip Columbus made to Portugal—delayed the council's work.

CHRONOLOGY

1451
Christopher Columbus is born in Genoa.

1480
Columbus's first son, Diego, is born.

1485
Columbus's wife, Felipa, dies; Columbus leaves Portugal for Spain.

1488
Columbus's mistress, Beatriz Enriquez de Arana, bears his second son, Ferdinand.

October 12, 1492
Columbus lands on San Salvador, in the Bahamas.

1506
Dies in Valladolid at fifty-five years of age.

1509
Diego Columbus arrives in Santo Domingo to serve as governor of the Indies.

1571
The Life of the Admiral Christopher Columbus, written years earlier by Fernando Columbus, is published.

In 1491 Columbus was back in Spain attempting to promote his project. The king and queen again sent his proposal to a subcommittee. The results of the subcommittee's study were not positive. Nevertheless, despite the lack of scientific support for Columbus's project, Ferdinand and Isabella agreed to lend their backing. They also reluctantly approved his unprecedented demands, which were set down in the Santa Fe Capitulations. For his service Columbus would be elevated to the rank of admiral of the ocean sea, would receive 10 percent of the net profits he won for the crown in the Indies, and would be governor of all the lands that he might discover.

The First Voyage: Discovery of the New World

Few single events have had a greater impact on world history than did the first voyage across the Atlantic made by Christopher Columbus. After years of seeking support in the royal courts of Portugal and Spain, Columbus finally set sail from the Spanish port of Palos on the morning of August 3, 1492. The expedition included three vessels and a crew of almost ninety men. The *Niña* and the *Pinta* were caravels—small, quick, and highly maneuverable ships particularly suited to costal exploration. The ships were captained by two brothers, Vicente Yañez Pinzón (c. 1460–c. 1523) and Martín Alonso Pinzón (c. 1441–1493). Columbus was captain of the third vessel, the flagship *Santa María.* This ship was a *nao,* a bulky merchant vessel less suited to the demands of coastal exploration.

The three ships set a course for the Canary Islands, off the coast of northwestern Africa. The stopover at the Canaries allowed Columbus's men to make repairs to the ships and to restock supplies. The voyage did not get underway again until September 6, more than a month after the departure from Spain.

By the first days of October, the crew was becoming anxious. Even Columbus had some doubts. According to his calculations, the three ships should already have landed in Cipango (Japan). The men gained confidence, however, when they sighted floating debris and flocks of birds. Around 10:00 p.m. on October 11, Columbus thought he saw lights in the distance. Four hours later, at two in the morning on October 12, Rodrigo de Triana, a seaman on watch aboard the *Pinta,* spotted the sandy beaches of a small island. The *Pinta* fired its cannon to announce the sighting, and the three ships anchored to wait for morning.

In this fresco by Daniel Vasquez, Columbus is depicted departing from Palos in 1492 on his historic crossing of the Atlantic Ocean.

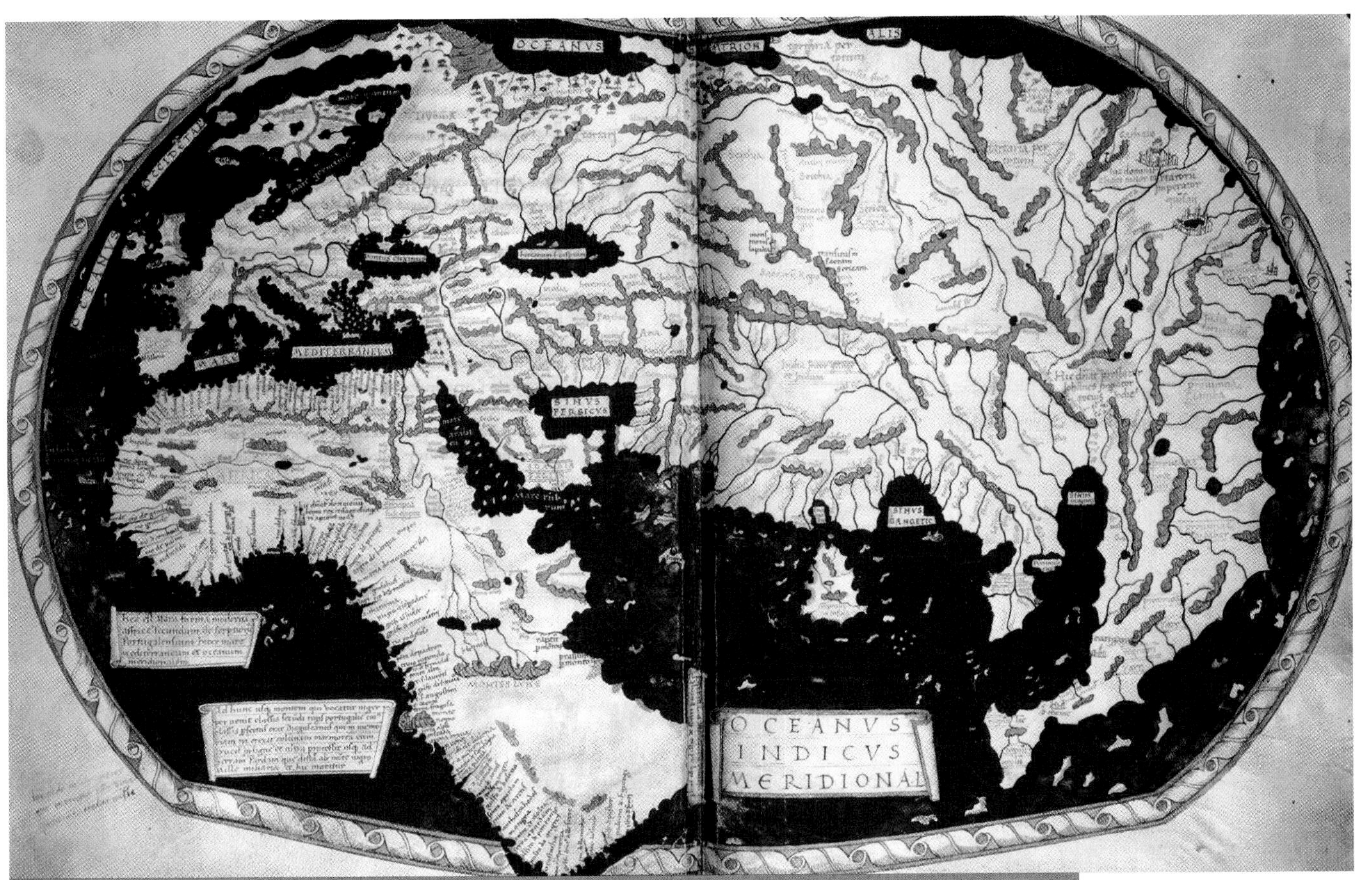

This 1489 world map by Henricus Martellus shows the world as Columbus and his contemporaries pictured it: the western edges of Europe and Africa are separated from the eastern edge of Asia only by ocean.

COLUMBUS'S WORLDVIEW

Columbus is seen by some as an early representative of the Renaissance: a man of science who stood against the ignorance of those around him and against the prevailing superstitions that were rooted in a medieval view of the world. A number of historians, however, see Columbus as a late embodiment of a medieval sensibility.

On the medieval map of the world, geography, religion, and superstition were combined. Columbus believed he would find the mythical lands and beings that populated the medieval imagination. He looked for monsters and men with tails and claimed to know of an island populated by the Amazon women of Greek myth. He believed that divine intervention had guided his discovery and often described the people and places of the Americas as remnants of the Garden of Eden, the earthly paradise in which, according to the book of Genesis, God placed the first man and woman.

The strength of Columbus's religious beliefs manifested itself more and more intensely in the later voyages. In August 1498 he was anchored off the coast of present-day Venezuela. As he gazed upon the marvelous scene that lay before him, he recalled, "I have always read, that the world comprising the land and the water was spherical, as is testified by the investigations of Ptolemy. . . . But I have now seen so much irregularity . . . that I have come to another conclusion respecting the earth, namely, that it is not round as they describe, but of the form of a pear, which is very round except where the stalk grows, at which part it is most prominent. . . . I am convinced that [this] is the spot of the earthly paradise. . . ." Columbus was suggesting that he had discovered the Garden of Eden on a bulge on the globe. He supported his theory by arguing that this bulge would place paradise closer to heaven. Thus, the Garden of Eden would have been spared during the Flood that, according to Genesis, destroyed all of the earth except Noah and the inhabitants of the Ark.

Indeed, despite his extensive practical knowledge of navigation, Columbus's view of the globe was greatly distorted from the outset. In both Portugal and Spain, Columbus's plan was rejected on the grounds that he had understimated the size of the earth and the distance that he would have to sail west in order to reach the Indies. Columbus landed in the Americas at approximately the same location in which he expected to find Japan. Therefore, he was never forced to acknowledge his error.

In this unattributed painting, a confident and vindicated Columbus shows his astonished sailors land. Unknown to Columbus, the land is not Asia but Guanahani Island in the Bahamian archipelago.

Columbus and his men had landed on a small island in the Bahama island chain (the local Taino Indians called their island Guanahani). Columbus took possession of the island in the name of the king and queen of Spain, planted a cross, and renamed the island San Salvador. He would repeat this ritual each time he made a new discovery. Many Caribbean islands still carry the names given by Columbus during his four voyages to the New World.

Columbus's landing was, on the one hand, the triumph of one man's determination to explore the unknown and the culmination of years of progress in the field of maritime navigation. On the other hand, his achievement might be described as an accidental encounter. Columbus was convinced that his view of the world had been accurate and that he had landed on the outer islands of Asia. He called the natives *indios* (inhabitants of India or Asia). Native peoples throughout the Americas are still widely called Indians. The islands of the Caribbean are still referred to as the West Indies.

Columbus left San Salvador two days later in search of other lands. Having sailed past several small islands, on October 28 Columbus found a land of significant size that he believed to be part of the Asian mainland. He christened the area Juana, although the island would later revert to its indigenous name of Colba, or Cuba. Eventually Columbus left in search of a an isle that the native peoples called Bohío. On December 12, Columbus landed on this island. Because it reminded him of the beauties of Spain (in Spanish, España), he named the island La Española. (Present-day Hispaniola is shared between Haiti and the Dominican Republic).

On Christmas Eve, Columbus began heading east along the coast of Hispaniola. Late that evening, after he had retired to his cabin, the *Santa María* lodged on a coral reef. In an attempt to lighten his flagship, Columbus even cut down the bulky mainmast. However, his efforts were unsuccessful, and the ship began taking on water. Columbus was left with no other option than to transfer his men to the *Niña* (Martín Alonso Pinzón had defiantly set off on his own some days earlier aboard the *Pinta*) and rescue as much of the wounded ship and its cargo as possible. Columbus sent for Guacanagari, a Taino chief

Many of Columbus's descriptions of the New World are an interesting combination of practical insight and creative exaggeration. The following passage from the letter Columbus wrote in 1493 to announce his discovery is typical.

Española is a marvel. The sierras and mountains, the plains and arable lands and pastures, are so lovely and rich for planting and sowing, for breeding cattle of every kind, for building towns and villages. The harbors of the sea here are such as cannot be believed to exist unless they have been seen, and so with the rivers, many and great, and good waters, the majority of which contain gold.

Letter to Luis de Santángel

with whom he had become friendly and whose village he had left recently. Guacanagari sent a number of men in large canoes to help unload the *Santa María.* Columbus would later claim that divine intervention had caused the accident in order to show him where to build a settlement. He ordered that a fort be built and, since it was Christmas, named it La Navidad (Nativity). He chose some forty men to stay behind, explore the region, and collect gold and other riches.

Columbus, now aboard the *Niña,* left La Navidad on January 4, 1493. Two days later he spotted Martín Pinzón aboard the missing *Pinta.* Columbus chose to forgive his wayward captain since he would need his help on the return voyage. On January 16, after a few more days of exploration, the two ships began the trip home. It was at this time that Columbus demonstrated the value of his extensive practical knowledge of Atlantic wind patterns. He had always been confident that no matter how far west he traveled, he would be able to return home. He understood that the Atlantic winds were circular in nature. To cross the ocean from Europe, he had traveled south via the Canary Islands to a region of the ocean where the winds blew to the west. On the return voyage he headed north to catch the westerlies, winds that swept him east back toward Europe.

Despite a severe storm that nearly destroyed the tiny vessels and an inopportune landing on the Portuguese-controlled Azores, where he was briefly arrested, Columbus managed to return to Europe. He arrived first in the Portuguese capital of Lisbon. On March 13 he left for Spain, and two days later he arrived to a hero's welcome in Palos, the Spanish port from which he had sailed more than seven months earlier.

▲ *In this engraving from Theodore de Bry's 1594 work,* America Tertia Pars, *Columbus receives gifts from Guacanagari, a cacique (chief) of the Taino people of Hispaniola. Guacanagari gave assistance to Columbus and refused to join with neighboring caciques in their attempts to wage war against the Spaniards.*

The Second Voyage: Colonization of the New World

Although Columbus's first voyage is his most recognized achievement, it was during his three subsequent journeys that he would make a permanent impact on the lands that came to be known as the Americas. Only six months after his return to Spain, Columbus headed west once again. A fleet of seventeen ships, carrying as many as 1,500 men, left the port of Cádiz on the morning of September 25, 1493. This was no voyage of discovery. After the success of the first expedition, Columbus's standing had risen dramatically, and he was now entrusted with the task of establishing and governing a trading colony.

It had been eleven months since the *Santa María* had lodged on a coral reef on Hispaniola. Columbus had hoped in that time that the men left behind in a makeshift fort would have gathered large amounts of gold and other riches to send back to Spain. What he discovered, however, would force him to alter his earlier view of a passive native population. La Navidad had been destroyed, and its occupants massacred. Columbus and his new band of colonizers—by now tired, hungry, and infirm—slowly sailed east along the coast of Hispaniola against the wind. They stopped at a location that included a large natural port. The Spaniards disembarked and began construction of Spain's first permanent settlement in the Americas, which Columbus christened La Isabela.

Columbus would spend the next two years at La Isabela as the community's founder and governor. The settlement struggled from the beginning. Colonizers, many of whom had joined the expedition in the hope of obtaining wealth quickly and easily, suffered in the heat of the tropical climate, struggled to adjust to new food sources, and despised the hard work. Columbus was seen as a foreigner by the class-conscious Spaniards. Complaints about his rule began almost immediately and soon escalated into open rebellion. The insubordination that revealed itself so acutely at La Isabela would reappear often during the rest of Columbus's life and on each of his final voyages.

In addition to La Isabela on the coast, Columbus began a process of colonizing the fertile interior of the island. His intention was to find a way to make his floundering expedition profitable. Although Columbus never found the amounts of gold that he claimed his discoveries would produce, there were mines to be exploited. To resolve the problem of a shortage of workers, Columbus turned an eye toward the native population. He established a system of forced labor by demanding tributes of gold and other commodities from the Tainos and backed up his policies with military might. In the most impressive indigenous rebellion to resist Columbus's domination, thousands of natives gathered in the Vega Real, the island's vast central plain. Columbus

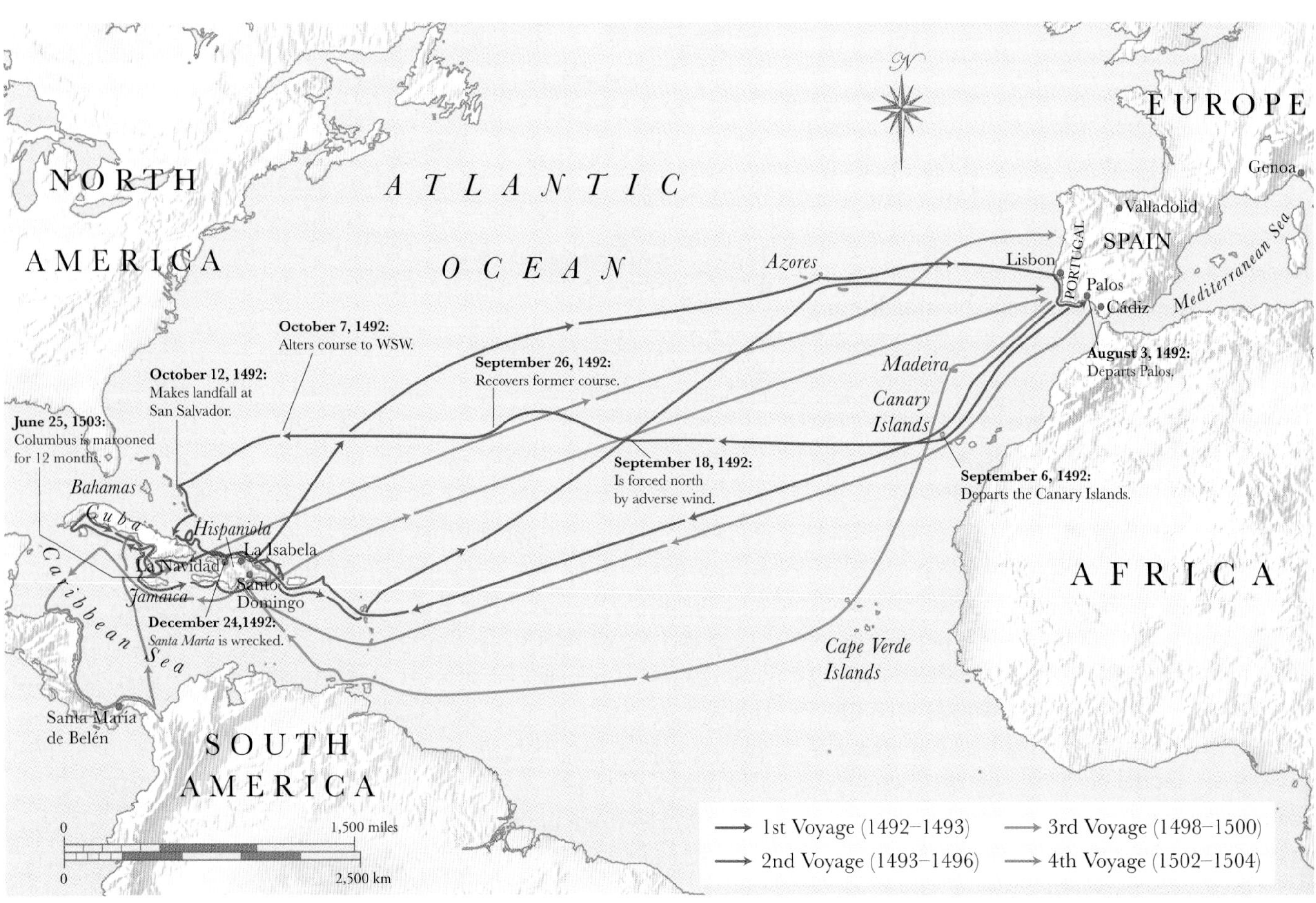

▼ The precise route of Columbus's ships on the last part of their first voyage cannot be reconstructed with certainty. What is certain, however, is that Columbus's four voyages together constitute a watershed in world history.

COLUMBUS'S WRITINGS

Columbus was a polyglot who, in addition to Italian (his native tongue), apparently spoke Portuguese, Spanish, and Latin. The vast majority of surviving writings that can be attributed to Columbus are written in Spanish. Unfortunately, none of Columbus's original journals of discovery have survived to the present day. Publications that purport to be Columbus's diary of the first voyage are, in fact, notes made by the Dominican friar Bartolomé de las Casas (1484–1566) while he was researching his vast *Historia de las Indias (History of the Indies)*. A personal friend of the Columbus family in the Caribbean, Bartolomé de las Casas was given access to the family's papers and made a summary of the diary that Columbus kept on the first voyage. Although the original document has been lost, Bartolomé's summary survives.

Of the many existing letters that Columbus penned, the most famous is the one he wrote in 1493 to Luis de Santángel (d. 1505), a financial adviser to King Ferdinand. This letter was published throughout Europe as an announcement of Columbus's discovery. This fascinating correspondence testifies to Columbus's fanciful imagination and his tendency to mystify the lands and the people that he discovered. It also demonstrates, however, the pragmatic nature of his endeavor. Columbus mentions gold and other riches, identifies locations suitable for colonization, and suggests the ease with which the native population could be defeated and even enslaved.

The fact that Columbus fails to mention God in this early document has led some readers to reject the sincerity of his later appeals to the religious nature of his endeavor. Nonetheless, in many of his papers, especially those written after his second voyage, Columbus seems obsessed with his spirituality and suggests a divine purpose in his past and continuing explorations. These texts (including the seldom-read *Book of Prophecies*) make fascinating reading and convey an often overlooked aspect of Columbus's worldview. Although skeptics emphasize the sense of disappointment and desperation that characterized Columbus's life at the time he wrote these documents, it would be a mistake to ignore the complex nature of Columbus's motivations and to discount his deep religiosity.

met the resistance with two hundred soldiers. In addition to their crude firearms, the Spaniards had twenty horses and the same number of bloodhounds. The natives, terrified by the fearsome Spanish weaponry and tactics, were routed.

While governing La Isabela, Columbus, who had seen the profitability of the Portuguese slave markets and was familiar with the practice of slavery in many countries, opted for what must have seemed the easiest method of raising capital. On February 25, 1495, he sent a fleet of ships back to Spain that included five hundred male and female Indians intended for sale at the slave market in Seville. Most died en route.

Meanwhile, the complaints against Columbus grew in intensity and reached Ferdinand and Isabella back in Spain. Columbus decided to abandon the failing community of La Isabela and ordered his brother Bartolomé to search for a new location for the island's capital (Bartolomé would choose Santo Domingo, the present-day capital of the Dominican Republic). Columbus then headed for Spain to defend his actions in the Americas. His departure on March 10, 1496, ended his second voyage.

An unattributed portrait of Bartolomé de las Casas (1474–1566), a Dominican friar, missionary, and historian who arrived in Hispaniola in 1502. By 1514 Bartolomé was campaigning against enslavement of native peoples in the Americas. Although his campaign was unsuccessful, during his impressive career Bartolomé did much to ensure better treatment of native peoples by Spanish colonists.

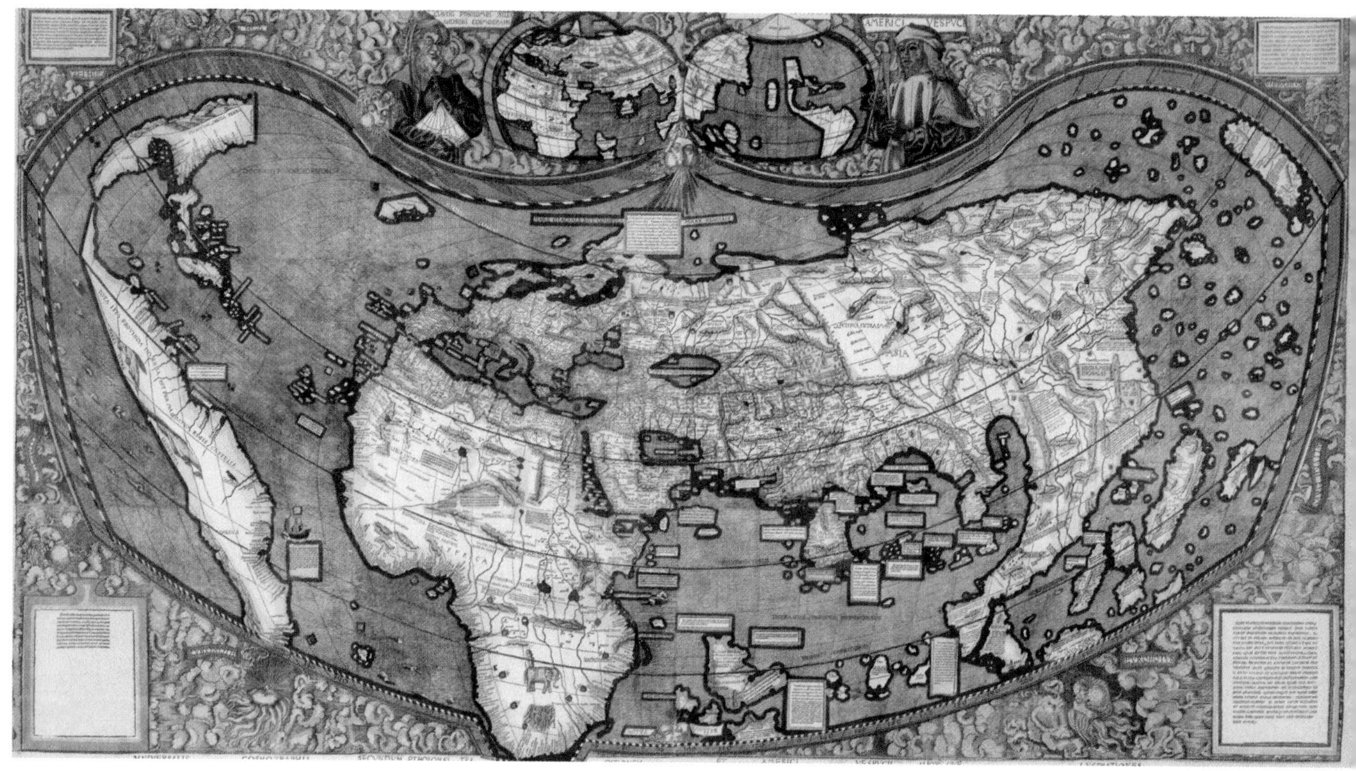

▲ *The world map drawn by Martin Waldseemüller in 1507 included one of the first depictions of the Americas, together with a suggestion that the New World be named "ab Americo inventore" ("after Amerigo [Vespucci] the discoverer"). By 1513 Waldseemüller had recognized that the credit belonged not to Vespucci (whose portrait is included at the top of this map) but to Columbus.*

The Third and Fourth Voyages: Shipwrecked in the New World

Although he would be granted two more voyages to the New World, Columbus's prestige in Spain would never fully recover from his failures in governing La Isabela. Columbus left on his third voyage on May 30, 1498. While a number of ships carrying supplies and new settlers—including, for the first time, a significant number of women—left for Hispaniola, Columbus took three ships on a more southerly route and discovered the South American continent. In August, after a two-year absence from Hispaniola, Columbus arrived at Santo Domingo and resumed his responsibilities as governor of the island. Conditions had not improved for the settlers, however, and a handful of dissidents (both Spanish and indigenous) used the general discontent to launch significant rebellions against Columbus's authority. In the summer of 1500, Francisco de Bobadilla (d. 1502) arrived from Spain with authority to investigate the situation of the colony. Sympathetic to the complaints, Bobadilla had Columbus arrested and returned in chains to Spain.

Despite their exasperation that Columbus had been treated so poorly, at first Ferdinand and Isabella were not interested in allowing Columbus to return to the lands that he had managed so unsuccessfully. In 1502, however, they agreed to allow him to make a fourth voyage. Their permission came with important limitations. Columbus was not to land on Hispaniola, and he was not to take any slaves. Columbus had high expectations and called this voyage, which began on May 9, 1502, his *Alto Viaje* ("high voyage"). He explored the coast of Central America and began building a settlement, which he named Santa María de Belén, by a bay in present-day Panama. A revolt by native peoples forced the would-be settlers to abandon their colony and one of their four ships. The remaining vessels were in desperate need of repairs, and Columbus had to ditch another. With his two remaining ships taking on water, Columbus was forced to run the vessels aground on the island of Jamaica, where he and his men would spend the next year waiting to be rescued.

The Death of Christopher Columbus

Columbus left the Americas for the last time and arrived back in Spain in November of 1504. He was fifty-five years old, in poor health, and generally shunned or ignored. He must have felt acutely the waning of his influence and reputation: a Spaniard now governed on Hispaniola,

THE COLUMBIAN EXCHANGE

When Columbus returned to Spain in 1493, he displayed to curious Spanish audiences a sample of the wonders he had encountered on his first voyage. Among these wonders were handicrafts, plants, birds, animals, and even a few Indians (as he thought they were) that he had gathered on the other side of the Atlantic. In this way Columbus began a process of exchange between the New World and the Old that would have far-reaching effects on all parts of the globe.

The phrase *Columbian exchange* was coined by the American historian Alfred Crosby in 1972. Civilizations with no previous knowledge of each other were introduced in an instant to each other's culture, ideas, and products. Europeans, to cite only a few examples, brought wheat, onions, sugar, rice, chickens, and horses to the Americas. They received in return corn, tomatoes, turkeys, cocoa, and potatoes. In many ways the sharing of these products has improved the lot of humankind as a whole.

However, some of the commodities exchanged between Europe and America had less positive repercussions. Diseases ran rife among populations that had had no previous exposure—and therefore no natural immunity—to them. Some have theorized that an outbreak of syphilis in Europe at the turn of the sixteenth century might have originated in the first sexual contacts between European men and women of the Americas. On the other side of the Atlantic, great swaths of the native population were wiped out by such European diseases as smallpox, influenza, measles, and chicken pox. As numbers dwindled, the European mine and plantation owners looked to Africa for forced labor. From 1505 to 1852, some 8 to 11 million enslaved Africans were shipped across the Atlantic. This particularly brutal legacy of the Columbian exchange permanently changed the demography of the Americas.

and the discovery and conquest of the Americas would continue without him. Emblematic of Columbus's travails at the end of his life was the failure of Martin Waldseemüller, a German mapmaker, to credit Columbus with having discovered the American mainland. Instead, Waldseemüller named the land America in honor of the Italian explorer Amerigo Vespucci. (1454–1512). By the time Waldseemüller recognized his error, it was too late: the name America had come to stay. Christopher Columbus died in Valladolid, Spain, on May 20, 1506.

FURTHER READING

Bedini, Silvio A., ed. *Christopher Columbus and the Age of Exploration: An Encyclopedia.* New York, 1998.

Columbus, Christopher. *Four Voyages to the New World: Letters and Selected Documents.* Translated and edited by R. H. Major. Secaucus, NJ, 1992.

Morison, Samuel Eliot. *Admiral of the Ocean Sea: A Life of Christopher Columbus.* New York, 1997. First published 1942.

Sale, Kirkpatrick. *The Conquest of Paradise: Christopher Columbus and the Columbian Legacy.* New York, 1991.

Douglas J. Weatherford

▲ *The funerary monument of Columbus in Seville, Spain. Columbus's bones were transferred to the Caribbean some years after he died in Spain. Although many believe that Columbus's remains are now buried in Seville, the Dominican Republic maintains a second sepulchre in Santo Domingo. Recent DNA tests failed to resolve the dispute.*

SEE ALSO

• Exploration • Ferdinand and Isabella • Portugal • Spain

Constantinople

As the capital of the Eastern Roman Empire, which stretched from Syria to Spain, Constantinople preserved for a thousand years the Greek Christian culture that inspired the Renaissance in western Europe.

The Imperial City

When the Renaissance began in Europe, around 1350, Constantinople was a thousand years old. The founding of the city had been the project of Emperor Constantine the Great (reigned 306–337), who inaugurated Constantinople in 330 as the new Christian capital of the Roman Empire. The site Constantine chose was Byzantium, a town on the northwestern shore of the Sea of Marmara. Among Constantine's reasons for leaving Rome were his desire to move closer to the empire's eastern frontier, where the Persians posed a grave threat, his wish to found a city bearing his name, and perhaps not least, a desire to have a Christian capital. Constantine's new city would enable more efficient government, immortalize the emperor's name, and provide a showcase for the new religion.

Constantinople was built on a triangular piece of land bounded on the south by the Sea of Marmara and on the north by the Golden Horn, a narrow bay four miles in length and shaped like a stag's horn that provided a sheltered anchorage. On the west the city was protected by a wall running from the Sea of Marmara to an area close to the Golden Horn. The first city wall was built by Constantine. Constantinople grew, and a new wall was built by Theodosius II in 413. Sea walls were added later, and soon there were suburbs across the Golden Horn and to the east across the Sea of Marmara.

Made in Switzerland in 1436, just seventeen years before the city fell to the Turks, this somewhat impressionistic drawing of Constantinople includes the city walls, the great domed Church of Hagia Sophia, and the equestrian statue of the emperor Justinian.

Priest and King

A feature of the political and religious life of Constantinople that distinguished the Byzantine (Eastern Roman) Empire from the West was the role of the emperor as head of both the church and the empire. Constantine and his successors until 1453 exemplified a system later called caesaropapism: the ruler, the caesar, was also the papa, the father of the church. (In the early church *papa* was the title of a bishop.) The view of the Eastern church was that God gave all authority to the emperor, who was ultimately responsible for both church and empire. The Western church, on the other hand, held that all authority was given to Christ, who had in turn given it to the church in the person of Saint Peter. Peter's successor, the patriarch of Rome, the pope, thus ruled over all the churches. The pope was the agent through whom kings were crowned. Although no single authority in the Eastern church was analogous to the pope in the West, deference was always shown to the patriarch of Constantinople.

The Byzantine theory would have some influence during the Reformation, when kings and princes began to see themselves as the head of their respective national churches and when Western theologians began to argue that a general council was the highest authority. The book that popularized this theory in the West was *Defender of the Peace* (1324), by Marsilius of Padua (c. 1280–c. 1343). While Marsilius's theory did not reproduce the Byzantine theory in all respects, it gave such kings as Henry VIII and Louis XIV a historical precedent for their claims to govern the church within their respective territory.

SPIRITUAL AND TEMPORAL POWER

There are significant differences between the religious art produced in the Eastern and Western Roman Empires. These differences reflect the alternative views held by the Eastern and Western churches of the role and relationship of church and empire. For example, a tenth-century Byzantine ivory plaque depicts Christ crowning the Eastern Roman emperor Romanus II (reigned 959–963) and the empress Eudocia. An eighteenth-century mosaic in the apse of the old Lateran Palace, occupied by the popes of Rome until the sixteenth century, offers a different perspective. The mosaic depicts Saint Peter giving temporal power, symbolized by a sword, to Charlemagne (who ruled as emperor of the West from 800 to 814), while at the same time giving spiritual power, represented by a set of keys, to Pope Leo III (795–816).

In Constantinople the emperor, in whom both temporal and spiritual power were joined, was thought of as having been crowned directly by Christ. In Rome the source of power was Saint Peter, to whom Christ had given all authority, and spiritual power and temporal power were vested in different authorities.

▲ Protected by the Sea of Marmara to the south, the Bosporus to the east, the Golden Horn to the north, and the walls of Constantine and Theodosius to the west, Constantinople was invaded only once in a thousand years—by European crusaders in 1204.

A Cultural Capital

The intellectual culture of Constantinople exemplified the union of Christian theology and classical learning that would mark the pattern of education in Christian Europe and its colonies until the nineteenth century. In a book entitled *How a Christian Youth Can Benefit from the Study of the Classics* (362), the theologian and bishop Basil the Great advocated the principle that a student should read the classics in order to develop good morals but should ignore accounts of evil deeds or persons.

In 425 a university, the first in the Christian Roman world, was established in Constantinople by Theodosius II. It included faculties of Greek grammar and rhetoric, Latin grammar, Latin rhetoric, law, and philosophy. Boys would have begun with such rudiments as spelling and reading before progressing to grammar and then to rhetoric and philosophy.

Michael Constantine Psellus 1018–c. 1078

Although there were exceptions, most Eastern Roman emperors valued learning and encouraged scholarship. The philosopher and theologian Michael Constantine Psellus served the emperors Michael V (reigned 1041–1042) and Constantine X (1042–1054), who in 1045 appointed Psellus to head the philosophy faculty at Constantinople's university. The empress Theodora (1055–1056) employed Psellus as chief minister, in which position he continued to serve under Michael VII (1071–1078), his former student. Renowned for his encyclopedic knowledge, Psellus integrated the philosophy of Plato (c. 428–c. 348 BCE) with Christian thought (as the fathers of the Greek church had done in the first centuries after Christ). He initiated a revival in the study of Homer and other ancient Greek authors. A statesman as well as a scholar, Psellus also wrote treatises on mathematics, physics, and metaphysics, in addition to verses and paraphrases of Homer's *Iliad* and Aristotle's *On Interpretation*.

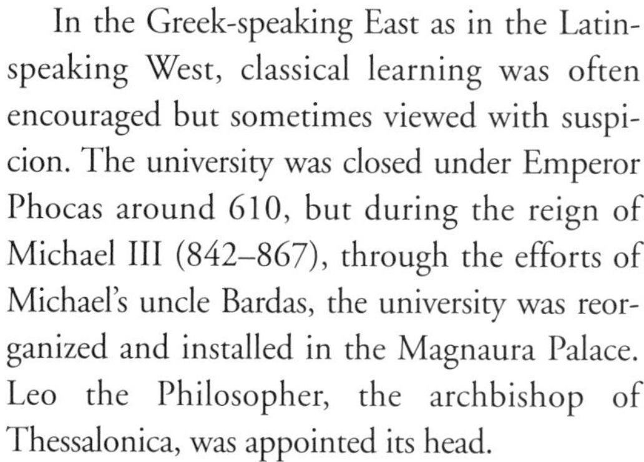

In the Greek-speaking East as in the Latin-speaking West, classical learning was often encouraged but sometimes viewed with suspicion. The university was closed under Emperor Phocas around 610, but during the reign of Michael III (842–867), through the efforts of Michael's uncle Bardas, the university was reorganized and installed in the Magnaura Palace. Leo the Philosopher, the archbishop of Thessalonica, was appointed its head.

By 1025 the refounded university had again closed, but in 1045 Emperor Constantine IX, concerned that there was no school of law, founded a law school that also employed a professor of philosophy. Michael Constantine Psellus (1018–c. 1078) was the first to hold this post. The university sometimes faltered and was sometimes overshadowed by the school of the patriarch. As often as the university fell into decay, however, it was refounded, as happened during the reign of Michael VIII Palaeologus (1261–1282). Although rivaled by such western university towns as Padua and Bologna in Italy and Paris in France, Constantinople would remain the world's greatest center of learning until the conquest of the city by the Muslims in 1453.

▼ *Kariye Cami, the church of the Chora monastery, was built around 1050 on a square plan with small domes at the corners and a large central dome, all raised on drums that allowed room for windows to let in light. With the Church of the Apostles, Kariye Cami became the model for Saint Mark's Basilica in Venice, built between 1041 and 1072. The frescos of Kariye Cami survived Ottoman occupation.*

Constantinople and the West

In the fourteenth century, when the Renaissance in the West heralded a revival in classical scholarship, Constantinople and its shrinking empire had been more or less cut off from the ideas current in Italy and the West for four hundred years. East and West spoke different languages; Greek was not known even by scholars in the West, and until the fourteenth-century revival of Byzantine interest in the West, Latin was not widely known in Constantinople.

This mutual isolation was rooted in political differences. Pope Gregory I the Great (540–604) had acted as the ambassador of the Roman church to the emperor in Constantinople. Gregory had learned from his stay at the Byzantine court that the eastern empire, represented in Italy by the exarch (viceroy) in Ravenna, lacked the military power to help the Romans. He made a separate peace with the Visigoths that set aside the authority of the exarch, an action that aroused resentment in Constantinople. In 800 Pope Leo III, by crowning Charlemagne emperor of his western territories, had formally removed the West from

◀ *This painting by Tintoretto (c. 1518–1594) celebrates the conquest of Constantinople by crusaders in 1204. The crusading army was unrepentant, but when Pope Innocent III heard of the destruction of Constantinople, he wept. The event remains a cause of much ill feeling between Roman Catholicism and Eastern Orthodoxy.*

Byzantine jurisdiction (parts of southern Italy and Sicily remained Greek-speaking until the eighteenth century, however). Then in 858 the Byzantine emperor Michael III, ignoring the objections of Pope Nicholas I, deposed the patriarch of Constantinople, Ignatius, and installed his own choice, Photius (c. 810–c. 895). This dispute was on the point of being resolved when the controversy as to whether Bulgaria, a newly converted land that lay between Rome and Constantinople, should fall under the ecclesiastical jurisdiction of one city or the other arose. Finally, in 1054 there was what proved to be a decisive break between Rome and Constantinople. From then on, East and West each considered the other to have abandoned a given point of doctrine. The East held that the Latins had made an unauthorized addition of the phrase *filioque* ("and the son") to the Creed of Nicaea and repudiated their use at the Eucharist of unleavened rather than leavened bread (unleavened bread is baked without yeast). The controversy also involved power and reputation; the pope of Rome claimed authority over the whole church, while the Byzantines insisted that the emperor was head of both church and empire and that a general council was the supreme authority in matters of faith.

The Fourth Crusade

The actions of the knights of the Fourth Crusade made eastern hostility to the West and to the Roman church permanent. The Crusades, armed expeditions of knights motivated in part by piety and in part by an undisguised desire for land and pillage, had as their announced purpose the securing of Christian access to the holy places in Jerusalem, Nazareth, and Bethlehem, sites occupied by the Muslims since the eighth century. The land route from Europe to the Holy

This Bohemian miniature commemorates the visit of the Byzantine emperor Manuel II Palaeologus to Charles VII of France in an unsuccessful attempt to secure aid for the embattled empire.

Land lay through Constantinople. When the Crusades began in 1096, the Eastern Roman emperor allowed the European knights to pass through the city, asking in return only that any territory recaptured be considered part of his empire. However, Syria and Palestine proved too great a temptation for the Europeans. Latin kingdoms were established at Jerusalem, Antioch, Tripoli, and Edessa. Then in 1204, during their journey through Constantinople, the knights of the Fourth Crusade became involved in a local quarrel and pillaged the city under the pretext of punishing the supposed heresy of the Greeks. Pope Innocent III is said to have been reduced to tears when he heard that the crusaders had occupied and wrecked the city, but the damage was done, and from 1204 to 1261 Constantinople was nominally a Latin city with a Latin patriarch.

Renaissance and Reunion

Although Constantinople continued to feel aggrieved about the events of the Fourth Crusade, soon after the Latin occupation of Constantinople ended in 1261, the Second Council of Lyons was convened to heal the rift between the Greek and Latin churches. The delegates of the Greek emperor Michael VIII Palaeologus agreed to the formula of reunion, which was proclaimed in 1274 but repudiated in 1289 in Constantinople. By 1400 it had become clear that Constantinople and the territories it still controlled would fall to the Turkish armies unless the West lent military support. If the West's support were to be secured, the rift would have to be closed more permanently.

The Council of Florence, which met at Ferrara (1438), Florence (1439–1443), and Rome (1443–1445), was convened by Pope Eugenius IV. In attendance were Joseph, the patriarch of Constantinople, John VIII Palaeologus, the emperor, and Bessarion (1403–1472), a Greek statesman and theologian. A decree of union was signed in July 1439 by the Greek delegates. However, one Greek bishop, Mark of Ephesus, refused to assent to the decree, and after the Greek delegates returned to the East, other bishops changed their minds. Ultimately, reunion with Rome proved so unpopular that it was abandoned. With the Latin conquest of 1204 so fresh in the memory, Constantinople and its people did not want the West's assistance at any price.

Although these two attempts to achieve reunion were unsuccessful, they brought Latin and Greek scholars together, and at Florence especially, Greek learning was welcomed.

Constantinople and the Renaissance

The Councils of Lyons and Florence were not the only important contact between Greeks and Latins. The Latin occupation of Constantinople in 1204, though it greatly widened the rift between East and West, had opened Constantinople to Latin learning and made the West aware of the treasures of Greek philosophy and literature. Greek learning and manuscripts were carried to the West by Greeks fleeing the Muslim advance as well as by those who came to the West trading or seeking aid.

Venetians and Genoese had traded extensively with Constantinople since the Crusades

Bessarion 1403–1472

Born in 1403 in Trebizond, on the southeastern shore of the Black Sea, Bessarion became a monk at age twenty. He studied under the most famous scholar of his day, Gemistus Plethon, from 1431 to 1436. In 1437 he was made bishop of Niceạ by John VIII Palaeologus. Bessarion accompanied the emperor to the Council of Florence, where he argued in favor of a reunion of Greek and Latin churches. When Bessarion left the council for Constantinople, he believed his advocacy of reunion had been successful, and while he was at sea, the pope made him a cardinal.

Soon after Bessarion reached Constantinople, it became clear that reunion was too unpopular to become effective. He returned to Italy in 1440. In 1450 he was made governor of the troubled city of Bologna, the first of many diplomatic posts he would hold. At Bologna he restored the university, repaired its buildings, and provided for scholars who would teach the Latin and Greek classics. Among his pupils was the famous Greek scholar John Lascaris (c. 1445–c. 1535), whom Bessarion sent to learn Latin at Padua. Lascaris, commissioned by Lorenzo de' Medici to collect Greek manuscripts, was among the first to publish books printed in Greek.

Bessarion's own scholarly achievements included translations of Greek works into Latin and an attempt to reconcile Plato and Aristotle by arguing against the extreme anti-Aristotelianism of George of Trebizond. In 1453, upon the death of Nicholas V, Bessarion narrowly missed being elected pope.

began, and the Venetian occupation of Greek islands brought the two cultures together. The emperor Manuel II spent the years 1399 to 1403 touring the western courts as a guest of the Venetians, King Charles VI of France, and King Henry IV of England. The purpose of Manuel's tour was to seek western aid for the embattled eastern empire. Manuel later advocated the study of Latin and insisted that it be included in the curriculum of Constantinople's university.

Bessarion translated into Latin Aristotle's *Metaphysics* and Xenophon's *Anabasis.* Around 1380 Demitrius Cydones translated the most important apologetic work of the English theologian Thomas Aquinas into Greek. Gennadius II Scholarios (c. 1405–c. 1473), who studied at the School of the Patriarch in Constantinople, attended the Council of Florence, where he, too, became familiar with the works of Thomas Aquinas; he translated some of them into Greek. Bessarion and Manuel Chrysoloras lectured on Plato in Florence, where Cosimo de' Medici's Florentine Academy sponsored a revival of Platonism. Gemistus Plethon (c. 1355–1450) repudiated Christianity in favor of Platonism and attempted to assimilate Christianity and the worship of the ancient gods. This attempt to rediscover the pagan influences that underlay Greek philosophy found an echo in the work of Pietro Pomponazzi (1462–1525) and other Italian philosophers. Bessarion, whose education had begun in Constantinople, left his collection of mostly Greek manuscripts to Venice, where they still form the nucleus of the civic library, the Marciana. The universities of the West were dominated by Scholasticism, a brand of philosophical and theological enquiry that was heavily influenced by Aristotle's work. The Platonism newly imported from the Byzantine world gave western scholars an alternative to Scholasticism.

▲ *The scholarly Cardinal Bessarion, the subject of this 1540 portrait, led those easterners attending the Council of Florence in 1439 who thought the theological and historical differences that separated East and West could be reconciled.*

Constantinople and the Reformation

As the Reformation matured in Europe, representatives of the Reformed churches contacted the patriarch of Constantinople. The Eastern church, also called the Orthodox Church, was attractive to the Reformers because it offered access to ancient Christian tradition independent of what Protestants saw as the erroneous doctrine and unacceptable claims to authority of Rome. In the early 1570s the Lutheran Martin Kraus, the leading professor of Greek in Germany, entered into correspondence with the patriarch Jeremias II. Copies of the Augsburg Confession, the basic statement of Lutheran doctrine, were sent eastward. Answering each of its twenty-one articles, the patriarch politely pointed out the differences between Orthodox and Lutheran doctrine. The correspondence ended with the gently worded invitation of the patriarch to the German correspondents to adhere to orthodoxy.

This detail from a painting by Benozzo Gozzolo (c. 1421–1497) depicts John VII Palaeologus, who inherited the empire from his father, Andronicus IV, but was deposed by his uncle Manuel II. During Manuel's tour of western courts from 1399 to 1403, John ruled in Constantinople, and after Manuel's return, he was emperor in Thessalonica.

The relationship between the patriarchate and the Church of England followed a similar pattern. In England there was much admiration for Greek Christianity. A Greek church was begun in London in 1677 with the assistance of King Charles II. English churchmen generously sponsored the education of Greek boys, the first of whom, Christopher Angelos, showed up at Great Yarmouth in 1608 and was sent to Trinity College, Cambridge, by the bishop of Norwich. With the encouragement of the Levant Company, a college for the education of young Greeks was begun at Oxford in 1695 with the enthusiastic help of the principal of Gloucester Hall, Dr. Benjamin Woodroffe. The scheme for funding the enterprise was vague, and although several of the students fared well, the Greeks seldom stayed long, and the experiment was abandoned in 1705.

Contacts between Greek Christians and English churchmen also sparked a correspondence between the patriarchate of Constantinople and the nonjurors. The nonjurors were Church of England clerics who had refused to swear allegiance to King William and Queen Mary in 1689 on the grounds that they had already sworn loyalty to James II, who had been forced to flee to France after showing excessive tolerance toward Roman Catholics. Nonjurors were high churchmen with a deep interest in the ancient church; their unusual position would have been strengthened by some token of recognition from Constantinople. There was a slow correspondence between the patriarch Jeremias III and the nonjurors in 1716 and 1717. The nonjurors received a disappointing answer from the patriarch, who restated the Orthodox position regarding tradition and the Eucharist. The conversation ceased, and the last nonjuror bishop, Thomas Ken, died in 1711.

The English correspondence with the church of Constantinople from 1650 to 1718 had two lasting consequences. The first, an enthusiasm in Britain for all things Greek, helped make Britain the sponsor of Greek independence in 1830. The second was the theory, advocated by Thomas

Ken and others, that the Catholic Church has three branches: Greek, Roman, and English. This idea would become important in the nineteenth century, when a broad interest in the relationship of the Church of England to the apostolic origins of Christianity surfaced.

The third Reformation tradition, Calvinism, touched Eastern Orthodoxy through the career of Cyril Lucaris (in Greek, Kyrillis Loukaris), the patriarch of Constantinople from 1620 to 1638. A Cretan who had studied at Venice and Padua, Cyril was an able scholar who traveled in the West and became a convinced Calvinist. His *Confession of Faith* (1629) alienated the Orthodox, as did his suspected sympathies toward Rome. One of the ablest men to hold the patriarchal chair, Cyril Lucaris was put to death at the order of the sultan in 1638.

▲ *Sultan Mehmed II, the subject of this portrait by Gentile Bellini (c. 1429–1507), conquered not only Constantinople but also Bosnia, much of Serbia, and several ports on the Adriatic. He drove the Genoese from their trading stations on the Black Sea and met defeat only once, in his attempt to take Rhodes from the Knights of Malta in 1480.*

After the Conquest

The gradual Turkish conquest of the Balkan Peninsula culminated in victory over the Serbs at the Battle of Kosovo in 1444. The Turks moved in on Constantinople until its territory barely extended beyond the city itself. The defenders of the city walls, who numbered around 7,000, included monks, volunteers, and foreigners. The Turkish leader Mehmed II commanded an army of around 60,000 fighting men and had at his disposal the finest navy Islam had yet assembled. Constantinople's citizens tried in vain to defend their city; on May 29, 1453, Constantinople fell. Its last emperor, Constantine XI, died fighting at the gate.

CONSTANTINOPLE IN 1400

Constantinople controlled sea traffic between the Black Sea and the Mediterranean Sea and land traffic between Asia and Europe. The city was built at the mouth of the Bosporus, the narrow channel that connects the Black Sea to the Sea of Marmara and beyond to the Aegean and the Mediterranean. The east–west road built by the Persians in the 490s had long been replaced by a slightly different route, but it was still necessary for travelers from Asia Minor bound for Greece or Italy to cross at either the Hellespont, at the southern entrance to the Sea of Marmara, or at the narrow Bosporus, both of which came under the control of Constantinople.

When Constantinople fell to Muslim invaders in 1453, it was still the greatest city in the Mediterranean world. It was dominated by such great churches as Hagia Sophia (the Church of the Holy Wisdom) and the Church of the Holy Apostles. The fourteenth century had seen a revival of icon painting and architecture, as represented by the church of the Chora monastery and Saint Mary Pammakaristos. In comparison, London was an overgrown village of wooden buildings, and the Rome of the Renaissance did not yet exist.

Manuel Chrysoloras c. 1350–1415

With the exception of the Irish monasteries, where scholars preserved some knowledge of Greek, and southern Italy, where Greek had never quite died out, the Greek language was not well known in western Europe. The teaching and writing of the Byzantine nobleman Manuel Chrysoloras began a process that made Greek the emblem of Renaissance scholarship. Chrysoloras came to the West in 1393 seeking support against a threatened Turkish invasion of Constantinople. In 1396 he became professor of Greek in Florence. After three years he returned briefly to Constantinople before settling in Italy, where he taught at Venice, Milan, Padua, and Rome and served as an official in the court of Pope Gregory XII. Chrysoloras died while on his way to the Council of Constance, which had been convened to further reunion between the Eastern and Western churches. His writings include Latin translations of the Greek authors Homer and Plato, a work comparing the cities of Rome and Constantinople, and a Greek grammar. One of his pupils, Leonardi Bruni (c. 1370–1444), wrote that Chrysoloras had renewed knowledge of a language no Italian had understood for seven hundred years.

▲ *This print by Bertrandon de la Broquière, made just two years after the city fell, depicts Constantinople under siege in 1453. The Ottoman tents are at the western wall, and the Bosporus is occupied by Mehmed's fleet.*

After the fall of the Western Roman Empire, Constantinople and its culture remained vivid in the western imagination. The influence of the Church of the Holy Apostles in Constantinople reached Ravenna, a Byzantine possession in Italy, where it was the pattern for the exarch's church. In Germany, Emperor Charlemagne used the exarch's church as the model for his own. Upon his death in 840, Charlemagne left to Saint Peter's Basilica in Rome a square silver table that bore a map of Constantinople. The golden solidus, the coin of Constantinople, was the currency of the Mediterranean; solidi have been found as far away as Britain. Greek persisted in the monasteries of Ireland.

As the shadow of defeat fell across the great Byzantine civilization, Constantinople transmitted to the West its rich linguistic and intellectual heritage. After 1453, although the Greek language would no longer dominate the largely Muslim culture of its homeland, Greek culture was as fundamental to the Western humanist revival of classical learning as was Latin. Greek culture thus played a pivotal role in the Renaissance.

Further Reading

Downey, Glanville. *Constantinople in the Age of Justinian.* Norman, OK, 1960.

Geanakoplos, Deno John. *Greek Scholars in Venice: Studies in the Dissemination of Greek Learning from Byzantium to Western Europe.* Cambridge, MA, 1962.

Jacobs, David. *Constantinople: City on the Golden Horn.* New York, 1969.

Philippides, Marios, trans. *Emperors, Patriarchs, and Sultans of Constantinople, 1373–1513.* Brookline, MA, 1990.

Phillips, James. *Early Christian and Byzantine Constantinople.* Monticello, IL, 1982.

James A. Patrick

SEE ALSO

• Byzantium • Humanism and Learning
• Languages, Classical • Platonism • Renaissance
• Venice

Copernicus, Nicolaus

THE POLISH ASTRONOMER NICOLAUS COPERNICUS IS REMEMBERED CHIEFLY FOR HIS DISCOVERY THAT THE EARTH AND THE OTHER PLANETS REVOLVE AROUND THE SUN.

Nicolaus Copernicus was born Mikolaj Kopernik in 1473 into a wealthy merchant family in the Prussian town of Torun (in present-day Poland). After the death of his parents, he was brought up by an uncle, Lucas Watzenrode; they moved to northern Poland when Watzenrode was made bishop of the diocese of Varmia. Copernicus's first studies at the university of Kraców were in mathematics, astronomy, and astrology. Having failed to gain a degree, in 1496 he moved to Italy to study law and medicine at the universities of Bologna, Padua, and Ferrara. He is known to have served as an assistant to the professor of astronomy at Padua, where he made his first recorded astronomical observation in March 1497. It was apparently at Padua that Copernicus came upon the *Epitome,* a digest of the *Almagest,* the great work of astronomy compiled in the second century CE by the Greek scientist and mathematician Ptolemy. The *Epitome,* which had been produced some twenty years earlier by the German scholar Johann Müller (known as Regiomontanus), criticized some of Ptolemy's findings. Thus, Copernicus would have been aware of unresolved questions in the field of astronomy. He returned to Varmia to serve as his uncle's physician and in 1510 moved north to the coastal town of Frauenberg, where, as a canon of the cathedral, he undertook the administrative duties of the diocese. Very little is known of Copernicus's personality or private life. From 1510 astronomy seems to have been his main preoccupation, and by 1514 he had competed a critique of Ptolemy known as the *Commentariolus,* which was circulated only in manuscript form.

▼ One of the few surviving portraits (the artist is unknown) of Nicolaus Copernicus, who did not rise to prominence during his lifetime. The significance of his work was recognized only some fifty years after his death.

Ptolemy and Greek Astronomy

The achievements of the Greek astronomers were extraordinary. One astronomer, Aristarchus of Samos (third century BCE) has been credited as the first to hypothesize that the sun was at the center of the universe. However, the majority of Greek astronomers held that the earth was the center of the universe. While they knew that the earth was a sphere (they could see its shadow on the moon), they also believed it was stationary. The philosopher Aristotle (fourth century BCE) argued that the universe was composed of four elements: earth, toward which heavy objects were naturally drawn; water, which rested on the earth; air, which formed a layer above the water; and fire, which formed a layer between the air and the moon. Beyond was a celestial region that was very different from the earth and its immediate elements in being geometrically perfect. In this celestial region the stars revolved in circles that had the earth at their center.

The problem for the Greeks lay in understanding how the stars moved. Most of those that could be observed from the earth were fixed in relation to one another and seemed to move around the earth together. Some stars, however, apparently followed an independent path. The sun and moon were two of the most obvious of what the Greeks called wandering stars (in Greek, *planetes*). Mercury, Venus, Mars, Saturn, and Jupiter were others that the Greeks could observe with the naked eye. The path of these planets seemed anything but circular. For any given planet, there were periods when it appeared to be moving quickly across the sky, moments when it seemed motionless, and even times when it appeared to backtrack. Such phenomena could not easily be accommodated within the theory that the stars moved in circles.

By the second century BCE, the Greeks had gained access to Babylonian trackings of the stars and were adding these observations to their own. Thus, there was no shortage of observations from which to work. The observations were put together in the most ingenious ways. By the time of Ptolemy, who worked in Alexandria between 127 and 141 CE, a geometrical model had evolved. The model supposed that, for each planet, there was a circle that ran around the

CHRONOLOGY

1473
Nicolaus Copernicus is born in Torun.

1491–1495
Studies mathematics and astronomy in Kraców.

1495
Becomes a canon at the cathedral of the diocese of Varmia.

1500
Gives a lecture in Rome, possibly on an astronomical theme.

1503
Achieves a degree in canon law; returns to Poland and takes up a position as physician to his uncle, the bishop of Varmia.

1510
Takes up post as canon at Frauenberg.

c. 1512–1529
Combines administrative work as canon with observational and computational work.

1539
Is encouraged by Georg Joachim Rheticus to complete the manuscript of *De revolutionibus*.

1543
De revolutionibus is published; Copernicus dies.

After his return to Frauenberg (modern-day Frombork, Poland) in 1510, Copernicus began astronomical observations in earnest. He worked in a tower in the fortifications that surrounded the cathedral; his study, photographed here, has been reconstructed to look much as it did when he used it.

PTOLEMY AND CHRISTIANITY

One of the reasons why Ptolemy's work was so difficult to supplant was that it had been integrated into mainstream Christian thought. Ptolemy had proposed seven planetary spheres, with the fixed stars making up an eighth sphere. In order to find a place for God in the Ptolemaic system, theologians went back to the Old Testament book of Genesis. The firmament brought forth by God on the second day of the Creation was equated with the fixed stars—that is, with the eighth sphere. The description in Genesis of waters created by God above the firmament necessitated a ninth sphere, and the heavens created on the first day must occupy a tenth sphere. According to Aristotle, the ultimate source of all motion in the universe was an Unmoving Mover, which Christians equated with God and placed in the tenth Ptolemaic sphere.

Christian theologians gave this model of the universe yet more credence by connecting it to the work of the Greek philosopher Plato. Plato had described a material world in a continual state of flux—the world inhabited by humans, where nothing is certain. However, the material world was merely a shadow of a more fundamental, unchanging reality, whose truths could be grasped only through the use of reason. The tenth Ptolemaic sphere was equated with Plato's unchanging reality, where the Supreme Good—for Christians, God—existed. Thus, an astronomer who overthrew Ptolemy risked overthrowing Christian orthodoxy.

earth (termed the deferent) that carried on its circumference a moving point. This moving point was the center of another smaller circle, known as the epicycle. It was argued that each given planet moved round the circumference of such an epicycle. The combination of these two circular paths could, it was argued, explain the variety of movements of the planets as seen from the earth.

However, as Ptolemy accumulated more observations, he realized that it was still impossible to create a model that could accurately predict the movement of each planet. Instead, he argued that there must be another point in the universe from which a planet would appear to the observer to be moving at a uniform speed. He called this hypothetical point the equant. If a direct line was drawn between the equant and the center of the earth, then the center of the circle on which the planet moved would be the point exactly halfway between the two. Though highly ingenious, this theory assumed that the planets varied their speed as they moved along their path and also suggested that the earth was not in fact the center of the universe. With deferent circles, epicycles, and equant points, each different for each planet, the theory was also enormously cumbersome. Ptolemy wrote up his theory in the *Mathematical Compilation,* a vast work full of observations and calculations. Later Islamic astronomers were so impressed that they named it *Al-majisti* ("the greatest"); it is still known from this Arabic title as the *Almagest.*

De ſanctificatione ſeptime diei

Conſummato igitur mundo: per fabricam diuine ſolercie ſex dierum. Creati enim diſpoſiti et ornati tandem perfecti ſunt celi et terra. Compleuit deus glorioſus opus ſuum: et requieuit die ſeptimo ab operibus manuum ſuarum: poſtquam cunctum mundum: et omnia que in eo ſunt creaſſet: non quaſi operando laſſus: ſed nouam creaturam facere ceſſauit: cuius materia vel ſimilitudo non preceſſerit. Opus enim propagationis operari non deſinit. Et dominus eidem diei benedixit: et ſanctificauit illum: vocauitque ipſum Sabatum quod nomen hebraica lingua requiem ſignificat. Eo quod in ipſo ceſſauerat ab omni opere quod patrarat. Unde et Judei eo die a laboribus proprijs vacare dignoſcuntur. Quem et ante legem certe gentes celebrem obſeruarunt. Jamque ad calcem ventum eſt operum diuinorum. Illum ergo timeamus: amemus: et veneremur. In quo ſunt omnia ſiue viſibilia ſiue inuiſibilia. Et a domino celi: domino bonorum omnium. Cui data omnis poteſtas in celo et in terra. Et preſentia bona: quatenus bona ſint. Et veram eterne vite felicitatem queramus.

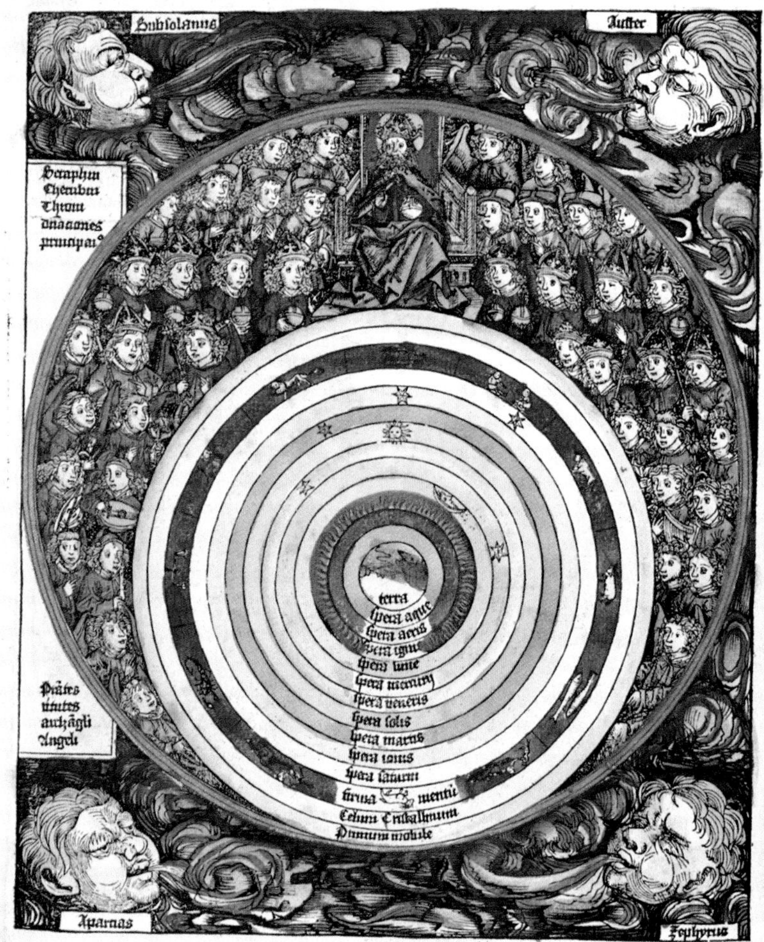

▼ *An illustration of the cosmos with Ptolemy's universe placed within a Christian setting. At the center are Aristotle's four elements surrounded by seven planetary spheres, the fixed stars (including depictions of the signs of the zodiac), and finally, heaven, with God and the angels encompassing the whole. The illustration comes from the* Nuremberg Chronicle, *a world history published in 1493.*

▶ *The Danish astronomer Tycho Brahe (1546–1601) was troubled by Copernicus's argument for a moving earth. Brahe pioneered more accurate observations of the stars but interpreted their movements in such a way as to leave the earth motionless in the center of the universe with the sun and moon revolving around it and the other planets revolving around the sun. This illustration from a 1661 celestial atlas combines Ptolemy and Brahe's alternative cosmologies.*

Having found a model that appeared to explain the movements of the individual planets, Ptolemy then tried to work out how everything fitted together in the universe. His results were brought together in his work *Planetary Hypotheses.* He assumed that each planet moved around the earth within a sphere. With the epicycles in operation, each planet would, while staying within its sphere, vary in its distance from the earth at different times in its cycle. Each sphere would have an inner edge and an outer edge that marked the nearest and farthest edges, respective to the earth, of the path each of the other planets followed. The spheres would lock together, one outside the other, with no space in between—in other words, there would be no space that did not have a planet allocated to it. An outer sphere would contain the fixed stars. Ptolemy next worked out the order of the planets in distance from the earth. The moon was the closest, followed by Mercury, Venus, the sun, Mars, Jupiter, and finally Saturn. Although this was the only order that fitted in with his observations, there was one immediate problem. According to the model, the moon would double its distance from the earth during its monthly cycle as it moved from the inner to the outer edge of its epicycle. If it did so, it would also appear to halve in size as it moved away from the earth. Yet the moon clearly appeared the same size throughout the month. Thus, the most elementary observation apparently contradicted the entire hypothesis.

For its time Ptolemy's achievement was remarkable. No other astronomer could match the sophistication of his work, and it is hardly surprising that, despite its deficiencies, Ptolemy's theory was respected by Christian and Islamic astronomers alike for 1,200 years after it first appeared. Copernicus himself praised Ptolemy as follows: "Ptolemy stands far in front of all the others on account of his care and industry and with the help of more than forty years of observations brought this art to such a high point that there seemed nothing left he had not touched upon" *(De revolutionibus).*

The Path to *De Revolutionibus*

The *Almagest* was lost to the West until a Latin translation of the Arabic version became available in the twelfth century. Texts in the original Greek did not reappear in Europe until the fall of Constantinople in 1453. (It was from the original Greek texts that Regiomontanus worked.) However, most astronomers by now rejected Ptolemy's equant points, and the problem of the moon's size also cast doubt on the underlying assumptions of his work. In his *Commentariolus,* Copernicus concentrated his criticism on the equants and went on to suggest that in a heliocentric (sun-centered) universe, the planets might be placed in a more acceptable order. However, he could offer no proof for his insight that the sun was the center of the universe, and between 1512 and 1529 he appears to have absorbed himself in making astronomical observations that might support his hypothesis. The next step was to perform the requisite mathematical computation. Eventually—and very hesitantly, as he was still unsure of many of his observations—Copernicus began writing *De revolutionibus orbium coelestium (On the Revolution of Heavenly Spheres).*

De revolutionibus might never have been published if word had not spread among astronomers about Copernicus's new theory. One astronomer, Georg Joachim Rheticus (1514–1576), a professor of mathematics at Wittenberg, Germany, visited Copernicus in 1539. Rheticus was so convinced by the theory that he even wrote his own description of it, the so-called *First Account* (1540). He encouraged Copernicus, now an old man, to finish the manuscript. In 1542 Rheticus took the manuscript to Nuremberg to be printed, but he was forced to hand over supervision of the printing to one Andreas Osiander, a Lutheran minister. Osiander, understandably shocked by the implications of the new theory, wrote his own unsigned preface to the work in which he suggested that Copernicus's theory did not necessarily represent the truth but merely provided a mathematical model that allowed for more efficient calculations. Copernicus was powerlesss to act, since he had lapsed into a coma (according to one story, a copy of *De revolutionibus* was placed in his hands as he lay dying). The true significance of his great work was masked by Osiander's preface.

▲ *Copernicus's map of the heavens places the sun firmly at the center of the universe and the planets in orbit around it in the correct order. Earth is given prominence; the progression of day and night is illustrated, and the landmasses are clearly delineated.*

The culmination of Copernicus's great work—the conclusion that the sun must be at the center of the universe—is a key moment in the history of modern science:

Therefore we are not ashamed to say that the center of the Earth traverses that great orbital circle among the other wandering stars in an annual revolution around the sun; and that the center of the world is around the sun. I also say that the sun remains forever immobile.... And though all these things are difficult, almost inconceivable, and quite contrary to the opinion of the multitude, nevertheless in what follows we will with God's help make them clearer than day—at least for those who are not ignorant of the art of mathematics.

Nicolaus Copernicus, *On the Revolution of Heavenly Spheres*

Copernicus's Theory

The ancient Greek mathematicians had prided themselves on the elegance of their field of study; Copernicus followed in this tradition. Indeed, one of Copernicus's main criticisms of Ptolemy was that his system was so inelegant and unwieldy. Each planet needed a completely different model to explain its movements. It was, said Copernicus, akin to having to create a human body from limbs belonging to different people: the result would be a monster, not a man. What drove Copernicus was the desire to find a harmonious model of the universe—one still based on perfect circles—that would fit with what could be observed. Copernicus opens the first book of *De revolutionibus* by setting out his vision of a cosmos with the sun at the center and goes on to provide the detailed mathematical calculations that prove that a heliocentric model of the universe can account for observed astronomical phenomena.

The heliocentric universe worked for Copernicus not only because it was more elegant but also because it made the universe easier to understand. It was clear from observations that the earth traveled once around the sun each year. Assuming that the other planets also traveled around the sun, by observing their movement, Copernicus could calculate their orbit—Mercury, for instance, took eighty-eight days to travel around the sun. If the planets were ordered according to the length of time they took to circle the sun, then the sun (at the center) would be followed by Mercury, Venus, Earth, Mars, Jupiter, and finally Saturn. A different approach was to calculate the relative distance of each planet from the sun. Once Copernicus discovered that the order that resulted was exactly the same as the order produced by calculating the length of the planets' orbits, he knew he had found what he was looking for: a harmonious model of the universe that was corroborated by all his observations. The problem of why the planets seemed at some times to be motionless and sometimes to be moving back along their path was also explained. If the earth is moving and spinning at the same time as the other planets are traveling along their path, then the other planets are bound to appear to move in this way. A planet that appears to be motionless is in fact moving directly toward or directly away from the earth.

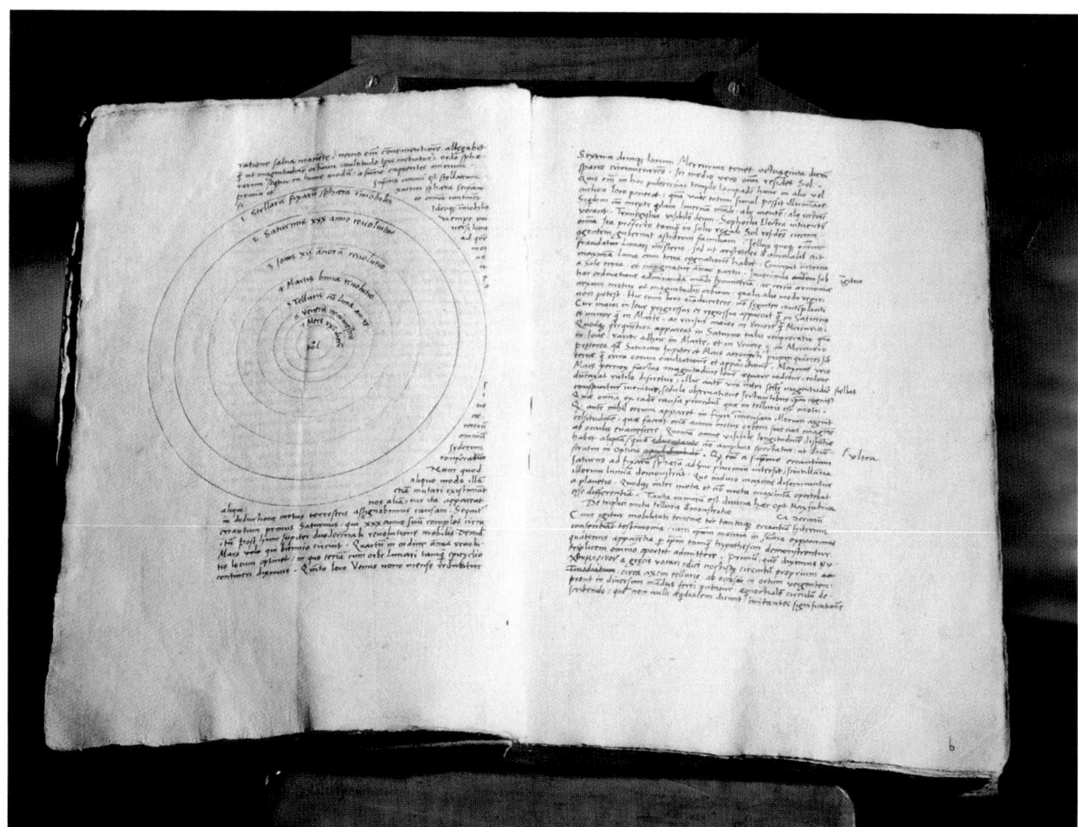

▶ *This manuscript of* De revolutionibus *is preserved in the Collegium Maius in Kraków, where Copernicus studied between 1491 and 1494. It is open at a page on which Copernicus provided an illustration of a sun-centered universe.*

COPERNICUS AND ISLAMIC ASTRONOMY

While astronomy in Europe was locked in the Ptolemaic model, in the Islamic world critical and innovative thinking continued. One of the most important Islamic observatories was the one founded at Maragha, in northwestern Iran, in 1259. Maragha's library was supposed to have some 40,000 volumes as well as astronomical instruments, including quadrants, armillary spheres, and astrolabes. Its astronomers were clearly concerned about Ptolemy's use of the equant; one of them, Nasir al-Din al-Tusi (1201–1274), put forward an alternative model that included further small circles. A century later, one of the great figures of Islamic astronomy, Ibn al-Shatir, who worked at the observatory at Damascus, used his own observations to undermine much of Ptolemy's work. Only in the 1950s was his work, *The Final Quest concerning the Rectification of Principles,* reassessed. It was discovered that the observations used by al-Shatir were identical to those used by Copernicus. Somehow—how exactly has not been conclusively shown—these achievements by Islamic astronomers had arrived in western Europe. The most likely explanation is that they were carried by Italian traders, who had extensive contacts with the Islamic world.

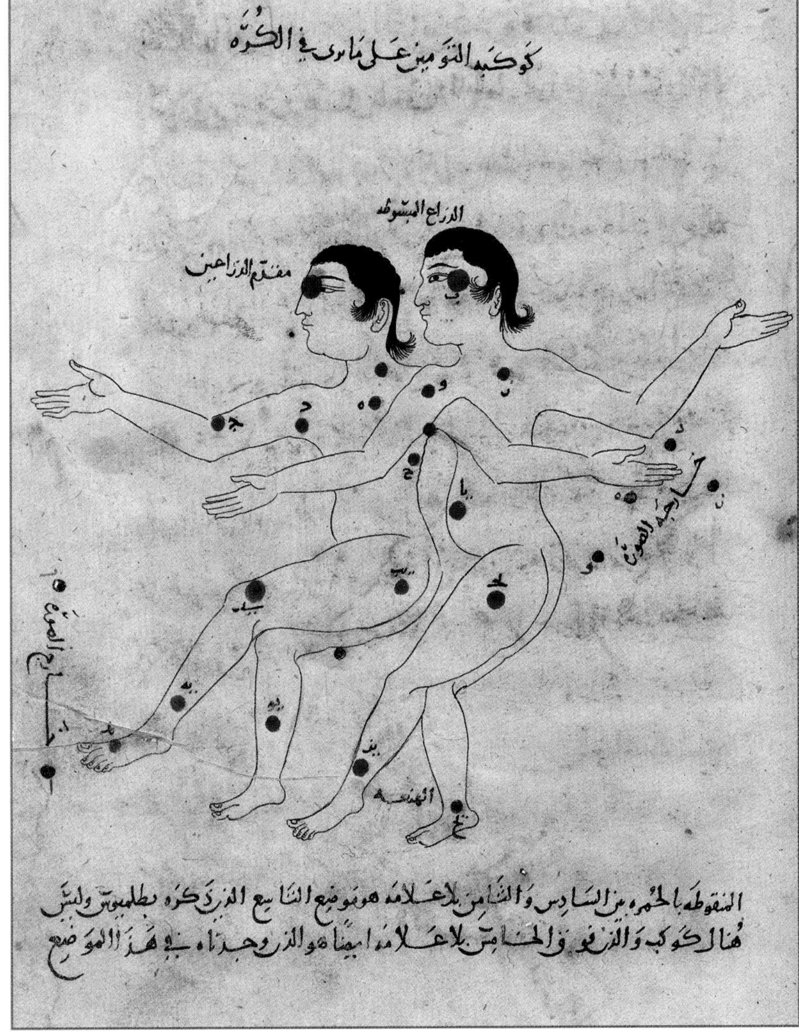

Before the Copernican revival, the last recorded astronomical observation in the West was made by the Athenian Proclus in 475 CE. While scientific life in Europe stagnated, however, Arab astronomers continued to build on the works of the ancient Greeks; Copernicus may well have used the Arabs' findings. This star chart of Gemini (the twins) is from a manuscript by al-Sufi (1009).

Copernicus's theory of the movement of the moon also fitted much more closely with what could be observed of its size, and even if a full understanding of the moon had to wait until the work of the Danish astronomer Tycho Brahe (1546–1601), Copernicus's work on the moon gave his model immediate credibility.

What Copernicus Failed to Explain

Although Copernicus's theory made much more sense of the universe, he still relied heavily on Ptolemy's observations and even retained epicycles and equants in his own work. The German astronomer Johannes Kepler (1571–1630), whose *Cosmographic Mystery* (1596) was the first work to take on the full implications of a heliocentric universe, wrote, "Copernicus, ignorant of his own riches, took it upon himself for the most part to represent Ptolemy, not nature, to which he had nevertheless come closest of all."

One immediate problem resulted from Copernicus's acceptance of Ptolemy's figures. In the *Planetary Hypotheses,* taking the radius of the earth as a standard unit of distance, Ptolemy argued that the sun lay some 1,200 radii from the earth, while the sphere of fixed stars was some 20,000 radii distant. In a sun-centered universe, these figures would suggest quite a large variation in the position of the fixed stars each year, but only a small one was noted. Copernicus argued that the stars were some eight million radii from the planets—much farther than anyone had thought. For Tycho Brahe, this distance seemed impossibly large—not least because it would have been absurd for God to have wasted so much space. Furthermore, given their apparent size when viewed from the earth, if the stars were so far away, they would be enormous. (In 1610 Galileo's telescope showed that the stars were not as big as they looked to the naked eye.)

THE AFTERLIFE OF *DE REVOLUTIONIBUS*

De revolutionibus was published in an edition of only four hundred copies, and even this small number did not sell out. Many early readers did not take on board its central hypothesis and quarried the work only for those calculations that most interested them. For instance, some scholars accepted that the earth spun on its own axis but continued to believe that it was at the center of the universe. Copernicus left enough unsolved issues for adherents of the traditional view to feel justified in rejecting his whole thesis.

In his *Commentariolus,* Copernicus did not seem concerned about the reaction of the Catholic Church to his hypothesis, though *De revolutionibus* did arouse the opposition of Protestants. Until 1600 Rome appears to have ignored *De revolutionibus,* but when an opponent of traditional Catholicism, the Italian philosopher Giordano Bruno (1548–1600), included a heliocentric universe among his beliefs, the church took notice (Bruno was eventually burned as a heretic). *De revolutionibus* was placed on the Index of Forbidden Books in 1616 and stayed there until 1835.

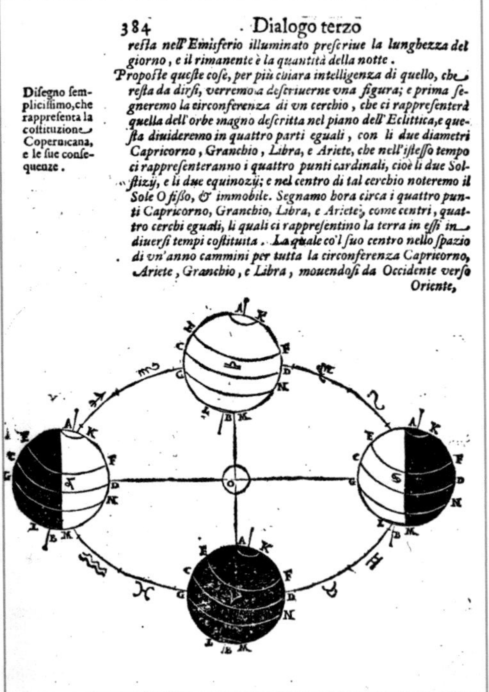

384 Dialogo terzo

reſta nell'Emiſferio illuminato preſcriue la lunghezza del giorno, e il rimanente è la quantità della notte.

Propoſte queſte coſe, per più chiara intelligenza di quello, che reſta da dirſi, verremo a deſcriuerne vna figura; e prima ſegneremo la circonferenza di vn cerchio, che ci rappreſenterà quella dell'orbe magno deſcritta nel piano dell'Eclittica, e queſta diuideremo in quattro parti eguali, con li due diametri Capricorno, Granchio, Libra, e Ariete, che nell'iſteſſo tempo ci rappreſenteranno i quattro punti cardinali, cioè li due Solſtizij, e li due equinozij; e nel centro di tal cerchio noteremo il Sole O fiſſo, & immobile. Segnamo hora circa i quattro punti Capricorno, Granchio, Libra, e Ariete, come centri, quattro cerchi eguali, li quali ci rappreſentino la terra in eſſi in diuerſi tempi coſtituita. La quale co'l ſuo centro nello ſpazio di vn'anno cammini per tutta la circonferenza Capricorno, Ariete, Granchio, e Libra, mouendoſi da Occidente verſo Oriente,

Diſegno ſempliciſſimo, che rappreſenta la coſtituzione Copernicana, e le ſue conſequenze.

▶ *In Galileo's* Dialogue concerning the Two Chief World Systems *(1632), a number of disputants discuss the different ways of portraying the heavens. In the "Third Dialogue," a page of which is pictured here, Galileo demonstrates how Copernicus's observations provide a better model for the universe than Ptolemy's. Galileo provides an illustration of Copernicus's system to prove the point.*

Copernicus's opponents argued that he had failed to explain how the universe stayed in place without everything falling toward the sun or how the earth could be spinning around without everything on it being dislodged. His followers countered with the theory that everything in the immediate vicinity of the earth is somehow connected to the earth and therefore remains in place despite the earth's motion. (Unable to give a cogent explanation of why the earth was spinning, they simply argued that it was in the nature of a sphere to spin). The fact that each planet remained at the same distance from the other planets was explained by the weak argument that the universe was made of different kinds of materials, each attracted to its own planet.

After Copernicus

The Copernican revolution is seen, in hindsight, as a milestone in the history of science. In fact, Copernicus remained embedded in the world of Ptolemy and would hardly have seen himself as a revolutionary. It took the work of later astronomers and mathematicians—Tycho Brahe, Johannes Kepler, the Italian Galileo Galilei (1564–1642), and the Englishman Isaac Newton (1642–1727)—to provide the observations, calculations, and theories that explained how the universe actually sustained itself as a physical entity. Yet Copernicus's original insight remained crucial to their work, and he deserves his reputation as a pioneer of modern science.

Further Reading

Armitage, Angus. *Copernicus, the Founder of Modern Astronomy.* New York, 1957.

Copernicus, Nicolaus. *On the Revolution of Heavenly Spheres.* Translated by Charles Glenn Wallis. Amherst, NY, 1995.

Gingerich, Owen. *The Book Nobody Read: Chasing the Revolutions of Nicolaus Copernicus.* New York, 2004.

———. *The Eye of Heaven: Ptolemy, Copernicus, Kepler.* New York, 1993.

Hoskin, Michael, ed. *The Cambridge Concise History of Astronomy.* New York, 1999.

Charles Freeman

SEE ALSO

- Astrology
- Galilei, Galileo
- Science and Technology

Dams and Drainage

RENAISSANCE ENGINEERS, ARCHITECTS, AND ARTISANS DESIGNED DAMS AND DEVELOPED DRAINAGE TECHNIQUES THAT WERE CRUCIAL FOR AGRICULTURAL, COMMERCIAL, AND MILITARY SUCCESSES AND FOR THE SURVIVAL OF THREATENED POPULATIONS.

During the Renaissance people strove more than ever before to control water. By using scientific knowledge to establish human mastery over the natural world, dam and drainage engineers were giving expression to the high estimation of humans that was one of the hallmarks of the Renaissance.

Some areas suffered because of the lack of an adequate water supply, while others endured flooding that destroyed crops and drowned entire communities. Hydraulic (water-powered) technology enabled people to manage water resources and transform watery landscapes. By borrowing and improving on the basic principles of dam construction used by Greek and Roman engineers, European engineers and architects found practical solutions to the age-old problems of storing water and irrigating farmland. They also invented new methods of draining waterlogged land and reclaiming it for settlement and agricultural use. During the period, the amount of land increased in order to meet the demands of growing populations. Millwrights and laborers contributed to advances in hydraulic technology by adapting the equipment and methods used for other applications.

Joseph Heinz the Younger (c. 1600–1678) captured the community effort to build dikes in this painting, which depicts a court visit to the construction site of a dike at Orléans, France. French rulers were mostly concerned with protecting riverside communities from floodwaters and draining marshy areas to reclaim agricultural lands.

Whether in the city or in the countryside, a consistent supply of clean water was essential for communities to survive. Without water, people could not remain in good health, cook, or clean. Water was essential for domestic sanitation, public health, and agriculture and industry. Hydraulic projects and other waterworks stored and delivered water for the irrigation of farmland, increased the rate of urbanization, improved conditions for people living in rural environments, contributed to civic improvements, such as parks with fountains, and were used as a renewable source of energy. Although droughts (sustained periods of dry weather) and a basic insufficiency of water supplies threatened the well-being and survival of populations throughout the world, it was also the case that too much water was devastating. Floods drenched many acres of farmland and often caused famines. Those who survived floodwaters frequently starved to death.

The Low Countries

People living in the Low Countries (present-day Belgium and the Netherlands) lived at an altitude at or below sea level. Before dikes protected the Low Countries, high tides frequently inundated the land. The North Sea breached defenses, spread across farmland, and altered the shape of the coast: a village might suddenly find itself cut off on an island. Lakes and rivers within the Netherlands frequently overflowed their banks. The Dutch people called such events water wolves, since they devoured land. Water flooded as much as approximately half of the Low Countries during the Renaissance and made the terrain swampy, uninhabitable, and unsuitable for livestock and crops.

In ancient times the Frisians settled on the peat marshes along the coast of the North Sea in northwestern Europe (the region became known as Friesland). They attempted to defend their territory against high tides by building earthen mounds and reinforcing them with local timber, seaweed, and natural fibers. When the Romans settled those regions, they improved the primitive mounds and, during the first century CE, erected seawalls. Approximately nine hundred years later, residents of the Low Countries began building dikes inland to supplement the sea walls. Groups of people in a given area joined together to gather rocks, clay, sand, jute (a strong fiber produced from a plant of the linden family), willow branches, and other materials and constructed dikes at sites vulnerable to flooding.

During the Middle Ages people in Friesland had continually fought to keep the water from seizing their land. In 1228 a flood killed 100,000 people. Around the year 1300 storms enlarged the Zuider Zee in the Low Countries to the extent that the lake reached the sea; areas that had previously lain inland were transformed into ports. Water surging from the south and north almost cut the Low Countries in half. In 1421 floodwater covered approximately sixty-five villages in Dordrecht and left 100,000 people dead.

By 1600, dikes protected most of the coast and waterways of the Netherlands from flooding as well as from erosion. The latter problem was exacerbated by deforestation—timber was needed in large quantities to support such industries as shipbuilding and construction and even for the building of dike frameworks. Coastal erosion made the land even more vulnerable to flooding, and dike masters vigilantly watched for gaps in dikes and seawalls that needed to be filled and reinforced. A dike master by the name of Andries Vierlingh (1507–1579) extolled the virtues of the dikes: "Look at the dammekens, they are but wattled twigs of willow, weighed down with clay sods but what great benefit they bring at low cost! You can do wonders with them . . . [as bricks] are but baked clay, but you can

Balthasar Florisz van Berckenrode (1591–1645), surveyor to the States General, produced this engraving of Rotterdam in 1626. The map shows how dikes protected the city's coastal areas from flooding and provided water traffic consistent access to its ports and markets. Outside the city, on land guarded from inundations, crops were grown to feed Rotterdam's residents.

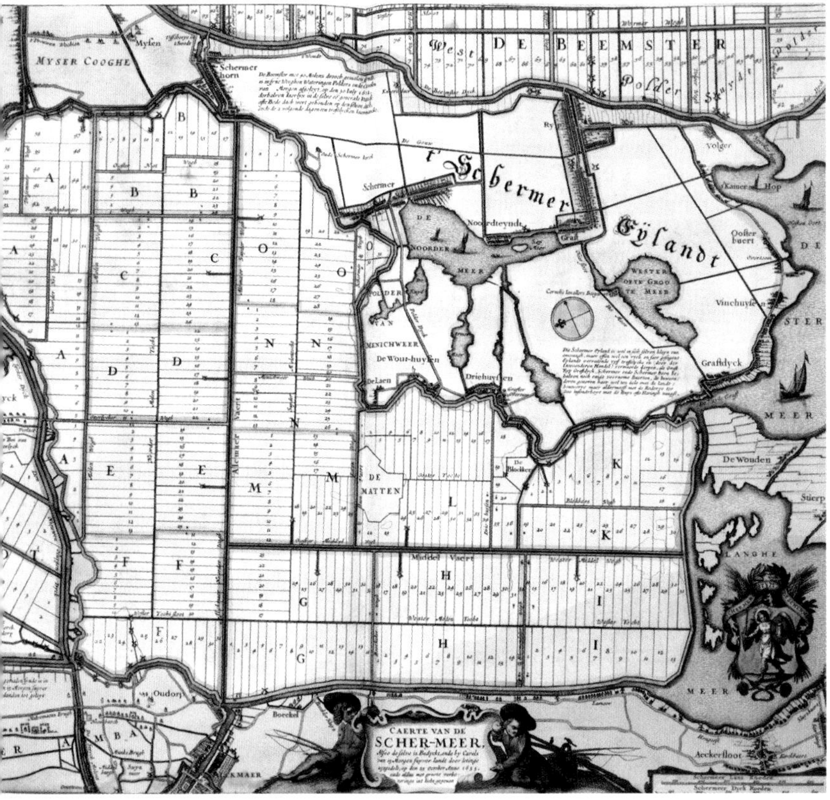

▲ The cartographer Jan Blaeu drew this map of the Schermer, in northern Holland, in 1635. The map shows how the forty mills located near Schermer polder, which Jan Adriaanszoon Leeghwater helped create, successfully drained a large area by generating energy to power water pumps. Drainage increased available farmland throughout the Low Countries.

build a castle with them." He advised growing plants close to dikes to stabilize them.

Innovators continually studied existing hydraulic techniques and strove to improve water management by advancing tool and dike design, revising their methods of construction, and appropriating and adapting technology successfully used for other purposes. For example, craftsmen modified windmills, traditionally used to grind grain, to power machines that pumped water from flooded land and from swollen lakes. Because the landscape was flat, the windmill-powered pumps transferred water into human- or machine-dug canals, along which the excess water could be channeled to the sea. Records suggest that people had first used windmills to power pumps for drainage in 1408. This drainage method had become established by 1600, when *droogmakerij,* the "laying dry" of meers (lakes) throughout the Netherlands, increased demand for drainage mills.

People built *ringdijk* (banks) for a windmill's base by the lake and *ringvaart* (channels) to carry water pumped from the meer. Inventors filed more than one hundred patents for drainage mill designs. Most incorporated scoop-wheels to transfer water. Around 1617 Simon Stevin, who understood the static behavior as well as the dynamic properties of water, wrote the pioneering treatises *Van de molens (On Mills)* and *Nieuwe maniere van sterctebou, door spilsluysen (New Manner of Fortification by Sluices).* Because Dutch windmill builders traveled throughout Europe to discuss their work and demonstrate their techniques, people built drainage windmills all over the continent.

Lakes and areas flooded by high tides, once drained, provided new land for growing populations to settle and develop. Settlers established such towns as Amsterdam and Rotterdam (the suffix *dam* indicates the importance of dams to those settlements). Functioning since the Middle Ages, *Hoogheemradschappen* (Main Polder Boards) oversaw local efforts to reclaim land from the sea and lakes by dike building and draining. People learned how to use dikes to

Jan Adriaanszoon Leeghwater c. 1575–1650

Appropriately enough for a man who devoted his life to draining lakes, Jan Adriaanszoon Leeghwater's adopted surname means "low water." Leeghwater grew up near Amsterdam and, while young, received a patent for an underwater tool to repair sluices. Identifying himself as an engineer and windmill builder, Leeghwater gained fame for draining Beemster Lake by 1612. His work resulted in the creation of two polders (tracts of reclaimed land), called Purmer and Schermer. Because he was an expert at pumping water from lakes, Leeghwater traveled throughout Europe as a consultant and occasionally risked drowning in areas with weak dikes.

In his *Haarlemmermeerboek* (1641), Leeghwater described how the 40,000-acre Haarlem Lake could be drained with 160 windmills. Owing to public demand, this book was reprinted seventeen times. In a second book, *Kleyne Chronycke* (1649), he recorded his drainage techniques and experiences. He wrote that "the draining of lakes is one of the most necessary, most profitable and most holy works in Holland." Officials delayed the draining of Haarlem Lake until the nineteenth century, when the Leeghwater pumping station was built. In the present day, the lake bed is home to Schipol airport.

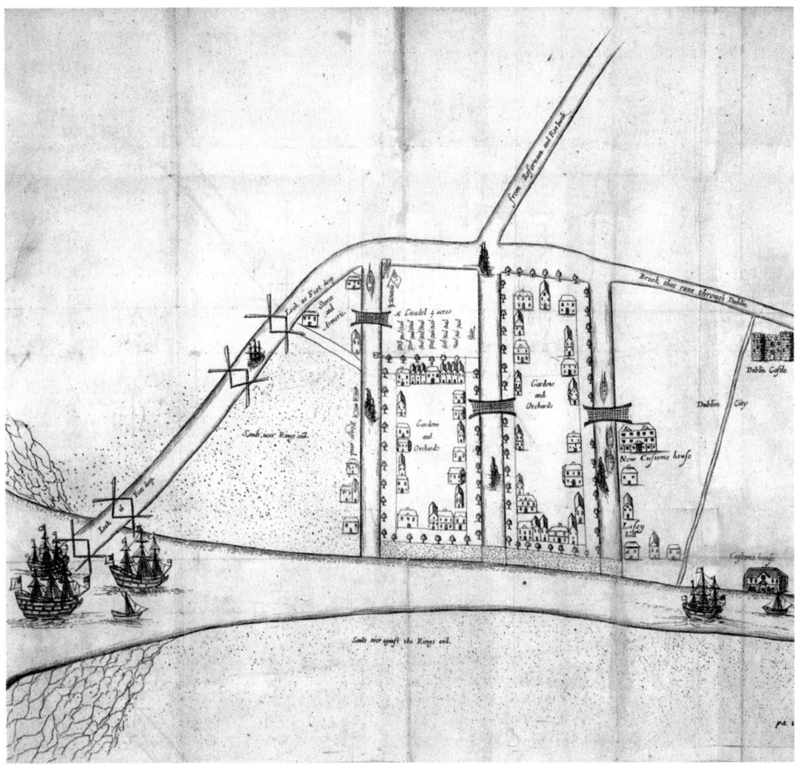

▲ *During his travels throughout northern Europe in the seventeenth century, Andrew Yarranton, the owner of an English ironworks, surveyed rivers and pursued waterway and harbor improvements, including the construction of canals, for better navigation. This copper engraving, depicting his canal and lock system in Dublin, was printed in Yarranton's book,* England's Improvement by Sea and Land.

contain water and how to drain land dry in order to expose soil to the elements so that the sun evaporated any traces of moisture and rainfall washed away salts, pollutants, and debris. The drained soil was exceptionally rich farmland. Men and women of all ages worked together within communities to build and maintain dikes and drain land for neighbors as needed. Reclamation enabled more people to earn an income from livestock and plants, both edible and ornamental. Property values increased as royalty and nobles sought this verdant land. Vierlingh noted, "Tidal sands, even those one foot above low water; they cry to be made into a fertile corn field!"

Elsewhere in Europe

In 1589 Humphrey Bradley proposed draining the Great Level, a huge swath of low-lying and waterlogged fenland in eastern England. Unlike the Netherlands, the Great Level was above sea level, and so water could flow naturally down channels without being pumped. Although Bradley's plan was sound, officials rejected it owing to financial and political reasons. The Dutch-born Englishman Cornelius Vermuyden finally directed this work four decades later, in the 1630s.

Dikes also guarded areas adjacent to rivers elsewhere in Europe—the Loire River in France is a notable example. In 1596 Humphrey Bradley and other dike experts traveled to France to help King Henry IV drain marshes and reclaim land. French marshes were not as extensive as England's were, and the sea did not cover much French land. Henry IV was most concerned to prevent rivers from flooding low-lying areas. Royal edicts sanctioned drainage work by l'Association pour le dessèchement des marais et lacs de France (the Association for the Draining of the Marshes and Lakes of France).

Venice and Padua

Italian rivers ran faster and were rougher than Dutch and other northern European waterways. Withstanding the torrents of Italian rivers required different approaches to the design and placement of dikes. In Italy the low-lying swampy city of Venice was a beacon of successful water management during the Renaissance. Venetian hydraulic experts and civil engineers ran drainage and irrigation programs, known collectively as *la bonifaca* (land reclamation), to manage the city's natural water resources, which were crucial for trade and economic prosperity in one of the busiest and most important European ports. During the sixteenth century, marsh officers, formally named *ufficiales paludum,* and officials representing Italian cities oversaw *la bonifaca* and encouraged the development of new hydraulic technology.

In the sixteenth century various engineers worked on improving and correcting the flow of rivers that flowed south from the Dolomite Mountains to Venice and studied how tides in the Adriatic Sea affected water movement in the city. Bernardo Timante Buontalenti, for example, investigated the Arno River, and Antonio Lupicinia worked on the Po River. Sediment deposited by the rivers in Venice's lagoon was clogging water channels and trapping stagnant water around the city. Engineers built dams and canal drainage systems that changed the course of rivers and, most important, changed the location of their mouth (the place at which a river empties into the sea). Maps incorporated these alterations to guide travelers.

DRAINING THE PONTINE MARSHES

Located in an area of central Italy that extends from the Lepini Mountains to the Tyrrhenian Sea, the Pontine Marshes were crossed by a Roman roadway, the Appian Way, and the adjacent remains of a Roman canal. Periodically soaked by rivers and a haven for mosquitoes and disease, the marshes were frequently all but inaccessible to travelers. Successive emperors and popes endorsed draining the marshes but had not completed that process by the beginning of the Renaissance. By 1514, Pope Leo X had authorized the Fiume Giuliano canal (named after his brother, Giuliano de' Medici). Leonardo da Vinci, who was working for the Medicis, drew a mapped proposal that included restoring the Roman canal and digging other channels for drainage. Pope Leo X died before da Vinci's Pontine Marshes drainage work began.

Toward the end of the sixteenth century, Pope Sixtus V approved a plan drawn up by the engineer Ascania Fenizi to secure patrons to finance marsh drainage. By 1589 crews had constructed canals and sluices, but their achievements were in vain: the plan was abandoned when the pope died the following year. Successful drainage finally took place in the 1930s. The story of the Pontine Marshes encompasses all the political and social factors that influenced the success or failure of Renaissance drainage efforts throughout Italy.

This detail from a sixteenth-century painting, entitled Prospect of Venice, *reveals how Saint Mark's Square relied on adequate water supplies for the daily activities and movement of people, who traveled by canals to the square's religious, commercial, and social sites. Dams and dredges provided sufficient navigable water to support transportation demands throughout Venice.*

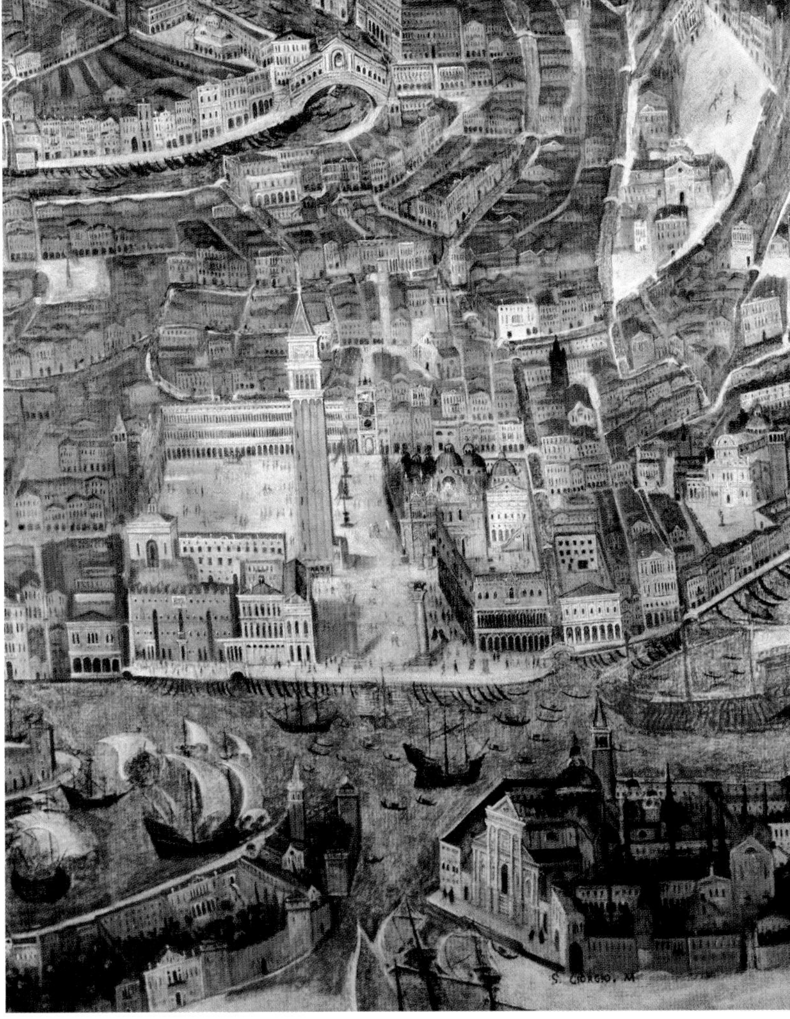

Venice's managed waterways were used as transportation routes for commercial, religious, social, and military purposes. The diversion of the Brenta River, for example, resulted in the construction of the Brenta Canal. Equipped with locks for boats to pass through at different water levels along the river, the canal offered a direct route from Venice to Padua. Venice's canals hosted regatta races and festivals held to celebrate Venetian events and welcome such royal visitors as King Henry III of France, who visited in 1574. Galileo Galilei studied the scientific aspects of water dynamics when he taught in Padua in the late sixteenth century. One of his students, Benedetto Castelli, focused on examining river flow and, in the groundbreaking *Della misura dell'acque correnti* (*On the Measurement of Running Waters;* 1628), discussed his observations and greatly contributed to knowledge of hydrodynamics.

Rural Italy

Drainage enlarged Italy's habitable area of land. During the Renaissance wealthy Italians bought homes and land in the countryside for purposes of financial investment or recreation, to elevate their social status, and to escape urban crowding and diseases. The city folk relied on vernacular reprints of classics, written by such authors as Marcus Varro and Lucius Columella, that gave instructions on how to drain and develop land for agriculture, build and maintain irrigation systems, dam streams, and use basic hydraulics to address other rural necessities associated with the reclamation and improvement of land. People profited from their rural crop yields and transformed boggy and marshy landscape into vineyards and livestock meadows.

Innovations

Engineers produced a number of innovations or enhancements to existing designs in order to manage seas, rivers, and lakes. Dikes were strengthened by automatic wooden sluice gates, which had a hinged upper edge that swung open during ebb tides to release water back to the sea. During high tides the water pressure kept the gates closed.

In 1498 Ludovico Sforza appointed Leonardo da Vinci Italy's state engineer. Fascinated by hydraulic engineering, da Vinci sketched designs for canals, weirs, and dredges, sketched possible methods for repairing dams, and hypothesized how to change the course of the Arno River. He innovated pairing lock gates that swung open from the sides and that, when closed, formed a point that kept water from leaking out. He added sluice doors to lock gates in order to release small amounts of water while the gates remained closed.

The silting up of riverbeds was a major problem. Engineers improved dredging and earth-moving machines to clear riverbeds of muck and silt and thereby increase water flow. Previously, people had used poles with buckets to scoop up silt from waterways. Dredging became more sophisticated when engineers outfitted boats with rakes to loosen silt that was then washed out to sea. Engineers later devised boats and barges whose decks were outfitted with treadmills on which humans or horses walked to move gears and rotate a line of buckets through the water. The first such mud mills were fitted with wooden buckets; later, copper became the preferred material. By dredging and pumping silt from riverbeds, natural and artificial waterways became consistently navigable, and the movement of people and goods from one place to another became far easier.

Not all progress was beneficial or well received, however. Extensive drainage threatened the balance of ecosystems. Hunters and fishers resented the drainage of wetlands that had previously provided a habitat for game, fish, and turtles. Some hunters and fishers sabotaged drainage windmills.

Renaissance Dams

Hundreds of years before the Renaissance, in ancient Rome and Persia, people were building dams across streams, rivers, and other bodies of water in an attempt to control the flow of water and direct it for specific ends. Renaissance dam builders adapted these ancient models and techniques when designing and constructing their

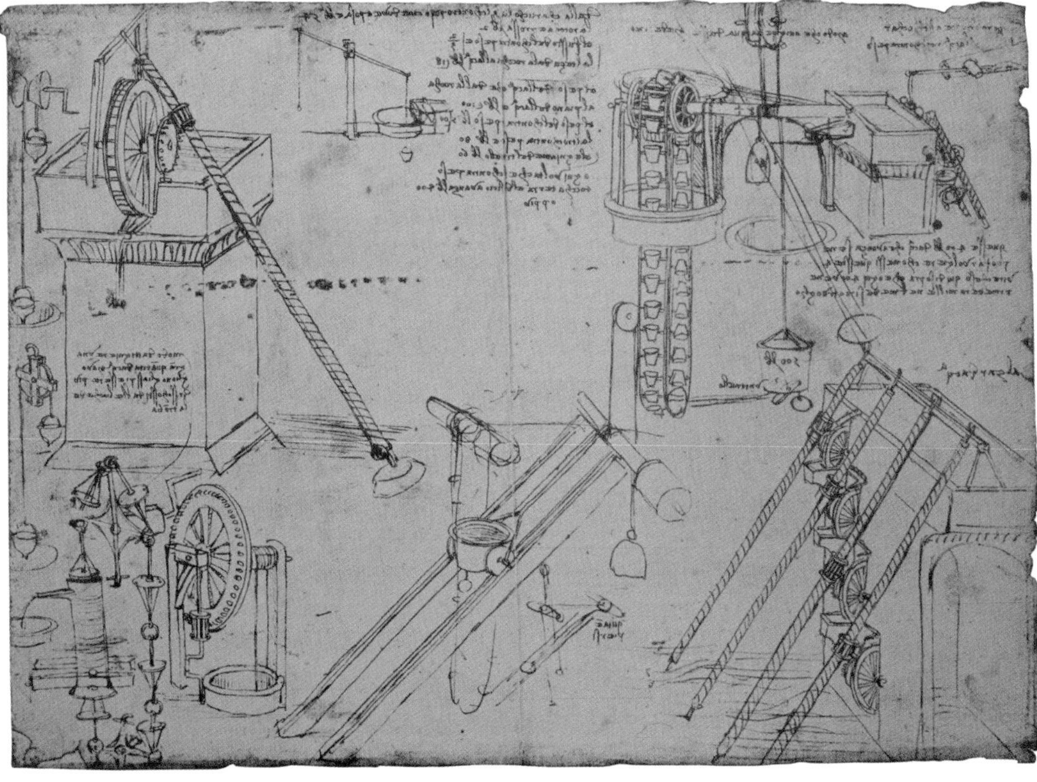

Leonardo da Vinci (1452–1519) envisioned many devices to control and move water, including a waterwheel with cups. He accompanied his sketches of possible designs with detailed annotations.

MILITARY STRATEGIES

Dams and drainage helped military forces invade or defend territory during the religious wars of the Reformation period. People occasionally broke dikes to flood land and prevent enemy armies from attacking. Defending the Netherlands in the Wars of Independence from 1568 to 1648, Dutch Protestants deployed water to combat Catholic Spaniards. When necessary, the Dutch troops built dikes and drained water to create strategically advantageous fighting grounds. Luring the Spanish soldiers to battlegrounds, the Protestants released water from dikes to drown their enemies.

During Renaissance-era conflicts, Italian forces also used the control of the flow of rivers as a military strategy. They increased flow to thwart their enemies' movements and restricted flow to expose riverbeds for Italian foot soldiers and cavalry to invade and recapture enemy-held cities. For instance, Leonardo da Vinci tried to control the Arno River during the Pisan Wars. The Italian strategies, though, were rarely successful. Other European troops recognized the strategic merits of stationing forces to control dams, sluices, and other hydraulic devices as offensive and defensive weapons.

dams, which were usually built from local materials and in a manner compatible with local surroundings. After a site was selected, often in a river valley, laborers accumulated stores of wood, bricks, stones, sand, and lime materials; cleared the ground; and dug a foundation.

Types of dams included palisade, masonry, gravity, and cofferdam. To make palisade dams, laborers placed stakes and fences, resembling military fortifications, across waterways. To make a cofferdam, a temporary dam to keep water away from parts of a river while the permanent dam was being built, a log frame was filled with clay. Masonry dams, composed of a wooden framework covered with lime, gravel, and stones, usually incorporated a sluice gate to release water. Buttresses often reinforced earthen dams. Gravity dams stood perpendicular to the riverbed and withstood water pressure by virtue of their weight. Arches, chutes, and sloping spillways achieve the desired water behavior and ensured the durability of dams.

Georg Bauer, known as Agricola, included this engraving in De re metallica *(1561) to illustrate how a winch removed water from mines. Dams were often built near mines and industrial sites to manage water and prevent damage to minerals and raw goods or to convert water into energy to run machinery and maneuver tools.*

A principal reason for the contruction of dams during the Renaissance was to prevent flooding. In Italy, Franco Recamati's 1537 wooden Ponte Alto Dam on the Fersina River protected the nearby city, Trento. When a flood ruined that dam five years later, builders erected a stone-and-mortar dam in the same place.

Other dams provided energy to power such mining equipment as pumps and hoists. The German Filz Dam, built in the Ore Mountains near Leipzig in 1485, provided power for mining machinery by channeling water into waterwheels. In the mid-sixteenth century, two dams were built in the Harz Mountains for the same purpose. In 1596, the Kobila Dam was built in Slovenia. Similar structures were built during the Renaissance at numerous other European sites.

Dams also powered other industrial processes. The architect Francisco Becerra designed the 1570 Casillas II Dam in Spain to supply a stable energy source. The 1610 Eastern Kreuz Dam and 1615 Knaben Dam powered mills and linen-bleaching machinery for textiles manufacturers in Saint Gall, Switzerland.

▲ The Khadjou barrage bridge across the Zayandeh River at Isfahan, Iran, was built on top of a dam during Shah Abbas II's reign (1642–1647). The stone, brick, and tile dam served several purposes. It held water in an artificial lake and diverted water into irrigation channels for agriculture. Tea rooms and entertainment sites were located on the bridge for the benefit of pedestrians crossing the river.

More than seven hundred fishpond dams were built in Switzerland, Italy, and throughout central Europe during the Renaissance to provide consistent sources of fish, a protein staple, for inland populations. Transportation of fish from the coasts was difficult, expensive, and time-consuming. Ice usually melted before fish deliveries arrived in towns, and fish would begin to decay. Around 1460, people in the area of present-day Austria built an earthen fishpond dam to create the *Spiegelfreudersee.* Jan Skála, using the pseudonymn Dubraius, wrote a sixteenth-century treatise entitled *Five Books on Fish Ponds,* which described Bohemian fish farming. John Taverner described fishpond dams that resembled mining dams in *Certaine Experiments concerning Fish and Fruite* (1600).

Storage dams collected and stored river water, snowmelt, and precipitation for urban usage, for the irrigation of crops, and to supply livestock, especially sheep and cattle. In France, Adam de Craponne designed an irrigation dam on the Durance River in 1554. Turkish and Spanish engineers built similar dams. Indeed, Spain was the world's primary dam builder during the Renaissance. In 1586 Spanish builders added a gravity dam to the 1384 Almansa Dam to make it higher and sturdier. A decade later, builders completed the Alicante Dam, also known as the Tibi Dam. The world's tallest dam during the Renaissance, it remained so for three centuries.

Other Spanish dams included the Castellar Dam, finished in 1500, and the Trujillo Dam, completed in 1572. Among the prominent Spanish dam engineers was Juanelo Turriano, who designed the waterworks for King Phillip II that raised the level of the Tagus River. Many of the dam engineers working in Spain were Italians who lived in Spanish-ruled areas. Ambrosio Mariano Azaro, for example, participated in the construction of the artificial reservoir known as the Sea of Ontígola, also on the Tagus River. King Phillip II had planned this reservoir for his court's amusement. It was also a source of water for canals and for the irrigation of gardens in the adjacent royal park, Reales Sitios, at Aranjuez.

An Italian dam completed in 1600 formed the Lago di Ternavasso, a reservoir that irrigated an adjacent estate. Other Italian dams included the Remole weir on the Arno River, which powered a mill; the Fucecchio Dam, which stored water; the brick-and-mortar Cento Dam on the Po River, which provided water for canals and irrigation; and the Lucca Dam, which held water in the Lago di Sesto and increased the acreage of nearby farmland.

Several Renaissance engineers recorded their impressions of hydrodynamics in pioneering manuscripts. In Italy an early-fifteenth-century manuscript by Mariano Taccola gave instructions on how to control rivers, strengthen banks, and divert water. By the end of the century, Francesco di Giorgio Martini had written a treatise that covered the same subject. Sometime in the first half of the sixteenth century, Jerónimo Giraba of Spain produced his manuscript about water engineering, the *Declaration of the Use and Fabrication of Water Instruments, Mills and Other Things.* The Milanese engineer Giovanni Francesco Sitoni worked on Spanish hydraulics projects in Aragon during the mid-1560s. He told readers how to build irrigation dams and drain fields in his *Treatise of the Virtues and Properties of Waters and How to Find Them, Move Them, Level Them and Channel Them, and Some Other of Their Characteristics.*

Travelers introduced Renaissance dam designs and construction techniques to the New World. Diego de Chávez Alvardo devised a gravity dam, Yuriria, in a Mexican volcano crater in 1550 to form a reservoir. Spanish engineers introduced dams and canals to South America for purposes of irrigation, mining, and the creation of reservoirs.

In a manuscript on dikes, dams, and drainage systems, a renowned sixteenth-century Dutch dike master offered the following advice to engineers working in the same field:

Do something every year, make your work grow steadily. The art is not to make expensive large dams but to work gently and cleverly trying to obtain great advantage. What is needed is patience and the use of time.

Andries Vierlingh, *Tractaet van Dyckague (Tract on Diking)*

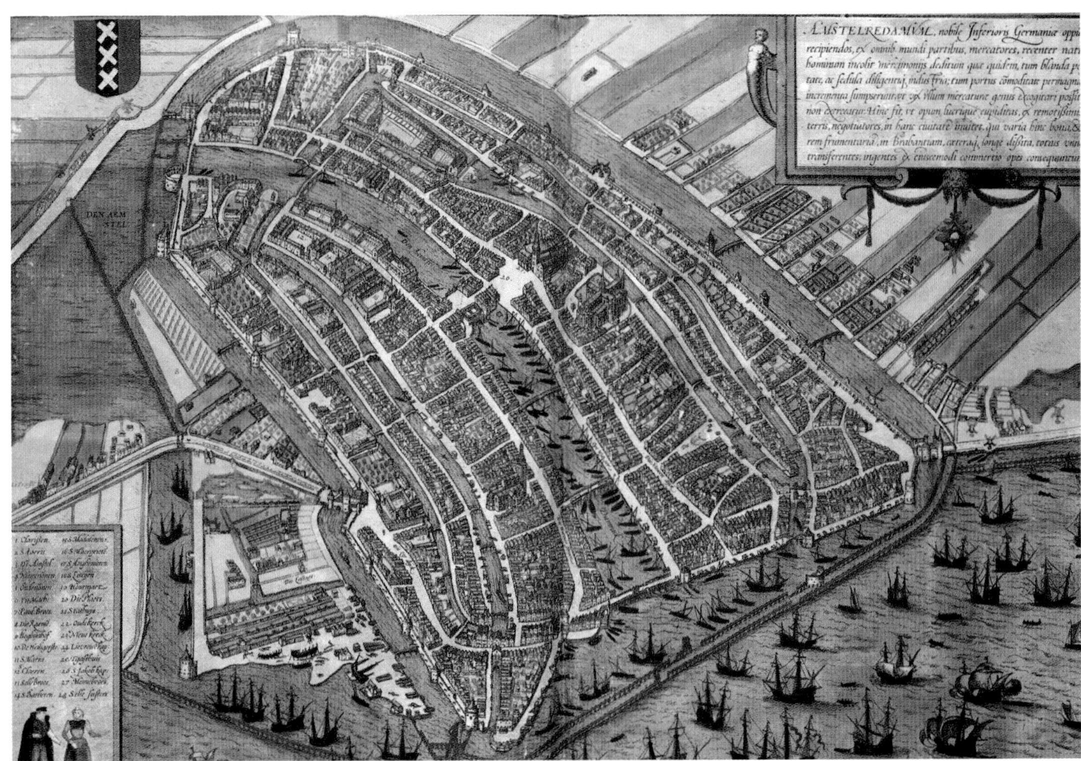

Georg Braun and Franz Hogenberg included this engraved map of Amsterdam in their atlas collection, Civitates orbis terrarum *(c. 1572). The city's name was derived from Amstelledamme, the fishing community established when the Amstel River was dammed in the thirteenth century.*

Failed Projects

In 1470 construction began on the Bruna River dam project on a reclaimed swampy site in the Republic of Siena where a previous dam had failed. Having spent two decades building the dam, workers were dismayed in 1492 when it cracked and then shattered. Hinting of corruption on the site, the diarist Allegretto Allegretti wrote, "the wall fell down and flooded much of the countryside. Men and beasts have died and this was the fault of those who completed it, since they bungled it for gain." Engineers and architects, including Baldassarre Peruzzi, submitted elaborate proposals to rebuild the dam with stronger materials and a sturdier structure, but it was not completed. Many Renaissance dams failed because architects lacked sufficient experience in hydraulic engineering and scientists did not yet have a full understanding of the mechanics of soil, the properties of materials, and the dynamics of water. Such knowledge improved future dams.

Further Reading

Ciriacono, Salvatore, ed. *Land Drainage and Irrigation.* Brookfield, VT, 1998.

Schnitter, Nicholas J. *A History of Dams: The Useful Pyramids.* Rotterdam, 1994.

Smith, Norman Alfred Fisher. *A History of Dams.* London, 1971.

Spier, Peter. *Of Dikes and Windmills.* Garden City, NY, 1969.

Veen, Johan van. *Dredge, Drain, Reclaim: The Art of a Nation.* The Hague, 1962.

Elizabeth D. Schafer

SEE ALSO

• Agriculture • Leonardo da Vinci • Machines
• Science and Technology • Venice

Index

Page numbers in **boldface** type refer to entire articles.
Page numbers in *italic* type refer to illustrations.

Q

R

S

T

U

V

W

Z

Illustration Credits

akg-images: 36 (Erich Lessing), 40 (Joseph Martin), 44 (Bildarchiv Monheim), 50 (Erich Lessing), 55, 60, 74, 75, 80, 82, 88, 99 (Erich Lessing), 103, 110, 117 (Erich Lessing), 123, 124 (Erich Lessing), 125 (Electa), 126, 127, 140 (Hervé Champollion), 141, 145 & 172 (Erich Lessing), 173, 214 & 215 (Bibliothèque Nationale, Paris), 217 (Erich Lessing), 243, 261 (Cameraphoto), 264 & 270 (Erich Lessing), 272, 276 (British Library, London).

Art Archive: 16 (Bibliothèque Nationale, Paris), 17 (Private Collection/ Dagli Orti), 19 (Victoria and Albert Museum, London/Harper Collins Publishers), 22 (Torre Aquila, Trento, Italy/Dagli Orti [A]), 23 (Issogne Castle, Valle d'Aosta, Italy/Dagli Orti), 24 (Bodleian Library, Oxford [Bodley 164 folio 81r]), 25 (University Library, Prague/Dagli Orti), 26 (British Library, London), 27 (Eileen Tweedy), 28 (Bodleian Library, Oxford [C 17 .48 (9) pt 4 Laxton Map]), 29 (Linnean Society), 30 & 33–35 (Dagli Orti), 38 (Palazzo del Tè, Mantua/Dagli Orti), 43 & 45 & 46 (Dagli Orti), 47 (Jarrold Publishing), 48 (Bibliothèque des Arts Décoratifs, Paris/Dagli Orti), 51 (Topkapi Museum, Istanbul/Dagli Orti), 52 (Musée du Louvre, Paris/Dagli Orti), 53 & 61 (Musée Condé, Chantilly, France/Dagli Orti), 63 (Bodleian Library, Oxford [MS Raw I A 102 folio 20r]), 64 (University Library, Geneva/Dagli Orti), 66 (Eileen Tweedy), 67 (John Webb), 68 (Private Collection/Marc Charmet), 69 (Museum of Turkish and Islamic Art, Istanbul/Dagli Orti [A]), 71 (British Library, London/Eileen Tweedy), 72 (British Library, London), 77 (Historisches Museum, Vienna/Dagli Orti), 84 (Musée du Louvre, Paris/Harper Collins Publishers), 85 (Musée Condé, Chantilly, France/Dagli Orti), 86 (Archivio di Stato di Siena/Dagli Orti), 89 (Museo Correr, Venice/Dagli Orti [A]), 90 (British Museum, London), 95 (Museo del Prado, Madrid/Dagli Orti), 97 & 98 (Galleria Borghese, Rome/Dagli Orti [A]), 101 (Joseph Martin), 102 (Biblioteca Estense, Modena, Italy/Dagli Orti [A]), 104 (Bodleian Library, Oxford [Bodley 270 b folio 192r]), 108 (Eileen Tweedy), 111 (Galleria degli Uffizi, Florence/Dagli Orti [A]), 112 (Bodleian Library, Oxford [Douce 331 fol 15r]), 113 (Bodleian Library, Oxford [Canon Ital 85 folio 67r]), 114 (Museo del Prado, Madrid/Dagli Orti), 115 (Musée Condé, Chantilly, France/Dagli Orti), 119 (University Library, Prague/Dagli Orti), 122 (Eileen Tweedy), 129 (Museo del Prado, Madrid/Joseph Martin), 131 (Museum of Fine Art, Ghent, Belgium/Joseph Martin), 132 (Musée du Louvre, Paris/Dagli Orti [A]), 134–136 (Galleria degli Uffizi, Florence/Dagli Orti [A]), 137 (National Gallery, London/Eileen Tweedy), 138 (Galleria degli Uffizi, Florence/Dagli Orti [A]), 146 (Metropolitan Museum of Art, New York/Joseph Martin), 148 (Kunsthistorisches Museum, Vienna), 151 & 153 (Dagli Orti), 154 (Dagli Orti [A]), 155 (Dagli Orti), 156 (Album/J. Enrique Molina), 157 (Musée du Château de Versailles/Dagli Orti), 158 (University Library, Prague/Dagli Orti), 159 (Bibliothèque des Arts Décoratifs, Paris/Harper Collins Publishers), 161 (Musée des Beaux Arts, Dijon/Dagli Orti), 162 (Bodleian Library, Oxford [Douce 383 folio 15r]), 163 (Galleria degli Uffizi, Florence/Dagli Orti [A]), 164 (Bodleian Library, Oxford [Douce 93 folio 100-101r]), 166 (San Vitale, Ravenna/Dagli Orti [A]), 167 (Archaeological Museum, Naples/Dagli Orti [A]), 170 (Museo della Civiltà Romana, Rome/ Dagli Orti), 171 (Dagli Orti [A]), 175 (Archivio di Stato di Siena/Dagli Orti), 177 (Ashmolean Museum, Oxford), 178 (University Library, Geneva/Dagli Orti), 179 (Musée Carnavalet, Paris/Dagli Orti), 180 (Bach House, Leipzig/Dagli Orti [A]), 181 (Musée du Louvre, Paris/Dagli Orti), 182 (Musée des Beaux Arts, Dijon/Dagli Orti), 183–185 (University Library, Geneva/Dagli Orti), 186 (Museo Tridentino Arte Sacra, Trento/ Dagli Orti [A]), 187 (University Library, Geneva/Dagli Orti), 188 (British Library, London), 190, 191 (Galleria degli Uffizi, Florence/Dagli Orti [A]), 194 (Musée du Louvre, Paris/Dagli Orti [A]), 195 (Dagli Orti), 196 (Musée des Beaux Arts, Rouen/Dagli Orti [A]), 199 (Château de Chaumont/Dagli Orti), 200 (Musée des Beaux Arts, Lausanne/Dagli Orti), 201 (Musée du Château de Versailles/Dagli Orti), 203 (Accademia, Venice/Dagli Orti [A]), 205 (Bibliothèque des Arts Décoratifs, Paris/Dagli Orti), 206 (Mohammed Khalil Museum, Cairo/Dagli Orti), 207 (Musée de l'Ain Bourg-en-Bresse/ Dagli Orti), 208, 210 (Farnese Palace Caprarola/Dagli Orti [A]), 211 (University Library, Geneva/Dagli Orti), 212 (Victoria and Albert Museum, London/Eileen Tweedy), 216 (Galleria degli Uffizi, Florence/Dagli Orti [A]), 218 & 220 (Jarrold Publishing), 222 (Musée Condé, Chantilly/Dagli Orti), 223 (British Museum, London), 225 (Museo di Roma, Palazzo Braschi/ Dagli Orti [A]), 227 (Museo del Prado, Madrid/Joseph Martin), 228, 229 (Musée Carnavalet, Paris/Dagli Orti), 231 (Dagli Orti), 235 (The Trustees of the Weston Park Foundation, UK), 236 (Museo del Prado, Madrid/Dagli Orti), 228, 239, 242 (Museo di Capodimonte, Naples/Dagli Orti), 245 (Dagli Orti [A]), 247 (Naval Museum, Genoa/Dagli Orti [A]), 248 (Fondation Thiers, Paris/Dagli Orti [A]), 249 (British Library, London), 250 (Monastery of the Rabida, Palos, Spain/Dagli Orti), 253 (General Archive of the Indies, Seville/Dagli Orti), 255 (Seville Cathedral/Dagli Orti), 256 (Bodleian Library, Oxford [Canon Misc 378 folio 84r]), 258 (Dagli Orti), 262 (Medici Riccardi Chapel, Florence/Dagli Orti [A]), 265 (Galleria degli Uffizi, Florence/Dagli Orti [A]), 269 (British Library, London), 271 (Bodleian Library, Oxford [Marsh 144 folio 210]), 273 (Museo Franz Mayer, Mexico/Dagli Orti), 274 (Maritiem Museum Prins Hendrik, Rotterdam/Dagli Orti), 277 (Museo Correr, Venice/Dagli Orti [A]), 280 (Dagli Orti).

Bridgeman Art Library: 20 (British Museum, London), 21 (Bibliothèque de l'Arsenal, Paris), 31 (Private Collection), 32 (Bibliothèque Nationale, Paris), 37 (Bibliothèque Nationale, Paris), 39 (Musée du Louvre, Paris), 41 (Villa Farnesina, Rome), 42 (Private Collection), 49 (Lauros/Giraudon), 54 (Bibliothèque de l'Académie de Médecine, Paris), 56 (Private Collection), 57 (Bibliothèque Nationale, Paris), 58 (Hermitage Museum, Saint Petersburg, Russia), 59 (Metropolitan Museum of Art, New York), 62 (Victoria and Albert Museum, London), 76 (Georgenkirche, Eisenach, Germany), 78 (Private Collection), 79 (Collection of the earl of Pembroke, Wilton House, Wiltshire, England), 81 (Private Collection), 87 (Galleria dell'Accademia, Venice/Giraudon), 91 (Scuola di San Giorgio degli Schiavoni, Venice), 93 & 94 & 96 (Private Collection), 100 (Joseph Martin), 105 (Bible Society, London), 107 (Bibliothèque Nationale, Paris), 109 (Bible Society, London), 120, 121 (Lobkowicz Collections, Nelahozeves Castle, Czech Republic), 128 (National Museum of Ancient Art, Lisbon/Giraudon), 130 (Museo del Prado, Madrid), 133 (Galleria degli Uffizi, Florence), 143 (British Museum, London), 144 (Giraudon/Musées Royaux des Beaux-Arts de Belgique, Brussels), 147 (Kunsthistorisches Museum, Vienna), 149 (Galleria dell'Accademia, Florence), 152, 165 (British Library, London), 168 (Museum of Art, Novgorod, Russia), 169 (Topkapi Palace Museum, Istanbul), 174 (British Library, London), 189, 192 (Contarelli Chapel, San Luigi dei Francesi, Rome), 193 (Santa Maria del Popolo, Rome), 197 (Villa della Petraia, Florence/Lauros/Giraudon), 198 (Victoria and Albert Museum, London), 202 (Real Academia de la Historia, Madrid/Index), 204 (Giraudon), 209 & 213 (Private Collection), 219 (Huntington Library and Art Gallery, San Marino, CA), 221 (Musées Royaux des Beaux-Arts de Belgique, Brussels/Giraudon), 224 (Palazzo Ducale, Mantua), 226 (British Library, London), 230 (Lungarno Corsini, Florence/Guido Mannucci), 232 (Private Collection), 233 (Private Collection of Philip Mould Historical Portraits Ltd., London), 234 (Civiche Raccolte d'Arte, Pavia/Dagli Orti [A]), 237 (Lambeth Palace, London), 240 (British Library, London), 241 (Museo di Capodimonte, Naples/Dagli Orti), 244 (Bibliothèque Nationale, Paris), 251 (Bibliothèque Nationale, Paris/Giraudon), 259 (Palazzo Ducale, Venice), 260 (British Library, London), 263 (National Gallery, London), 264 (Bibliothèque Nationale, Paris), 267 (Bibliothèque Sainte-Genevieve, Paris/Archives Charmet), 268 (Stapleton Collection, UK), 275 (Royal Geographical Society, London), 278 (Private Collection), 279 (Bibliothèque du Musée d'Histoire Naturelle, Paris), 281 (Stapleton Collection, UK).

Corbis: 92 (Hulton-Deutsch Collection), 139 (Archivo Iconografico, S.A.), 142 (Robert van der Hilst), 176 (Archivo Iconografico, S.A.), 246.

Digital Vision: 150.

Mary Evans Picture Library: 83.

Topfoto: 70 (Roger-Viollet), 73 (British Library, London/HIP), 106 (British Library, London), 118 (uppa.co.uk), 254 (British Library, London/HIP).